Surveys in Economics

VOLUME I

on behalf of the
Royal Economic Society

Edited by
ANDREW J. OSWALD

BLACKWELL
Oxford UK & Cambridge USA

Copyright © Royal Economic Society 1991

First published 1991

Basil Blackwell Ltd
108 Cowley Road, Oxford, OX4 1JF, UK

Basil Blackwell, Inc.
3 Cambridge Center
Cambridge, Massachusetts 02142, USA

British Library Cataloguing in Publication Data
A CIP catalogue record for this book is available from the British Library.

Library of Congress Cataloging in Publication Data
Surveys in economics/edited by Andrew J. Oswald on behalf of the
    Royal Economic Society.
    p. cm.
    Includes bibliographical references and index.
    ISBN 0–631–17972–0 (v. 1): ISBN 0–631–17973–9 (pbk.:
v. 1): ISBN 0–631–17974–7 (v. 2): ISBN
0–631–17975–5 (pbk.: v. 2)
    1. Economics.   I. Oswald, Andrew J.   II. Royal Economic Society
(Great Britain)
HB171.5.S9615   1991
330—dc20   90–19344   CIP

1655917

Printed in Great Britain at the University Press, Cambridge

SURVEYS IN ECONOMICS

VOLUME I

£14.95

B

CONTENTS

PREFACE

In 1986 the Royal Economic Society decided to commission a set of survey papers in Economics. It was the incoming editor, John Hey, who suggested that it was time to revive this tradition. I was given the task of selecting authors and topics.

The ECONOMIC JOURNAL has published surveys for fifty years, but the last papers appeared in the journal more than a decade ago. Many of the articles – such as Hahn and Matthews on growth in 1964 and Laidler and Parkin on inflation in 1975 – became instant classics. Most defined the reading lists, and moulded the thinking, of generations of students.

Survey articles are valuable. They help to focus debates; they teach; they allow the experienced to point out avenues that the young might miss. None of this means that survey papers could or should play a dominant role in academic research.

Twelve papers seemed a good number. However, a very few of those people invited were unable to accept. The survey series moved rapidly towards a natural equilibrium of ten papers, and there it has remained. I have taken the view throughout that the ECONOMIC JOURNAL should be as able to stop publishing surveys as to start. Although there is no doubt that one could include an article per issue forever, it is not clear (at least to me) that this would be appropriate for a research journal.

I should like to express my gratitude to the eleven economists who contributed papers and to the dozens who acted as referees. We all discovered the difficulties of running consecutive articles. With luck the results have been worthwhile.

Each author was given identical instructions. The aim of the series was to provide surveys that could be read fairly easily by researchers in other sub-disciplines of Economics. As readers will see, the styles of the surveys differ somewhat, and this was to be expected. Subjects are different. Experts are, by and large, best left alone. To those who find article X too polemical, article Y too theoretical or article Z too informal, I apologize. It should be borne in mind that the ECONOMIC JOURNAL has one of the most diverse readerships in the world of economics journals.

In choosing authors, my view was that two criteria had to be met. First, an author should have an international research reputation. Second, he or she should be able to cover both theoretical and empirical aspects of the chosen topic. My hope is that readers will sympathise with these aims and see the group as satisfying them.

A special word of thanks is due to Professor John Black of the University of Exeter. His careful reading helped improve these volumes.

I was delighted when these eleven economists – busy people all – generously consented to write survey papers in their specialist fields.

ANDREW J. OSWALD

I

RECENT DEVELOPMENTS IN MACROECONOMICS*

Stanley Fischer

Underlying the existence of macroeconomics as a separate field of study are the phenomena of economy-wide fluctuations of output and prices, and sometimes persistent high levels of unemployment. Two basic views of macroeconomic behaviour have persisted even as conceptual innovations and the application of more powerful analytic and empirical techniques have brought significant changes in macroeconomics.

One view and school of thought, associated with Keynes, Keynesians and new Keynesians, is that the private economy is subject to co-ordination failures that can produce excessive levels of unemployment and excessive fluctuations in real activity. The other view, attributed to classical economists, and espoused by monetarists and equilibrium business cycle theorists, is that the private economy reaches as good an equilibrium as is possible given government policy.

Any twofold division of a complex, large and developing field of study is inevitably a caricature, which cannot do justice to the subtleties of the views of different individuals at a moment of time, the intricacies of the development of the field over time, and the remarkable range of research topics that fall under the heading of macroeconomics. For instance, although the protagonists in the sixties were Keynesians and monetarists, and in the eighties are new Keynesians and equilibrium business cycle theorists, there is a clear sense in which the views of Milton Friedman or Karl Brunner and Allan Meltzer are closer to those of Keynesians than those of equilibrium business cycle theorists.[1] Nonetheless, the caricature captures the essence of macroeconomic controversies and provides a useful organising framework within which to attempt a survey of a field that is too large for such an enterprise.

It appears that macroeconomics as such has not been surveyed. The classic 1962 Harry Johnson survey is of monetary economics; Barro and Fischer (1976) also survey monetary economics, though their definition of the subject is sufficiently broad to encompass disequilibrium theory, which is more

* This chapter was first published in the Economic Journal, vol. 98, June 1988. I am grateful to Charles Bean, Olivier Blanchard, Martin Prachowny, Rudiger Dornbusch, Andrew Oswald, Danny Quah, Julio Rotemberg and the referees for helpful comments and/or discussions, and the National Science Foundation for research support. I am especially indebted to Olivier Blanchard, for I draw freely in this survey on material contained in our recent book (1989). (I have taken the opportunity of this reprinting to correct some references and interpretations of the literature, but have not attempted a systematic updating of the paper. I am grateful to Jean-Pascal Benassy, J. Black and Fumio Hayashi for comments.)

[1] Milton Friedman's theoretical framework (1970) is close to the standard IS-LM model; Brunner and Meltzer's (1976) basic analytic model is not dissimilar to Tobin's (1969) three asset model. Friedman's view of the macroeconomy as adjusting slowly and unpredictably to monetary policy is very far from the modern real business cycle view that monetary policy plays at most a minor role in macroeconomic fluctuations and that markets are continually in equilibrium.

macroeconomics than monetary economics. Rotemberg (1987) and Blanchard (1988) each provide excellent surveys of part of the material discussed in this paper.[2]

The focus in this survey is on the core issue, of the reasons for macroeconomic fluctuations and sometimes persistent unemployment. To provide continuity, and perspective on how promising research leads of the past turned out, I start by summarising in Sections I and II developments since the Barro–Fischer survey. The core of the survey is contained in Sections III and IV which describe the current representations of the two basic approaches to macro-economics; the equilibrium business cycle approach and new Keynesianism respectively. Brief sketches of developments in several areas of research in Section V broaden the perspective on the field. Section VI contains concluding comments.

I. UPDATE FROM 1975

Barro and Fischer (1976, written in 1975) describe their survey as complementary with Harry Johnson's 1962 paper. This survey in turn can be regarded as complementary with Barro and Fischer, which classified research into seven topics.

The Theory of Money Demand

Theoretical work on the demand for money was a declining industry in 1975, and there has been only a brief subsequent revival. Akerlof and Milbourne (1980) develop a target-threshold model of the demand for money, related to $s-S$ models (Miller and Orr, 1966), in which money balances adjust passively to inflows and outflows of cash until they hit a lower bound, at which point the balance is restored to a higher level. Akerlof and Milbourne show that the short-run income elasticity of money demand in this model is very small, so long as the target and threshold stay fixed, and argue that their model accounts for the very low short-run income elasticities of demand found in empirical studies.

The collapse of the empirical demand for money function in the United States (Goldfeld, 1976; Rasche, 1987) led to a largely empirical re-examination of the basics of money demand. Most attention has been commanded by the work of Barnett and others (e.g. Barnett *et al.* 1984) creating Divisia aggregated money stock measures. The change in the Divisia quantity index is equal to a weighted sum of the changes of the components, with the weights corresponding to the share of spending on that component of the aggregate. In the case of monetary assets, the spending on a particular component is priced at user cost, equal to the difference between the maximum expected holding period yield available in the economy and the expected yield on the particular asset – it thus corresponds closely to the notion of non-pecuniary returns. The Divisia aggregates are contrasted with the simple sum aggregates such as M_1, which weight components of each measure equally. The empirical success of the new

---

[2] Fischer (1987) also contains survey-like material.

measures has been mixed. Monetary targeting in terms of Divisia aggregates is complicated by the fact that the aggregates themselves depend on interest rates, so that achieving a targeted Divisia aggregate implies achieving a specific level of a non-linear function of different asset stocks and interest rates. Poterba and Rotemberg (1987) develop and estimate a more explicit related approach in which money and other assets enter the utility function, with differing liquidity characteristics and risk premia accounting for interest differentials.

Technical and regulatory changes in definitions of the money stock are responsible for many of the shifts in the demand for money function (Porter *et al.* 1979). Nonetheless, these shifts have significantly reduced belief in the efficacy of a constant growth rate monetary rule and in monetarism.

Even though interest rate controls have been lifted, there is more deregulation of the United States financial system to come, for instance in interstate and international banking. Whether stability will return to the demand for money function, for any of the conventional monetary aggregates or some Divisia aggregate, as deregulation of the banking and financial systems slows, remains to be seen. Continued deregulation and technical progress in the payments mechanism – heading in the direction of, but not reaching, the cashless society – are likely to make for future unpredictable and significant changes in velocity.

Money, Inflation and Growth

In the 1976 survey this topic was devoted largely to the question of the effect of an increase in money growth on capital intensity. Whereas Tobin (1965) showed in a non-maximising model that a higher growth rate of money produced both more inflation and higher capital intensity – and thus a lower real interest rate, money in Sidrauski's optimising model (1967) is superneutral in the sense that higher rates of inflation do not affect steady state capital intensity and thus the real interest rate.

The effect of higher inflation in reducing the real interest rate is known as the Mundell–Tobin effect. In fact, the mechanisms that produce this effect in Mundell (1963) and Tobin (1965) are not identical. In Mundell, a higher inflation rate reduces real balances and thereby, through a wealth effect, consumption; the interest rate falls to ensure goods market equilibrium. In Tobin, new money is introduced into the economy through transfer payments, the net real value of which is $(g-\pi)m$, where g is the growth rate of nominal balances, π the inflation rate, and m is real balances. In the steady state $(g-\pi)$ is equal to the economy's growth rate (assuming unitary income elasticity of money demand) which is independent of the inflation rate, whereas m falls with the inflation rate. The real value of monetary transfers thus falls with the inflation rate, reducing consumption demand and the real interest rate. Back-of-the-envelope calculations suggest that both these effects are empirically very small.

Subsequent analysis showed that dynamic adjustment towards the steady state capital stock is typically faster in the Sidrauski model the higher the

growth rate of money, thus reinstating the Mundell–Tobin result in the
Sidrauski model, at least for the adjustment path (Fischer, 1979). A variety of
results on the relationship between capital intensity and inflation have been
obtained in other models of money, including for instance Stockman's (1981)
model with a Clower constraint in which investment goods have to be paid for
with cash in advance. The cost of investing rises with the inflation rate, and
inflation therefore reduces capital intensity. However, this result is not robust
to the precise details of the assumed Clower constraint (Abel, 1985a). In
overlapping generations models inflation generally reduces capital intensity
(e.g. Weiss, 1980).

The most important development in this area is the incorporation of details
of the tax system into the analysis of the effects of inflation on interest rates and
capital accumulation (e.g. Feldstein and Summers, 1978). Mainly because
it erodes the value of depreciation allowances, these analyses generally indicate
that inflation reduces capital intensity and capital accumulation. Tax effects
also disturb the Fisher effect on nominal interest rates, implying that the
nominal rate should rise more than one-for-one with inflation if the after-tax
real rate is to remain constant (Feldstein, 1976).

The empirical evidence supports the view that inflation adversely affects
capital accumulation; in a cross-section of countries, the predominant
relationship between inflation and the share of investment in GNP is negative
(Fischer, 1983).

Empirical evidence on the Fisher effect has had an unusually chequered
history. After Fama's striking 1975 demonstration that, on the assumptions of
a constant real interest rate and rational expectations, the Fisher effect held
one-for-one in the U.S. for the period 1951–73, it soon became clear that the
result was period specific (Begg, 1977). Further, the tax effects should have
produced a greater than one-for-one effect of inflation on nominal interest
rates. Subsequently Summers (1983) showed that ex post decadal average real
interest rates have a strong negative correlation with inflation, and argued that
this implied that ex ante rates are also negatively related to anticipated
inflation.[3]

Changes in the real interest rate in the United States in the first half of the
1980s were in the direction implied by Summers' regressions. Indeed, it was
common to account for the high real rates as a regular feature of disinflations
– which while true is hardly an explanation. The high real rates of the early
1980s made the assumption of a constant ex ante real rate implausible if the
rational expectations hypothesis is maintained.[4]

Welfare Costs of Inflation, the Optimum Quantity of Money, and Inflationary Finance

By 1975 the Phelps (1973) analysis of the inflation tax in the context of optimal
tax analysis was becoming well known. Subsequent work was directed to

---

[3] However, McCallum (1984) has pointed out problems with the Summers argument. See also the
subsequent debate between Summers and McCallum in the July 1986 *Journal of Monetary Economics*.

[4] It is always possible and possibly plausible to account for high long rates as consistent with unchanged
real rates at the start of a disinflation, but high short rates cannot be consistent with an unchanged ex ante
real rate.

answering the question of whether there were conditions under which the inflation tax would not be used, so that the optimum quantity of money result – that the nominal interest rate should be driven to zero – would still hold. Drazen (1979) showed, using a representative family infinite horizon model that there was no general presumption that money should be taxed, the result depending on cross-elasticities of demand between real balances and other goods. Faig (1985) proved in the case where money is modelled as an intermediate good that it would be optimal not to tax it. The question of how optimally to finance government spending among bonds, money issue and taxes received was analysed by Helpman and Sadka (1979).

The topic of the welfare costs of inflation received empirical attention. The conclusion of attempts to enumerate and quantify the costs of inflation (Fischer and Modigliani, 1978; Fischer, 1981) was that the costs of even moderate inflation could in practice amount to 1 or 2 % of GNP in developed economies, but that these costs were largely the result of institutional non-adaptation to inflation.

As inflations in several countries rose to three digit annual rates in the 1980s, monetary financing of budget deficits became central to the analysis of the inflationary process. Seigniorage revenue can amount to several percent of GNP for governments operating at high rates of inflation, and could thus be an important factor in the perpetuation of high inflation in countries with rudimentary tax systems.

As a result of the Laffer curve, there may be two inflation rates at which a given amount of seigniorage revenue can be collected. The stability properties of the two equilibria differ, the high inflation equilibrium typically being stable under rational expectations (Bruno and Fischer, 1985; Sargent and Wallace, 1987). Governments could then find themselves operating at an unnecessarily high inflation rate.

Despite the fact that seigniorage *per se* can produce significant amounts of revenue for the government, the inflation tax analysis that focuses on seigniorage may be seriously misleading. The Keynes–Olivera–Tanzi (1977) effect whereby tax revenues decline at high inflation[5] reduces the net revenue effects of inflation on government revenues. Remarkably, in the Israeli case there is evidence that on net inflation reduced government revenues during parts of the inflationary period, because the government was a net creditor on nominal terms and debtor on real terms (Sokoler, 1987). These considerations strongly suggest that something other than rational revenue considerations is driving the money-creation process in high inflation economies; one possibility is that the government has put in place a set of operating rules that leaves money creation as the residual source of government finance.[6]

---

[5] The effect is more likely a function of the change than the level of the inflation rate, for once the inflation level stabilises tax rates are usually adjusted.

[6] Mankiw (1987) examines the determination of the inflation rate in the United States from an optimal tax viewpoint.

Disequilibrium Theory

In 1975 disequilibrium theory was a live area of research that had already produced insights, particularly into the notion of effective demand, into the fact that behaviour in any one market depends on whether other markets clear, and into the effects of changes in the real wage on the macro equilibrium. The distinction between classical unemployment, resulting from too high real wages, and Keynesian unemployment, resulting from a lack of aggregate demand, which can be clearly understood from standard disequilibrium models, also proved useful, for example in empirical analyses of the European unemployment problem (Bruno and Sachs, 1985).

Beyond those insights, and despite the elegant statement of the approach in Malinvaud (1976) and other contributions reviewed in Drazen (1980), interest in disequilibrium theory *per se* has waned. The difficulty, already evident in 1975, was that the careful maximising analysis that underlay the derivation of demand and supply functions at given prices was not generally extended to price dynamics itself. Benassy (1976) provided an important interpretation of this approach as representing a monopolistic competition equilibrium reached as a result of price adjustment. The 1976 Benassy analysis establishes the close link between disequilibrium theory and the new Keynesian analysis to be reviewed in Section IV, where price and quantity determination are treated symmetrically.

General Equilibrium Approach to Monetary Theory

The 'general equilibrium' discussed under this heading in the 1976 survey was the equilibrium of the assets markets, with attention focused on the Brainard–Tobin supply and demand framework for asset pricing and the analysis of monetary policy. That approach has been integrated with the capital asset pricing model, in an attempt to identify the effects of changes in asset supplies on risk premia (e.g. B. Friedman, 1985; Frankel, 1985).

The modern approach to asset pricing deploys various forms of the capital asset pricing model, mainly derived through representative consumer models (e.g. Lucas, 1978*a*; Breeden, 1979; Cox *et al.*, 1985). Asset supplies are exogenous in the Lucas model; it is difficult to obtain closed form solutions for asset prices in models in which supplies are endogenous. The Lucas model has been used for studying relative asset returns (Campbell, 1986) and the size of the equity premium (Mehra and Prescott, 1985); Mehra and Prescott's results raise the question of whether the historical size of the equity premium can be rationalised in such models.

The term structure has continued as an active area of research, with the development of rational expectations econometrics making formal testing of the joint hypothesis of the expectations theory of term structure and rational expectations possible. The recent literature is surveyed by Shiller (1987), who states that there has been much progress in understanding the term structure in the last twenty years, but that empirical work has produced very little consensus.

The New Microfoundations of Money

Covered under this heading was fundamental work attempting to explain the need for and use of money (e.g. Brunner and Meltzer, 1971; Kurz, 1974; Starr, 1974). Lucas (1980) and Townsend (1980) have pursued models in which the lack of a double coincidence of wants necessitates the use of an asset for making exchanges, but by and large work on the reasons for the use of money has not gone much further than it had in 1975. Rather the modern trend has been to impose the use of money on the model, rather than to allow it to emerge from within the model.

There are two approaches: the Clower or cash-in-advance constraint; and money in the utility function. The Clower constraint imposes the requirement that money has to be used in making some or all transactions. The usual cash-in-advance constraint in discrete time models is that current income is not available for making current purchases, so that money for this period's purchases has to be held from the end of the previous period. By imposing unitary velocity on money holding this rules out the important systematic effects of inflation and interest rates on money holding.

Lucas and Stokey (1987) restore interest elasticity to money holding in a cash-in-advance constraint model by introducing a distinction between credit and cash goods, the former of which can be purchased with an interest free one period loan, the latter requiring the use of cash. Shifts in demand between cash and credit goods as their relative prices change then make it possible for inflation to produce systematic effects on velocity. However, the distinction between cash and credit goods is unlikely to be independent of the inflation rate and interest rates. Svensson (1985) relaxes the unitary velocity assumption by assuming that individuals face uncertainty about their spending and have to decide on money holdings before the uncertainty is resolved.

The Clower constraint has also been imposed in general equilibrium continuous time models (Jovanovic, 1982; D. Romer 1986) where lump sum transactions costs generate a demand for money, as in the original partial equilibrium Baumol–Tobin models. There is a Clower constraint in the innovative continuous time model of Diamond (1984), in which both multiple and inefficient equilibria arise from the increase in the efficiency with which sellers search for buyers when there are more buyers. The constraint has been used constructively to explain asset pricing anomalies (Svensson, 1985; Townsend, 1987) and price level determinacy with pegged nominal interest rates (Woodford, 1985).

The money in the utility or production function approach has the benefit of greater generality in producing a demand for money. Indeed, as the theory of revealed preference shows, specifying that a good enters the utility or production function is merely the assumption that there is a demand for that good. Restrictions on the demand function emerge from the functional form of the utility function and from the precise way in which money balances are put into the utility function (Feenstra, 1986).

Rational Expectations and the Phillips Curve

The longest section of the 1976 survey discusses the rational expectations hypothesis and its applications in monetary models. A sample Phillips curve along Lucas (1973) lines, but more explicitly emphasising intertemporal substitution on both the supply and demand sides, is presented and used both to illustrate the information assumptions needed to generate a Phillips curve in an equilibrium model and the monetary policy ineffectiveness theorem.

The 1976 survey draws a clear distinction between the rational expectations hypothesis as a theory of expectations, and the type of equilibrium model in which the hypothesis was typically embodied at the time. Rational expectations has indeed become the dominant expectations hypothesis in macroeconomics, despite the evidence by Kahneman and Tversky (1979) of systematic errors in expectations, and repeated failures of joint tests of rational expectations and subsidiary hypotheses. The rational expectations hypothesis is the dominant paradigm because it is the natural benchmark model of expectations[7] and because the technology now exists to do rational expectations econometrics.

However, the need to couple the weak form of the rational expectations assumption – that individuals make the optimal use of the information available to them – with an explicit learning model is well recognised. De Canio (1979) showed convergence to rational expectations for a plausible learning process; the topic has been the subject of considerable recent research, (e.g. Bray and Savin, 1986, Marcet and Sargent, 1987), and will no doubt generate further results on conditions for convergence to a rational expectations equilibrium, and the nature of the alternative equilibria.

The further difficulty of dealing with the rational expectations assumption in a many-agent model in which each agent's expectations depend on his beliefs about the expectations of others has been wrestled with by Frydman and Phelps (1983). The problem of infinite regress can be cut through by assuming each agent's expectations of actual outcomes is correct. However, in situations such as the inception of an inflation stabilisation programme, the process of learning about the new situation where there are other agents whose actions depend on their beliefs is neither conceptually nor in practice straightforward.

The subsequent history of the Phillips curve component of the Lucas model is discussed in the next section.

II. MONEY AND EQUILIBRIUM BUSINESS CYCLE THEORY

The Lucas (1973) Phillips curve model[8] was the dominant equilibrium model for almost a decade. The distinguishing features of the model are that it builds the Phillips curve on imperfect information, and that the exposition though not necessarily the structure of the model emphasises a monetary cause of economic fluctuations.

---

[7] Or, what is almost the same thing, because there is as yet no clear way of choosing among alternative assumptions.

[8] Lucas (1972) is a more fully specified general equilibrium model that generates a non-exploitable Phillips curve trade-off. It is possible that this model contains multiple equilibria.

A third feature distinguishes the model as a prototype equilibrium model: prices move instantly to clear markets which are fully competitive. By contrast, Phillips (1958) rationalised his curve as an expression of the response of wages to labour market disequilibrium. If the expectations of individuals in the Lucas model were correct, the equilibrium would be a Pareto optimum. More even than the assumption of equilibrium, it is the assumption of competition that distinguishes the equilibrium business cycle approach from other analyses of economic fluctuations.[9]

Lucas derived several important results in his 1973 paper. The first is the Phillips curve-but result; there is a tradeoff between output and inflation, but the tradeoff is only with unanticipated inflation. This implies the *policy ineffectiveness result*, later developed by Sargent and Wallace (1975), that anticipated monetary policy has no real effects in models of this type. This was the main empirical implication of the model tested by later researchers.

The third result is that the slope of the Phillips curve in the Lucas model consists of a combination of a structural parameter, the elasticity of supply in each market, and a variance ratio that is affected by policy. Thus an apparently structural parameter, the slope of the Phillips curve, would change if policy changed in a particular way.[10] Such possibilities are at the heart of Lucas's famous *econometric policy evaluation critique* (1976), which asserts that because apparently structural parameters may change when policy changes, existing econometric models cannot be used to study alternative policy regimes.

The policy evaluation critique has had a devastating impact on both econometric policy evaluation and the seriousness with which large scale macroeconometric models are treated by researchers, at least in the United States. Into the mid-seventies, serious academic researchers were putting major efforts into large-scale models; state-of-the-art empirical versions of major behavioural functions were as likely to be found in the MPS (MIT-Penn-SSRC) model as anywhere.

Such models are now routinely dismissed as 'subject to the Lucas critique' – though remarkably, that critique has not been shown to be of any empirical significance in accounting for the failures of the econometric models in the seventies. Lucas himself (e.g. 1976) has repeatedly referred to the massive empirical failure of these models in including a long-run inflation–unemployment tradeoff that was falsified in the seventies.[11] But that was a failure of theory, which was repaired in the late sixties, following work by Friedman and Phelps, by adding the expected inflation rate to the Phillips curve. The 1973 supply shock also led to an underprediction of inflation in the major models, but that has nothing to do with the Lucas critique – unless the Lucas critique is reduced to the statement that models are inevitably misspecified.

---

[9] Equilibrium theorists frequently rely on the result that a Pareto optimum can be supported by a competitive equilibrium to analyse quantity movements in representative agent models without having to examine price behaviour.

[10] In the 1973 article Lucas attempted to test this implication using international cross-sectional data.

[11] See also Lucas and Sargent (1978) who refer to 'empirical failure on a grand scale' and the evaluation of that claim by Blanchard (1988).

From a theoretical viewpoint, the Lucas (1972 and 1973) model is of interest for its demonstration of the information-conveying role of prices. Lucas included two disturbances and one source of information about them – the price in the local market. Some of the subsequent theoretical developments elaborated on the information structure, for example by adding a capital market. The basic result in models in which money would be neutral with full information is that it will be neutral (non-superneutrality, such as the Mundell–Tobin effect aside) if there is sufficient information to identify the disturbances in the economy; so long as monetary disturbances (which may come from the demand as well as the supply of money) cannot be fully identified, unanticipated changes in money will have real effects.

Despite the elegance and intellectual power of the original model, subsequent intensive theoretical development, and some empirical successes, the imperfect information about current monetary variables approach to the monetary business cycle has met with severe difficulties. The basic problem is that it is difficult to believe that a lack of information about current nominal variables, particularly the price level, can be the source of monetary non-neutrality, when the lags in producing money stock and price level data are of the order of weeks. Further, if those lags were important, they could be reduced to seconds. It would be entirely possible to produce an on-line estimate of the current price level at low cost by providing terminals to businesses, which would enter price changes as they took place. The failure of the CPI futures market set up in the United States in 1985 also suggests that short term aggregate price level uncertainty is not a significant problem in the US economy.

Beyond this problem, empirical support for the model was not robust. Despite early work by Barro (1978) indicating that only unanticipated changes in the money stock affected output, later research by Gordon (1982) and Mishkin (1983) suggested that both anticipated and unanticipated money mattered. Results by Boschen and Grossman (1982) showing that output appeared to be affected by the currently perceived money stock, and related conclusions reached by Barro and Hercowitz (1980), coming as they did from proponents of the equilibrium approach, had a significant impact on supporters of the approach.

The Lucas model was set up to model the Phillips curve, or the apparent association between inflation and output. The non-neutrality of money is a problem for monetary theory precisely because money is neutral in most clearly specified models in which markets clear quickly. If sticky prices are ruled out on methodological grounds, and the implausibility of the information assumptions rule out the information-confusion assumption of the 1973 Lucas model, then it becomes difficult (this is an empirical statement) to provide a convincing theoretical account of a causal Phillips curve relationship.

The most influential demonstration of the real effects of money on output is no doubt Friedman and Schwartz's (1963a) account of the Great Depression; their more systematic attempt to address this issue (1963b) by working with cyclical average data and timing relationships was less persuasive because of the evident variability of the timing relationships and the question of causation.

Confidence in a causal role of money was increased by Sims' (1972) result in a two variable (nominal GNP and the money stock) system that money Granger-causes output, and by the previously noted results on the effects of unanticipated money on output. However, the disappearance of Granger causation for money in a vector autoregression to which the nominal interest rates was added (Sims, 1980 a, b) raised doubts about the role of money, even though no clear explanation for the latter finding emerged. Combined with the theoretical difficulties, this 1980 result led to exploration of the implications of endogeneity of the money stock.[12]

Money may be endogenous either because central banks pursue accommodating policies, or because most of the money stock is inside money, the real volume of which adjusts to the level of economic activity. Tobin (1970) showed in a model of endogenous money that particular money supply rules may generate the appearance that money Granger-causes (a concept that was not yet used in economics) output even in a context where it has no effects on real output (Tobin presented this result as an example of the *post hoc, ergo propter hoc* fallacy).

One approach to modelling the role of inside money is to include transactions services as a factor of production, and to assume that banks are involved in the production of such services, using labour, capital, and perhaps outside money as factors of production (King and Plosser, 1984).[13] In the absence of outside money, it is difficult to see why the price level or inflation rate as opposed to real activity is procyclical in such models. Once outside money is introduced, the behaviour of the price level follows from the interactions of the real demand for outside money and the nominal supply: this approach like that of Tobin (1970) relies on central bank behaviour to determine the correlation between the price level, the money stock, and output.

With regard to money, the equilibrium approach appears to be squeezed between the theoretical difficulty of finding a route through which monetary policy can affect output and the fact that changes in aggregate demand do appear in practice to affect output. The real business cycle approach sidesteps the money issue and attempts to account for the major characteristics of the cycle in a purely non-monetary framework.

III. BUSINESS CYCLES AND REAL BUSINESS CYCLES

Four sets of stylised facts are the central focus of business cycle analysis:

(1) There are fluctuations over time in both employment and unemployment, correlated across industries, associated with only small changes in the real wage, and apparently correlated with demand disturbances.

---

[12] Both Rotemberg (1987) and Blanchard (1988) examine and extend the evidence, concluding that it supports the view that monetary shocks affect output.

[13] However, there is no inherent reason that outside money is needed in such a system.

(2) These fluctuations, along with fluctuations in output, are serially correlated, which is the essence of the business cycle.

(3) Business cycle fluctuations appear to be correlated with monetary disturbances: there is a Phillips curve. The two approaches to building equilibrium models consistent with this fact have already been described.

(4) A final fact to note at this stage is that consumption, income, and employment are positively correlated over the cycle.

The work of Nelson and Plosser (1982) and subsequent research by among others Rose (1986), Cochrane (1986), Campbell and Mankiw (1987) and Quah (1987) has cast doubt on the conventional characterisation of the cycle as consisting of serially correlated divergences of output from a smooth trend. Rather it is argued there is a unit root in the stochastic process for output – and that there is little dynamics other than that. If there were no dynamics other than the unit root – that is, if output followed a random walk – then it would not be possible to talk of a business cycle in output. However, Campbell and Mankiw cannot reject the characterisation of output as a second order hump-shaped process around a deterministic trend. Further, Cochrane (1986) finds some evidence that the dominant root is less than one.

More fundamentally, even if there were a unit root in output, the business cycle could be defined as consisting of fluctuations of the unemployment rate about a slowly moving trend. There is little evidence of a unit root in unemployment, except perhaps for some European countries (Blanchard and Summers, 1986). Thus the existence of the business cycle does not seem threatened by the finding of a unit root in the stochastic process for output.

Business-cycle theory was a major branch of economics until the Keynesian revolution. Early business cycle theorists saw the cycle as largely self-sustaining, with each boom containing the seeds of the subsequent recession and slump, the slump in turn containing the seeds of the recovery and boom.[14] The business cycle continued to be a subject of research following the Keynesian revolution; Samuelson's (1939) multiplier-accelerator model, Kaldor's non-linear cycle (1940), and Hicks' non-linear models (1950) are all firmly in the Keynesian tradition. The Keynesian revolution did shift the focus of macroeconomics from the inevitability of the cycle to methods of improving macroeconomic performance.

During the long expansion of the sixties, it was even possible to think that the business cycle had been cured.[15] Poor economic performance during the seventies, reflected in the increased frequency and depth of recessions, together with the forceful advocacy of Robert Lucas (1977) renewed interest in the business cycle as a specific field of research. But modern approaches are not a continuation of the main line of earlier business cycle analysis.

Rather, modern theorists have followed the stochastic approach of Frisch (1933) and Slutsky (1937), which distinguishes between the shocks that

---

[14] Haberler (1937) contains an authoritative account of the earlier approaches.

[15] No doubt economic fluctuations will always be with us; the cycle would be cured if deviations from full employment output were small and serially uncorrelated.

impinge on the economy, causing variables to differ from their steady state values, and the propagation mechanisms that convert the shocks into longer-lived divergences from steady state values.[16] The modern approach is especially convenient for econometric implementation. Further – and this was the basic point of Frisch and Slutsky – the time series behaviour of economic variables produced when shocks disturb relatively simple linear difference equation systems is broadly consistent with business cycle characteristics. Adelman and Adelman in 1959 showed that the Klein–Goldberger econometric model (the forerunner of the Wharton model) generated output movements similar to those observed in the US business cycle when subjected to stochastic disturbances.

Shocks may hit the economy on the demand side, for instance a stochastic change in private sector or government demand for goods, perhaps resulting from a change in fiscal or monetary policy. Or they can come from the supply side, as productivity shocks, or shifts in the supply functions of factors of production. The shocks, for instance productivity shocks, may be serially correlated.

A variety of propagation mechanisms can carry the effects of the shocks forward through time:

(1) Because individuals prefer smooth consumption streams, temporarily high output today generates high saving, thus high investment, and a larger capital stock and higher output tomorrow.

(2) Lags in the investment process may mean that increased investment demand today increases investment demand and output in future periods as well.

(3) Firms carry inventories in part to meet unexpected changes in demand. A demand shock today will cause firms both to draw down inventories and increase production, and in future periods they will increase production to restore inventories. Thus production will be serially correlated.

(4) Individuals may work harder when wages are temporarily higher – the intertemporal substitution of leisure – and thus both magnify the effects of productivity shocks on current output and tend to produce negative serial correlation of labour input.

(5) Because it is costly for firms to adjust their labour forces, firms tend to adjust the labour force gradually in response to changes in wages and prices.

(6) Because individuals may take time to understand the nature of the shocks hitting them (in particular whether they are permanent or transitory) their responses to shocks may be distributed over time.

(7) Because it takes time for individuals to search for and find jobs, shocks to demand and supply lead to prolonged labour force adjustments.

Both the shocks and the propagation mechanisms identified in the preceding paragraphs can be embodied in either market clearing or non-market clearing

---

[16] Zarnowitz (1985) compares earlier and later approaches, not always to the benefit of the latter, which he suggests has become excessively fragmented.

cycle models.[17] Proponents of the *equilibrium real business cycle approach*[18] are distinguished by their view that virtually all business cycle phenomena are the result of productivity shocks hitting an economy in which markets are continuously in equilibrium.

In general, though, real business cycle theorists do not examine markets explicitly, rather drawing on the equivalence of market and planning solutions to deduce the behaviour of quantities that would be seen if resources were allocated optimally. They typically also work with representative agent models. In the remainder of this section I concentrate on the real business cycle approach, best exemplified in the paper by Kydland and Prescott (1982).

Serial correlation of output in an equilibrium model can be generated most simply by assuming that productivity disturbances are serially correlated – as they undoubtedly are. A priori it seems reasonable to posit that productivity shocks are a mixture of permanent changes that come from improvements in knowledge[19] and transitory changes such as those that come from the weather. If factor inputs were constant, any pattern of output correlation could be derived purely by specifying the stochastic process for productivity. Kydland and Prescott do assume productivity is serially correlated, though there is no indication in the description of their results how much the different shocks and propagation mechanisms in their model each contribute to the overall variability of output. Whether their assumption about productivity is a satisfactory basis for explaining cyclical and trend behaviour depends on whether independent evidence can be found for the assumed formulation (McCallum, 1986). Research attempting to identify supply and demand disturbances (Shapiro, 1987; and Blanchard and Quah, 1987) is currently under way.

I now briefly discuss propagation mechanisms; it will turn out that the key issue is that of the intertemporal substitution of leisure, without which shifts in aggregate demand have no impact on output and supply shocks have no impact on labour input.

The Role of Capital

It is straightforward to obtain a stochastic first order difference equation for output from an overlapping generations model of two-period lived people who supply work inelastically in the first period of life and save by buying capital that is used up in retirement. A positive productivity shock in the current period raises output and the income of the employed, therefore saving, and therefore future capital stocks. This produces positive serial correlation of output, through the supply side.

---

[17] Capital accumulation, inventory dynamics and slow adjustment of factors of production were all components of the MPS model.

[18] See for example the case made by Prescott (1986); Summers (1986 b) attacks Prescott's claims for the approach. Fischer Black (1982) was an early proponent.

[19] By definition, the stock of genuine knowledge must always be increasing, apparently implying that technical knowledge as represented by the production function should have only positive increments. However, mistakes may be made in choosing technologies to use. In the field of economics, monetarists would argue there was technical regress when the Keynesian revolution was adopted, Keynesians would argue there was technical regress when monetarism temporarily triumphed in the seventies.

However, the supply of capital route to serial correlation cannot be empirically significant. Suppose that a shock raises GNP this year by 1 % and that saving increases by as much as 0·5 % of GNP. With the real return on capital equal to about 10 %, the extra saving would increase output by 0·05 % in the following year, implying very little persistence of the effects of the productivity shock.

Long and Plosser (1983) develop a simple multi-sector capital model. With an n-sector input–output structure, and a one-period production lag between inputs and outputs, the system has n roots and is therefore capable of interesting dynamic behaviour when disturbed by productivity shocks. This model too will not generate high serial correlation of output unless the share of capital in output is high.

Nonetheless, it has long been observed that booms in economic activity are typically accompanied by investment booms; the multiplier-accelerator mechanism has for long been part of most accounts of the cycle. Kydland and Prescott (1982) emphasise 'time to build' – investment projects require inputs in several earlier periods before they come into operation. However, it is not clear from their exposition how much of their dynamics results from the time to build assumptions.

Inventories

It is well known (see for example Dornbusch and Fischer (1987), Chapter 9) that inventory decumulation accounts for a significant proportion of the decline in real GNP in periods following cyclical peaks. In every post-1948 US business cycle except one (1980–1), a large part of the decline in demand during the recession consisted of a decline in inventory accumulation.

The intuitive explanation for the role of inventories is that a decline in demand causes an inventory build-up, perhaps slowly if producers do not notice the demand shift immediately, and that production is then cut back to work off the excess inventories. In a model with a multiplier, this cutback in production itself reduces demand further, accentuating the decline in output.

Inventory accumulation is usually motivated in equilibrium models by production smoothing. Increasing marginal costs of production imply that it is cheaper to meet shifts in demand by changes in production that are distributed over several periods than by increasing production solely in the period of the demand shift.[20] A shock to demand causes an increase in consumption in the current period, which is met in part by increased production and in part by drawing down inventories. Then in subsequent periods production stays high as inventories are restored to their target level. In the case of cost shocks, a temporary cost reduction should lead to an increase in output and buildup of inventories, followed by lower output that allows inventories to return to their target level.

In the real business cycle approach, which emphasises productivity shocks,

[20] The insight goes back at least to Holt, Modigliani, Muth and Simon (1960). Blinder and Fischer (1981) embed production-smoothing-based inventory behaviour in an equilibrium model.

inventories tend to create negative serial correlation of output. A favourable temporary productivity shock results in higher output today, partly for consumption and also to build up inventories. Then in future periods output is lower than normal as the inventories are consumed, creating the possibility of negative serial correlation of output.

Although inventory dynamics is not helpful in explaining positive serial correlation in real business cycle theory, I briefly review recent work. The production smoothing model implies that if shocks are to demand, output is smoother than consumption; if shocks are to supply, output is more variable than consumption. Several researchers have found that the variability of production exceeds that of sales or consumption[21] implying either that the production smoothing model is inappropriate or that cost shocks play a larger role in explaining inventory behaviour than most researchers are willing to allow.

At least two other models have been proposed to account for the cyclical behaviour of inventories. One builds on production lags (Abel, 1985b; Kahn, 1987).[22] Suppose that the sales process takes at least one period, and that goods have to be in place at the beginning of any period in which they are to be sold, and that demand is serially correlated. Then high sales this period imply that inventories have to be restored, and that production has also to increase to meet higher than average demand next period.

A second approach, initiated by Blinder (1981), and followed by Caplin (1985) and Mosser (1986), explores the implications of models in which inventory policy is $s-S$. The policy is to order inventories only when the inventory level hits a trigger point, s, and then to order an amount that restores the inventory level to S.

If the average order size $(S-s)$ is large relative to sales, then this ordering policy, which is frequently used in practice, creates the possibility that production can vary more than sales. Whether it does depends significantly on the cost function of ultimate suppliers. If the supplier has constant costs of production, the $s-S$ policy may well lead to more variable output. Alternatively, suppose demand for the final good were relatively constant, and that the $s-S$ orders come in quite regularly to the producing firm. With concave production costs the producing firm would produce smoothly to meet expected orders, and the $s-S$ policy would determine only where inventories were held – by producer or by seller – rather than the production pattern (Caplin, 1985).

Intertemporal Labour Supply Substitution

Both capital accumulation and inventory dynamics undoubtedly play a role in business cycle dynamics, and both illustrate that entirely neoclassical economies in which markets are always in equilibrium can be expected to produce serially

---

[21] See for example Blinder (1984) and West (1985).

[22] Although the Kahn and Abel models are related, Abel examined conditions under which production smoothing still took place, whereas Kahn was looking for conditions that explain the 'excess' volatility of inventories.

correlated movements in output around trend. But none of the models we have developed so far accounts explicitly for the first stylised fact set out above, the pro-cyclical pattern of hours of labour.

If shocks are assumed not to come from the labour supply function itself, then the cyclical pattern of labour supply in an equilibrium model is determined by the cyclical behaviour of the real wage. The question of whether the real wage is pro- or counter-cyclical has been the subject of research for at least a half-century, since Keynes assumed in the *General Theory* that firms were always on their demand function for labour.[23]

Geary and Kennan (1982) test and are unable to reject the hypothesis that the real wage and employment are independent across a sample of twelve industrial countries. They show that results on the cyclical properties of the real wage depend on whether the CPI or WPI is used to define the real wage. However, the weight of the evidence by now is that the real wage is slightly pro-cyclical. Schor (1985) finds evidence of pro-cyclical wages in nine industrialised countries for the period 1955–70, with less pro-cyclicality in the subsequent decade. Basing his argument on overtime premia, Bils (1985) also finds significantly pro-cyclical real wages. We shall in the following discussion assume that the real wage is mildly pro-cyclical, but that it would require large elasticities of labour supply for these real wage movements to be interpreted as movements over the cycle along a simple labour supply curve.

There have been three approaches to explaining the cyclical behaviour of the real wage. One is to argue that the labour market is not in equilibrium, that, for instance, there is always excess supply of labour, and that the business cycle is driven by shifts in aggregate demand. The pattern of the real wage then depends on assumptions about pricing. In the *General Theory* and early Keynesian models, in which firms were assumed to be always on a stable demand function for labour, the real wage would be counter-cyclical if aggregate demand disturbances are the predominant cause of the cycle.[24] In mark-up pricing models, in which the price is a mark-up on the wage, the real wage may be independent of the state of the cycle.

The second argues that observed real wages have very little to do with the allocation of labour.[25] The wage is set either to provide insurance to workers, or as part of a long-term bargain between the firm and the worker, and need not vary with employment. Nonetheless, because it is efficient to do so, work at all times is pushed to the point where the marginal product of labour is equal to the marginal utility of leisure.

Proponents of equilibrium business cycles have however largely pursued a third route, the *intertemporal substitution (of leisure) approach*. The approach, which can be traced to an influential 1969 paper by Lucas and Rapping, argues that labour supply responds extremely sensitively to transitory incipient changes in

[23] It is well known that Dunlop (1938) showed the real wage was pro-cyclical in fact. Tarshis (1939) is often credited with supporting Dunlop's results, though as noted by Blanchard (1988) in fact he showed a negative correlation between changes in manhours and changes in real wages.

[24] When in the 1970s supply disturbances made their entry into standard macroeconomic models, it became clear that the cyclical pattern of the real wage depends on the predominant source of disturbances.

[25] This is implied by Azariadis (1975) and developed in Hall and Lilien (1979).

the real wage, and that this high elasticity reduces movements in the real wage. Whatever movements there might be in the real wage could easily be obscured by small disturbances to the supply of labour function.

Consider a person who consumes and works in two periods. The utility function is:

$$U(c_1, c_2, x_1, x_2) = \ln c_1 - \gamma(1+\beta)^{-1} x_1^{1+\beta} + (1+\theta)^{-1}[\ln c_2 - \gamma(1+\beta)^{-1} x_2^{1+\beta}], \quad (1)$$

where c_i is consumption, and x_i is labour; $\beta > 0$. The greater is β the greater is the curvature of the disutility of labour function and the less willing are individuals to substitute labour (and thus leisure) intertemporally. The individual maximises (1) subject to the budget constraint

$$c_1 + c_2/R = w_1 x_1 + w_2 x_2/R, \quad (2)$$

where R is one plus the interest rate.

Solving the resultant first order conditions, the ratio of labour inputs in the two periods is:

$$x_1/x_2 = \{w_1/[w_2(1+\theta)/R]\}^{1/\beta}. \quad (3)$$

The ratio of labour inputs is determined by the relative wages in the two periods w_1 and w_2/R, with an elasticity $1/\beta$ that depends on the curvature of the disutility of labour function, and which for β small (in which case the marginal disutility of labour is virtually constant) may be extremely large. Thus, depending on the utility function, a small increase in the wage in one period relative to the wage in the other may cause the individual to work much more in that period relative to the amount of work done in the other period.

When w_1 and w_2 change in the same proportion, (3) shows that there is no change in the ratio of work done in the two periods. It can also be shown that a proportional increase in wages in the two periods leaves total hours of work in each period unchanged as the income and substitution effects of the change in the wage just balance each other. That is, individuals may respond sensitively to transitory changes in the real wage, while not responding at all to permanent changes.

This result is the essence of the intertemporal substitution explanation of the behaviour of hours of work over the cycle: that individuals respond sensitively to the small pro-cyclical variations that can sometimes be detected in the real wage. Such variations could for instance be caused by productivity shocks. Hence, if the cycle were driven largely by productivity or supply shocks, and if intertemporal substitution were to be established as a major force in determining hours of work, the puzzle of large movements in the quantity of labour accompanied by small wage changes could be solved in an equilibrium framework.[26]

The empirical evidence on the intertemporal substitution hypothesis is mixed, though mainly unfavourable. Work by Altonji (1982) and Ashenfelter

---

[26] Note that the real interest rate plays a role in determining the intertemporal allocation of labour: a pro-cyclical pattern of the real interest rate could therefore account for cyclical changes in the quantity of labour that occur despite constant real wages.

(1984) finds little evidence to support strong intertemporal substitution effects in labour supply. Heckman and MaCurdy (1987) suggest that the evidence is still in its infancy, and that it is not inconsistent with equilibrium models that admit considerable worker heterogeneity.

Consumption and leisure over the cycle. Even if the intertemporal leisure substitution explanation of the cyclical behaviour of real wages and employment is accepted, the final stylised fact – the negative covariance of consumption of goods and consumption of leisure – has to be accounted for. More work is done in booms than in recessions; there is also more consumption (or at least purchases of consumption goods) in booms.

The standard utility function used to study intertemporal allocation problems is additively separable (over time). Assuming both consumption and leisure are normal, Barro and King (1984) show that such functions have the very strong implication that both consumption and leisure should move in the same direction in response to all disturbances except those that change the terms of trade between consumption and leisure within a given period, that is the real wage. Without real wage movements the cyclical pattern of consumption and leisure cannot be explained by the standard form of utility function. But since real wage changes are, if at all, only mildly pro-cyclical, the additively separable formulation cannot be a good one – if one insists on an equilibrium interpretation of the business cycle.

Mankiw *et al.* (1985) examine the Euler equations derived from the standard intertemporal optimisation problem based on a particular additively separable utility function. Using aggregate time series data they find no support for the intertemporal substitution model. The essential problem is the cyclical pattern of leisure and consumption, for they typically find that one or the other is inferior.

Equilibrium business cycle proponents have suggested two alternatives to the standard formulation. The first, due to Kydland and Prescott (1982), allows for habit formation or fatigue in the utility function, by replacing the leisure argument in the utility function by a distributed lag on leisure.

The second formulation builds on the fact that most variation in hours takes the form of changes in numbers employed rather than hours per employee. Staying within the representative agent framework, Hansen (1985) and Rogerson (1985) have built models in which individuals work either zero hours or full time (say forty hours).

Solving the central planning problem in such an economy, Hansen shows that 'wage' or consumption variability over time does not depend on the properties of the underlying utility of leisure function. Rather, the cyclical pattern of the wage reflects the properties of the marginal utility of consumption function and not the marginal utility of leisure function – after all, hours of work are not set to equate the marginal utility of leisure[27] to the real wage.

---

[27] If the utility function is separable between leisure and consumption, then the marginal utility of leisure at 40 hours of work per week is constant.

What is the market set-up corresponding to this central planning problem? It is that everyone owns a share of the firm or firms in the economy, and receives the same share of profits; in addition, every potential worker signs a contract with a firm, which guarantees a given utility level in exchange for the individual's willingness to work a specified number of hours if his or her number is drawn. If there is disutility to work, then each worker will receive a payment for signing, and an additional payment if he or she works.

It is not clear what should be regarded as the wage in this setting. If it is the marginal product of labour, then that may not change over the cycle – for instance if the utility function is separable, and there is the appearance of large changes in output with no change in the wage. Alternatively, if everyone who signs a contract with the firm receives a payment, and there is an additional payment for those who work, that marginal payment may be regarded as the wage – and it could be constant over the cycle. It is also possible though that the wage is measured as the per capita payment (averaged over employed and unemployed) received from the firm by each worker, which increases with the aggregate amount of work done in this model. Further, if the marginal utility of consumption were decreasing, the average payment per worker would be even more pro-cyclical.

Two issues are relevant in judging the potential value of the Rogerson–Hansen amendment to the standard equilibrium model. First, it is necessary to detail the factors determining the length of the workweek, and the possibilities of part-time and overtime work. It is clear that there is some fixed cost of taking a job and thus that the approach starts from a useful fact; it is also clear that the workweek in fact varies over the cycle, and that part-time work has become increasingly common. Second, the implication of full private insurance against unemployment and the fact that the unemployed are in no way worse off than the employed are both unsatisfactory, the first because there is very little private unemployment insurance, the second because it violates everyday observation. Whether by invoking moral hazard and non-homogeneities of the labour force it becomes possible to explain the absence of such private insurance in an equilibrium model remains to be seen.

The more important lesson of a model of this type may be that the representative agent assumption is unsatisfactory, and that labour force heterogeneity may play an important role in determining the cyclical pattern of wages. Suppose that for technological reasons individuals can work either full time or not at all. Suppose also that workers differ. Then variations in employment take place at the extensive margin where new individuals enter employment or leave it, rather than at the intensive margin of hours of work. Then the responsiveness of hours of work to changes in the real wage have nothing to do with individual utility functions, but rather with the distribution of reservation wages of those near the employment margin.[28]

Variation in numbers employed across the cycle is reflected also in the pattern of unemployment. Very little in the equilibrium business cycle

---

[28] This point is emphasised by Heckman (1984) and Heckman and MaCurdy (1987).

framework addresses the issue of unemployment.[29] Indeed, it has been common in this approach to work with the level of output as the key macroeconomic variable, and to treat unemployment as a secondary and not very interesting issue.[30]

Even if the unemployment issue is left aside, the equilibrium approach to the business cycle runs into its greatest problem in the labour market. Real wages simply do not show the movements that are needed for this theory to explain the facts, and it is unclear that the assumption of indivisible labour solves the problem.[31] What then could explain the facts? We have already noted that theories that do not require labour market equilibrium may do the job.

Alternatively, the reported real wage may not accurately reflect the marginal product of labour and marginal disutility of work. For instance, imperfect capital markets may result in firms paying workers a constant real wage over the cycle, with the allocation of labour nonetheless sensitively reflecting shifts in the productivity of labour and marginal valuation of time.

Labour Adjustment Costs

The real wage may differ from the marginal product of labour in the short run when there are costs of adjusting inputs.[32] Labour adjustment costs reduce the response of hours of work to the real wage: the firm changes its labour input in response to a transitory shock to productivity or the wage, by less than it would without costs of adjustment. In response to a permanent shock to the wage or productivity, the firm eventually adjusts all the way, setting the marginal product equal to the wage. But the adjustment takes time.

With respect to cyclical adjustments to real wage movements, this model has exactly the opposite implications to the intertemporal substitution model. Costs of adjustment therefore do not help account for the cyclical pattern of real wages and employment.[33]

Search Unemployment

Unemployment is modelled in an equilibrium framework as resulting from search, where the search is not only that of unemployed workers looking for jobs but also that of vacancies looking for workers. Mortensen (1970) develops a search-theoretic unemployment model and derives an explicit expression for the natural rate of unemployment as a function of the determinants of rates of

---

[29] Ham (1986) argues that the unemployed cannot be interpreted as being on their labour supply functions in any useful sense.

[30] This tradition goes back at least to Friedman's Presidential Address (1968). For an examination of the issue of involuntary unemployment, see Lucas (1978b).

[31] This claim is a matter of judgment. Heckman (1984) and Bils (1985) present evidence of pro-cyclical real wages.

[32] Models with labour adjustment costs have been studied by Solow (1965) and Sargent (1978).

[33] An extended version of the adjustment cost model is often used in explaining the cyclical pattern of labour productivity. In that version not only are there costs of adjusting the input of labour, but also the existing labour force may work harder at times of high demand, or may be used in times of slack on maintenance and other investment-like tasks.

job loss and acceptance. Lucas and Prescott (1974) present a complete model of the unemployment process generated by stochastic shifts in demand among sectors and a one-period lag by workers in moving between sectors. More recently Diamond (1981, 1984) and Pissarides (1985) have developed and worked with sophisticated continuous time search models.[34] Howitt (1987) is a particularly tractable search model, embodying adjustment costs for labour, and generating dynamic adjustment of employment and unemployment to productivity and demand shocks.

One theme of modern search theories of unemployment is that because job matches require an explicit search process, there is no market to set the wage (Mortensen, 1982). Rather it is assumed that the wage is set in a bargain which divides the surplus from the job between the workers and the firm.

Typically equilibrium is inefficient in these models, reflecting a search externality which arises because a worker's decision to search makes it easier for a firm to fill its vacancy – but there is no direct compensation from the hiring firm to the searching worker for his or her decision to become unemployed. The inefficiency may make a case for unemployment compensation. In the opposite direction, the congestion externality created for the unemployed by the decision of a worker to join their ranks could suggest a tax on unemployment.

Lilien (1982) argued that most of the variance of unemployment in the United States in the period 1958–77 was a result of relative rather than aggregate shocks to the economy, which set off shifts of workers between sectors and thereby affected the aggregate unemployment rate. Abraham and Katz (1986) and Murphy and Topel (1987) question this interpretation of the data: the former because differing supply and demand elasticities in any event imply differences in sectoral responses to aggregate shocks, and because the behaviour of vacancies is inconsistent with the relative disturbance hypothesis; the latter because rising unemployment is associated with a decline in the mobility of labour between sectors.

More direct evidence on the role of search in unemployment comes from surveys showing that the time of the unemployed is mostly spent waiting. The notion that individuals can search more efficiently when they are unemployed, and therefore optimally enter unemployment to seek new jobs has little empirical support. They could as well be working at MacDonald's. The theory of search unemployment might thus be replaced by a theory of optimal wait unemployment, which would presumably stress the influence of aggregate demand on the creation of job opportunities.

IV. THE NEW-KEYNESIAN REVIVAL:
PRICE-SETTING WITHOUT THE AUCTIONEER

Evaluating the contribution of the *General Theory*, Keynes remarked that the disappearance of the notion of aggregate demand for almost a century was an extraordinary episode in the history of economic thought (Patinkin, 1988). Much of the sophisticated development of the microeconomic foundations of

---

[34] Sargent (1987) presents several search theoretic models, mostly from the side of the worker or consumer.

macroeconomics in the 1950s, such as the permanent income–life-cycle theory of consumption, inventory and portfolio theories of the demand for money, and flexible accelerator theories of investment, elaborated on the determinants of demand.

There have been significant developments in the empirical modelling of aggregate demand since 1975, though no real departures from earlier theoretical approaches. The life-cycle–permanent-income consumption function remains the mainstay of consumption theory, with new testing methods having developed following the key contribution of Hall (1978). Hall tested the implications of the Euler equation or first order condition for intertemporal consumer optimisation, which under specified conditions implies that consumption should follow a random walk. It is not yet clear whether consumption is excessively variable or excessively smooth, the issue turning on whether detrended income follows a stationary process or not.[35] Empirical work on liquidity constraints and other causes of potential deviations from the permanent income hypothesis has turned to cross-sectional data (e.g. Zeldes, 1985). Tobin's Q theory of investment has received much attention and is widely used, though empirical results relating investment to stock prices are still far from satisfactory (Summers, 1981).

The last decade has seen real progress in the theory of aggregate supply on Keynesian lines. The Phillips curve was exactly the empirical construction the Keynesian model needed to model the supply side, endogenising the dynamics of the wage rate and the price level. But the theory of aggregate supply underlying the Phillips curve remained underdeveloped. Although Phillips (1958) and Lipsey (1960) both explained the Phillips curve as an application of the law of supply and demand, the law itself lacked microfoundations. Arrow (1959), discussing price setting, argued that the assumption of competition made explicit study of price-determination difficult.

The Friedman–Phelps addition of the expected rate of inflation to the Phillips curve both stimulated further work on the microfoundations of price setting, and tended to focus the reasons for the real effects of shifts in demand on output on errors in expectations. By 1970, Phelps and Winter were able to announce in the landmark Phelps volume that a 'landing on the non-Walrasian continent has been made'. The papers in the Phelps volume were mainly search theoretic, and implied that anticipated changes in prices would have no effects on output.[36] The radical implications of that result did not become clear until Lucas (1972, 1973) combined the Friedman–Phelps Phillips curve with the assumption of rational expectations.

Sticky Wages

The contributions of Fischer (1977a) and Taylor (1980)[37] clarified the distinction between the implications of rational expectations and of wage or price stickiness in accounting for real effects of money and aggregate demand

---

[35] For a review of the issues see Hall (1988).

[36] Nordhaus (1972) worked on the microfoundations of the Phillips curve, showing that there was no necessary inconsistency between mark-up pricing and competition.

[37] Phelps and Taylor (1977) also showed that nominal disturbances could produce real effects in a rational expectations setting with sticky prices.

on output. In each case sticky nominal wages determined in long-term labour contracts were the source of nominal inertia. Each model implied a potential stabilising role for monetary or aggregate demand policy even in the presence of rational expectations, and provided a framework for examining the dynamic effects of changes in policy on prices and output.[38]

Contractual wage setting allows for potentially interesting price and output dynamics in response to disturbances to supply or demand. Particularly in the Taylor model, where workers are concerned over relative wages and wages are held at a constant level throughout each contract, wage leapfrogging can produce protracted adjustments.[39] Because the dynamics depends significantly on whether contracts are staggered or co-ordinated, there has been extensive investigation of the determinants of the staggering structure.[40] Since real world contracts are co-ordinated in some countries (e.g. Japan) and staggered in others, it is likely that both structures may be stable, depending on the predominant sources of disturbances to the economy (Fethke and Policano, 1986). The efficiency of different staggering structures has also been investigated (e.g. Ball, 1987).

Although the contract wage setting approach has been fruitful, it too lacks microfoundations. In particular, as pointed out by Barro (1977), it leaves open the question of why quantities are determined by demand.[41] More generally, the fundamental question posed by any non-equilibrium approach to fluctuations in which wages or prices are sticky is why, if fluctuations are economically costly, private agents do not make arrangements that avoid such costs.[42] The notion that there must be some market failure, an externality or coordination failure, is an old one that has not until recently received satisfactory formal treatment, despite the suggestive analysis by Okun (1981).

When sticky wages are responsible for unemployment, the obvious question is: 'Why don't the unemployed bid down wages?' Keynes argued that wage flexibility would not in any case help maintain full employment, because of adverse effects of expected deflation on demand and employment. More recently, de Long and Summers (1986) have re-examined this argument, finding for some parameter values in the Taylor overlapping contracts model that wage flexibility is indeed destabilising.[43]

[38] For simplicity adjustment in both models is built entirely on the dynamics of wages and prices. In practice, other propagation mechanisms, such as inventory adjustment and others described in Section II above, affect the dynamic adjustment of the economy to demand and supply shocks.

[39] Calvo (1983) develops a very tractable contract model.

[40] These are reviewed in Blanchard (1988).

[41] Fischer used the *General Theory* assumption that firms are always on the demand curve for labour, while Taylor assumed markup pricing and the aggregate demand determination of output.

[42] Lucas (1987) has argued that the costs of aggregate fluctuations, as measured by the variance of consumption, are small. In the post-World War II period, elimination of all variability of aggregate consumption around trend would have raised utility, in a representative agent model, by the same amount as an increase in the level of consumption of one-tenth of one per cent. McCallum (1986) questions this estimate on the grounds that it assumes the trend is independent of stabilisation policy.

[43] Taylor (1986) claimed on the basis of an empirical analysis comparing the periods 1891–1914 and post-World War II that greater stickiness of wages and prices in the United States in the latter period increased the amplitude of fluctuations given the disturbances affecting the economy.

Solow (1979) forcefully addressed the question of wage stickiness, arguing that several causes each tend to create sticky wages and/or prices, and that the stickiness is a key fact in understanding business cycle fluctuations. We examine theoretical developments of three of the causes of wage stickiness that he discussed: long-term labour contracts,[44] the role of unions, and efficiency wages. In reviewing these topics, we should note the distinction between nominal and real rigidity of wages and prices: whereas the Fischer and Taylor models build on sticky nominal wages or prices, in order to develop models in which monetary policy has real effects, some of the work to be reviewed produces real but not nominal price stickiness.

Labour contracts. Baily (1974) showed that for any pattern of employment, an individual without access to the capital markets would prefer more stable to less stable income. Azariadis (1975) examined optimal labour contracts between risk averse workers without access to income insurance markets, and risk neutral firms, finding that the real wage in the optimal contract was state-independent, with the firm essentially smoothing the individual's consumption stream by paying a constant real wage. Azariadis assumed that workers worked either full time or not at all, and that firms made payments only to the employed, the unemployed receiving unemployment compensation or some other source of income.

The Baily–Azariadis result seemed to provide a reason for stickiness of real wages and variability of real output: with real wages sticky rather than increasing with output, perhaps increases in demand would call forth a greater increase in output than in competitive markets. However, it turns out that with constant marginal utility of income, output in the Azariadis model would be the same in each state of nature as in a competitive labour market.[45] Further, if payments could be made to the unemployed, employed and unemployed workers in the Azariadis model would receive the same income and the employed would envy the unemployed.

Insight into the output results in the Azariadis model was provided by Hall and Lilien (1979), following an earlier contribution of Leontief (1946): in any bargaining situation between workers and a firm, the employment contract should in each state of nature satisfy the efficiency condition that the marginal value product of labour be equal to the marginal disutility of work. The terms of compensation can then be set separately, and do not necessarily imply that the wage is equal to the marginal value product of labour in each state.

The mid-seventies approach, which built labour contracts around differences in risk-aversion and access to capital markets, does not account for the fact that firms set employment decisions. The later asymmetric information approach assumes that the firm knows the state of nature but the worker does not.[46] The firm and the employees agree on an optimal contract that specifies wage-

---

[44] This is a much- and well-surveyed field. See Azariadis (1979), Hart (1983), Rosen (1985), Stiglitz (1986), Hart and Holmstrom (1986).

[45] If workers' utility functions are such as to produce an upward sloping labour supply curve, employment varies more with labour contracts than in a competitive market.

[46] See the surveys noted above; Hart and Holmstrom provide a concise summary.

employment combinations in each state of nature. Because of the asymmetric information, contracts have to satisfy an incentive compatibility constraint whereby the firm does not have an incentive to misrepresent the state.

These contracts do imply that the firm sets the employment level. In general they do not satisfy the ex post efficiency condition, and thus can account for departures from Walrasian quantity levels. However, it also turns out that unless firms are more risk averse than workers, optimal asymmetric information contracts generally imply more employment in bad states of nature than would occur in a competitive non-contract labour market. This – together with the difficulty of deriving results – has led to some discouragement over the contract route to explaining economic fluctuations.[47] Nonetheless, the fact that asymmetric information – which certainly exists – makes for inefficient employment levels, is itself an important result.

Unions. The labour contracting approach to wage and output determination assumes that there is free entry into the labour pool attached to each firm. When workers are unionised, the union may control access to the firm's labour force, and may have its own utility function.[48]

McDonald and Solow (1981) showed that in contracts between a union (with given membership) and a firm, and given certain assumptions on the determinants of the bargaining outcome, the behaviour of the real wage over the cycle is determined by the cyclical behaviour of the wage elasticity of demand for labour. Thus with a constant elasticity of labour demand, the real wage would be invariant over the cycle, so long as not all members of the union were employed. This is another potential reason for real wage stickiness.

However, as noted by McDonald and Solow, their model is partial equilibrium and deals with wage and quantity determination in a single period. Unemployment occurs within the period when the demand for labour is low. But the average level of unemployment in a succession of one-period models realisations would depend on the dynamics of the reservation wage. If unions are to produce a higher average rate of unemployment than would occur in competitive markets, they have somehow to maintain a higher reservation wage than the competitive wage.

If unions succeed in obtaining high wages that cause unemployment in the short run, the dynamics of employment depends on whether it is possible for a non-unionised sector to develop. The existence of a pool of unemployed workers provides the opportunity for new firms to undercut existing firms by employing the current unemployed at wages below union rates. If this process works slowly, the presence of unions may account for slow adjustment of unemployment towards the natural rate. If unions rigorously control entry, they may be responsible for permanently higher unemployment.

There has been much interest, particularly in Europe, in using union models or related insider-outsider models to explain persistent high unemployment

---

[47] Grossman *et al.* (1983) have embedded asymmetric information labour contracts in a general equilibrium model and shown that shocks that change the variance of a variable relevant to firms' employment decisions may affect the aggregate level of employment.

[48] For surveys on unions, see Farber (1986), Oswald (1986) and Pencavel (1986).

(Lindbeck and Snower, 1984). Unions may be able to affect the average level of unemployment if they control entry into the workforce. The key issue then is what is the union utility function. For instance, if unions are concerned only with the interests of their current membership, they may totally ignore the unemployed, and can produce long-term unemployment (Blanchard and Summers, 1986).

The policy implications of insider-outsider models are not unambiguous. Presumably they justify open shop legislation and other steps to break union control over entry into the workforce; alternatively, Layard (1986) argues for subsidisation of the unemployed outsiders to allow them to break in.

Efficiency wages. The efficiency wage hypothesis is that the wage affects worker productivity.[49] In underdeveloped countries, low wages may impair strength and concentration and raising the wage may reduce the unit cost of the effective labour input.

There are several rationales for the efficiency wage hypothesis even where physical strength is not an issue. The simplest is the sociological explanation, that firms that pay higher wages generate a more loyal and therefore more productive work force. In the shirking model (e.g. Shapiro and Stiglitz, 1984) firms can only imperfectly monitor worker performance. Workers who are caught shirking can be punished only by being fired, in which case they receive the alternative wage. By paying wages above the alternative rate, firms provide an incentive to workers not to shirk. One criticism of this model is that shirking can also be prevented by alternative mechanisms, such as the posting by workers of performance bonds.

The shirking model provides an explanation for dual labour markets, in which higher wages are paid for primary jobs than for secondary (in which shirking is difficult) perhaps even for workers with the same ability. Whether the shirking model generates unemployment depends on how large the secondary market is relative to the primary; certainly it is possible to generate wait unemployment in a dual labour market if workers are willing to work at the primary but not the secondary wage (Hall, 1975).[50]

The implications of efficiency wage theories for macroeconomic fluctuations depend on their rationale.[51] Solow (1979) showed that the wage may be constant (at the unit labour cost minimising level) in an efficiency wage model. In underdeveloped economies, this would peg the real wage at a level determined by physical efficiency. In the shirking model, the efficiency wage would be set as a differential above the secondary wage. It would not then provide a justification for sticky real or nominal wages without further explanation for the stickiness of the secondary wage, or some explanation of why the primary wage itself was sticky. In both these cases, it is, if anything, the real wage rather than the nominal wage that would be sticky.

Sociological theories that build on the adverse effects of wage cuts on morale

---

[49] Katz (1986) presents an excellent survey and empirical examination of the efficiency wage hypothesis.

[50] Katz (1986) also discusses turnover, adverse selection, and union threat efficiency wage models.

[51] Startz (1984) builds an almost-textbook style Keynesian model with an efficiency wage as the only departure from a classical model.

could account for either nominal or real wage stickiness. Casual observation certainly supports the notion that wage cutting has an adverse effect on morale, but the deep reasons for that are unclear. Conceivably this is a self-justifying convention. Alternatively, relative wages may affect morale,[52] and wage stickiness may result from the difficulty of co-ordinating wage cuts across decentralised firms.[53]

Summary. With one possible exception, contract theory, union wage models and efficiency wage theories account for real rather than nominal wage rigidity. The possible exception is the nominal wage version of the argument that wage cutting reduces worker morale – but this hypothesis amounts to little more than restating the puzzle of the apparent inflexibility of wages.[54]

The union and efficiency wage models may also help account for unemployment.[55] To the extent that they produce both unemployment and rigid real wages, they also account for the fact that cyclical changes in the rate of employment are accompanied by only small changes in the real wage.

Sticky Prices

The Keynesian tradition and the Phillips curve emphasise nominal wage stickiness. Strictly interpreted, the aggregate supply theories outlined above account for real wage stickiness. Coordination problems – the fact that given other wages and prices, any change in a wage is a change in both the real and relative wage – could perhaps generate nominal wage stickiness out of real wage stickiness. However, co-ordination problems fail to explain why all wages are not routinely indexed. The conclusion is either that the original emphasis on nominal wage stickiness was misplaced, or that nominal wage stickiness still awaits an explanation. The preoccupation with nominal wage rigidity could be misleading though, a reflection of hysteresis in the development of macro-economic models, for rigid real wages are also a real world problem with important macroeconomic consequences (e.g. Bruno and Sachs, 1985).

More recently the emphasis has shifted from sticky wages to sticky prices. The new approaches generally start from a now widely-used model of imperfect competition in the goods markets that builds on the work of Dixit and Stiglitz (1977).[56] That imperfect competition is widespread is suggested both by observation and by the work of Hall (1986) on markups in US industry.

Imperfect competition general equilibrium. The *General Theory* and the monopolistic or imperfect competition revolutions occurred simultaneously. The notion that there should be close connections between them is an old one,

[52] Certainly observation of the economics profession suggests a keen interest in relative wages, and sometimes discontent over relative wage reductions that are also absolute wage increases.

[53] This is the *General Theory* argument that the aggregate wage level may be sticky because workers concerned with their relative wages resist cuts in their own wages which, given other wages, would imply a reduced relative wage.

[54] Nominal wage cuts in the early eighties in the United States certainly establish that nominal wages are not completely inflexible downward, but those cuts nonetheless appear to have been regarded as exceptional rather than the establishment of a new norm.

[55] Bulow and Summers (1986) press the case for the efficiency wage as an explanation of unemployment and other ailments.

[56] See also Hart (1982) and Weitzman (1982). I draw here on Blanchard and Fischer (1988, Chapter 7), which in turn is based on Blanchard and Kiyotaki (1987).

but the connection has only recently been made explicit (e.g. Startz, 1986). The intuitive reason there may be a link is that the Keynesian assumption that suppliers are always willing to sell more if demand at the existing price increases is a characteristic of a monopolistic equilibrium. The reason to doubt the link, at least in the case of nominal disturbances, is that monopolistic equilibrium determines a set of relative prices, which will surely be invariant to nominal shocks.

In the following general equilibrium model monopolistic competition can be used to make both points. There are n producer-consumers, each consuming all goods but producing only one, with the following utility functions:

$$U_i = (C_i/\gamma)^\gamma \left[(M_i/P)/(1-\gamma)\right]^{1-\gamma} - (d/b)\, Y_i^\beta \quad (1 > \gamma > 0; d > 0; \beta \geq 1), \quad (4)$$

where

$$C_i = n^{1/(1-\theta)} \left[\sum_{j=1}^{n} C_{ji}^{(\theta-1)/\gamma}\right]^{\theta/(\theta-1)}$$

and

$$P = \left[(1/n)\sum_{i=1}^{n} P_i^{(1-\theta)}\right]^{1/(1-\theta)}.$$

Utility depends positively on consumption, C_i and on real money balances M_i/P, and negatively on the output of good i, Y_i. The production of good i uses labour; the labour input enters the utility function in the form shown either because production is subject to diminishing returns or because labour is subject to increasing marginal disutility. The consumption of all goods enters the utility function symmetrically. The utility function implies a constant elasticity of substitution between goods, equal to θ. Constant terms in the utility function are introduced for convenience. Real money balances enter the utility function, and play a key role in transmitting effects of money stock disturbances to demand.[57]

Each individual faces the budget constraint

$$\sum_{i}^{n} P_j C_{ji} + M_i = P_i Y_i + \underline{M_i} \equiv I_i \quad (5)$$

where $\underline{M_i}$ is initial holdings of nominal balances.

Working from the first order conditions of the consumer, and making some substitutions, the demand curve facing each producer can be shown to be,

$$Y_i = (P_i/P)^{-\theta} [\gamma/(1-\gamma)n] (\underline{M}/P) \equiv (P_i/P)^{-\theta}(M'/P) \quad (6)$$

where unsubscripted variables represent aggregates.

Producer i sets price to maximise utility, taking the actions of other producers (their prices) as given. This implies the relative price:

$$P_i/P = \{[d\theta/(\theta-1)] (M'/P)^{\beta-1}\}^{1/[1+\theta(\beta-1)]}. \quad (7)$$

So long as there are increasing marginal costs of production $(\beta > 1)$, an increase in (M/P) results in both a higher relative price and higher output.

---

[57] Ball and Romer (1987) derive the same results using a Clower constraint.

With constant costs of production an increase in (M/P) would result in no change in the relative price, and an increase in output.

Finally, recognising the symmetry, all relative prices are equal to one, which implies from (7) the equilibrium value of the aggregate price level P, and the level of output of each producer:

$$P = [(\theta-1)/\theta d]^{1/(1-\beta)} M$$

$$Y_i = [(\theta-1)/\theta d]^{1/(\beta-1)}.$$

(8)

Note first that in equilibrium the quantity theory holds; the nominal price level is proportional to the money stock. It is also true though that if M' were to increase, and producers for some reason were to keep their nominal prices constant, the utility of each would increase. This is because price exceeds marginal cost. That is the source of an aggregate demand externality; if prices are fully flexible, each producer raises price when the money stock rises, and all producers acting together thereby reduce aggregate demand and welfare.

The PAYM insight. The derivative of the profit function of a price setting firm with respect to price is zero at the optimum. Thus divergences of price from the optimum produce only second order reductions of profits. Parkin (1986), Akerlof and Yellen (1985) and Mankiw (1985) observed that, combined with even small costs of changing prices, this implies that changes in demand may lead monopolistically competitive firms not to change price and instead to satisfy demand.[58] Thus shifts in aggregate demand may lead to changes in output. Further, the increase in demand may make everyone better off, in a first order way, because of the excess of price over marginal cost in the initial situation.

More precisely, the PAYM insight is that if all firms are at their optimal price, and there are some fixed costs of changing price, a sufficiently small increase in aggregate demand will lead to a welfare-increasing expansion of output.

Costs of price change are often described as menu costs, implying a physical cost of resetting a price. It is difficult to think of many goods for which such costs could be non-trivial. There may be a fixed decision cost to the firm of reconsidering the price it charges for a particular good. Or there may be a loss of goodwill for firms that change price. Okun (1981) argued that the goodwill cost is incurred by firms that change prices in response to demand shocks, but not by firms whose price rises merely pass cost increases on to customers.

The assumption in these cases is that there is a fixed cost to changing price. Rotemberg (1987) investigates the effects on price and output dynamics of quadratic costs of price change. Whereas with fixed costs of changing price, a large enough shift in demand will produce small effects on output because most firms will adjust price, with quadratic costs of price change, larger shifts in demand cause larger changes in output.

More careful examination of the PAYM insight raises several other interesting issues. First, there may be multiple equilibria. In response to a given shift in demand, both no change in price by any firm and full response in price

---

[58] Rotemberg (1987) named this the PAYM insight.

by all firms may be Nash equilibria (Rotemberg, 1987; Ball and Romer, 1987). In this sense, Ball and Romer argue that sticky prices may represent a coordination failure.[59] Second, there is the question of why firms would find it more costly to adjust price than quantity. Changing production plans too appears to involve decision costs. One possibility for a large firm selling to sophisticated buyers is that whereas the production decision is internal and has to be made daily, the price decision has to be communicated to a large group of actual and potential buyers, and is thus more costly.

Third, there is the question of the effects of aggregate demand shifts on output and prices when not all firms are at their optimum price at any one time. Caplin and Spulber (1987) show that if firms are uniformly distributed over the interval in which prices are set, and if the firms follow $s-S$ pricing policies,[60] then the distribution is maintained even after demand changes, and the average price level changes smoothly in response to demand changes. This appears to destroy the effects of the PAYM insight that produces Keynesian results in the monopolistic competition model. However, the Caplin and Spulber result appears not to be robust either to the effects of a monetary shock (Rotemberg, 1987), or to the possibility that prices may fall as well as rise (Blanchard, 1988).

It is not yet known what form optimal pricing behaviour takes when the aggregate price level is not growing steadily. An interesting result has been obtained by Tsiddon (1986), who examines the adjustment to an unexpected change in the aggregate inflation rate. When the inflation rate falls, the s-S range falls. This means that at the moment of the change, a number of firms find themselves below the new optimal s, and should therefore raise price to the new S. Some firms will be above the new S; they however may find it optimal to let their excessively high price be eroded by inflation rather than adjust it. The implication is that a reduction in the growth rate of money may initially lead to an increase in the price level.

Staggering and price dynamics. Blanchard (1988) draws the distinction between state dependent pricing rules, such as the $s-S$ rule, and time-dependent rules, in which prices are reset at particular times. The extent of time dependency varies across firms, for example between firms that print catalogues and those that sell perishables. Further, even for firms that usually set prices at particular times, large shocks may well disturb the regular pattern.[61]

Nonetheless, it is interesting to explore the implications of time-dependency of price setting. A key issue for dynamics in this case, as in the case of wage setting, is whether price setting is staggered or synchronised. Blanchard (1983) has used a stage of processing model to show how even short lags in adjusting prices can produce long aggregate lags if price setting is staggered.

Also, as in the case of wage setting, the question of the stability of the

[59] See also Cooper and John (1985) on coordination failures.

[60] Barro (1972) introduced s-S pricing rules for a monopolist. Sheshinski and Weiss (1977) show that if the aggregate price level is increasing at a constant rate, and if there are fixed costs of changing price, then it is optimal for firms to use an s-S pricing policy in which relative price is allowed to drop to a level s before being adjusted upwards to level S. See Rotemberg (1987) for discussion of optimal pricing policy.

[61] Time-dependent wage setting appears to be relatively more widespread than time-dependent price setting.

staggering structure arises. If an increase in the aggregate price level increases the desired price of a given firm, price staggering is unlikely to be stable. For instance, where prices are fixed for two periods, if more than half the prices are adjusted in even periods, those who adjust price in odd periods have an incentive to move their adjustment to the even period – because the price rise that they observe after the first period causes them to want to raise price. Of course, price adjustments are not synchronised in practice; the staggering may to some extent be due to seasonality and the non-synchronisation to the idiosyncratic shocks hitting the firm (Ball and Romer, 1986).

Real wages and the PAYM insight. It is not obvious in the monopolistic competition model outlined above why workers/firms are willing to supply more output when demand increases. In that model, increases in labour input are called forth by increases in the real wage, with larger β implying greater sensitivity of the real wage to output.

If β were close to one, output would change without much change in the real wage. But if β were close to one, equilibrium business cycle theory would have no difficulty accounting for the observed real wage-employment relationship. New Keynesians have taken two alternative routes in explaining the cyclical behaviour of the real wage in monopolistic competition models. Blanchard and Kiyotaki (1987) model each worker as a monopolistically competitive seller of labour. At their optimum quantity of labour sold, workers suffer little change in utility from working slightly more or less. That could explain the cyclical real-wage employment relationship if all variations in labour input were in hours, but is less persuasive when a considerable part of the variation takes the form of unemployment of the worker.

Akerlof and Yellen (1985) instead assume monopolistic competition in the goods markets and an efficiency wage model in the labour markets. The real wage is held constant at the efficient level, and variations in demand for goods are translated into shifts in output at the same real wage.

V. OTHER DEVELOPMENTS

In this section I briefly review recent developments in areas that have not so far been discussed.

Multiple Equilibria

There are now many rational expectations models with multiple equilibria.[62] There is nothing exceptional in the result that changes in expectations affect the equilibrium of the economy; the interesting feature is that those changed expectations (animal spirits) may be correct and thus self-justifying. This is a rigorous justification of the notion that optimism itself may be sufficient to create a boom, or that all we have to fear is fear itself.

Rotemberg (1987) reviews the varieties of multiple equilibria and their implications. Among the striking results are those by Kehoe and Levine (1985),

[62] Rotemberg (1987) categorises and concisely reviews these models, which include contributions by Azariadis (1981), Cass and Shell (1983), Diamond and Fudenberg (1982) and Shleifer (1986).

showing an extreme multiplicity of equilibria in overlapping generations models; by Grandmont (1985) showing that deterministic cycles of virtually any order can – under some restrictions on utility functions – be generated as rational expectations equilibria in an overlapping generations model with money as the only asset; and by Roberts (1986) producing a multiplicity of unemployment equilibria at Walrasian prices.

Policy analysis appears difficult when it is not clear at which equilibrium the model will start, nor to which equilibrium a policy change or other shocks will move it. One possibility is that multiple equilibria enhance the role of policy, because the government may be able to provide some focus for expectations about which is the relevant equilibrium (for instance the full employment equilibrium). An alternative view is that models with multiple equilibria are incomplete, awaiting the improved specification that will remove the multiplicities.

Credit Rationing

The recent concentration on the aggregate supply question of why output varies with only small variations in real wages has supplanted a similar earlier question, of how monetary policy affects real activity when interest rate movements are relatively small. In part the earlier question has been obscured because interest rate movements – both nominal and real – have become much larger in the 1970s and 1980s than in earlier decades; in addition, doubts have arisen about the effects of monetary policy on real output, as the rise of the real business cycle approach testifies.

Participants in credit markets believe that credit is rationed, in the sense that individuals or firms cannot typically borrow as much as they want to at the going interest rate. Credit rationing was part of the transmission mechanism for monetary policy in the MIT-Penn-SSRC model; with sticky interest rates, monetary policy affects the availability of bank credit and thus the volume of investment without necessarily affecting interest rates.

Credit rationing is certainly understandable when interest rates are controlled, say by usury ceilings.[63] But credit is likely to be rationed even without interest rate controls, for at least two reasons arising from incomplete information under uncertainty.[64] First is adverse selection: as interest rates rise, banks are likely to attract riskier borrowers. The second is moral hazard: as interest rates rise, borrowers tend to undertake more risky projects. In each case an increase in the interest rate may reduce the bank's expected return; the bank therefore rations credit. In his innovative thesis, Keeton (1979) demonstrates these two effects. He also draws a distinction between Type I and Type II rationing: the former applies when each individual receives less than the amount he or she would want at the going interest rate; the latter when among identical individuals some are rationed and some are not.

[63] Allen (1987) provides a comprehensive survey of the credit rationing literature. Stiglitz and Weiss (1987) review their earlier contributions and criticisms of them.
[64] The case for the importance of credit market phenomena, arising from imperfect information, in accounting for economic fluctuations and the apparent role of money in them has been made most vigorously by Greenwald and Stiglitz (1987).

Although credit rationing produces the appearance of non-clearing markets, it does not necessarily imply an inefficient allocation of resources (English, 1986). Along similar lines, Hayashi (1987) and Yotsuzuka (1987) have shown that even with credit rationing, Ricardian equivalence may hold.

The sense that credit rationing is an important component of the monetary mechanism was reinforced by the findings of Friedman (1983) that the debt-GNP ratio was among the most stable of macro ratios. However, in an example of Goodhart's or Murphy's Law, the debt-GNP ratio began to diverge from previous behaviour shortly after the Federal Reserve started announcing targets for the growth rate of debt.

Bernanke (1983), re-examining the Great Depression, argues that the increased cost of financial intermediation was largely responsible for the collapse of investment. Beyond the effects of credit on demand, Blinder (1985) claims that credit rationing affects aggregate supply. This is a variant on the familiar Keyserling–Patman–Cavallo-and-many-others argument that higher interest rates are inflationary because they increase costs. A sophisticated general equilibrium model of credit rationing and its impact on the macroeconomy has been developed by Bernanke and Gertler (1987), who start from asymmetric information between borrowers and lenders and show that firms' balance sheets matter, and that in some circumstances government bailouts of weak firms may be appropriate.

Banking

Fama (1980) and Fischer Black (1975) re-examined the theory of the banking firm, providing an abstract view of its role, as portfolio manager and operator of the accounting system. By and large this so-called new view of banking had no implications for the monetary mechanism beyond those already clear from Patinkin (1965).

The common literary notion that bank runs may be self-justifying prophecies was confirmed by Diamond and Dybvig (1983), who also discussed how deposit insurance could be a self-denying prophecy.[65] King (1983) assessed theoretical issues that have to be faced in analysing the nineteenth century question of whether a competitive banking system with free entry would be viable – an issue that the banking deregulation movement makes more than academic.

Bubbles and Excess Volatility

Shiller (1981) inaugurated a protracted and fierce debate over the issue of excess volatility of the stock market. The simple-minded observer watching the US stock market rise by a factor of almost three between 1982 and 1987 asks whether anything objective could possibly account for that increase, or whether some bubble or other irrationality might be responsible.[66]

It was Shiller's considerable achievement to propose a way of answering that question: because a rational stock price is the present discounted value of

---

[65] Jacklin (1986) describes and extends subsequent developments.
[66] This sentence appears in the first draft of this paper, which was written before October 1987.

dividends, the variance of stock prices should be related to characteristics of the joint stochastic processes for dividends and the discount factor. Shiller assumed the discount factor constant, and argued that stock prices fluctuated excessively. The Shiller tests were rapidly applied to the term structure of interest and exchange rates, with asset prices typically being found to fluctuate excessively.

The subsequent debate seemed to pit finance economists against macro-economists, with the advantage shifting over time to finance.[67] The key issue is the stationarity of the dividend process; most recent work tends to find that the stock market does not necessarily fluctuate excessively (see for example Kleidon, 1986 and Marsh and Merton, 1986), though anomalies remain in stock price behaviour.

At the same time as the empirical literature on excess volatility developed, so did a theoretical literature on the possibility of bubbles in asset prices. A bubble is a self-justifying departure of the stochastic process for an asset price from its fundamentals, and is another example of multiple equilibria. At a given rate of return, r, on an asset, the expected value of the bubble component of price has to grow at rate r. The first bubbles were deterministic: but a bubble could typically not be expected to grow at rate r if the economy was efficient, because it would eventually come to dominate the economy. Blanchard (1979) produced partial equilibrium examples of stochastic or bursting bubbles which would be expected to grow at rate r but would almost surely have burst by some point. In general equilibrium, Tirole (1985) has shown that bubbles can exist only in inefficient equilibria in which the growth rate exceeds the interest rate, and that bubbles tend to be welfare-increasing.

Ricardian Equivalence and Fiscal Policy

Barro (1974) inaugurated another protracted debate, this one over the question of whether individuals treat government bonds as net wealth. Patinkin (1965, p. 289) had discussed the implications of the issue for the neutrality of money and the effects of open market operations on interest rates. It seemed clear that if the debt floated by the government is to be paid off by future generations, then the future taxes implied by current debt would not offset the asset value of the debt. Barro's contribution was to show that finite lived individuals concerned about the welfare of their descendants might nonetheless behave as effectively infinitely lived, and thus take into account the taxes to be levied on future generations.

Although the issue was posed as 'is the debt wealth', the answer is also key to the questions of whether in fully neoclassical models fiscal policy affects real interest rates, whether federal budget deficits affect national saving and the trade account, whether open market operations are neutral, whether social security affects the capital stock, and so forth.

Bernheim (1987) presents an account of the analytic and empirical literature; it is clear that there are many reasons that Ricardian equivalence could fail to hold, and it is also clear that the evidence at this stage is insufficient to change

---

[67] This sentence too was written before October 1987; it remains to be seen how the 1987 crash will affect both the statistical and the polemical debates.

the prior views of most economists by very much. Poterba and Summers (1987) argue that the concentration on finite horizons is misleading, in that typically most of the debt will be paid off by those currently alive. The US fiscal policy experiment of the early 1980s should, one might hope, have settled the issue once-for-all: the major change in the deficit raised real interest rates and did not increase private saving. However, that is only one episode, and its influence in regressions appears insufficient to reject Ricardian equivalence (Evans, 1987).

Sargent and Wallace's (1981) startling claim that bond financing of a government budget deficit could produce a higher inflation rate than monetary financing increased the awareness of the intertemporal implications of the government budget constraint. The argument is that if the deficit will ultimately be financed by money printing, then the accumulation of interest on the debt will require higher seigniorage revenue in the future – which would imply a higher steady state inflation rate with bond financing, and could even imply higher inflation now. The subsequent debate clarified not only the reasonably general conditions under which the result holds, but also the relationship between budget deficits and inflation (Drazen and Helpman, 1986), which depends on the policies that are expected to be used to reduce the deficit to a sustainable level.

Indexation

In 1974 Milton Friedman returned from Brazil convinced that indexation would protect the real economy from monetary disturbances and thereby reduce the costs of inflation. Gray (1976) and Fischer (1977b) confirmed that indexation indeed neutralised the effects of monetary shocks on real variables; indexation in the capital markets would also neutralise the effects of nominal shocks. But indexation might amplify the real effects of real shocks to the economy.

Given the clear results on indexation and nominal shocks, the minimal adoption of indexation in private contracts remains difficult to explain. Evidently there are major advantages to nominal contracting that are not captured by existing models. One possibility is that nominal shocks account for only a small part of the uncertainty about the outcomes of contracts, which, together with small costs of adding complexity to contracts, prevents indexation.

The experience of accelerating inflation in heavily indexed economies such as Brazil and Israel has been a chastening experience for proponents of indexation. The fact that high inflation reflects problems in policy making was not taken sufficiently into account; if as a result of indexation the real effects of inflation are reduced, the result may be an increase in the rate of inflation to achieve similar real effects.

Weitzman's much-discussed proposal that workers take part of their compensation as a share of profits bears some similarity to indexing of the wage to profits, at the firm level. Weitzman (e.g. 1986) argues that firms are more willing to hire labour in a profit-sharing scheme, which would enhance macroeconomic stability. The extent to which superior Japanese unemployment experience reflects their bonus system is a key issue in evaluating profit-sharing. There has been intensive examination of the issue in Britain, where incentives for profit-sharing have been provided in the budget.[68]

The Theory of Growth

After rapid development in the fifties and sixties, the theories of economic growth and capital received relatively little attention for almost two decades, despite the absolutely central importance of growth to economic performance. The Ramsey–Solow and Samuelson overlapping generations models became workhorses of micro-based macroeconomics, but the theory of growth as such was neglected. The worldwide growth slowdown made it inevitable that interest in growth would revive, though neither theory nor intensive empirical work has yet provided a persuasive explanation for the slowdown. Recent work has emphasised the role of economies of scale in the growth process (e.g. P. Romer, 1986).

The Theory of Policy

The rational expectations revolution in macroeconomics and game theory have combined to produce a far more sophisticated approach to the analysis of policy than was state of the art a decade ago. A key paper here is Kydland and Prescott (1977), which introduced the problem of dynamic inconsistency of optimal policy and argued that the dynamic inconsistency arising from discretionary policy-making could be prevented by adopting policy rules. Developing the game theory approach, Prescott (1978) dismissed the use of optimal control theory for the design of optimal policy on the grounds that economic agents do not respond mechanistically to changes in policy rules.

The game theoretic approach to policy makes it possible to model notions such as reputation and credibility that have long been staples of policymakers' own discussions of their actions.[69] The predictive content of these applications, as opposed to their usefulness in providing insights, remains to be developed. Barro and Gordon (1983) showed that discretionary monetary policy-making could produce an inflationary bias, but subsequent developments that allow for reputational effects have weakened that result; nor is it clear how to test it.

VI. CONCLUDING COMMENTS

Any comparison of the contents of this survey with that of Barro and Fischer (1976) must conclude that there has been a tremendous increase in the breadth and depth of macroeconomics in the past decade. Technical progress from the side of both theory and econometrics has made it possible to address and illuminate issues that were simply too difficult before – such as the excess

[68] Blanchflower and Oswald (1986), who present evidence that profit-sharing has been widely used in Britain, and Estrin, et al. (1987) take a sceptical view of the stabilising and other beneficial effects of profit-sharing.

[69] This large and rapidly growing literature receives little space here because it has been surveyed at length by, among others, Fischer (1986) and Rogoff (1987).

volatility of asset prices, the macroeconomic implications of monopolistic competition, co-ordination problems in the macroeconomy, bank runs, and the existence of multiple equilibria, to pick just a few examples.

There is no question that macroeconomics is far more microeconomics-based than it used to be. In a sense the microeconomic foundations of macro now exist, in equilibrium models of the Prescott–Kydland type in the equilibrium approach, and in models such as the Akerlof and Yellen model in the post-Keynesian approach. But to a considerable extent the earlier notion that once the microeconomic foundations had been laid, a set of standard macro models could be used, has not been justified. Rather the tendency has been to build a variety of micro-based models, each making or emphasising a specific point.

A three equation macromodel, consisting of the IS-LM apparatus plus an aggregate supply equation is frequently used. In the simplest version the IS-LM side is reduced to the quantity equation or a Clower constraint, and a Lucas aggregate supply equation, or one in which exogenous productivity shocks drive output, is added. In the more Keynesian versions, velocity becomes a function of the interest rate, and there is more detail on the demand side. In terms of this model, there has been advance in testing of the aggregate demand side (e.g. Hall, 1978 on consumption) but not to the same extent in understanding of the structural determinants of demand; there has been real progress in analysis of the financial markets, though not necessarily in understanding of the transmission mechanism of monetary policy; and there is greater understanding of the theoretical underpinnings of the supply side.

Has macroeconomics progressed? Yes: there has been remarkable progress in understanding many theoretical issues, some specified above, that were only imprecisely understood before. There has also been progress in understanding the structure of the basic macro model.

And yet: there is greater not less confusion at the business end of macroeconomics, in understanding the actual causes of macroeconomic fluctuations, and in applying macroeconomics to policy-making. Revealing untruths is of course progress, and it is possible that the greater uncertainty that now exists is part of the process of rubble-clearing that precedes the erection of a new structure.

Probably it is not. Rather there are two factors at work. One is the increasing realisation of the extraordinary difficulty of settling disputes with econometric evidence. Take for instance the issues of Ricardian equivalence and excess volatility of asset prices. Both are quite fundamental, both have been the subjects of intensive empirical scrutiny, but neither has yielded to the time series evidence brought to bear.

What the implications of the lack of cutting power of time series macroeconometrics may be remains to be seen. The use of panel data, statistical events studies as in finance, and careful case studies of particular episodes, are all obvious possibilities.

The second factor is that it has become fashionable, at least in the United States, to claim that economists have little to say on the policy issues of the day, beyond recommending institutional reforms. That is the comparative advantage of some. But it would not be progress for macroeconomists in general to avoid current policy issues, for instance by arguing that while we can (perhaps) design a good budget rule, we cannot answer the question of whether the budget deficit should be cut now or not. The decision will be made, one way or the other, and the abdication of serious macroeconomists leaves the policy advice business to those either ignorant or unscrupulous enough to claim full understanding of the issues. Macroeconomists will not be able to participate seriously in such analyses without the use of models, small or large, that attempt to quantify the impact of policy decisions.

Finally one has to ask where the field is heading. There are two correct answers. One is that the field is no longer a field, that it is too big for any researcher to describe her or himself as a specialist in it, and that much of macroeconomics will gradually meld into subspecialities and partly be absorbed in existing fields.

The second is that macroeconomics will continue just as long as macroeconomic fluctuations. If one further takes the (appropriate) view that business fluctuations are not caused by one major set of shocks, nor propagated mainly by a single important mechanism, then progress will have to be made in evaluating the significance of each mechanism and fitting the pieces together. That is what macroeconometric models attempt to do; it is also what Kydland and Prescott attempt in their calibrated (1982) model. Within such models, the aggregate supply side remains the outstanding challenge.

BIBLIOGRAPHY

Abel, Andrew B. (1985 a). 'Dynamic behavior of capital accumulation in a cash-in-advance model.' *Journal of Monetary Economics*, vol. 16, no. 1, pp. 55–71.
—— (1985 b). 'Inventories, stock-outs and production smoothing.' *Review of Economic Studies*, vol. 52, pp. 283–93.
Abraham, Katherine G. and Katz, Lawrence F. (1986). 'Cyclical unemployment: sectoral shifts or aggregate disturbances?' *Journal of Political Economy*, vol. 94, no. 3, pp. 507–22.
Adelman, Irma and Adelman, Frank (1959). 'The dynamic properties of the Klein–Goldberger model.' *Econometrica*, vol. 27, no. 4, October, pp. 596–625.
Akerlof, George, A. and Milbourne, Ross D. (1980). 'The short run demand for money.' ECONOMIC JOURNAL, vol. 90, December, pp. 885–900.
—— and Yellen, Janet (1985). 'A near-rational model of the business cycle with wage and price inertia.' *Quarterly Journal of Economics*, vol. 100, Supplement, pp. 176–213.
Allen, Linda (1987). 'The credit rationing phenomenon: a survey of the literature.' Occasional Papers in Business and Finance no. 7, Salomon Brothers Center, New York University.
Altonji, Joseph G. (1982). 'The intertemporal substitution model of labour market fluctuations: an empirical analysis.' *Review of Economic Studies*, vol. 49, no. 5, Special Issue, pp. 783–824.
Arrow Kenneth J. (1959). 'Towards a theory of price adjustment.' In *The Allocation of Economic Resources* (ed. M. Abramowitz *et al.*). Stanford, CA: Stanford University Press.
Ashenfelter, Orley (1984). 'Macroeconomic analyses and microeconomic analyses of labour supply.' In Carnegie-Rochester Conference Series, vol. 21 (ed. K. Brunner and A. Meltzer).
Azariadis, Costas (1975). 'Implicit contracts and underemployment equilibria.' *Journal of Political Economy*, vol. 83, no. 6, pp. 1183–202.
—— (1979). 'Implicit contracts and related topics.' In *The Economics of the Labour Market* (ed. Z. Hornstein), London: Her Majesty's Stationery Office.
—— (1981). 'Self-fulfilling prophecies.' *Journal of Economic Theory*, vol. 25, no. 3, pp. 380–96.
Baily, Martin N. (1974). 'Wages and employment under uncertain demand.' *Review of Economic Studies*, vol. 41, no. 1, pp. 37–50.
Ball, Laurence (1987). 'Externalities from contract length.' *American Economic Review*, vol. 77, no. 4 pp. 615–29.

—— and Romer, David (1986). 'The equilibrium and optimal timing of prices changes.' Mimeo, New York University.

—— and —— (1987). 'Sticky prices as coordination failure.' NBER Working Paper no. 2327 (July).

Barnett, William A., Offenbacher, Edward K. and Spindt, Paul A. (1984). 'The new Divisia monetary aggregates.' *Journal of Political Economy*, vol. 92, no. 6, pp. 1049–85.

Barro, Robert J. (1972). 'A theory of monopolistic price adjustment.' *Review of Economic Studies*, vol. 39, no. 1, pp. 93–110.

—— (1974). 'Are government bonds net wealth?' *Journal of Political Economy*, vol. 81, no. 6, pp. 1095–117.

—— (1977). 'Long-term contracting, sticky prices, and monetary policy.' *Journal of Monetary Economics*, vol. 3, no. 3, pp. 305–16.

—— (1978). 'Unanticipated money, output, and the price level in the United States.' *Journal of Political Economy*, vol. 86, no. 4, pp. 549–80.

—— and Gordon, David B. (1983). 'A positive theory of monetary policy in a natural rate model.' *Journal of Political Economy*, vol. 91, no. 4, pp. 589–610.

—— and Fischer, Stanley (1976). 'Recent developments in monetary theory.' *Journal of Monetary Economics*, vol. 2, no. 2, pp. 133–67.

—— and Hercowitz, Zvi (1980). 'Money stock revisions and unanticipated money growth.' *Journal of Monetary Economics*, vol. 6, April, pp. 257–67.

—— and King, Robert G. (1984). 'Time-separable preferences and intertemporal-substitution models of business cycles.' *Quarterly Journal of Economics*, vol. 99, no. 4, pp. 817–40.

Begg, David (1977). 'Rational expectations of inflation and the behavior of asset returns in a stochastic macroeconomic model.' Ph.D. dissertation, Department of Economics, MIT.

Benassy, Jean-Pascal (1976). 'The disequilibrium approach to monopolistic price setting and general monopolistic equilibrium.' *Review of Economic Studies*, vol. 43, no. 1, pp. 69–81.

Bernanke, Ben (1983). 'Non-monetary effects of the financial crisis in the propagation of the Great Depression.' *American Economic Review*, vol. 73, no. 3, pp. 257–76.

—— and Gertler, Mark (1987). 'Financial fragility and economic performance.' NBER Working Paper no. 2318 (July).

Bernheim, B. Douglas (1987). 'Ricardian equivalence: an evaluation of theory and evidence.' *NBER Macroeconomics Annual*, vol. 2, pp. 263–303.

Bils, Mark J. (1985). 'Real wages over the business cycle: evidence from panel data.' *Journal of Political Economy*, vol. 93, no. 4, pp. 666–89.

Black, Fischer (1975). 'Bank funds management in an efficient market.' *Journal of Financial Economics*, vol. 2, pp. 323–39.

—— (1982). 'General equilibrium and business cycles.' NBER Working Paper no. 950.

Blanchard, Olivier J. (1979). 'Speculative bubbles, crashes and rational expectations.' *Economics Letters*, vol. 3, pp. 387–9.

—— (1983). 'Price asynchronization and price level inertia.' In *Inflation, Debt, and Indexation* (ed. R. Dornbusch and M. H. Simonsen). Cambridge, MA: MIT Press.

—— (1988). 'Why does money affect output? A survey.' In *Handbook of Monetary Economics* (ed. B. M. Friedman and F. H. Hahn). North Holland. (In the Press.)

—— and Fischer, Stanley (1989). *Lectures on Macroeconomics*. Cambridge, MA: MIT Press.

—— and Kiyotaki, Nobuhiro (1987). 'Monopolistic competition and the effects of aggregate demand.' *American Economic Review*, vol. 77, no. 4, pp. 647–66.

—— and Quah, Danny (1987). 'The dynamic effects of aggregate demand and supply disturbances.' Mimeo, Department of Economics, MIT.

—— and Summers, Lawrence H. (1986). 'Hysteresis and the European unemployment problem.' *NBER Macroeconomics Annual*, pp. 15–78.

Blanchflower D. G. and Oswald A. J. (1986). 'Profit Related Pay: Prose Discovered?' Centre for Labour Economics, London School of Economics.

Blinder, Alan S. (1981). 'Retail inventory behavior and business fluctuations.' *Brookings Papers on Economic Activity*, vol. 2, pp. 443–505.

—— (1984). 'Can the production smoothing model of inventory behavior be saved?' NBER Working Paper no. 1257.

—— and Fischer, Stanley (1981). 'Inventories, rational expectations and the business cycle.' *Journal of Monetary Economics*, vol. 8, pp. 277–304.

—— (1985). 'Credit rationing and effective supply failures.' NBER Working Paper no. 1619.

Boschen, John and Grossman, Herschel (1982). 'Tests of equilibrium macroeconomics with contemporaneous monetary data.' *Journal of Monetary Economics*, vol. 10, November, pp. 309–33.

Bray, M. M. and Savin, N. E. (1986). 'Rational expectations equilibria, learning, and model specification.' *Econometrica*, vol. 54, no. 5, pp. 1129–60.

Breeden, Douglas (1979). 'An intertemporal asset pricing model with stochastic consumption and investment opportunities.' *Journal of Financial Economics*, vol. 7, September, pp. 265–96.

Brunner, Karl and Meltzer, Allan H. (1971). 'The uses of money: money in the theory of an exchange economy.' *American Economic Review*, vol. 61, no. 5, pp. 784–805.

—— and —— (1976). 'An aggregate theory for a closed economy.' In *Monetarism* (ed. J. Stein). New York: North-Holland.

Bruno, Michael and Fischer, Stanley (1985). 'Expectations and the high inflation trap.' Mimeo, Department of Economics, MIT.

—— and Sachs, Jeffrey (1985). *The Economics of Worldwide Stagflation*. Cambridge, MA: Harvard University Press.

Bulow, Jeremy I. and Summers, Lawrence H. (1986). 'A theory of dual labor markets with application to industrial policy, discrimination, and Keynesian unemployment.' *Journal of Labor Economics*, vol. 4, no. 3, pp. 376–414.

Calvo, Guillermo A. (1983). 'Staggered prices in a utility-maximizing framework.' *Journal of Monetary Economics*, vol. 12, no. 3, pp. 383–98.

Campbell, John Y. (1986) 'Bond and stock returns in a simple exchange model.' *Quarterly Journal of Economics*, vol. 101, no. 4, pp. 785–803.

—— and Mankiw, N. Gregory (1987). 'Are output fluctuations transitory?' *Quarterly Journal of Economics*, forthcoming.

Caplin, Andrew S. (1985). 'The variability of aggregate demand with (S, s) inventory policies.' *Econometrica*, vol. 53, no. 6, pp. 1395–410.

—— and Spulber, Daniel (1987). 'Menu costs and the neutrality of money.' *Quarterly Journal of Economics*, vol. 102, no. 4, pp. 703–26.

Cass, David and Shell, Karl (1983). 'Do sunspots matter?' *Journal of Political Economy*, vol. 91, no. 2, pp. 193–227.

Cochrane, John (1986). 'How big is the random walk component in GNP?' Mimeo, University of Chicago.

Cooper, Russell and John, Andrew (1985). 'Coordinating coordination failures in Keynesian models.' Cowles Foundation Discussion Paper no. 745R, Yale University.

Cox, John C., Ingersoll, Jonathan E. and Ross, Stephen A. (1985). 'A theory of the term structure of interest rates.' *Econometrica*, vol. 53, no. 2, pp. 385–408.

De Canio, Stephen (1979). 'Rational expectations and learning from experience.' *Quarterly Journal of Economics*, vol. 93, no. 1, pp. 47–58.

De Long, J. Bradford and Summers, Lawrence H. (1986). 'Is increased price flexibility destabilizing?' *American Economic Review*, vol. 76, no. 5, pp. 1031–44.

Diamond, Douglas W. and Dybvig, Philip (1983). 'Bank runs, deposit insurance and liquidity', *Journal of Political Economy*, vol. 91, no. 3, June, pp. 401–19.

Diamond, Peter A. (1981). 'Mobility costs, frictional unemployment, and efficiency.' *Journal of Political Economy*, vol. 89, no. 4, pp. 798–812.

—— (1984). 'Money in search equilibrium.' *Econometrica*, vol. 52, no. 1, pp. 1–20.

—— and Fudenberg, Drew (1982). 'An example of animal spirits equilibrium.' Mimeo, Department of Economics, MIT.

Dixit, Avinash and Stiglitz, Joseph E. (1977). 'Monopolistic competition and optimum product diversity.' *American Economic Review*, vol. 67, no. 3, pp. 297–308.

Dornbusch, Rudiger and Fischer, Stanley (1987). *Macroeconomics* (4th edition). New York: McGraw Hill.

Drazen, Allan (1979). 'The optimal rate of inflation revisited.' *Journal of Monetary Economics*, vol. 5, no. 2, pp. 231–48.

—— (1980). 'Recent developments in macroeconomic disequilibrium theory.' *Econometrica*, vol. 48, no. 2, pp. 283–306.

—— and Helpman, Elhanan (1986). 'Inflationary consequences of anticipated macroeconomic policies.' NBER Working Paper no. 2006.

Dunlop, John T. (1938). 'The movements of real and money wages.' ECONOMIC JOURNAL, pp. 413–34.

English, William B. (1986). 'Credit rationing in general equilibrium.' CARESS Working Paper no. 86–20, University of Pennsylvania.

Estrin, Saul, Grout, Paul and Wadwhani, Sushil (1987). 'Profit-sharing and employee share ownership.' *Economic Policy*, vol. 2, no. 1, April, pp. 13–52.

Evans, Paul (1987). 'Interest rates and expected future budget deficits in the United States.' *Journal of Political Economy*, vol. 95, no. 1, pp. 34–58.

Faig, Miguel (1985). 'Optimal taxation of money balances.' Mimeo, Economics Department, Stanford University.

Fama, Eugene F. (1975). 'Short-term interest rates as predictors of inflation.' *American Economic Review*, vol. 65, no. 3, pp. 269–82.

—— (1980). 'Banking in the theory of finance.' *Journal of Monetary Economics*, vol. 6, no. 1, pp. 39–57.

Farber, Henry (1986). 'The analysis of union behavior.' In *Handbook of Labor Economics* (ed. O. Ashenfelter and R. Layard).

Feenstra, Robert C. (1986). 'Functional equivalence between liquidity costs and the utility of money.' *Journal of Monetary Economics*, vol. 17, pp. 271–91.

Feldstein, Martin (1976). 'Inflation, income taxes, and the rate of interest.' *American Economic Review*, vol. 66, no. 5, pp. 809–20.

—— and Summers, Lawrence H. (1978). 'Inflation, tax rules, and the long-term interest rate.' *Brookings Papers on Economic Activity*, vol. 1, pp. 61–99.

Fethke, Gary and Policano, Andrew (1986). 'Will wage setters ever stagger decisions?' *Quarterly Journal of Economics*, vol. 101, no. 4, pp. 867–77.

Fischer, Stanley (1977 a). 'Long-term contracts, rational expectations, and the optimal money supply rule.' *Journal of Political Economy*, vol. 85, no. 1, pp. 191–206.

—— (1977 b). 'Wage indexation and macroeconomic stability.' In Carnegie-Rochester Conference Series on Public Policy, vol. 5 (ed. K. Brunner and A. Meltzer).

—— (1979). 'Capital accumulation on the transition path in a monetary optimizing model.' *Econometrica*, vol. 47, no. 6, pp. 1433–9.

—— (1981). 'Towards an understanding of the costs of inflation: II.' In *The Costs and Consequences of Inflation* (ed. K. Brunner and A. Meltzer). Carnegie-Rochester Conference Series on Public Policy, vol. 15, pp. 5–42.

—— (1982). 'Seigniorage and the case for a national money.' *Journal of Political Economy*, vol. 90, no. 2, pp. 295–313.

—— (1983) 'Inflacion y crecimiento.' *Cuadernos de Economia*, vol. 20, December, pp. 267–78.

—— (1986). 'Time consistent monetary and fiscal policy: a survey.' Mimeo, Department of Economics, MIT.

—— (1987). '1944, 1963, and 1985.' In *Macroeconomics and Finance: Essays in Honor of Franco Modigliani*. (ed. R. Dornbusch, S. Fischer and J. Bossons). Cambridge, MA: MIT Press.

—— and Modigliani, Franco (1978). 'Towards an understanding of the real effects and costs of inflation.' *Welwirtschaftliches Archiv*, pp. 810–32.

Frankel, Jeffrey A. (1985). 'Portfolio crowding-out empirically estimated.' *Quarterly Journal of Economics*, vol. 100 (Supplement), pp. 1041–65.

Friedman, Benjamin M. (1983). 'The roles of money and credit in macroeconomic analysis.' In *Macroeconomics, Prices, and Quantities* (ed. J. Tobin). Washington, DC: Brookings Institution.

—— (1985). 'Crowding out or crowding in? Evidence on debt-equity substitutability.' Mimeo, Department of Economics, Harvard University.

Friedman, Milton (1968). 'The role of monetary policy.' *American Economic Review*, vol. 58, no. 1, pp. 1–17.

—— (1970). 'A theoretical framework for monetary analysis.' *Journal of Political Economy*, vol. 78, no. 2, pp. 193–238.

—— and Schwartz, Anna J. (1963 a). *A Monetary History of the United States, 1867–1960*. Princeton University Press.

—— and —— (1963 b). 'Money and business cycles.' *Review of Economics and Statistics*, vol. 45, no. 1, part 2, pp. 32–64.

Frisch, Ragnar (1933). 'Propagation problems and impulse problems in dynamic economics.' In *Economic Essays in Honor of Gustav Cassel*, pp. 171–205.

Frydman, Roman and Phelps, Edmund S. (1983) (eds.). *Individual Forecasting and Aggregate Outcomes*. New York: Cambridge University Press.

Geary, Patrick T. and Kennan, John (1982). 'The employment-real wage relationship: an international study.' *Journal of Political Economy*, vol. 90, no. 4, pp. 854–71.

Goldfeld, Stephen M. (1976). 'The case of the missing money.' *Brookings Papers on Economic Activity*, vol. 3, pp. 683–730.

Gordon, Robert J. (1982). 'Price inertia and policy ineffectiveness in the United States, 1890–1980.' *Journal of Political Economy*, vol. 90, no. 6, pp. 1087–117.

Grandmont, Jean-Michel (1985). 'On endogenous competitive business cycles.' *Econometrica*, vol. 53, no. 5, pp. 995–1046.

Gray, JoAnna (1976). 'Wage indexation: a macroeconomic approach.' *Journal of Monetary Economics*, vol. 2, pp. 221–35.

Greenwald, Bruce and Stiglitz, Joseph E. (1987). 'Money, imperfect information and economic fluctuations.' NBER Working Paper no. 2188.

Grossman, Sanford, Hart, Oliver and Maskin, Eric (1983). 'Unemployment with observable aggregate shocks.' *Journal of Political Economy*, vol. 91, no. 6, pp. 907–28.

Haberler, Gottfried (1937). *Prosperity and Depression*. Geneva: League of Nations.

Hall, Robert E. (1975). 'The rigidity of wages and the persistence of unemployment.' *Brookings Papers on Economic Activity*, vol. 2, pp. 301–35.

—— (1978). 'Stochastic implications of the life cycle-permanent income hypothesis: theory and evidence.' *Journal of Political Economy*, vol. 86, no. 6.

—— (1986). 'Market structure and macroeconomic fluctuations.' *Brookings Papers on Economic Activity*, vol. 2, pp. 285–338.

—— (1988). 'Consumption.' In *Handbook of Monetary Economics*. (In the Press.)

—— and Lilien, David (1979). 'Efficient wage bargains under uncertain supply.' *American Economic Review*, vol. 69, no. 5, pp. 868–79.

Ham, John (1986). 'Testing whether unemployment represents intertemporal labour supply substitution.' *Review of Economic Studies*, vol. 53, no. 4, pp. 559–78.

Hansen, Gary D. (1985). 'Indivisible labor and the business cycle.' *Journal of Monetary Economics*, vol. 1, no. 3, pp. 309–28.

Hart, Oliver (1982). 'A model of imperfect competition with Keynesian features.' *Quarterly Journal of Economics*, vol. 97, no. 1, pp. 109–38.

—— (1983). 'Optimal labour contracts under asymmetric information: an introduction.' *Review of Economic Studies*, vol. 50, pp. 3–35.

—— and Holmstrom, Bengt (1986). 'The theory of contracts.' MIT Department of Economics, Working Paper no. 418.

Hayashi, Fumio (1987). 'Tests for liquidity constraints: a critical survey and some new observations.' In *Advances in Econometrics* (ed. T. Bewley). Cambridge University Press.

Heckman, James J. (1984). 'Comments on the Ashenfelter and Kydland papers.' In Carnegie-Rochester Conference Series on Public Policy, vol. 21 (ed. K. Brunner and A. Meltzer).

—— and MaCurdy, Thomas E. (1987). 'Empirical tests of labor market equilibrium: a microeconomic perspective.' Mimeo, Department of Economics, University of Chicago.

Helpman, Elhanan and Sadka, Ephraim (1979). 'Optimal financing of the government's budget: taxes, bonds, or money?' *American Economic Review*, vol. 69, no. 1, pp. 152–60.

Hicks, John R. (1950). *A Contribution to the Theory of the Trade Cycle*. Oxford: Clarendon Press.

Holt, Charles C., Modigliani, Franco, Muth, John S. and Simon, Herbert S. (1960). *Planning, Production, Inventories and Workforce*. Englewood Cliffs: Prentice-Hall.

Howitt, Peter (1987). 'Business cycles with costly search and recruiting.' *Quarterly Journal of Economics*. (In the Press.)

Jacklin, Charles J. (1986). 'Banks and risk sharing: instabilities and coordination.' Center for Research in Security Prices, University of Chicago, Working Paper no. 185.

Johnson, Harry G. (1962). 'Monetary theory and policy.' *American Economic Review*, vol. 52, no. 3, pp. 335–84.

Jovanovic, Boyan (1982). 'Inflation and welfare in the steady state.' *Journal of Political Economy*, vol. 90, no. 3, pp. 561–77.

Kahn, James (1987). 'Inventories and the volatility of production.' *American Economic Review*, vol. 77, no. 4, pp. 667–79.

Kahneman, D. and Tversky, A. (1979). 'Prospect theory: an analysis of decision under risk.' *Econometrica*, vol. 47, no. 2, pp. 263–91.

Kaldor, Nicholas (1940). 'A model of the trade cycle.' ECONOMIC JOURNAL, vol. 50, pp. 78–92.

Katz, Lawrence F. (1986). 'Efficiency wage theories: a partial explanation.' *NBER Macroeconomic Annual*, pp. 235–76.

Keeton, William (1979). *Equilibrium Credit Rationing*. New York: Garland.

Kehoe, Timothy J., and Levine, David K. (1985). 'Comparative statics and perfect foresight in infinite horizon models.' *Econometrica*, vol. 53, no. 2, pp. 433–53.

King, Robert G. (1983). 'On the economics of private money.' *Journal of Monetary Economics*, vol. 12, no. 1, pp. 127–58.

—— and Plosser, Charles I. (1984). 'Money, credit and prices in a real business cycle.' *American Economic Review*, vol. 74, no. 3, pp. 363–80.

Kleidon, Allan W. (1986). 'Variance bounds tests and stock price valuation models. *Journal of Political Economy*, vol. 94, no. 5, pp. 953–1001.

Kydland, Finn and Prescott, Edward C. (1977). 'Rules rather than discretion: the inconsistency of optimal plans.' *Journal of Political Economy*, vol. 85, no. 3, pp. 473–92.

—— and —— (1982). 'Time to build and aggregate fluctuations. *Econometrica*, vol. 50, no. 6, pp. 1345–70.

Kurz, Mordecai (1974). 'Equilibrium in a finite sequence of markets with transaction costs.' *Econometrica*, vol. 42, no. 1, pp. 1–20.

Layard, Richard (1986). *How to Beat Unemployment*. Oxford University Press.

Leontief, Wassily (1946). 'The pure theory of the guaranteed annual wage contract.' *Journal of Political Economy*, vol. 54, pp. 76–9.

Lilien, David (1982). 'Sectoral shifts and cyclical unemployment.' *Journal of Political Economy*, vol. 90, no. 4, pp. 777–93.

Lindbeck, Assar and Snower, Dennis (1984). 'Involuntary unemployment as an insider-outsider dilemma.' Working Paper no. 282, Institute for International Economic Studies, University of Stockholm.

Lipsey, Richard G. (1960). 'The relationship between unemployment and the rate of change of money wage rates in the United Kingdom, 1861–1957; a further analysis.' *Economica*, vol. 27, February, pp. 1–31.

Long, John B. and Plosser, Charles I. (1983). 'Real business cycles.' *Journal of Political Economy*, vol. 91, no. 1, pp. 39–69.

Lucas, Robert E. Jr. (1972). 'Expectations and the neutrality of money.' *Journal of Economic Theory*, vol. 4, April, pp. 103–24.

—— (1973). 'Some international evidence on output–inflation tradeoffs.' *American Economic Review*, vol. 63, June, pp. 326–34.

—— (1976). 'Econometric policy evaluation: a critique.' In *The Phillips Curve and Labor Markets* (ed. K. Brunner and A. Meltzer). Carnegie-Rochester Conference Series, vol. 1.

—— (1977). 'Understanding business cycles.' In *Stabilization of the Domestic and International Economy* (ed. K. Brunner and A. Meltzer). Carnegie-Rochester Conference Series, vol. 5.

—— (1978a). 'Asset prices in an exchange economy.' *Econometrica*, vol. 46, pp. 1429–45.

—— (1978b). 'Unemployment policy.' *American Economic Review*, Papers and Proceedings, vol. 68, no. 2, pp. 353–7.

—— (1980). 'Equilibrium in a pure currency economy.' In *Models of Monetary Economies* (ed. J. H. Kareken and N. Wallace). Federal Reserve Bank of Minneapolis.

—— (1987). *Models of Business Cycles*. Oxford: Basil Blackwell.

—— and Prescott, Edward C. (1974). 'Equilibrium search and unemployment.' *Journal of Economic Theory*, vol. 7, no. 1, pp. 188–209.

—— and Rapping, Leonard (1969). 'Real wages, employment, and inflation.' *Journal of Political Economy*, vol. 77, no. 5, pp. 721–54.

—— and Sargent, Thomas J. (1978). 'After Keynesian Economics.' In *After the Phillips Curve: Persistence of High Inflation and High Unemployment*. Federal Reserve Bank of Boston.

—— and Stokey, Nancy (1987). 'Money and interest in a cash-in-advance economy.' *Econometrica*, vol. 55, no. 3, pp. 491–514.

Malinvaud, Edmund (1976). *The Theory of Unemployment Reconsidered*. New York: Halsted Press.

Mankiw, N. Gregory (1985). 'Small menu costs and large business cycles: a macroeconomic model of monopoly.' *Quarterly Journal of Economics*, vol. 100, no. 2, pp. 528–39.

—— (1987). 'The optimal collection of seigniorage: theory and evidence.' NBER Working Paper no. 2270 (May).

——, Rotemberg, Julio and Summers, Lawrence (1985). 'Intertemporal substitution in macroeconomics.' *Quarterly Journal of Economics*, vol. 100, no. 1, pp. 225–51.

Marcet, A., and Sargent, Thomas J. (1987). 'Convergence of least squares learning mechanisms in self referential linear stochastic models.' Mimeo, Stanford University.

Marsh, Terry A. and Merton, Robert C. (1986). 'Dividend variability and variance bounds tests for the rationality of stock market prices.' *American Economic Review*, vol. 76, no. 3, pp. 483–98.

McCallum, Bennett T. (1984). 'On low-frequency estimates of long-run relationships in macroeconomics.' *Journal of Monetary Economics*, vol. 14, no. 1, pp. 3–14.

—— (1986). 'On "real" and "sticky-price" theories of the business cycle.' *Journal of Money, Credit, and Banking*, vol. 18, no. 4, pp. 397–414.

McDonald, Ian and Solow, Robert M. (1981). 'Wage bargaining and employment.' *American Economic Review*, vol. 71, no. 5, pp. 896–908.

Mehra, Rajnish and Prescott, Edward C. (1985). 'The equity premium: a puzzle.' *Journal of Monetary Economics*, vol. 15, pp. 145–62.

Miller, Merton H. and Orr, Daniel (1966). 'A model of the demand for money by firms.' *Quarterly Journal of Economics*, vol. 81, no. 3, pp. 413–35.

Mishkin, Frederic S. (1983). *A Rational Expectations Approach to Macroeconometrics*. NBER: University of Chicago Press.

Mosser, Patricia C. (1986). 'Essays on inventory behavior and excess volatility.' Ph.D. dissertation, Department of Economics, MIT.

Mortensen, Dale T. (1970). 'A theory of wage and employment dynamics.' In Phelps (1970).

—— (1982). 'The matching process as a noncooperative bargaining game.' In *The Economics of Information and Uncertainty* (ed. J. McCall). Chicago: University of Chicago Press.

Mundell, Robert A. (1963). 'Inflation and real interest.' *Journal of Political Economy*, vol. 71, no. 3, pp. 280–3.

Murphy, Kevin M. and Topel, Robert H. (1987). 'The evolution of unemployment in the United States: 1968–1985.' *NBER Macroeconomics Annual*, vol. 2, pp. 11–57.

Nelson, Charles R. and Plosser, Charles I. (1982). 'Trends and random walks in macroeconomic time series.' *Journal of Monetary Economics*, vol. 10, pp. 139–62.

Nordhaus, William (1972). 'Recent developments in price dynamics.' In *The Econometrics of Price Determination* (ed. O. Eckstein). Washington, DC: Board of Governors of the Federal Reserve System.

Okun, Arthur (1981). *Prices and Quantities. A Macroeconomic Analysis*. Washington, DC: Brookings Institution.

Oswald, Andrew (1986). 'The economic theory of trade unions: an introductory survey.' In *Trade Unions, Wage Formation and Macroeconomic Stability* (ed. L. Calmførs and H. Horn). London: Macmillan.

Parkin, Michael (1986). 'The output-inflation tradeoff when prices are costly to change.' *Journal of Political Economy*, vol. 94, no. 1, pp. 200–24.

Patinkin, Don (1965). *Money, Interest, and Prices*. Evanston, Ill.: Harper and Row.

—— (1988). 'John Maynard Keynes.' In *The New Palgrave*.

Pencavel, John (1986). 'Wages and employment under trade unionism: microeconomic models and macroeconomic applications.' In *Trade Unions, Wage Formation and Macroeconomic Stability* (ed. L. Calmfors and H. Horn). London: Macmillan.

Phelps, Edmund S. (1968). 'Money wage dynamics and labor market equilibrium.' *Journal of Political Economy*, vol. 76, no. 4, pp. 687–711.

—— (1970) (ed.). *Microeconomic Foundations of Employment and Inflation Theory.* New York: Norton.

—— (1973). 'Inflation in the theory of public finance.' *Swedish Journal of Economics*, vol. 75, no. 1, pp. 67–82.

—— and Winter, Sidney G. (1970). 'Optimal price policy under atomistic competition.' In Phelps (1970).

—— and Taylor, John B. (1977). 'Stabilizing powers of monetary policy under rational expectations.' *Journal of Political Economy*, vol. 85, no. 1, pp. 163–90.

Phillips, A. W. (1958). 'The relation between unemployment and the rate of change of money wage rates in the United Kingdom, 1861–1957.' *Economica*, vol. 25, November, pp. 283–99.

Pissarides, Christopher A. (1985). 'Short-run equilibrium dynamics of unemployment, vacancies, and real wages,' *American Economic Review*, vol. 75, no. 4, pp. 676–90.

Porter, Richard D., Simpson, Thomas D. and Mauskopf, Eileen (1979). 'Financial innovation and the monetary aggregates.' *Brookings Papers on Economic Activity*, vol. 1, pp. 213–29.

Poterba, James and Rotemberg, Julio (1987). 'Money in the utility function: an empirical implementation.' In *New Developments in Monetary Economics* (ed. W. Barnett and K. Singleton). Cambridge University Press.

—— and Summers, Lawrence H. (1987). 'Finite lifetimes and effects of budget deficits on national saving.' *Journal of Monetary Economics*, vol. 20, no. 2, pp. 369–92.

Prescott, Edward C. (1978). 'Should control theory be used for economic stabilization?' In Carnegie-Rochester Conference Series on Public Policy, vol. 7 (ed. K. Brunner and A. Meltzer).

—— (1986). 'Theory ahead of business cycle measurement.' Federal Reserve Bank of Minneapolis, *Quarterly Review*, Fall, pp. 9–22.

Quah, Danny (1987). 'What do we learn from unit roots in macroeconomic time series?' Mimeo, Department of Economics, MIT.

Rasche, Robert (1987). 'Velocity and money demand functions: do stable relationships exist?' Carnegie-Rochester Conference Series, vol. 27 (ed. K. Brunner and A. Meltzer). Forthcoming.

Roberts, John (1986). 'An equilibrium model with Keynesian unemployment at Walrasian prices.' Mimeo, Graduate School of Business, Stanford University.

Rogerson, Richard (1985). 'Indivisible labor, lotteries, and equilibrium.' Mimeo, Department of Economics, University of Rochester.

Rogoff, Kenneth (1987). 'Reputational constraints on monetary policy.' In *Bubbles and Other Essays* (ed. K. Brunner and A. Meltzer). Carnegie-Rochester Conference Series on Public Policy, vol 26. North-Holland.

Romer, David (1986). 'A simple general equilibrium version of the Baumol–Tobin model.' *Quarterly Journal of Economics*, vol. 101, no. 4, pp. 663–86.

Romer, Paul M. (1986). 'Increasing returns and long-run growth.' *Journal of Political Economy*, vol. 94, no. 5, pp. 1002–37.

Rose, Andrew (1986). 'The autoregressivity paradox in macroeconomics.' Ph.D. dissertation, Department of Economics, MIT.

Rosen, Sherwin (1985). 'Implicit contracts: a survey.' *Journal of Economic Literature*, vol. 23, pp. 1144–75.

Rotemberg, Julio (1987). 'The New Keynesian microfoundations.' *NBER Macroeconomics Annual*, vol. 2, pp. 69–104.

Samuelson, Paul A. (1939). 'Interactions between the multiplier analysis and the principle of acceleration.' *Review of Economics and Statistics*, vol. 21, May, pp. 75–8.

Sargent, Thomas J. (1978). 'Estimation of labor demand schedules under rational expectations.' *Journal of Political Economy*, vol. 86, no. 6, pp. 1009–44.

—— (1987). *Dynamic Macroeconomic Theory.* Cambridge, MA: Harvard University Press.

—— and Wallace, Neil (1975). '"Rational" expectations, the optimal monetary instrument, and the optimal money supply rule.' *Journal of Political Economy*, vol. 83, no. 2, pp. 241–54.

—— and —— (1981). 'Some unpleasant monetarist arithmetic.' Federal Reserve Bank of Minneapolis *Quarterly Review*, Fall, pp. 1–17.

—— and —— (1987). 'Inflation and the government budget constraint.' In *Economic Policy in Theory and Practice* (ed. Razin and E. Sadka). London: Macmillan.

Schor, Julia B. (1985). 'Changes in the cyclical pattern of real wages: evidence from nine countries, 1955–80.' ECONOMIC JOURNAL, vol. 95, June, pp. 452–68.

Shapiro, Carl and Stiglitz, Joseph E. (1984). 'Equilibrium unemployment as a worker discipline device.' *American Economic Review*, vol. 74, no. 3, pp. 433–44.

Shapiro, Matthew D. (1987). 'Are cyclical fluctuations in productivity due more to supply shocks or demand shocks?' NBER Working Paper no. 2147, February.

Sheshinski, Eytan and Weiss, Yoram (1977). 'Inflation and costs of price adjustment.' *Review of Economic Studies*, vol. 44, no. 2, pp. 287–303.

Shiller, Robert J. (1981). 'Do stock prices move too much to be justified by subsequent changes in dividends?' *American Economic Review*, vol. 71, no. 3, pp. 421–36.
—— (1987). 'The term structure of interest rates.' Yale University, Cowles Foundation Discussion Paper no. 843, (July).
Shleifer, Andre (1986). 'Implementation cycles.' *Journal of Political Economy*, vol. 94, no. 6, pp. 1163–90.
Sidrauski, Miguel (1967). 'Rational choice and patterns of growth in a monetary economy.' *American Economic Review*, Papers and Proceedings, vol. 57, May, pp. 534–44.
Sims, Christopher (1972). 'Money, income, and causality.' *American Economic Review*, vol. 62, no. 4, pp. 540–52.
—— (1980a). 'Comparison of interwar and postwar business cycles: monetarism reconsidered.' *American Economic Review*, Papers and Proceedings, vol. 70, no. 2, pp. 250–7.
—— (1980b). 'Macroeconomics and reality.' *Econometrica*, vol. 48, no. 1, pp. 1–48.
Slutsky, Eugen (1937). 'The summation of random causes as the source of cyclic processes.' *Econometrica*, pp. 105–46.
Sokoler, Meir (1987). 'The inflation tax on real balances, the inflation subsidy on credit, and the inflationary process in Israel.' *Bank of Israel Economic Review*, vol. 59, April, pp. 1–26.
Solow, Robert M. (1965). 'Short-run adjustment of employment to output.' In *Value, Capital and Growth* (ed. J. N. Wolfe). Chicago: Aldine.
—— (1979). 'Another possible source of wage stickiness.' *Journal of Macroeconomics*, Winter, vol. 1, pp. 79–82.
Starr, Ross (1974). 'The price of money in a pure exchange economy with taxation.' *Econometrica*, vol. 42, no. 1, pp. 45–54.
Startz, Richard (1984). 'Prelude to macroeconomics.' *American Economic Review*, vol. 74, no. 5, December, pp. 881–92.
—— (1986). 'Monopolistic competition as a foundation for Keynesian macroeconomics.' Mimeo, University of Washington.
Stiglitz, Joseph E. (1986). 'Theories of wage rigidity.' In *Keynes' Economic Legacy: Contemporary Economic Theories* (ed. Butkiewicz *et al.*). New York: Praeger.
—— and Weiss, Andrew (1987). 'Macro-economic equilibrium and credit rationing.' NBER Working Paper no. 2164, February.
Stockman, Alan C. (1981). 'Anticipated inflation and the capital stock in a cash-in-advance economy.' *Journal of Monetary Economics*, vol. 8, no. 3, pp. 387–93.
Summers, Lawrence H. (1981). 'Taxation and corporate investment: a q-theory approach.' *Brookings Papers on Economic Activity*, no. 1, pp. 67–140.
—— (1983). 'The non-adjustment of nominal interest rates: a study of the Fisher effect.' In *Macroeconomics, Prices and Quantities* (ed. J. Tobin). Washington, DC: Brookings Institution.
—— (1986a). 'Estimating the long-run relationship between interest rates and inflation: a response to McCallum.' *Journal of Monetary Economics*, vol. 18, no. 1, pp. 77–86.
—— (1986b). 'Some skeptical observations on real business cycle theory.' Federal Reserve Bank of Minneapolis. *Quarterly Review*, Fall, pp. 23–7.
Svensson, Lars E. O. (1985). 'Money and asset prices in a cash-in-advance economy.' *Journal of Political Economy*, vol. 93, no. 5, pp. 919–44.
Tanzi, Vito (1977). 'Inflation lags in collection and the real value of tax revenue.' *IMF Staff Papers*, vol. 24, no. 1.
Tarshis, Lorie (1939). 'Changes in real and money wages.' ECONOMIC JOURNAL, pp. 150–4.
Taylor, John B. (1980). 'Aggregate dynamics and staggered contracts.' *Journal of Political Economy*, vol. 88, no. 1, pp. 1–24.
—— (1986). 'Improvements in macroeconomic stability: the role of wages and prices.' In *The American Business Cycle: Continuity and Change* (ed. R. J. Gordon). Chicago: University of Chicago Press.
Tirole, Jean (1985). 'Asset bubbles and overlapping generations.' *Econometrica*, vol. 53, no. 5, pp. 1071–100.
Tobin, James (1965). 'Money and economic growth.' *Econometrica*, vol. 33, no. 4, pp. 671–84.
—— (1969). 'A general equilibrium approach to monetary theory.' *Journal of Money, Credit, and Banking*, vol. 1, no. 1, pp. 15–29.
—— (1970). 'Post hoc, ergo propter hoc.' *Quarterly Journal of Economics*, vol. 84, May, pp. 310–7.
Townsend, Robert M. (1980). 'Models of money with spatially separated agents.' In *Models of Monetary Economies* (ed. J. H. Kareken and N. Wallace). Federal Reserve Bank of Minneapolis.
—— (1987). 'Asset-return anomalies in a monetary economy.' *Journal of Economic Theory*, forthcoming.
Tsiddon, Daniel (1986). 'On the stubbornness of sticky prices.' Mimeo, Department of Economics, Columbia University.
Weiss, Laurence (1980). 'The effects of money supply on economic welfare in the steady state.' *Econometrica*, vol. 48, no. 3, pp. 565–76.
Weitzman, Martin L. (1982). 'Increasing returns and the foundations of unemployment theory.' ECONOMIC JOURNAL, vol. 92, no. 4, pp. 787–804.

—— (1986). 'Macroeconomic implications of profit-sharing.' *NBER Macroeconomics Annual*, pp. 291–335.

West, Kenneth D. (1985). 'A variance bounds test of the linear quadratic inventory model.' NBER Working Paper no. 1581.

Woodford, Michael (1985). 'Interest and prices in a cash-in-advance economy.' Department of Economics, Columbia University Discussion Paper no. 281 (February).

Yotsuzuka, Toshiki (1987). 'Ricardian equivalence in the presence of capital market imperfections' *Journal of Monetary Economics*, vol. 20, no. 2, pp. 411–36.

Zarnowitz, Victor (1985). 'Recent work on business cycles in historical perspective: a review of theories and evidence.' *Journal of Economic Literature*, vol. 23, no. 2, pp. 523–80.

Zeldes, Stephen (1985). Ph.D. dissertation, Department of Economics, MIT.

MACROECONOMIC FORECASTING: A SURVEY*

Kenneth F. Wallis

Developments in macroeconomic forecasting over the last twenty years are surveyed in this paper, which takes the 1969 Presidential Address to the Royal Economic Society (Cairncross, 1969) as its starting point. Sir Alec Cairncross had found no previous occasion on which the Royal Economic Society had discussed 'this new activity', and so selected economic forecasting as the topic for his address. As retiring Chief Economic Adviser to the Treasury he had been preoccupied with forecasting for the preceding few years, and was well placed to reflect on the new kind of economic forecasting that was emerging and the new ways in which it was being organised. At the time these were changing fast, with forecasting becoming in particular more heavily based on computable models. A conference in April 1969 heard that in the Treasury 'a more elaborate fully formalised model is being programmed for a computer' (Roy, 1970); in August 1969, at the National Institute of Economic and Social Research (NIESR), an econometric model of the whole economy became an integral part of the quarterly forecasting exercises that had begun, with the publication of the *National Institute Economic Review*, in 1959. These developments followed the inauguration by the London Business School (LBS) in 1966 of the first series of published forecasts based on the direct application of a complete statistical model of the economy.

In the late 1960s and early 1970s confidence in forecasting was growing. 'Extra resources were put in, and there were hopes that the accumulation of data and more sophisticated techniques would lead to major improvements in accuracy of forecasts and understanding of the economy' (Burns, 1986). This confidence rested in part on the wide acceptance of the neoclassical synthesis as a framework for macroeconomic analysis. The phrase originated with Samuelson, who was largely instrumental in constructing and promulgating the 'grand neoclassical synthesis', which was given considerable prominence in the third edition of his textbook. Here it was noted that economists, instead of being Keynesian or anti-Keynesian, 'have worked toward a synthesis of whatever is valuable in older economics and in modern theories of income determination. The result might be called neo-classical economics and is accepted in its broad outlines by all but about 5 per cent of extreme left wing and right wing writers' (Samuelson, 1955, p. 212). In his *New Palgrave* entry on the neoclassical synthesis, Blanchard (1987) observes that it 'did not expect full employment to occur under *laissez-faire*; it believed however that, by proper use of monetary and fiscal policy, the old classical truths would come back into

* This chapter was first published in the ECONOMIC JOURNAL, vol. 99, March 1989. The support of the Economic and Social Research Council is gratefully acknowledged, as are the helpful comments and/or research assistance of M. J. Artis, A. J. C. Britton, P. G. Fisher, C. W. J. Granger, C. L. Melliss, A. J. Oswald, S. K. Tanna, D. S. Turner, J. D. Whitley and two anonymous referees.

relevance. This synthesis was to remain the dominant paradigm for another twenty years, in which most of the important contributions, by Hicks, Modigliani, Solow, Tobin and others, were to fit quite naturally.' The neoclassical synthesis enjoyed considerable empirical success in the 1960s: as a result Heller *et al.* (1968, p. 16) could conclude that 'governments have, to a large extent, succeeded in subduing or overcoming the rhythmic fluctuations which used to be called the trade cycle' and Cairncross (1969, p. 805) could 'doubt whether bad theory has played a major part in forecasting errors in this country over the past decade or two'.

Growing confidence in the use of more sophisticated techniques rested on developments in econometric modelling and forecasting that had taken place largely outside the United Kingdom. The construction of economy-wide models had been pioneered by Tinbergen, who had subsequently served as the first director of the Central Planning Bureau of the Netherlands; this had become the official forecasting agency whose activities were the most heavily model-based. An account of the methods of short-term forecasting used by the governments of six member countries was published by the OECD in 1965, and in his introductory survey McMahon reported that 'All the participating countries except the United Kingdom use an econometric model; but except for the Netherlands it is used primarily as a consistency check, rather than as the primary method of making the forecast itself.' Theil's classic *Economic Forecasts and Policy* (1958) and *Applied Economic Forecasting* (1966) represented in part a contribution to the research programme of the Central Planning Bureau. In the United States Klein had led the way, and his brief stay in the United Kingdom had resulted in the first serious attempt to develop a large-scale quarterly model of any national economy, the model being estimated for the most part on seasonally unadjusted data (Klein *et al.*, 1961). The annual Klein–Goldberger model had been built at the University of Michigan in the early 1950s, and its descendants were subsequently used for forecasting by the Research Seminar in Quantitative Economics (Suits, 1962); forecasts based on a quarterly model of the US economy were distributed by the Wharton School at the University of Pennsylvania from 1963 onwards (see Klein, 1968 and references therein). Important work on the evaluation of forecasts came from an NBER project on short-term economic forecasting (Zarnowitz, 1967; Mincer and Zarnowitz, 1969). This literature provided a foundation for the initial developments indicated in the opening paragraph, and for subsequent developments that occurred in the period under consideration.

A feature of the last twenty years that is immediately apparent on attempting a survey is that the literature on forecasting has grown apace with forecasting activity. From the three groups in existence in the late 1960s, macroeconomic forecasting activity has grown to the point where the Treasury's monthly compilation *Forecasts for the UK Economy* now covers nineteen forecasts. As for the literature, it remains the case that forecasting has scarcely featured in this JOURNAL, no major article having dealt with the subject in the intervening period, but in this time two journals devoted entirely to forecasting have been established. Notable books on the production and use of macroeconomic forecasts have been published by leading practitioners, for example, Keating (1985), Klein and Young (1980), and Llewellyn *et al.* (1985), respectively from UK, US and international perspectives. More general textbooks have appeared, for example, Fair (1984), Granger and Newbold (1977), and Pindyck and Rubinfeld (1976). A substantial section of the literature deals with the assessment of forecasts, both in theory and in practice, and in turn with the use of forecasts in model evaluation. An early study of UK forecasts is that by Ash and Smyth (1973); subsequently numerous authors, including the forecasters themselves, have contributed assessments. Various aspects of macroeconomic forecasting are touched on in the international conference volumes edited by Chow and Corsi (1982), Kmenta and Ramsey (1981), and Malgrange and Muet (1984); the UK scene is represented by Hilton and Heathfield (1970), Renton (1975), Ormerod (1979*a*), and the sequence of reviews by the ESRC Macroeconomic Modelling Bureau (Wallis *et al.*, 1984–7).

The paper proceeds as follows. In the next section the essential ingredients of a forecast are described, by way of background, and some basic data on forecasts and outcomes are presented as a point of reference. The events and consequences of some important episodes are then considered: first 1974–5, when in many countries unprecedented forecast errors were made, which provided a focus for important challenges, both empirical and theoretical, to the prevailing consensus; next 1979–81, which saw a recession, a change of regime and notable forecasting errors, heralding further developments. Forecast evaluation is touched on as much as is necessary throughout this account, but is then treated more thoroughly in a separate section, which includes consideration of a final episode, namely 1986, when the dramatic fall in the world price of oil, fortunately for the forecasters, was not anticipated. Concluding comments follow, the paper closing, like Cairncross (1969), on the issue of the publication of forecasts. The principal orientation of the paper is towards the UK economy, with occasional glances elsewhere, although developments in economic analysis and econometric methods know no frontiers.

I. CONSTRUCTION OF FORECASTS

The need for forecasting in economic policy-making, and the essential ingredients of a forecast, have scarcely changed over twenty years. Thus Cairncross (1969, p. 798) notes that forecasts 'provide a frame of reference for policy decisions' and 'a base against which to judge how policies are working out', and the current Chief Economic Adviser to the Treasury similarly states 'Decisions have to be made against the background of an uncertain current position; they cannot easily be reversed, and many policy changes have consequences stretching years ahead. Some kind of forward look is therefore essential and it is best to do this in a consistent way. Once they are produced, forecasts have an important monitoring function as they provide a basis against which to judge subsequent developments' (Burns, 1986, p. 117). Outside the policy-making context, two further quite different motives for forecasting exist.

One is to anticipate events, whether for private gain or for public good, and it is largely in respect of the former that the growth in forecasting activity has occurred; the other is to put hypotheses about the behaviour of the world to test, which helps explain why independent research groups engage in forecasting.

Although the key ingredients of a forecast have remained quantitative data and a framework for their interpretation and analysis, substantial developments have occurred in respect of the methods of analysis. Early forecasts were based on a limited number of variables, which were analysed in the context of an implicit, perhaps informal model, not necessarily written down. The process relied on the assessment of data and the evaluation of new information by the experienced forecaster. 'A few people possess the extraordinary gift of being able to do this in their heads... The process involved is not well understood, but it seems to involve the checking of data against the predictions and workings of a mental model of how the economy works. The disadvantage of such a method is that the number of people truly gifted in this way is small, and the technique is difficult to explain and transmit to others' (Llewellyn *et al.*, 1985, p. 83) – and to replicate. In the 1960s the use of explicit, more formal models increased, with these models becoming increasingly based on estimated equations. The models distinguish between endogenous and exogenous variables, that is, those determined by the system of equations and those treated as being determined outside the system. In a forecasting context, these latter variables have to be set by projection or assumption, which leads to the further distinction between an unconditional and a conditional forecast. The former represents the conventional understanding of a forecast, namely a prediction of a future event, whereas the latter represents an if–then statement, resting on the occurrence of certain specified conditions. The pure prediction problem is the main concern of this paper, although the distinction is less clear-cut than might appear, since exogenous variables that are policy instruments may be treated in different ways. One possibility is to assume no change in policy instruments, irrespective of the forecast; another is to project a policy response to the forecasted developments.

With greater computerisation the size of the models could be increased, allowing attention to be paid to a greater number of variables, including the components of aggregates previously treated as one. The intervening years have seen such developments in computing that computer capability is no longer a constraint, either on the size and complexity of the model to be managed, or on the frequency with which forecasts and policy exercises can be constructed and revised, or on the econometric estimation and testing procedures applied to the models, these procedures themselves having been substantially developed over the last twenty years.

The removal of the computing constraint and the use of more fully elaborated accounting frameworks should not obscure the fact that some practical limitations, in particular concerning data, remain much as in Cairncross' (1969) description. 'First of all, the forecaster has to contend with the inevitable lag of statistics behind events... when the February forecasts are being prepared in advance of the Budget the latest available national accounts relate to the third quarter' of the preceding year. This remains the case today. Moreover, the inevitable lags differ from one variable to another, so there is not a clean break between periods for which data are available and those for which they are not; rather, the dataset has a 'ragged edge', presenting additional complications (Wallis, 1986). 'Next comes the issue of reliability', one indication of which is the frequency with which preliminary data are subsequently amended, and another is the frequency of changes in definition of a given series. Some errors are systematic and survive the revision process, the most notable current example being in international trade, where on a balance of payments basis imports considerably exceed exports, globally, by an amount which, as a proportion of total imports, is of the same order of magnitude as the UK current balance. Less frequently, reconstruction of the real national accounts data using revised relative price weights can lead to very substantial revision of data, going back perhaps to the origin of the data series, and affecting both the level of the series and its growth rate over given periods. Last, but not least, is the discrepancy between the statistician's measurement and the economist's concept. The problem of the valuation of stocks, and the decomposition of a given change into price and volume changes, arises in a number of areas, and is part of the well-known problem of the measurement of capital stock; a related problem is that of the measurement of capacity utilisation. In the absence of adequate direct measurements, indirect measurements or 'proxy' variables have to be used. Moreover 'even measures that in principle are equal to one another are often in flat contradiction. To take what may be an extreme example, between the first quarter of 1966 and the first quarter of 1967 the expenditure measure of GNP increased by 2 per cent, the income measure fell by $\frac{1}{2}$ per cent and the output measure was unchanged. Yet all these measure the same thing' (Cairncross, 1969, p. 803). Such contradictions remain in the 1980s. For example, in October 1983 it was estimated that the expenditure measure had risen by $1\frac{1}{4}\%$ between 1980 and 1982, while the output measure had fallen by $\frac{1}{2}\%$ and the income measure had not changed. Just one year later, in October 1984, the expenditure increase was revised to $\frac{1}{2}\%$, that of output to $\frac{1}{4}\%$ and income was estimated to have increased by $1\frac{3}{4}\%$!

The continuing presence of data discrepancies and delays is one reason why there remains a role for informed judgement in forecasting, often expressed through a process of adjustments to model-based forecasts. The use of such adjustments, variously termed constant adjustments, residual adjustments, add factors, etc. is widespread, despite the models having come to represent a more complete framework for analysis. Indeed, the more complete is the model, the greater is the internal consistency with which a given adjustment to a variable or an equation is carried through the forecast calculations. The use of 'conjunctural analysis' to supplement the official macroeconomic data and so to suggest adjustments is well described by Keating (1985); other reasons for making adjustments, based on knowledge of further developments not incorporated in the model or of other model deficiencies, feature in general terms in all practitioners' accounts of their art. An attempt to appraise the impact of these adjustments, *ex post*, is presented in Section IV.5 below.

As a point of reference for subsequent discussion, data on one-year-ahead forecasts of GDP and inflation published by independent UK forecasting groups, LBS, NIESR and LPL (the Liverpool University Research Group in Macroeconomics) are presented in Figs. 1 and 2. The upper panel of each figure shows the actual outcome, and the lower panel the forecast errors, defined as actual minus forecast. Public discussion usually focuses on the annual (real) GDP growth rate and the annual rate of inflation, so the data are presented in these terms, which also has the merit of reducing the basic GDP and price level variables to (near) stationarity. That is, the proportionate rates of change are trend-free, and their variances and autocovariances can be treated as time-invariant. The forecasts described as one-year-ahead are

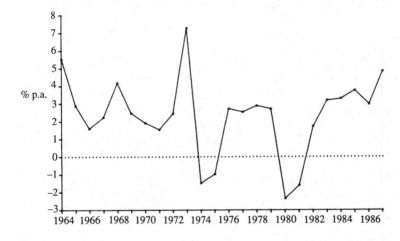

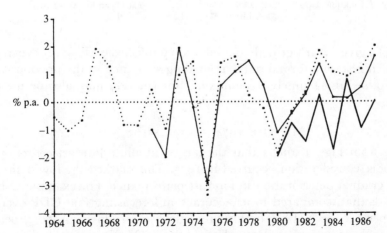

Fig. 1. GDP growth. Upper panel, actual; lower panel, one-year-ahead forecast errors.
Key: LBS (—■—), NIESR (··■··) and LPL (——).

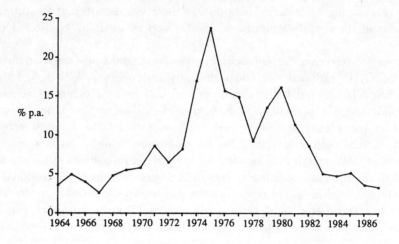

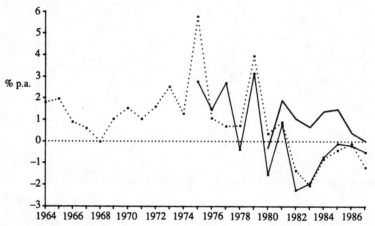

Fig. 2. Inflation. Upper panel, actual; lower panel, one-year-ahead forecast errors.
Key: —■—, LBS; ··■··, NIESR; ----, LPL.

forecasts of a given year's growth and inflation published early in that year, and
hence which rest on a formal database ending sometime in the previous year,
although other, more timely, conjunctural information may also be used, as
noted above.

II. THE 1974–5 RECESSION

It is clear from Figs. 1 and 2 that the largest absolute forecast errors in the
period under consideration occurred in 1975. This marked the low point of a
period of gradual deterioration in forecast performance. For example Osborn
(1979) finds that, compared to its accuracy in forecasting real GDP over the
1965–70 period, the NIESR performance deteriorates in the 1970–5 period,
most markedly so in 1974–5. In the United States, McNees (1979a) finds that,
for a sequence of quarterly one-year-ahead forecasts of real GNP growth

through the 1970s, all of the 'failures', with one minor exception, occurred in forecasts of the periods ending between 1974:1 and 1976:1, all but one of these nine forecasts being a 'failure': a 'failure' is defined as the median absolute error across five leading US forecasters substantially exceeding its average value over the entire period. For the OECD area, Llewellyn *et al.* (1985, ch. 6) find that, of the seventeen year-ahead forecasts of real OECD GNP growth over the period 1966–82, those for 1974 and 1975 exhibit the two largest errors. In the analytical framework of the time, an overestimate of real growth would be expected to be associated with an underestimate of unemployment, which indeed occurred: McNees (1979*a*) notes the 'extraordinarily large underestimates of unemployment in early 1975'. Emphasis on the absolute forecast errors may underestimate the ability of the forecasters, since, as indicated by Figs. 1 and 2, for example, the situation they were attempting to predict showed a sharp increase in variation. In these circumstances their relative performance, assessed more fully below, might even be considered laudable. It is clear from contemporary writings, however, that this provided little solace, and the absolute errors prompted a vigorous search for forecasting improvements.

The economic scenario in which these forecasting errors occurred was the coexistence, not previously experienced, of rapid inflation and high unemployment, leading into recession. Writing from a US perspective, Lucas and Sargent (1978) in their well-known polemic laid the blame for these reversals very clearly at the door of the neoclassical synthesis. That macroeconomic policies predicated on models in this tradition had not produced the predicted results represented 'econometric failure on a grand scale'. Moreover, not only were the predictions 'wildly incorrect' but 'the doctrine on which they were based is fundamentally flawed'; it was argued 'that the difficulties are *fatal*: that modern macroeconomic models are of *no* value in guiding policy and that this condition will not be remedied by modifications along any line which is currently being pursued'. The models should be replaced by equilibrium models (Lucas, 1975, 1977), which assume that prices and quantities continuously clear markets and that agents continuously optimise, which in turn leads to the imposition of the hypothesis of rational expectations. In such equilibrium or 'new classical' models, fluctuations are caused by agents' reactions to unanticipated shocks.

This recommendation was not followed by the forecasters, whose attention focused on other perceived inadequacies of their models. First among these was the models' oversimplified treatment of supply factors, since the 'first oil price shock', that is, the quadrupling of the price of imported oil in late 1973, was in particular blamed for the 1974–5 recession. 'This unique external supply-side shock provided a severe challenge to the conventional, demand-oriented forecasting techniques' (McNees, 1979*b*) not because it was unanticipated but because its repercussions were not understood and in consequence were underestimated. Thus, in revising their forecasts for 1974 after observing the oil price increase, US forecasters made adjustments to show more inflation and lower growth, but these, while in the right direction, were not nearly large enough, as McNees (1979b) notes: 'the upward pressure on prices and downward pressure on output were far stronger than...anticipated'. Writing at the time, Klein (1974) noted that 'The US models, which have been not only demand oriented, but also overly domestic in character have few provisions for indicating how high import prices (fuel in this case) contribute to domestic inflation. This is not a problem for European and UK model builders, however, because they have generally been alert to problems of imported inflation and allow for that factor in their domestic price formation equations'. Subsequently elaborate energy sectors were introduced into the Wharton model, to allow routine analysis of oil-price changes in particular. Likewise the DRI model moved into its third generation after 1975, to remedy the shortcomings in the existing ('second generation') models that became apparent during 1973–5. Specifically, the design of these models did not 'offer sufficient points of contact with external matters such as raw material prices, oil prices, worldwide booms and recessions, shortages and the financial instability which only became more evident during that period' (Eckstein, 1983, p. 8). They had been fitted over the sample period 1953–73, which enjoyed relatively smooth growth and 'did not reveal the full cyclical vulnerability of the economy'. Appropriate extensions to the model were accordingly made.

For the OECD area as a whole, forecast errors also reflected underestimates of the scale of the response to the oil-price shock. Again, once the oil price increase was known, growth forecasts for 1974 were revised downwards, but insufficiently so. 'Anyone who was involved in managing a macroeconometric model at the time of the 1973 oil-price rise will never forget the strain this supply shock placed on an apparatus largely attuned to coping with demand disturbances' (Higgins, 1988). Since the continuation of the recession into 1975 was not foreseen in forecasts prepared in late 1974, Llewellyn et al. (1985) emphasise the lack of understanding not only of the magnitude of the economic responses to the shock but also of their timing. An international analytic framework and an appropriate set of quantified relationships was not available at the time, and the oil shock provided a strong impetus for the development of globally consistent projections, as Higgins notes. Whereas it was immediately apparent that there would be large transfers of financial resources from oil-importing to oil-exporting countries through the current account of the balance of payments, their continuing consequences were unclear. As the OPEC countries began to react to their new wealth, work began on an international linkage model to focus on the effects of the various transmission mechanisms.

In the United Kingdom the inflationary explosion of 1974–5 was attributed not only to the oil-price shock but also, by monetarists in particular, to the surge in monetary growth in 1972–3. A rapid rise in public borrowing was associated with the expansionary fiscal policy of 1971–2, which produced unprecedented output growth in 1973, and rapid growth in bank lending followed the move towards a more liberal regulatory regime in 1971 (the 'competition and credit control' measures). The broad money measure in use at the time (M3) grew by 27·8% in 1972 and 27·6% in 1973, the inflationary explosion following with a two-year lag and an intervening temporary output rise, exactly as in the basic Friedmanite analysis, although the oil-price rise exaggerated the magnitude of the inflationary response. Foreign prices had a role in the models, as indicated by Klein (1974), quoted above, but no distinction was drawn between oil and other imports, nor between oil and other commodities, whose prices were also rising exceptionally quickly in 1973. The inclusion of foreign prices was by no means enough to prevent the 1975 forecasting errors shown in Figs. 1 and 2; similarly large errors were observed in other variables such as consumption and employment. As elsewhere, the depth of the recession was not correctly anticipated. Again as elsewhere, the response was a pragmatic one, with forecasters attempting to learn from the new information and new experience in order to improve future performance, rather than jettisoning their whole approach.

In the light of the events described above, and of the 1973 move to a system of floating exchange rates, attention concentrated on the modelling of the financial sector, exchange rate equations, and the influence of monetary policy. A new financial sector for the Treasury model became operational in 1978 (Spencer and Mowl, 1978; Spencer, 1986), and a simple financial system was introduced into the NIESR model (Ormerod, 1979b). The fullest account of their learning and respecification process or, in Flemming's (1978) phrase, their 'intellectual odyssey', is provided by the LBS group in papers presented at conferences in late 1977 and mid-1978 (Ball and Burns, 1978; Ball et al., 1979). The LBS approach followed the 'international monetarist' tradition (Dornbusch, 1976), that changes in relative money supplies affect prices via changes in the exchange rate, given long-run purchasing power parity. More generally, the LBS group undertook a 'fundamental reappraisal of the properties of the system as a whole'. In the personal sector, for example, failure to anticipate the sharp fall in consumers' expenditure in 1975 led to a reconsideration of the impact of inflation on real spending, in which consumers were assumed to save more as inflation increased in order to preserve the real value of their financial assets.

Given the central place of the consumption function in neoclassical synthesis econometrics, the rise in the savings ratio that occurred in the early to mid-1970s in association with a rising rate of inflation prompted much empirical research by forecasters and others, which continues to this day. Notable examples in this JOURNAL are the papers by Davidson et al. (1978) and Pesaran and Evans (1984), and the current forecasting models incorporate the effect of inflation on consumers' expenditure, occurring either directly, or indirectly via an adjustment to real income for the inflation loss on liquid assets and/or wealth. The detection of this effect provides a good example of the model development opportunities offered by turbulent periods of history, alluded to in the quotation by Eckstein, above.

The technical point is that forecasts based on a mis-specified model, for example, one that omits a relevant explanatory variable, will continue to perform as well as expected from past experience and hence arouse no suspicions as long as the omitted variable continues to behave in the same manner as before. Once its behaviour changes, however, then so does that of variables related to it, and forecasts of these variables based on the mis-specified model exhibit unexpected errors, so drawing attention to the model's inadequacy. Over the time span of this paper the changes have been from relatively smooth to relatively turbulent behaviour, and it may be that only after the perturbation of the data, and a period in which events appear inexplicable, is it possible to identify and estimate an appropriately extended model. On the other hand, there may have been enough information in the 'smooth' data to permit the satisfactory estimation of a revised model, once the inadequacies of the original model are revealed. In the case of the consumption function, Davidson *et al.* (1978) find that there is enough variation in the 1960s data to allow the estimation of a new equation, incorporating inflation effects, that does not suffer from the mid-1970s predictive failure of the old equation. The forecast errors in consumers' expenditure could have been avoided if the inflation effects had been looked for and, in an *ex ante* forecast context, if inflation itself had been well predicted.

In the case of the exchange rate, other UK forecasters, like the LBS group, introduced exchange rate equations and made other related changes post-1975. None of the exchange rate systems performed well when used for forecasting, however, and the exchange rate equations often had to be overridden or subject to heavy residual adjustments. In the first instance the modelling difficulties were not surprising, given the short series of data available for the 'floating' regime and the completely uninformative nature of the 'fixed' regime. These have persisted, however, Isard (1988) concluding in his international survey that 'empirical modeling of exchange rates over the past decade has been largely a failure', which is evident 'from documentation of the poor post sample forecasting accuracy of the models, from data that appear to reject important building blocks for the monetary models (in particular, the assumption of uncovered interest rate parity), and from the lack of statistically significant in-sample support for existing portfolio-balance models of the exchange risk premium'. Forecasting the exchange rate remains arguably the greatest single problem facing UK forecasters.

The experience of the 1974–5 recession was a major blow to the growing confidence in forecasting of the 1960s and early 1970s. It represented a valuable learning experience, however, and caused a sharp spurt in the continuing evolution of forecasting models, as existing systems were amended, not abandoned. In any event the advice that they should be abandoned was by the end of the decade itself amended, Lucas (1980) observing 'To what extent this forecast error should be interpreted as a "fatal" error in models based on the neoclassical synthesis or simply as one suggesting some modifications is not so easy to determine.'

III. THE 1979–81 RECESSION

The second oil-price shock occurred in several stages in 1979 and initiated a second recession in the OECD economies. 'Inflation re-accelerated, current account deficits increased, public sector deficits swelled, and unemployment rose yet further. Taken together, these presented a greater problem for policy in nearly all economies than in any previous post-war cycle' (Llewellyn *et al.*, 1985, p. 39), although unlike the first oil price shock, there was now no substantial disagreement among the OECD economies about the appropriate policy response. The UK experience differed from that of the rest of the OECD, however. Despite its near self-sufficiency in oil by 1979, the United Kingdom suffered a recession which started earlier than elsewhere and was of much greater severity. Many authors have compared this recession with the Great Depression of the 1930s, output falling by 5% in both 1929–31 and 1979–81. Unemployment rose from 1·2 million in mid-1979 to reach 2 million in late 1980 and 3 million by autumn 1982.

May 1979 had seen the election of a new Conservative government in the United Kingdom, committed to the reduction of inflation and the creation of conditions favourable to sustained economic growth, but no longer accepting responsibility for high employment. Inflation was to be controlled by restrictive monetary policy, not incomes policy, and the supply side was to be strengthened through fiscal measures such as a shift from direct to indirect taxation and a reduction in public expenditure, and through the liberalising of financial markets and the labour market. Thus in the June 1979 Budget monetary policy was tightened, public expenditure cuts were announced, income tax was reduced and the rate of indirect taxation (value added tax) was increased. In October 1979 exchange controls were abolished. The March 1980 Budget introduced the medium-term financial strategy (MTFS) comprising a four-year declining target path for the growth of a broad monetary aggregate (sterling M3) and an accompanying path for the public sector borrowing requirement (PSBR), which implied a declining PSBR/GDP ratio. The immediate result of these policies, in conjunction with external developments, was a major loss of competitiveness accompanied by a large fall in production and the rise in unemployment noted above. Company finances were adversely affected, real profitability falling to its lowest recorded level in the second half of 1980, and the reaction was a massive reduction in inventories. Arithmetically, the reduction in real GDP between 1979 and 1980 was more than accounted for by the reversal in stockbuilding; substantial destocking continued in 1981. Inflation increased to 18% in 1980, but then began to fall, reaching 5·4% by the end of 1982.

This brief description serves to set the scene for the discussion of forecast performance over this period, of which a good account is given by Barker (1985), and of subsequent developments. The 'Thatcher experiment', or what is now the 'Thatcher experience', has a considerable literature of its own, two notable early contributions being the Brookings papers of Buiter and Miller (1981, 1983), and that literature falls outside the scope of the present survey.

The recession was not well forecast, being unanticipated until mid-1979, although the errors were smaller than in 1974–5. As Barker (1985) points out, the difficulties are demonstrated by an exercise presented to the Bank of England Academic Panel (Worswick and Budd, 1981), in which the LBS and

NIESR models were used to explain the shortfall of output over 1978–80 relative to its trend. (Budd's contribution also includes a post-mortem analysis of LBS forecasts over this period; Surrey (1982) likewise examines the NIESR track record.) The shortfall in output was estimated at 4%, the main contributions being

    (i) policy changes in the June 1979 Budget, in particular the VAT increase and the planned cuts in public expenditure (1·6–1·7%);

   (ii) the deterioration in competitiveness (1·1–1·3%);

  (iii) the oil price rise (0·8–1·3%).

As all these factors appeared in the models as relevant exogenous variables, three possible explanations of the forecast errors remain. First, the movements in these variables may not have been correctly anticipated. Secondly, their effects on the economy may not have been accurately modelled. Thirdly, the model forecasts may have been adjusted to show less dramatic changes, although no evidence on this is available (an analysis of the impact of adjustments on later forecasts is presented in Section IV.5 below). After the onset of the oil price increases and the June 1979 Budget growth forecasts were revised downwards, with the LBS correctly forecasting that output would fall in 1980, although the extent of the fall, and in particular the collapse of GDP in the fourth quarter of 1980, was not anticipated. The NIESR forecast of growth in 1980 was revised to a negative number only in February 1980, and again the fall in output was considerably underestimated. By this time the full extent of the oil-price rise was appreciated, but the extent of the financial squeeze on the company sector was not. Cuts in public expenditure continued to be forecast into 1980, but these never materialised, and these errors served to offset the failure to capture the large volume of destocking. As Budd notes, to predict the speed of adjustment to major shocks, particularly financial shocks, is especially difficult, and the previous recession offered little guidance. Whereas companies allowed exceptionally high deficits to accrue in 1974 and did not adjust inventories and employment until 1975, in 1980 the adjustment occurred almost instantaneously. Thus the rise in unemployment was also underpredicted. Finally the exchange rate was underpredicted, and this would have remained the case even had the oil price increase been fully anticipated.

Once again the experience of forecasting through a relatively turbulent period led to a reappraisal of the forecasting models. While this resulted in further small steps in the continuing process of model evolution, such as the introduction of financial considerations into the determination of investment and stockbuilding, two major items appeared on the agenda, namely expectations and the supply side.

Expectations of future developments have long been recognised as important determinants of current behaviour and, as Klein (1987, p. 420) notes, forecasters have long endeavoured to use survey data on expectations and anticipations wherever possible. Reliable quantitative data on expectations are relatively rare, however, and auxiliary hypotheses about the way in which expectations are formed are commonly used in their place. In the forecasting models of the 1960s and 1970s expectations were assumed to be formed by extrapolating from past experience, usually in respect of the variable of interest alone. The simplest example of this approach is the adaptive expectations hypothesis, which was widely used, and in this and more general cases the resulting model can be described as backward-looking. The need to accommodate explicit forward-looking behaviour was increasingly recognised, at the theoretical level through the attention given to the rational expectations hypothesis and at the practical level through the experience of 1979–81. The role of expectations in the face of a change of policy regime and the associated questions of credibility began to feature in the discussion. Credibility featured without agreement, however. On the one hand Buiter and Miller (1981, p. 362) assert

> The government established the credibility of its restrictive policy stance at the start of its term of office. The perception that current and future monetary policy would be restrictive was reflected promptly in the exchange rate, interest rates, and financial markets generally, but only gradually in domestic costs, especially wages. This led to a major appreciation of the real exchange rate along the lines of the overshooting model, a rise in real interest rates, and a decline in Tobin's q.

On the other hand, Matthews and Minford (1987, p. 62) argue that 'in fact, most people had written off the early actions of the government as unlikely to be followed through,...so if anything people expected a "U-turn" towards much looser policies. It was for this reason, the lack of credibility, that prices and wages in 1979–80 were accelerating towards 20% p.a. growth.'

In March 1980 the first forecasts based on the Liverpool model (Minford *et al.*, 1984) were published. This model represented a break with the existing models of the UK economy, being a new classical equilibrium model, incorporating the hypothesis of rational expectations; it is a monetarist model in the sense that higher monetary growth directly increases inflation, with no role for cost factors. The rational expectations literature is usually assumed to start with Muth (1961), although following much older discussions of the influence of forecasts on outcomes, Grunberg and Modigliani (1954) had already shown that where agents react to forecasts and thereby alter the course of events, this reaction can be taken into account to yield a correct, self-fulfilling forecast. This same kind of internal consistency is imposed by the rational expectations algorithms used to calculate a sequence of forecasts based on a model containing explicit forward-looking expectations variables, in that each period's future expectations coincide with the model's forecasts for the future period. The approach is more appropriately and perhaps less controversially termed 'model-consistent' expectations. In policy evaluation exercises, the use of consistent expectations allows policies to be tested under conditions in which their effects are understood. As Currie (1985) argues, good performance in these conditions is a necessary condition for a satisfactory policy: 'a policy that performs badly when its effects are understood must be unsatisfactory'. In both forecasting and policy analysis, the explicit treatment of forward expectations allows such issues as the announcement effects of future policy changes, their credibility and, indeed, the consequences of false expectations to be dealt with.

Fischer (1988)[1] recalls that his 1976 survey with Barro drew 'a clear distinction between the rational expectations hypothesis as a theory of expectations, and the type of equilibrium model in which the hypothesis was typically embodied at the time'. This distinction was blurred by leading US forecasters, however; thus in discussing the 'rational expectations school', both Eckstein (1983) and Klein (1986) associate the rational expectations hypothesis with the policy ineffectiveness proposition, and Klein *et al.* (1983) describe the 'many ways in which the thinking of monetarists and proponents of rational expectations are congruent'. Given the opposition of the 'mainstream models' to the positions of the 'rational expectations school' and the extreme monetarists indicated in these writings, it is perhaps not surprising that consistent expectations were not widely embraced in the US models. In the United Kingdom, however, despite the first appearance of rational expectations being in the new classical Liverpool model, the distinction appears to have been more clearly appreciated, and the incorporation of explicit forward-looking expectations handled in a model-consistent manner was part of the post-1981 revision process of other, more mainstream 'sticky price' and quantity adjustment models.

In the case of the LBS model, the introduction of consistent expectations was associated with the introduction of a detailed financial sector, in which asset demands are determined in a general portfolio choice model featuring expected future prices of gilts, equities and overseas assets, and in which the exchange rate is determined as a market-clearing price. Various questions, now of increased importance, such as the conduct of monetary and exchange rate policy, the use of open-market operations and debt management, and the finance of fiscal deficits could then be addressed.

The introduction of forward-looking behaviour into the NIESR model (Hall and Henry, 1985) was motivated by its forecasting performance: backward-looking equations for employment, investment and stockbuilding, depending mainly on lagged output, missed the turning point in 1979, as noted above, and did not capture the speed and depth of the recession. Accordingly, forward-looking behaviour was introduced into these equations, together with wage equations, money demand and exchange rate equations. Not only do expectations of various prices appear, as in the LBS and Liverpool models, but also expectations of future output and personal income, so retaining the model's neo-Keynesian quantity adjustment approach.

The influence of the supply side on macroeconomic phenomena received increasing attention as a result of the major supply shocks of the 1970s and the criticisms of the new classical macroeconomists. Among US modellers and forecasters, for example, Klein (1978) in his AEA Presidential Address and Eckstein (1983), cited above, advocate a consensus approach in which mainstream models, now recognised to be over-emphasising effective demand, are extended by incorporating a full supply-side analysis into an appropriately

[1] See previous chapter.

elaborated IS–LM system. The over-emphasis on the demand side does not imply that supply theory had been neglected in the academic literature in preceding decades, as Eckstein (1983, p. 56) notes, but that body of work had had little impact on the macroeconomics used for policy. In the United Kingdom the Conservative government elected in May 1979 paid increasing attention to supply-side policies, and the Liverpool model contained powerful supply effects in its representation of the labour market. As Matthews and Minford (1987) note, the size of the effects attributed to variations in unemployment benefits, direct taxes and trade union membership (proxying the power of unions) remain controversial, and their claim that these are well-determined empirically has been rejected by other researchers (for example, Nickell, 1987; Wallis *et al.*, 1986, ch. 5). A further model, specifically designed as a supply-side model, namely that of the City University Business School (Beenstock *et al.*, 1986) was first used for forecasting at the time of the June 1983 general election. The CUBS model abandoned the usual income-expenditure framework and determined the supply of output through a KLEM production function (capital, labour, energy, materials); it also included a formal labour supply schedule, unlike other models. Like the Liverpool model, it is an annual, not quarterly model, and emphasises the medium-term development of the economy. In the quarterly models the consensus has been slower to arrive than in the United States, but the current version of the LBS model (Dinenis *et al.*, 1989) incorporates explicit supply influences into the income–expenditure framework. Output is determined not as the sum of the expenditure components but by both supply and demand factors at the sectoral level, with prices in the long run ensuring that the goods market clears.

IV. EVALUATION OF FORECASTS

The evaluation of past forecasting performance is an important input into the forecasting process and, since it provides a forecast of future performance, it is of interest to the users of forecasts. The forecasters themselves regularly publish accounts of their own performance, and occasionally contrast this with that of other groups. Several authors have undertaken independent studies of the performance of different forecasters with respect to a range of variables and forecast horizons, for example, in the United Kingdom Ash and Smyth (1973), Holden and Peel (1983, 1986) and Wallis *et al.* (1986, 1987), and in the United States McNees (1982, 1986) and Zarnowitz (1979, 1985) and references therein, including papers cited above; Artis (1988) examines the forecasting record of the IMF World Economic Outlook, and compares it with that of the separate national forecasting agencies. Evaluations range from descriptive accounts of forecasting ability in particular periods, especially turning points, as in the preceding sections, to the statistical analysis of forecast errors over a period of years, considered in this section. Evaluations are typically addressed to one variable at a time, whereas a multivariate assessment may be more relevant, particularly if trade-offs between different variables have a bearing on the specific decision problem.

Given time series of forecasts and outcomes, the first step is usually to calculate summary statistics such as the mean absolute error (MAE) and root mean square error (RMSE), or comparable statistics for the forecasts and outcomes separately, or even their correlation coefficient. An immediate difficulty is that there is no absolute measure of the forecastability of a series, and so there is no absolute standard against which to compare these summary statistics. For a given definition of optimality, usually linear least squares, statistical prediction theory provides the optimal forecast with respect to a given information set, but economic forecasters may not agree about the relevant information set, which in the widest sense is in any event unknown, *ex ante* and *ex post*, and unmanageably large. In the absence of an absolute standard, various comparative procedures have been developed, discussed in the following sections. The first approach is to test whether the forecast satisfies certain properties of an optimal forecast, other than that of minimum mean square error. The second approach is to limit attention to a particularly restricted information set, namely that comprising past values of the variable of interest alone, and to compare a given forecast with the 'pure time series' forecast based on this 'own-variable' information set. The proper interpretation of such comparisons is considered, together with some recent evidence on the variation over time of the performance of economic forecasts relative to a particularly simple time series forecast. A third possibility is to conduct comparisons across a number of models or forecasts, and the issues that these raise, together with the possibility of combining forecasts, are discussed next. Whereas all these approaches limit attention to the published *ex ante* forecast, some recent systematic appraisals of the major sources of forecast error, *ex post*, are then described. Finally, the assessment of forecast uncertainty is considered.

IV.1 *Properties of Optimal Forecasts*

An optimal forecast, which is the same thing as a rational expectation in the macroeconomic context, is unbiased and efficient. That is, the forecast error has an expected value of zero and cannot be predicted by any variable in the information set: full use of the given information has already been made in constructing the forecast.

A simple test of unbiasedness is to calculate the sample mean forecast error and compare it to its standard error. Many studies, instead or in addition, estimate the realisation-forecast regression

$$A_t = \alpha + \beta F_t + u_t,$$

where A and F denote actual value and forecast respectively, and test the (joint) hypothesis $\alpha = 0$, $\beta = 1$. While this is often interpreted as a test of unbiasedness, since if $\alpha = 0$ and $\beta = 1$ the forecasts are unbiased, it is in fact a stricter test, and was originally presented as a test of efficiency by Mincer and Zarnowitz (1969, p. 9). Since

$$A_t \equiv F_t + e_t,$$

where e_t is the forecast error, the estimate of β in the above regression only deviates from 1 if F_t and e_t are correlated. Such a correlation indicates an inefficient forecast, since the correlation could be exploited to help predict the forecast error and so improve the forecast. But a significant deviation of the estimates of α and β from 0 and 1, respectively, does not necessarily imply significant bias, for it is possible that the sample mean forecast error, $\bar{e}$, is nevertheless close to zero in such circumstances. Since the regression estimates of α and β are in general correlated, their individual t ratios provide inappropriate tests of the efficiency hypothesis, and a *joint* test is required: Artis (1988) presents examples in which the individual and joint tests are in conflict.

Granger and Newbold (1977, p. 284) raise a practical objection to the realisation-forecast regression, namely that the validity of the usual test procedures rests on the non-autocorrelation of u_t, which need not necessarily hold for sub-optimal one-step-ahead forecasts, and does not generally hold for optimal forecasts more than one step ahead: Hansen and Hodrick (1980) provide corrected estimates of the asymptotic covariance matrix to accommodate this possibility. These are used by Holden and Peel (1985), for example, who study NIESR forecasts of six variables one to four quarters ahead over the period 1975–80: the hypothesis $\alpha = 0$, $\beta = 1$ is rejected in only one of the twenty-four cases, namely for forecasts of inflation four quarters ahead. Zarnowitz (1985) studies ASA–NBER business outlook survey respondents and likewise finds that inflation is the difficult variable: across six variables, five horizons and 79 respondents, the hypothesis $\alpha = 0$, $\beta = 1$ is rejected at the 5% level in 15·4% of the tests, but nearly half of these rejections refer to the inflation forecasts. In both of these papers the hypothesis $\alpha = 0$, $\beta = 1$ is referred to as the unbiasedness hypothesis.

The NIESR inflation forecasts presented in Fig. 2 are similar to the four-quarter-ahead forecasts considered by Holden and Peel, but cover a longer period. It is clear from inspection that the forecast errors are positive during the period 1964–81 (except 1968, which has a zero error), indicating persistent underprediction of inflation, followed by persistently negative errors during 1982–87. Given this pattern it is not surprising that the realisation-forecast regression has a significant Durbin-Watson statistic, and in a joint test based on the corrected coefficient covariances the hypothesis $\alpha = 0$, $\beta = 1$ is rejected. The mean forecast error overall is 1·0% p.a. The GDP forecasts, however, are unbiased according to these tests.

It is now recognised that the concept of efficiency underlying the realisation-forecast regression is a relatively weak one. Granger and Newbold (1977, p. 284) argue that $\alpha = 0$, $\beta = 1$ 'constitutes a necessary condition for forecast efficiency, but according to any acceptable interpretation of that word it cannot be regarded as a *sufficient* condition'; in particular, it neglects possible autocorrelation of the forecast error, as their counter-example implicitly suggests. Autocorrelation of one-step-ahead forecast errors indicates that the forecast is not making efficient use at least of the own-variable information set, since knowledge of past forecast errors for the variable in question can then improve current forecasts. Errors in forecasts more than one step ahead cumulate step-by-step and so are autocorrelated, as noted above, but the errors in an optimal n-step-ahead forecast exhibit autocorrelation of order n-1, not n, so this cannot be exploited to improve the forecast: it is efficient with respect to the own-variable information set. This efficiency property can be tested in a variety of ways. Holden and Peel (1985) regress the forecast error on the four most recent values of the variable known when the forecast was made. Of the twenty-four cases considered, only the inflation forecasts over three and four quarters fail this test, and the remaining NIESR forecasts could not be improved by using own-variable information more efficiently.

Increased use of the rational expectations hypothesis has been associated with a further strengthening of the concept of efficiency, which in its most extreme form, 'full rationality', requires that all available information be used in an optimal manner in constructing a forecast. Efficiency with respect to an information set containing other variables can be tested as in the preceding paragraph, by regressing the forecast error on lagged values of these variables known at the time the forecast was prepared. But the notion of 'all available' information presents practical difficulties, and whereas a rejection of full rationality in such a test is convincing, a failure to reject does not dispel the thought that there might be a relevant variable, untested, lurking around the corner. Brown and Maital (1981) assess one of the best-known surveys of experts' anticipations, namely the Livingston data, over the period 1962–77. Of the nine variables considered, only the wholesale price inflation expectations were found to be inefficient with respect to own-variable information, and the forecast errors in this variable and consumer price inflation could each be partly explained by past values of the other variable, indicating that their interrelationship was not properly appreciated by the forecasters. The more interesting finding, however, was that monetary growth helped to explain the forecast errors in both inflation variables, indicating that had monetary growth been correctly understood and fully incorporated into expectations over this period, the forecasts would have been considerably improved. Neglect of monetary influences does not appear to be the explanation of the problems in the NIESR annual inflation forecasts described above, however.

IV.2 *Comparisons with Time-series Forecasts*

Forecasts based exclusively on the statistical time-series properties of the variable in question have often been used to provide a yardstick against which economic forecasts, whether model-based or not, can be assessed. At a conference in 1972, Granger and Newbold (1975) commented that 'so far the sparring partner [the time series forecast] is consistently out-pointing the potential champion [the econometric model]', but the potential champion quickly reached match-fitness. A typical result is that of McNees (1982), who finds that published model forecasts generally outperform their time series competitors, the margin being greater four quarters ahead than one quarter ahead.

Comparison of a given forecast with a particularly naive alternative is implicit in a widely used 'inequality coefficient', attributed to Theil, defined as the ratio of the RMSE of the forecast to the RMSE of a 'no-change' forecasting rule. This rule projects forward the last available observed value, and so the error in such a one-step-ahead forecast is simply the first difference of the variable in question. This inequality coefficient appears in Theil's *Applied Economic Forecasting* (1966), also in Ferber and Verdoorn (1962), Zarnowitz (1967), and elsewhere; in *Economic Forecasts and Policy* (1958) Theil had proposed a coefficient with a different denominator, designed to ensure that the coefficient lies between 0 and 1, but this has other disadvantages, as noted by Ferber and Verdoorn (1962, ch. 10.4), Sims (1967), Granger and Newbold (1977, pp. 281–2), and by Theil (1966, p. 28) himself. Sims (1967) and Zarnowitz (1967) also use inequality coefficients in which the denominator is the RMSE of less naive time series forecasts, initiating a trend in forecast comparisons that has continued since that time. After the initial use of no-change or 'same-change' forecasting rules, autoregressive models and the ARIMA models of Box and Jenkins (1970) were employed as benchmarks. The increased complexity of these time series methods itself indicates the progress that has occurred in forecasting models since their early development. Finally, moving to a multivariate context, vector autoregressive (VAR) models as used for forecasting by Litterman (1986) have entered the competition. In this last respect the US picture is somewhat mixed: VAR forecasts are part of the comparison carried out by McNees (1982), summarised above; with Litterman's Bayesian modification they also feature in the comparison of McNees (1986), where they are generally the most accurate or among the most accurate for real GNP, unemployment and investment. Curiously, for four of the seven variables considered by McNees, the RMSE of the VAR forecast declines as the forecast horizon increases from one to eight quarters. In the United Kingdom, however, VAR forecasts have not been found to dominate published model-based forecasts (Wallis *et al.*, 1986, 1987).

Formal comparisons between model-based forecasts and time series forecasts face two difficulties. First, since the data used in empirical specification and estimation of the two forms are the same, their forecasts, forecast errors and resulting summary measures are not statistically independent, hence a formal test based on a direct comparison of the two forecast error variances, such as an F test, cannot be employed. Secondly, at the theoretical level, a univariate ARIMA model can be regarded as an approximation to a solution form of an econometric model (its 'final equation'), and hence again cannot provide an independent check on the econometric model, in terms of forecast or any other comparison. Since the time series models emphasise dynamic and stochastic features of the data, early comparisons in which they outperformed econometric models simply suggest that the latter were deficient in these respects (Prothero and Wallis, 1976). Indeed, the equations of such models often exhibited substantial residual autocorrelation. Subsequently, the dynamic and stochastic specification of the large-scale econometric models has improved, through the application of developments in time-series econometrics. In the UK context, these stem from the classic Colston paper by Sargan (1964); see, for example, Wallis (1972), Hendry (1974) and Hendry and Richard (1983). In particular, comparisons with time series models now can be seen to represent a useful diagnostic device during the model specification process. The advice offered at that same 1972 conference, 'that a suggested specification should be tested in all possible ways, and only those specifications which survive and correspond to a reasonable economic model should be used' (Sargan, 1975) has been heeded, and a range of diagnostic tests is readily available in user-friendly micro-computer software (for example, Hendry, 1986).

Finally, an inequality coefficient based on a naive time-series forecast is reconsidered, for a different purpose. In his analysis of Treasury forecasts, Burns (1986) calculates five-year moving averages of absolute forecast errors and compares these to an index of variation which gives some impression of the difficulty of forecasting at different points in time. The index is defined as the five-year moving average of the absolute error of a no-change forecast of the growth rate or the inflation rate, that is, the average of the absolute difference between successive years' growth or inflation rates; appropriate extensions are needed for comparison with two-year-ahead forecasts. The resulting ratio modifies the Theil inequality coefficient for forecasts of growth and inflation in two ways: it replaces RMSEs by MAEs, and it replaces the overall sample means by five-year moving averages. Burns' results for Treasury forecasts over one-year and two-year horizons are shown, slightly updated, in Fig. 3, together with equivalent information for LBS and NIESR forecasts. His broad conclusion about Treasury forecasts over this period is that while there has not been any marked improvement in accuracy of the short-term forecasts, the results for the two-year-ahead forecasts are more encouraging, with some evidence of improvement over time. Over the shorter period for which data are available, the LBS and NIESR two-year forecasts show no substantial change in performance in respect of these two variables, and the Treasury forecasts appear to dominate, which may reflect their more effective incorporation of policy measures. For the one-year-ahead forecasts, however, the ranking of the three groups varies over time, and at any point in time is not consistent across the two variables considered. This is illustrative of a general finding in cross-model comparisons, discussed next.

IV.3 *Cross-model Comparisons and Combinations*

Comparisons of the *ex ante* forecasts published by different forecasting groups place all competitors on an equal footing with respect to information about the future. If one forecaster uses a model which treats as exogenous a variable which another treats as endogenous, then the former needs to provide an off-model projected value for that variable. The difference in classification of variables is immaterial, provided that it is recognised that a forecaster-model combination is under scrutiny. Remembering also the process of adjustments described in Section I, it is clear that *ex ante* forecasts do not provide useful evaluations of models alone. Furthermore, since models evolve, as discussed above, comparisons based on summary statistics such as MAE or RMSE over a period of years are in effect evaluating forecasting groups together with whatever model specification was in use at the time. Their personnel changes over time, too, although Burns (1986) attributes some of the improvement in Treasury medium-term forecasts to an increase in human capital: 'many

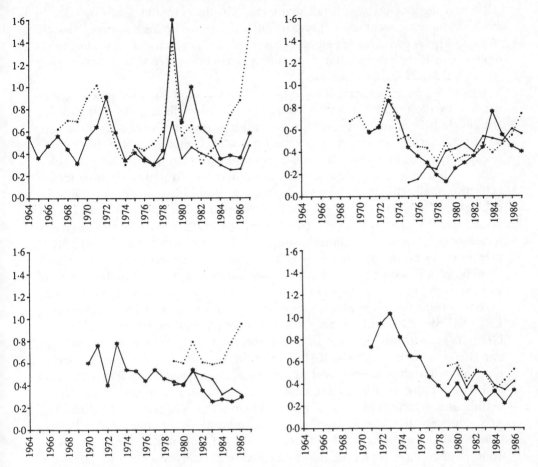

Fig. 3. Ratio of mean absolute error to index of variation (five-year moving averages shown against last year of period). Upper left, GDP growth, one-year-ahead forecast; lower left, GDP growth, two-year-ahead forecast; upper right, Inflation, one-year-ahead forecast; lower right, Inflation, two-year-ahead forecast. Key: ——■——, LBS; ··■··, NIESR; ——*——, HMT.

members of the forecasting teams were engaged in forecasting for many years'.

One practical use of forecasts is in informing decision-making, and in principle the evaluation of forecasts can be associated with any specified loss function, relevant to the particular objective. Given the dynamic multivariate nature of the forecasts, this would then help to specify the time horizon and the set of variables to be considered. In practice this does not feature in the literature, since decision makers and the users of forecasts seldom discuss such matters, at least not in public. As a result comparative studies usually focus on the small number of key macroeconomic indicators that feature in public discussion, and the possibility that one forecaster may offer information about a further group of variables about which another forecaster is completely silent is usually ignored. Clearly, however, if a user's interest is in that further group of variables, then there is no difficulty in deciding which forecaster is 'best'.

Although the loss function is not made explicit, the common measures used to evaluate forecast accuracy imply particular forms of the loss function, the use of mean square error, for example, implying that it is quadratic. Also the period over which these are calculated implies a particular interest in short-term or long-term forecasts, for example.

Given the rather general nature of the criteria, and the existence of a free market in data and economic ideas, the common finding of comparative studies that there are no unambiguous rankings is perhaps not surprising. For example, Zarnowitz (1979) finds that rankings among six US forecasting groups show appreciable differences with respect to particular variables, subperiods and forecast horizons, but the differences in summary statistics are typically small: 'the main lesson...is that the similarities greatly outweigh the differences between the forecasters' performance records'. In the United Kingdom, Holden and Peel (1986) compare LBS and NIESR quarterly forecasts of growth and inflation, and find that for both variables NIESR is preferred to LBS in 1975–9, whereas the ranking is reversed in 1980–4 (in each case both are superior to the forecasts published by a London firm of stockbrokers, however). As an example of a multivariate exercise, Wallis *et al.* (1987) consider a single forecast published in autumn 1984 by four groups – LBS, NIESR, LPL and CUBS – and study four variables, namely the level of GDP, its growth rate, the inflation rate and the unemployment rate. For each variable and each group the RMSE over the two years of the forecast period is calculated and then expressed as a ratio of the average for a given variable across all groups, in order to standardise the comparison in respect of the degree of difficulty of forecasting that variable. The relative RMSEs are shown in Fig. 4: a value less than one for a given group and a given variable implies better-than-average performance for that variable. If one tetrahedron lies inside another, then there is an unambiguous ranking not only when the variables are deemed to have equal importance, as in the illustration, but for all values of their relative weights. While this occurs in this particular short-term forecast for one pair, LBS and LPL, in all other pairwise comparisons the tetrahedra intersect and so no rankings that are invariant to the choice of weights on the different variables can be derived.

The statistical significance of differences in summary statistics such as the RMSE cannot be directly tested, as noted above, since the competing forecasts are not independent. The idea of combining forecasts (Bates and Granger, 1969) offers an alternative approach to testing the *ex post* performance of competing forecasts, and also a method of improving *ex ante* forecasting performance. Consider a combination of one forecast with its competitor: if the combined forecast has an error variance that is not significantly smaller than that of the first forecast then the competing forecast appears to offer no useful additional information. On the other hand, different forecasts based on different informations sets, different models, or even different approaches to data analysis, as in econometric vs. time series comparisons, in general may each be expected to contribute usefully to the forecasting problem, and so the combined forecast may be more accurate than any of the individual

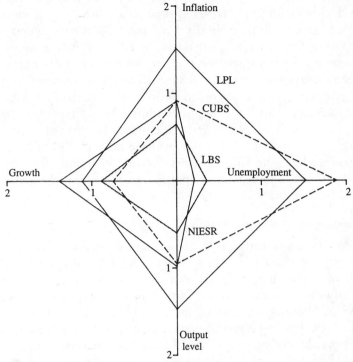

Fig. 4. Relative root mean square errors. The average root mean square errors are: GDP level, 2% of actual; GDP growth rate, 1·0% per annum; inflation rate 1·8% per annum; unemployment rate, 0·7%.

components. Thus an *ex post* comparison of two forecasts, F_{1t} and F_{2t}, may be based on the regression equation

$$A_t = \beta F_{1t} + (1 - \beta) F_{2t} + u_t$$

and a test of the null hypothesis $\beta = 1$, while a combination of *ex ante* forecasts for subsequent use may be based on the estimated coefficient.

Recent discussion (Granger and Ramanathan, 1984; Clemen, 1986; Holden and Peel, 1986) has focused on the general combination of k forecasts through the equation

$$A_t = \alpha + \beta_1 F_{1t} + \beta_2 F_{2t} + \ldots + \beta_k F_{kt} + u_t$$

and the question of whether or not the coefficient restrictions

$$\alpha = 0, \quad \beta_1 + \beta_2 + \ldots + \beta_k = 1$$

should be imposed. The unconstrained regression clearly achieves a smaller residual sum of squares *ex post*, as Granger and Ramanathan indicate, but the practical objective is to improve *ex ante* forecast performance, and Clemen shows that the imposition of the restrictions can improve forecast efficiency. Whereas some forecasts may be found to be biased, *ex post*, over certain periods, each individual *ex ante* forecast is offered as a best estimate of the future outcome, corrected for any past bias through the best endeavours of the forecaster. Holden and Peel (1986) estimate the above regression using only data available at a given point in the past, and with the estimated coefficients form a combined forecast of a future outcome, which is then compared with the actual outcomes: for quarterly forecasts of growth and inflation, a restricted combination always has a smaller RMSE than an unrestricted combination. The three 'economic' forecasts noted above are considered, along with three time series forecasts, and the winning combination is that based on the three economic forecasts. However, given the need to estimate the regression coefficients, the comparison is restricted to the later period of available data, namely 1980–4: here the LBS provides the best economic forecast, as noted above, and this single forecast also dominates the combined forecast over this period.

IV.4 *Decomposition of Forecast Error*

Ex ante forecasts are of little assistance in the evaluation of models, as noted above, since the forecast is a joint product of model and forecaster. Statistical summaries of errors in published forecasts provide no information about possible causes of forecast error. Errors may arise because the model is inadequate and because exogenous variables behave in a different manner to that on which the forecast is conditioned. Recomputation of the forecast, *ex post*, using realised values of exogenous variables, allows this latter source of error to be assessed. Forecasters make adjustments to the pure model forecasts in an attempt to overcome perceived model inadequacies and to improve the forecast in other ways, and the extent to which this succeeds may be assessed by recomputing the forecast with such adjustments removed. There is little consideration in the literature of these various sources of forecast error, an exception being Osborn and Teal (1979), who analyse two NIESR forecasts. In general, independent researchers have not been able to recompute forecasts under alternative assumptions, using the precise models on which the forecasts were based. An exception, however, is the ESRC Macroeconomic Modelling Bureau, which has taken successive deposits of models and forecasts since autumn 1983, and archived this information. With the passage of time comparative *ex post* forecast error decompositions become feasible, as described in this section, based on Wallis *et al.* (1986, ch. 4; 1987, ch. 4).

Ex post forecast comparisons give an advantage to a model that treats as exogenous a variable that is difficult to forecast, when other models are trying to explain its behaviour. Accordingly such comparisons are often criticised, because different models may have different degrees of exogeneity. Practical experience with the UK models, however, is that the broad classification of variables as endogenous or exogenous does not differ across models. In general, the variables treated as exogenous in models of small open economies fall into three main groups, describing respectively the economic environment in the rest of the world, domestic economic policy, and various natural resource and demographic trends, such as the growth of North Sea oil production and changes in the population of working age. Within these generally agreed exogenous areas differences of detail may arise, for the same reasons that apply in other areas of the models. For example, different models may measure an identical concept (the world price of oil, the real wage) in different ways; some concepts (world money supply) may appear in some models but not in others; the level of aggregation (distinguishing the price of oil from the general price level) may differ. Also, where the line is drawn between exogenous assumption and endogenous consequence may differ, particularly in respect of domestic economic policy: the more medium-term models tend to take as given a broad policy stance and allow the response of public expenditure and taxation to emerging pressures to be determined by the model, whereas the more short-term models take the detailed policy settings as given. Nevertheless these differences are not sufficient to inhibit cross-model comparisons.

Wallis *et al.* (1986, 1987) compute two variant forecasts after the event. First, the projected values of variables treated as exogenous are replaced by the actual outcomes: a comparison with the published forecast indicates the effect of incorrect anticipations about external developments. Secondly, by setting all residual adjustments to zero an *ex post* forecast, variously described as pure model-based, mechanical, or hands-off, is obtained. The error in this forecast includes the effect of model misspecification and the contribution of random disturbances in the forecast period, together with any effect of data revisions not explicitly accommodated elsewhere. The forecaster's residual adjustments represent an attempt to reduce this error and a comparison with the first variant indicates how successful this was. The error in the published forecast can then be decomposed as illustrated in Fig. 5, which describes the 1983 and 1984 forecasts of the price level, one and two years ahead, from four groups. In each segment of the figure the first block gives the error in the *ex post* hands-off forecast ('model error'), and the second block is the contribution of the forecaster's adjustments. These should be of opposite sign if the adjustments indeed act in an offsetting manner: in the majority of cases this has occurred, although the adjustment is seldom of the correct magnitude and sometimes rather large offsets were called for. The third block gives the contribution of errors in projecting exogenous variables, and these three contributions sum to the fourth block, namely, the error in the published forecast. In all cases these last errors increase as the forecast horizon increases, as expected. Overall the LPL group persistently underestimated inflation, that is, took an overoptimistic view in this respect, whereas the other three groups tended to be unduly pessimistic. It is often argued that a good track record in forecasting is a prerequisite for the use of a model in policy analysis, but it is important to disentangle the role of the model and the role of the forecaster, as in this illustration.

Perhaps the most striking feature of Fig. 5 is the contribution of exogenous uncertainty to the forecasts for 1986. In the first three cases the fortuitous choice of wrong exogenous assumptions has resulted in a relatively small final error, while in the LPL forecast the exogenous outcome transposes a pessimistic *ex post* adjusted forecast into an optimistic one. The principal cause is the unanticipated and unprecedented fall in the world oil price in 1986. This

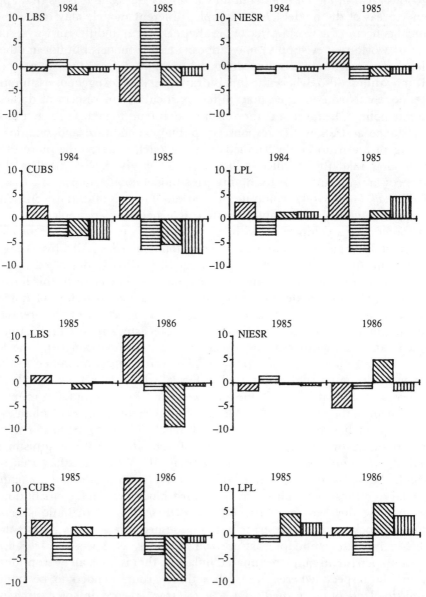

Fig. 5. Contributions to errors in price level forecasts, one and two years ahead (% of actual). Upper panel, autumn 1983 forecasts; lower panel, autumn 1984 forecasts. Key: ⊘, model error; ☰, contribution of residuals; ◩, contribution of exogenous uncertainty; ⊞, error in published forecast.

variable appears directly in the LBS, NIESR and CUBS models, which would have produced substantial forecast errors had its movements been anticipated, as the first block of the decomposition indicates. The fall in the world oil price was associated with a level of world demand lower than anticipated, the depressing impact of lower oil prices on the oil-producing countries being more immediate than the expansionary impact in the oil-importing countries, and this is the principal source of exogenous error in the LPL model, where oil prices do not appear. In the other three cases there is no agreement: LBS and CUBS show a large positive model error and knowledge of the forthcoming oil price fall would have led them to underestimate the domestic price level by a considerable amount, whereas in the NIESR forecast lower oil prices would have increased domestic prices via the lower exchange rate. This is the principal transmission mechanism in this case, and the actual impact on exchange rates of the oil price fall was much smaller than suggested by the then-current models. These were projecting forward from a different kind of sample experience and did not reflect whatever asymmetric effects were in operation. Once again, a change in data characteristics has been informative, and including this episode in the sample period has resulted in newly estimated equations that are much less sensitive to world oil prices.

A principal use of *ex post* forecast assessment is in studying the performance of models, as noted above. As far as the forecasts themselves are concerned, whereas calculations such as those that lie behind Fig. 5 permit discussion of what might have been, they cannot tell what would have been. The production of a forecast is an interactive process, and had the oil price fall been anticipated forecasters might have realised that its effects would not simply be the negative of the effects of the preceding oil price rise. Adjustments to the pure model-based forecast might then have been made, anticipating the model modifications that occurred subsequently. However forecasters seldom reveal the rationale for specific adjustments that they make (revelation of the adjustments themselves is a relatively new phenomenon, as discussed below), and it is not possible to reconstruct the forecasting team and its state of mind at the time in order to answer 'what-if' questions. Nevertheless a model that produces accurate *ex post* forecasts only after substantial adjustment must represent an unreliable vehicle for policy analysis.

IV.5 *Assessing Uncertainty*

Forecasts are subject to errors, and the user of forecasts needs to know the likely margin of error. Theoretical discussion of model-based forecasts usually takes the model as given and then analyses the forecast error in terms of its three sources: the model's random disturbance terms, its coefficient estimation errors, and forecast errors in exogenous variables. In the textbook linear model formal expressions for the variance attributable to each source are available, and in the practical nonlinear model stochastic simulation can be employed to estimate these quantities. This approach is of little help to the practitioner. It neglects the contribution of the forecaster's subjective adjustments, and its last element simply pushes the problem of assessing the margin of forecast error one stage further back, from endogenous to exogenous variables. More fundamentally, the model's specification is uncertain. At any point in time competing models coexist, over time model specifications evolve, and there is no way of assessing this uncertainty. Thus the only practical indication of the likely margin of future error is provided by the past forecast errors. Published evaluations of forecasts, such as those cited above, are a source of this information, and the forecasters themselves commonly provide an estimate of their past performance. For example, Treasury forecasts published in the annual *Financial Statement and Budget Report* (the 'Red Book') are accompanied by the MAE of the preceding ten years' forecasts.

Estimating the future margin of error is itself a forecasting problem, in that not only the first moment but also the second moment of the conditional probability distribution of future outcomes is now under consideration. As with the first moment, errors in forecasting the second moment are likely to occur at times of rapid change in the underlying situation, when the economy becomes harder or easier to forecast for some reason. Standardising measures of forecast performance with reference to the underlying variation, as in the examples in Fig. 3, accommodates such changes in the past, but in projecting forward the underlying variation is assumed to remain constant, unless this forecast is in turn subjectively adjusted. For example, in discussing the margin of error of Treasury forecasts, the *Financial Statement and Budget Report* that accompanied the June 1979 Budget noted the 'possibility that large changes in policy will affect the economy in ways which are not foreseen'.

The uncertainty of a single forecast, indicated by the spread of the probability distribution of possible outcomes, should be distinguished from disagreement among several (point) forecasts, as Zarnowitz and Lambros (1987) note. Consensus among forecasters need not imply a high degree of confidence about the commonly predicted outcome. To study this question, Zarnowitz and Lambros analyse the ASA-NBER survey responses on GNP growth and inflation, in which individual respondents provide their subjective (joint) probability distribution of outcomes. It is found that the variance of point forecasts tends to understate uncertainty as measured by the variance of the predictive probability distributions. The former varies much more over time than the latter, although these measures of consensus and uncertainty are positively correlated.

V. CONCLUDING COMMENTS

This paper surveys developments in macroeconomic forecasting over the last twenty years, during which forecasting methods have become more formalised and considerable progress has been made. 'Success in forecasting may be occasional and fortuitous or intuitive, but progress in forecasting, to the extent it is possible, can only come from advances of science, not art or chance' (Zarnowitz, 1979). Such advances have occurred gradually, with small improvements building on one another, 'but nothing really has been a complete breakthrough for solving the problems that confront us' (Klein, 1987). Forecasting disappointments led not to complete changes of direction but to constructive reappraisals and eventual improvements, also changes of emphasis. McNees (1988) concludes that 'annual forecasts of real GNP and the inflation rate have improved over time. Summary error measures have declined slightly in absolute terms but even more relative to either naive standards of comparison or the variability of the actual outcomes.'

The role of forecasts in macroeconomic policy-making, and the policy-making itself, have seen considerable changes during this period. Although the uncertainty in forecasting was clearly appreciated, Cairncross (1969) noting that 'the margins of error...even when small in relation to the magnitudes involved, remain large in relation to policy objectives and to the reserves held against contingencies', during the years of demand management short-term forecasts played an increasing role in fine tuning the level of demand. But by 1976, as Burns (1986) notes, 'there was not only disillusion with demand management; there was also growing frustration with the forecasts' as the increased level of noise in the economic system led to increased margins of error. In the 1980s the focus of the forecasts and policy analysis has shifted to a more medium-term horizon, and it is here that 'many of the developments in our understanding of the way economies work are likely to have their pay-off', again quoting Burns.

Cairncross (1969) concluded his Presidential Address by commenting on the issue of the publication of official forecasts. While acknowledging that there were 'great advantages in making official forecasts as widely available as possible', he also emphasised 'some of the inconveniences from the Ministerial point of view in putting official forecasts in front of an unsophisticated public' and expressed his own view 'that the issue is not nearly as important as it appears'. In any event, the Bray amendment to the 1975 Industry Act required the Treasury to publish forecasts produced with the aid of the model at least twice a year, and the first 'Industry Act forecast' was published in December 1976. As noted above, these are accompanied by indications of forecasting error, also as required by the Act. Five years after the Act, the Treasury could conclude that 'the impact of the Government's publishing forecasts has been, perhaps, more limited than was suggested by some of the strongly-held beliefs – pre-1976 – for and against publication' (HM Treasury, 1981).

Considerable improvements in publication and dissemination of forecasts have occurred in the period under review. Models and forecasts have become better documented and more widely accessible, most recently being disseminated for implementation on micro-computers. In the United Kingdom, forecast analysis such as that described in Section IV.4 is possible because the models, forecasts, and associated databases are made available to an independent research group (the ESRC Macroeconomic Modelling Bureau) charged with improving accessibility and undertaking comparative research. Before the establishment of the Bureau in 1983, the LBS forecasters had begun to publish the residual adjustments used in each forecast in their *Economic Outlook*. (Treasury forecasts do not enter such comparative analysis, however, since although the model is publicly available, again thanks to the Industry Act, the forecast assumptions and adjustments are not.) This degree of openness is unique, and perhaps could not be achieved in countries where the leading forecasting groups are commercial. Nevertheless in such countries public bodies are often among the main customers of commercial forecasters, and when such forecasts enter the public debate the same arguments about understanding the assumptions and replicating the results apply. Models and forecasts benefit from public discussion and assessment, and in most countries much more could be done.

REFERENCES

Artis, M. J. (1988). 'How accurate is the World Economic Outlook? A post mortem on short-term forecasting at the International Monetary Fund.' In *Staff Studies for the World Economic Outlook*, July 1988, pp. 1–49. Washington, DC: International Monetary Fund.

Ash, J. C. K. and Smyth, D. J. (1973). *Forecasting the United Kingdom Economy*. Farnborough: Saxon House.

Ball, R. J. and Burns, T. (1978). 'Stabilisation policy in Britain 1964–81.' In *Demand Management* (ed. M. V. Posner), pp. 66–100. London: Heinemann.

——, —— and Warburton, P. J. (1979). 'The London Business School model of the UK economy: an exercise in international monetarism.' In *Economic Modelling* (ed. P. A. Ormerod), pp. 86–114. London: Heinemann.

Barker, T. S. (1985). 'Forecasting the economic recession in the U.K. 1979–1982: a comparison of model-based *ex ante* forecasts.' *Journal of Forecasting*, vol. 4, pp. 133–51.

Barro, R. J. and Fischer, S. (1976). 'Recent developments in monetary theory.' *Journal of Monetary Economics*, vol. 2, pp. 133–67.

Bates, J. M. and Granger, C. W. J. (1969). 'The combination of forecasts.' *Operational Research Quarterly*, vol. 20, pp. 451–68.

Beenstock, M., Warburton, P., Lewington, P. and Dalziel, A. (1986). 'A macroeconomic model of aggregate supply and demand for the UK.' *Economic Modelling*, vol. 3, pp. 242–68.

Blanchard, O. J. (1987). 'Neoclassical synthesis.' In *The New Palgrave: A Dictionary of Economics*, vol. 3 (ed. J. Eatwell, M. Milgate and P. Newman), pp. 634–6. London: Macmillan.

Box, G. E. P. and Jenkins, G. M. (1970). *Time Series Analysis, Forecasting and Control*. San Francisco: Holden–Day.

Brown, B. W. and Maital, S. (1981). 'What do economists know? An empirical study of experts' expectations.' *Econometrica*, vol. 49, pp. 491–504.

Buiter, W. H. and Miller, M. H. (1981). 'The Thatcher experiment: the first two years.' *Brookings Papers on Economic Activity*, no. 2, pp. 315–67.

—— and —— (1983). 'Changing the rules: economic consequences of the Thatcher regime.' *Brookings Papers on Economic Activity*, no. 2, pp. 305–65.

Burns, T. (1986). 'The interpretation and use of economic predictions.' *Proceedings of the Royal Society of London*, A, no. 407, pp. 103–25. Reprinted in *Predictability in Science and Society* (ed. J. Mason, P. Mathias and J. H. Westcott). London: Royal Society and British Academy.

Cairncross, A. (1969). 'Economic forecasting.' ECONOMIC JOURNAL, vol. 79, pp. 797–812.

Chow, G. C. and Corsi, P. (eds.) (1982). *Evaluating the Reliability of Macroeconomic Models*. New York: Wiley.

Clemen, R. T. (1986). 'Linear constraints and the efficiency of combined forecasts.' *Journal of Forecasting*, vol. 5, pp. 31–8.

Currie, D. A. (1985). 'Macroeconomic policy design and control theory – a failed partnership?' ECONOMIC JOURNAL, vol. 95, pp. 285–306.

Davidson, J. E. H., Hendry, D. F., Srba, F. and Yeo, S. (1978). 'Econometric modelling of the aggregate time-series relationship between consumers' expenditure and income in the United Kingdom.' ECONOMIC JOURNAL, vol. 88, pp. 661–92.

Dinenis, E., Holly, S., Levine, P. and Smith, P. (1989). 'The London Business School econometric model: some recent developments.' *Economic Modelling*, vol. 6, pp. 243–351.

Dornbusch, R. (1976). 'Expectations and exchange rate dynamics.' *Journal of Political Economy*, vol. 84, pp. 1161–76.

Eckstein, O. (1983), *The DRI Model of the U.S. Economy*. New York: McGraw-Hill.

Fair, R. C. (1984). *Specification, Estimation and Analysis of Macroeconometric Models*. Cambridge, Mass: Harvard University Press.

Ferber, R. and Verdoorn, P. J. (1962). *Research Methods in Economics and Business*. New York: Macmillan.

Fischer, S. (1988). 'Recent developments in macroeconomics.' ECONOMIC JOURNAL, vol. 98, pp. 294–339.

Flemming, J. S. (1978). Review of *Demand Management* (ed. M. V. Posner), Heinemann, 1978. *Times Higher Educational Supplement*, 15 September.

Granger, C. W. J. and Newbold, P. (1975). 'Economic forecasting: the atheist's viewpoint.' In *Modelling the Economy* (ed. G. A. Renton), pp. 131–47. London: Heinemann.

—— and —— (1977). *Forecasting Economic Time Series*. New York: Academic Press. (Second edition, 1986.)

—— and Ramanathan, R. (1984). 'Improved methods of combining forecasts.' *Journal of Forecasting*, vol. 3, pp. 197–204.

Grunberg, E. and Modigliani, F. (1954). 'The predictability of social events.' *Journal of Political Economy*, vol. 62, pp. 465–78.

Hall, S. G. and Henry, S. G. B. (1985). 'Rational expectations in an econometric model: NIESR model 8.' *National Institute Economic Review*, No. 114, pp. 58–68.

Hansen, L. P. and Hodrick, R. J. (1980). 'Forward exchange rates as optimal predictors of future spot rates: an econometric analysis.' *Journal of Political Economy*, vol. 88, pp. 829–53.

Heller, W. W. *et al.* (1968). *Fiscal Policy for a Balanced Economy*. Paris: OECD.

Hendry, D. F. (1974). 'Stochastic specification in an aggregate demand model of the United Kingdom.' *Econometrica*, vol. 42, pp. 559–78.

—— (1986). 'Using PC-GIVE in econometrics teaching.' *Oxford Bulletin of Economics and Statistics*, vol. 48, pp. 87–98.

—— and Richard, J. F. (1983). 'The econometric analysis of economic time series.' *International Statistical Review*, vol. 51, pp. 111–63.

HM Treasury (1981). 'Forecasting in the Treasury.' *Economic Progress Report*, No. 134 (June), pp. 2–6.

Higgins, C. I. (1988). 'Empirical analysis and intergovernmental policy consultation.' In *Empirical Macroeconomics for Interdependent Economies* (ed. R. C. Bryant *et al.*), pp. 285–302. Washington, DC: Brookings Institution.

Hilton, K. and Heathfield, D. F. (eds.) (1970). *The Econometric Study of the United Kingdom*. London: Macmillan.

Holden, K. and Peel, D. A. (1983). 'Forecasts and expectations: some evidence for the UK.' *Journal of Forecasting*, vol. 2, pp. 51–8.

—— and —— (1985). 'An evaluation of quarterly National Institute forecasts.' *Journal of Forecasting*, vol. 4, pp. 227–34.

—— and —— (1986). 'An empirical investigation of combinations of economic forecasts.' *Journal of Forecasting*, vol. 5, pp. 229–42.

Isard, P. (1988). 'Exchange rate modeling: an assessment of alternative approaches.' In *Empirical Macroeconomics for Interdependent Economies* (ed. R. C. Bryant *et al.*), pp. 183–201. Washington, DC: Brookings Institution.

Keating, G. (1985). *The Production and Use of Economic Forecasts*. London: Methuen.

Klein, L. R. (1968). *An Essay on the Theory of Economic Prediction*. Helsinki: Yrjo Jahnsson Foundation.

—— (1974). 'Supply constraints in demand-oriented systems: an interpretation of the oil crisis.' *Zeitschrift fur Nationalokonomie*, vol. 34, pp. 45–56.

—— (1978). 'The supply side.' *American Economic Review*, vol. 68, pp. 1–7.

—— (1986). 'Economic policy formation: theory and implementation (applied econometrics in the public sector).' In *Handbook of Econometrics*, vol. 3 (ed. Z. Griliches and M. D. Intriligator), pp. 2057–93. Amsterdam: North-Holland.

—— (1987). 'The ET interview: Professor L. R. Klein interviewed by Roberto S. Mariano.' *Econometric Theory*, vol. 3, pp. 409–60.

—— Ball, R. J., Hazlewood, A. and Vandome, P. (1961). *An Econometric Model of the United Kingdom*. Oxford: Basil Blackwell.

—— Friedman, E. and Able, S. (1983). 'Money in the Wharton quarterly model.' *Journal of Money, Credit and Banking*, vol. 15, pp. 237–59.

—— and Young, R. M. (1980). *An Introduction to Econometric Forecasting and Forecasting Models*. Lexington, Mass: D. C. Heath.

Kmenta, J. and Ramsey, J. B. (eds.) (1981). *Large-Scale Macroeconometric Models: Theory and Practice*. Amsterdam: North-Holland.

Litterman, R. B. (1986). 'Forecasting with Bayesian vector autoregressions – five years of experience.' *Journal of Business and Economic Statistics*, vol. 4, pp. 25–38.

Llewellyn, J., Potter, S. and Samuelson, L. (1985). *Economic Forecasting and Policy – the International Dimension*. London: Routledge and Kegan Paul.

Lucas, R. E. (1975). 'An equilibrium model of the business cycle.' *Journal of Political Economy*, vol. 83, pp. 1113–44.

—— (1977). 'Understanding business cycles.' In *Stabilization of the Domestic and International Economy* (Carnegie-Rochester Series on Public Policy, vol. 5, ed. K. Brunner and A. H. Meltzer), pp. 7–29. Amsterdam: North-Holland.

—— (1980). 'Methods and problems in business cycle theory.' *Journal of Money, Credit and Banking*, vol. 12, pp. 696–715.

—— and Sargent, T. J. 'After Keynesian macroeconomics.' In *After the Phillips Curve: Persistence of High Inflation and High Unemployment*, pp. 44–72. Federal Reserve Bank of Boston, Conference Series No. 19.

McNees, S. K. (1979a). 'The forecasting record for the 1970s.' *New England Economic Review* (September/October), pp. 33–53.

—— (1979b). 'Lessons from the track record of macroeconomic forecasts in the 1970s.' In *Forecasting* (TIMS Studies in the Management Sciences, vol. 12, ed. S. Makridakis and S. C. Wheelwright), pp. 227–46. Amsterdam: North-Holland.

—— (1982). 'The role of macroeconometric models in forecasting and policy analysis in the United States.' *Journal of Forecasting*, vol. 1, pp. 37–48.

—— (1986). 'Forecasting accuracy of alternative techniques: a comparison of U.S. macroeconomic forecasts (with discussion).' *Journal of Business and Economic Statistics*, vol. 4, pp. 5–23.

—— (1988). 'How accurate are macroeconomic forecasts?' *New England Economic Review* (July/August), pp. 15–36.

Malgrange, P. and Muet, P. A. (eds.) (1984). *Contemporary Macroeconomic Modelling*. Oxford: Blackwell.

Matthews, K. G. P. and Minford, A. P. L. (1987). 'Mrs Thatcher's economic policies 1979–87 (with discussion).' *Economic Policy*, vol. 5, pp. 59–101.

Mincer, J. and Zarnowitz, V. (1969). 'The evaluation of economic forecasts.' In *Economic Forecasts and Expectations*, National Bureau of Economic Research Studies in Business Cycles No. 19 (ed. J. Mincer), pp. 3–46. New York: Columbia University Press.

Minford, A. P. L., Marwaha, S., Matthews, K. and Sprague, A. (1984). 'The Liverpool macroeconomic model of the United Kingdom.' *Economic Modelling*, vol. 1, pp. 24–62.

Muth, J. F. (1961). 'Rational expectations and the theory of price movements.' *Econometrica*, vol. 29, pp. 315–35.

Nickell, S. J. (1987). Discussion (of Matthews and Minford, 1987). *Economic Policy*, vol. 5, pp. 93–5.

Organisation for Economic Co-operation and Development (1965). *Techniques of Economic Forecasting*. Paris: OECD.

Ormerod, P. A. (ed.) (1979a). *Economic Modelling*. London: Heinemann.

—— (1979b). 'The National Institute model of the UK economy: some current problems.' In Ormerod (1979a), pp. 115–40.

Osborn, D. R. (1979). 'National Institute gross output forecasts: a comparison with US performance.' *National Institute Economic Review*, No. 88, pp. 40–9.

—— and Teal, F. (1979). 'An assessment and comparison of two NIESR econometric model forecasts.' *National Institute Economic Review*, No. 88, pp. 50–62.

Pesaran, M. H. and Evans, R, A. (1984). 'Inflation, capital gains and U.K. personal savings: 1953–1981.' ECONOMIC JOURNAL, vol. 94, pp. 237–57.

Pindyck, R. S. and Rubinfeld, D. L. (1976). *Econometric Models and Economic Forecasts*. New York: McGraw-Hill. (Second edition, 1981.)

Prothero, D. L. and Wallis, K. F. (1976). 'Modelling macroeconomic time series (with discussion).' *Journal of the Royal Statistical Society*, Series A, vol. 139, pp. 468–500.

Renton, G. A. (ed.) (1975). *Modelling the Economy*. London: Heinemann.

Roy, A. D. (1970). 'Short-term forecasting for central economic management of the U.K. economy.' In *The Econometric Study of the United Kingdom* (ed. K. Hilton and D. F. Heathfield), pp. 463–73. London: Macmillan.

Samuelson, P. A. (1955). *Economics* (3rd edn.). New York: McGraw-Hill.

Sargan, J. D. (1964). 'Wages and prices in the United Kingdom: a study in econometric methodology.' In *Econometric Analysis for National Economic Planning* (ed. P. E. Hart, G. Mills and J. K. Whitaker), pp. 22–54. London: Butterworth. Reprinted in *Econometrics and Quantitative Economics* (ed. D. F. Hendry and K. F. Wallis), pp. 275–314. Oxford: Basil Blackwell.

—— (1975). 'Discussion on misspecification.' In *Modelling the Economy* (ed. G. A. Renton), pp. 321–22. London: Heinemann.

Sims, C. A. (1967). 'Evaluating short-term macro-economic forecasts: the Dutch performance.' *Review of Economics and Statistics*, vol. 49, pp. 225–36.

Spencer, P. D. (1986). *Financial Innovation, Efficiency and Disequilibrium: Problems of Monetary Management in the United Kingdom 1971–1981*. Oxford: Clarendon Press.

—— and Mowl, C. J. (1978). 'A financial sector for the Treasury model.' Government Economic Service Working Paper No. 17.

Suits, D. B. (1962). 'Forecasting and analysis with an econometric model.' *American Economic Review*, vol. 52, pp. 104–32.

Surrey, M. J. C. (1982). 'Was the recession forecast?' *National Institute Economic Review*, No. 100, pp. 24–8.

Theil, H. (1958). *Economic Forecasts and Policy*. Amsterdam: North-Holland. (Second edition, 1961.)

—— (1966). *Applied Economic Forecasting*. Amsterdam: North-Holland.

Wallis, K. F. (1972). 'Testing for fourth order autocorrelation in quarterly regression equations.' *Econometrica*, vol. 40, pp. 617–36.

—— (1986). 'Forecasting with an econometric model: the "ragged edge" problem.' *Journal of Forecasting*, vol. 5, pp. 1–13.

—— (ed.), Andrews, M. J., Bell, D. N. F., Fisher, P. G. and Whitley, J. D. (1984). *Models of the UK Economy: A Review by the ESRC Macroeconomic Modelling Bureau*. Oxford: Oxford University Press.

—— (ed.), ——, ——, —— and —— (1985). *Models of the UK Economy: A Second Review by the ESRC Macroeconomic Modelling Bureau*. Oxford: Oxford University Press.

—— (ed.), —— Fisher, P. G., Longbottom, J. A. and Whitley, J. D. (1986). *Models of the UK Economy: A Third Review by the ESRC Macroeconomic Modelling Bureau*. Oxford: Oxford University Press.

—— (ed.), Fisher, P. G., Longbottom, J. A., Turner, D. S. and Whitley, J. D. (1987). *Models of the UK Economy: A Fourth Review by the ESRC Macroeconomic Modelling Bureau*. Oxford: Oxford University Press.

Worswick, G. D. N. and Budd, A. P. (1981). 'Factors underlying the recent recession.' Paper presented to the Panel of Academic Consultants, No. 15, Bank of England.

Zarnowitz, V. (1967). *An Appraisal of Short-Term Economic Forecasts*. National Bureau of Economic Research Occasional Paper, No. 104. New York: Columbia University Press.

—— (1979). 'An analysis of annual and multiperiod quarterly forecasts of aggregate income, output and the price level.' *Journal of Business*, vol. 52, pp. 1–33.

—— (1985). 'Rational expectations and macroeconomic forecasts.' *Journal of Business and Economic Statistics*, vol. 3, pp. 293–311.

—— and Lambros, L. A. (1987). 'Consensus and uncertainty in economic prediction.' *Journal of Political Economy*, vol. 95, pp. 591–621.

3

THE CONDUCT OF MONETARY POLICY*

Charles Goodhart

Nowadays the Central Bank is the monopoly supplier of legal tender currency. The commercial banks are committed to making their deposits convertible at par into such currency. So the banks need to keep reserves in the form of currency and deposits at the Central Bank. The Central Bank primarily conducts its policy by buying and selling financial securities, e.g. Treasury bills or foreign exchange, in exchange for its own liabilities, i.e. open market operations. Academic economists generally regard such operations as adjusting the quantitative volume of the banks' reserve base, and hence of the money stock, with rates (prices) in such markets simultaneously determined by the interplay of demand and supply. Central Bank practitioners, almost always, view themselves as unable to deny the banks the reserve base that the banking system requires, and see themselves as setting the level of interest rates, at which such reserve requirements are met, with the quantity of money then simultaneously determined by the portfolio preferences of private sector banks and non-banks. This difference in perceptions is discussed again in Section III.

Whether the monetary policy operations of Central Banks should be viewed primarily in terms of quantity, or rate, setting actions, (though, of course, one is the dual of the other), these had allowed inflation, and inflationary expectations, to become entrenched by the end of the 1970s. A selection of representative statistics for a number of the leading industrialised countries is given in Table 1 below.

This table indicates a common pattern, among the countries, of interaction between interest rates, inflation and the growth of output. The first period, 1969–78, is marked by high inflation, negative real interest rates, and slightly above average growth; the second period, 1979–82, by very high nominal, and high real, interest rates, high (but falling) inflation, and very low output growth. The final period, 1983–7, is marked by much lower inflation, lower nominal, but still high real, interest rates, and a recovery in output growth, in some cases to above average rates. In contrast, the relationship in these countries between the growth of their chosen key monetary aggregate and nominal incomes appears much weaker; also see Clinton and Chouraqui (1987), especially p. 7.

Whether measured in terms of monetary growth, or in terms of 'real' interest rates, i.e. after adjustment for prospective future inflation, policy during the

* This chapter was first published in the ECONOMIC JOURNAL, vol. 99, June 1989. My thanks for help and suggestions in its compilation go to Mike Artis, John Black, Peter Bull, Victoria Chick, Jean-Claude Chouraqui, Keith Cuthbertson, Dick Davis, Hermann-Joseph Dudler, Kim Frame, Chuck Freedman, Eric Hansen, David Hendry, Richard Jackman, David Laidler, David Lindsey, Ian Macfarlane, Gordon Midgley, Mark Mullins, Peter Nicholl, Andrew Oswald, Robert Raymond, Yoshio Suzuki, Richard Urwin and my referees, none of whom should be held responsible for my opinions or remaining errors.

Table 1

		1969 Q1 to 1987 Q4	1969 Q1 to 1978 Q4	1979 Q1 to 1987 Q4	1979 Q1 to 1982 Q4	1983 Q1 to 1987 Q4
		UK				
A	(£M3)	12·9	12·3	13·6	13·1	14·1
B	(Y)	11·9	14·0	9·6	11·6	8·0
C	(y)	2·1	2·1	2·1	0·3	3·5
D	(P)	9·8	11·9	7·6	11·4	4·5
E	(i_s)	10·7	9·4	12·2	14·1	10·6
F	(i_l)	11·7	11·6	11·8	13·6	10·3
		US				
A	(M1)	7·4	6·2	8·9	7·8	9·6
B	(Y)	9·0	10·0	7·9	8·0	7·8
C	(y)	2·7	3·0	2·5	−0·1	4·5
D	(P)	6·2	6·9	5·3	8·1	3·2
E	(i_s)	8·5	6·9	10·4	13·1	8·2
F	(i_l)	9·0	7·2	10·9	12·0	10·1
		West Germany				
A	(CBM)	7·6	9·3	5·8	4·9	6·2
B	(Y)	7·3	9·3	5·0	5·0	4·8
C	(y)	2·7	3·6	1·8	0·7	2·5
D	(P)	4·5	5·6	3·2	4·3	2·3
E	(i_s)	6·9	6·7	7·0	9·3	5·2
F	(i_l)	7·8	7·8	7·7	8·8	6·8
		Japan				
A	(M2)	12·7	16·4	8·7	8·7	8·9
B	(Y)	10·4	14·4	5·9	6·5	5·4
C	(y)	4·9	5·7	4·0	3·8	4·4
D	(P)	5·2	8·4	1·8	2·6	1·0
E	(i_s)	7·0	7·5	6·5	7·8	5·5
F	(i_l)	7·3	7·6	7·0	8·4	5·9
		France				
A	(M2)	12·2	14·7	9·2	11·3	7·2
B	(Y)	11·8	13·4	10·0	13·1	7·4
C	(y)	3·1	4·2	1·8	1·9	1·9
D	(P)	8·5	8·9	8·0	10·9	5·4
E	(i_s)	9·7	8·4	11·1	12·6	10·0
F	(i_l)	10·3	8·7	12·1	13·5	11·0
		Canada				
A	(M1)	8·2	10·3	6·1	5·3	6·4
B	(Y)	11·1	12·6	9·4	10·7	8·5
C	(y)	4·0	4·8	3·1	0·5	4·9
D	(P)	6·9	7·5	6·2	10·1	3·4
E	(i_s)	9·7	7·7	11·8	14·5	9·6
F	(i_l)	10·0	8·3	11·9	13·1	11·0
		Australia				
A	(M2)	12·9	12·9	12·9	11·6	13·7
B	(Y)	13·2	14·4	11·6	12·0	11·6
C	(y)	3·5	3·2	3·7	3·1	4·6
D	(P)	9·5	11·0	7·7	8·8	6·8
E	(i_s)	9·4	6·6	12·6	11·9	13·1
F	(i_l)	10·6	8·1	13·3	12·7	13·9

(A) Annualised mean % growth of key monetary aggregate.
(B) Annualised mean % growth of nominal income.
(C) Annualised mean % growth of real output.
(D) Annualised mean % growth of inflation.
(E) Annualised mean level of representative short-term (3-month) interest rate.
(F) Annualised mean level of representative long-term (10-year) interest rate.

1970s had become quite slack. Such accommodative policy had been accompanied by higher inflation than in previous decades, but not by particularly strong output growth. While it remained possible to argue, and was often so argued in the United Kingdom during the 1970s, that this conjuncture was caused by the adverse oil-related supply-side shocks of 1973 and 1979, the combination of the stagflation of this decade, together with the Lucas (1976) critique of Keynesian macro-models, as exemplified in the Friedman (1968)–Phelps (1968) analysis of the irrationality – and likely disappearance – of a downwards sloping Phillips curve, led to a downgrading of Keynesian demand-management, and associated monetary policy, strategies, (Mankiw, 1988). In addition, the demonstration effect of the comparative success of the West German and Swiss economies, which first adopted overtly quasi-monetarist policies, in reviving from the 1973 crisis led to a shift towards targetry and monetary rules. So, at the close of the 1970s most major industrialised countries had committed themselves to following targets, sometimes stretching into the medium term, for a selected monetary aggregate, a particular definition of the domestic money stock. With each country choosing its separate *domestic* target, the *international* relationship between the currencies was, perforce, flexibly determined through the foreign exchange market.

The power to conduct such monetary policy is not, however, concentrated solely in the Central Bank. In many countries, such as the United Kingdom, Australia and France, the Central Bank acts as the executive agent to carry out the strategic policy decisions of the Chancellor or Minister of Finance; meanwhile the Treasury and/or Ministry of Finance plays a major role in the formulation of such policy as well as the Central Bank. Even where the Central Bank is constitutionally independent of the Executive, as in the United States and West Germany, the decisions of the Central Bank are not, and can hardly be, taken in a political vacuum. Havrilesky (1988) provides a recent example (and an excellent reading list) of the entertaining US literature examining the degree to which the Fed's actions are affected by pressure from the Executive or Congress. Two more substantial works on this politico-economic borderline are, for the United States, Wooley (1984) and, for the United Kingdom, Moran (1984); Greider (1988) has written a more popular recent book about the Fed; for the United Kingdom, see Fay (1987); for West Germany, see Willms (1983) and Filc *et al.* (1988); for France, see Aftalion (1983); and for a wider survey of several countries, see Hodgman (1983).

In practice, the balance of power to determine monetary policy between the political Minister, the Ministry of Finance or Treasury, and the Central Bank varies both between countries, depending often as much on the wider political context as on the precise constitutional position of the Central Bank – viz. the comparatively powerful role of the Banca d'Italia and Banca d'Espana, – and also over time, depending greatly on the accident of personalities. Nevertheless, there has been some interest in the question whether the comparative susceptibility of Central Banks to political pressures has been a factor in their performance, e.g. in combating inflation, see Mayer (1987), Burdekin (1986), and Frey and Schneider (1981). For the purpose of this survey, I shall not pursue this question further; instead I shall explore the acts of the monetary authorities, without too much concern for the internal balance between Central Bank and Treasury.

Nevertheless the failure of the monetary authorities, whether Central Bankers or Ministers of Finance, to stem inflation in the 1970s led to reconsideration whether they were selflessly working for the public good – as implicit in much Keynesian theory – or might be swayed by other political and bureaucratic objectives. Such public-choice theorising about the incentives affecting the decision-making process of the authorities was for many monetarists (Friedman, 1984a) at the root of their preference for 'rules' rather than discretion.

A more analytically rigorous, and persuasive, reformulation of the arguments against discretionary intervention appeared somewhat later, in the guise of the 'Rules vs. Discretion' literature initially developed by Kydland and Prescott (1977), Calvo (1978), and made more accessible to the generality of economists by Barro and Gordon (1983a, b), and Barro (1986); also see McCallum (1987, 1988) and Isard and Rojas-Suarez (1986). In such models, if the authorities either assume (incorrectly) that expectations are relatively inflexible, or place excessive weight upon the short run, e.g. because of approaching elections, they will be led to introduce an expansionary (inflationary) policy which they would have previously pledged to abjure (time inconsistency). Unless the authorities are deterred from such actions by penalties arising from a loss of reputation in the future, leading to a reputational equilibrium, the ultimate outcome of discretion will be a higher inflation/same unemployment (time consistent) equilibrium than could be achieved by sticking to a monetary rule. It is doubtful how far those in charge of monetary policy followed the finer points of this analysis. But the general thrust of the importance of credibility, commitment, sticking to (simple) rules undoubtedly struck a resonant chord among them at the end of the 1970s.

So, at the outset of this decade (1980s) there was a considerable degree of concordance between (most) policy-makers and (most) academic economists. Monetary policy should be based on the achievement of monetary targets predicated on an assumed long-term stable relationship between the money stock and nominal incomes. Apart from setting and maintaining such quantitative monetary targets, the authorities should refrain from market intervention, e.g. in the foreign exchange market, since in conditions of efficient financial markets, in which agents were informed by rational expectations, such intervention could only destabilise the market to no good end.

By the latter part of the 1980s, however, the more *technical* elements, (as contrasted with the broader politico-economic ends), of this experiment were deemed, by the generality of policy-makers, to have comprehensively failed. The policies adopted in the early 1980s did, however, allow the authorities freedom to raise interest rates to levels that did subdue inflation, and the accompanying check to output growth, though severe, was indeed temporary. In terms of the mechanics, as contrasted with the ultimate objectives, of the policy, however, the crucial *long-term* relationships, i.e. the relationships between the money stock and nominal incomes (velocity), and between prices in two countries and their nominal exchange rate (purchasing power parity), appeared far more fragile than expected.[1] The extraordinary movements (misalignments) in foreign exchange markets and the crash of October 1987 put major question marks over the rational expectation, efficient market hypothesis.

Yet a large wing of mainstream (mostly US) macro-theoretical economists appear to have taken little notice of such historical experience in recent years, driving ever deeper into an artificial (Arrow/Debreu) world of perfectly clearing (complete) markets, in which money and finance do not matter, and business cycles are caused by real phenomena, e.g. Kydland and Prescott (1982), Long and Plosser (1983), King and Plosser (1984). Moreover, in a number of analytical studies of this kind, e.g. Lucas (1972), Sargent and Wallace (1975), the only reason why monetary policy may affect real variables is owing to an informational imperfection, which would seem simple and worthwhile to overcome. This leaves something of a gap between state-of-the-art macro-theory and practical policy analysis, see Laidler (1988 a, b).

It is not the function, or purpose, of this paper to examine the recent development of macro-economic theory, on which two recent surveys (Fischer, 1988; Mankiw, 1988), can be consulted. Both note the increasing divorce between theory and current practice. Thus Fischer, (p. 331), comments that 'there is greater not less confusion at the business end of macroeconomics, in understanding the actual causes of macroeconomic fluctuations, and in applying macroeconomics to policy-making'. Instead, the main aim of this paper is to document how, and why, policy makers in the main moved decisively away from the ideological (pragmatic monetarist) position adopted at the outset of the decade.

For this latter exercise I shall begin by examining the actual historical record of what policy makers have said and done, (Section I). In this Section, I shall somewhat arbitrarily divide up the recent decade into four periods: (*i*) The Shift of Policy towards Monetarism up till 1979; (*ii*) The High Tide of Monetarism, 1979–82; (*iii*) The Return to Pragmatism, 1982–85; (*iv*) The Increasing Concern with Exchange Rate Regimes, 1985 onwards.

A severe problem, occasioned by space limitations, concerns which countries' experience to record. Naturally, we focus primarily on the United Kingdom, but we must also review developments in the United States, not only since it has remained the central economic power, but also because US experience shapes the views of the dominant body of (American) monetary theorists.[2] Nevertheless, a number of references to papers on the experience of other

---

[1] For a reconsideration of rules for targetry in these new circumstances, and an advocacy of their reformulation in terms of a feed-back rule from nominal incomes (or some combination of price and output behaviour) to base money, see McCallum (1988) and Hall (1986). For a continuing critique of such rules, see Summers (1988), Tobin (1983) and Lamfalussy (1981).

[2] The continental parochialism of US economists is remarkable. Purely as an example, without wishing to impugn an otherwise admirable paper, B. Friedman's (1988 b) bibliography of approximately 100 citations has no reference to experience outside North America, and cites, by my count, only a couple of economists not primarily resident there.

countries will be added, in order to provide students with an entrée to the literature available on other major developed countries: there is no discussion of the monetary policy problems of LDCs.

The main reason for the progressive withdrawal of the monetary authorities from a public commitment to a pre-set monetary target was that such targetry was predicated on the existence of a predictable, and preferably stable, relationship between monetary growth and (subsequent) growth of nominal incomes. The previously estimated econometric relationships between movements in the money stock and in nominal incomes increasingly came apart at the seams during the course of the 1980s, though less dramatically in some countries, such as West Germany and France,[3] than in others, such as the United Kingdom, the United States and Canada. Since the purpose of monetary targetry was to seek to compress the rate of growth of nominal incomes (to a rate in line with the underlying potential rate of real growth), (see Lawson, 1986) the inability to predict what rate of growth of money would be consistent with the preferred path of nominal incomes removed the rationale for the authorities choosing, and seeking to maintain, some particular numerical target for monetary growth (Leigh-Pemberton, 1986). We record the main features of this story in Section II.

The breakdown of existing econometric relationships, e.g. in the form of demand-for-money functions, and the difficulties of replacing these earlier relationships with superior, and *credible*, more stable alternatives can be easily retold. What remains much harder is to explain just how, and why, such breakdowns occurred. During the last two decades, however, theoretical economists have emphasised that statistically estimated equations, such as demand-for-money functions, are not true, 'deep', structural equations, but are conditioned on the institutional structures and policy regimes – and the behaviour and expectations that these induce. The last decade has seen a wave of financial innovations (Solomon, 1981), again more so in the Anglo-Saxon countries than in continental Europe, in part in response to the various pressures within the financial system brought about by the earlier policy regime switch towards monetary targetry, and 'practical monetarism' (as described by Richardson, 1978). This is discussed in the second part of Section II.

One of the more important of such financial innovations was the spreading practice of banks offering market related interest rates on deposits that had earlier borne zero interest (i.e. sight/demand deposits), or whose interest rates had been administratively constrained. The increasing scope for liability management limited the authorities' capacity to control the volume of bank deposits by varying the general level of short-term interest rates, since they could no longer thereby control the relative differential between rates on deposits and on non-monetary assets. At the outset of the 1980s the ability of the authorities to control the money stock by this traditional method (interest rate adjustment) was the subject of sharp debate, and the alternative policy of

---

[3] 'Au fil du temps, l'évolution à longue terme de la vitesse de circulation de la monnaie a été suffisamment stable, en France, pour qu'un simple analyse de tendance fournisse une approximation correcte de sa valeur future,' Bordes and Strauss-Kahn (1988).

monetary base control (MBC) was strongly advocated, and, subject to some qualifications, partially adopted in the United States. We discuss such control issues in Section III. As policy makers came to place less weight on the achievement of monetary targets, public concern with the techniques of monetary control abated. Even so, reliance on interest rate adjustments, (whether occasioned directly by the authorities or indirectly through the market under MBC), in order to stabilise monetary growth, appeared to entail sizeable fluctuations in such rates. There remained, therefore, some interest in other possible methods of monetary control, notably the policy of 'over-funding' which was peculiar to the UK.

Nevertheless, especially following the removal of exchange controls (abolished in the United Kingdom in October 1979, see Lawson (1980) for the rationale) and other barriers to the free movement of capital between countries, it became generally accepted that adjustments to the general level of short-term interest rates formed just about the only effective monetary instrument, viz. for the United Kingdom Leigh-Pemberton (1987) and Lawson (1986, 1988); for France, Conseil National du Crédit (1987), Banque de France (1987); for Japan, Suzuki (1988) and Bank of Japan (1985). With monetary targets falling out of favour as key intermediate objectives, concern shifted away from the question of how interest rate adjustments might affect the monetary aggregates back towards the more traditional question of how they might affect nominal incomes and inflation.

This latter is considered in Section IV, but only briefly and mainly by reference to other survey papers. The subject of the transmission mechanism of monetary policy is both too large, and impinges too much on general macro-economic issues, to cover adequately here. Even so, we regard it as important to distinguish in this respect between the standard Keynesian IS–LM, approach, (which views the transmission mechanism as being restricted to a limited channel running from short-term interest rates, to long-term interest rates and equity prices, and hence to expenditures), and both the monetarist and neo-Keynesian approaches, wherein monetary/credit shocks can directly affect expenditures, e.g. by relaxing market imperfections. While most economists would probably now accept some aspects of this latter position, there remains great uncertainty on the relative importance of credit and monetary shocks.

So, this paper has the following structure; Section I: Historical Overview; Section II: Demand for Money; Section III: Supply of Money; Section IV: Transmission Mechanism.

The paper is intended for the general, non-technical reader. Some technical references to current econometric methodology creep into Section II, but, even so, the literary description is meant to give everyone some understanding of what is afoot.

As evidenced in Section I, policy makers became increasingly concerned, as the 1980s progressed, with the wayward behaviour of the foreign exchange market, and concerned to re-establish co-operative exchange rate regimes, either regionally (EMS) or internationally (e.g. at the meetings of the G7

Finance Ministers), to restore some 'order' to the international system. Although germane, and indeed increasingly central, to the story of the conduct of monetary policy in these years, space limitations have regretfully precluded a satisfactory coverage of this further extensive subject here.

I. AN HISTORICAL OVERVIEW

(i) The 1970s – The Policy Shifts

During the course of the mid-1970s, the monetary authorities in a growing number of countries adopted published monetary targets, starting with West Germany late in 1974, and then quite rapidly followed by the United States, Switzerland and Canada in 1975, and the United Kingdom, France and Australia in 1976, see Chouraqui et al. (1988, Table 3, p. 45), Hoskins (1985), and Foot (1981). Nevertheless the commitment of the authorities in a number of these countries remained doubted by sceptical commentators. Indeed, 'Judged solely by whether or not the targets were met, the results [in the earlier years were] generally poor,' (Foot, 1981, p. 28). In the United States the authorities initially shifted the target period forward one quarter at a time until the end of 1978, when, under the terms of the Humphrey-Hawkins Act of that year, targets were generally set for a full year at a time. The earlier approach in particular proved fertile ground for 'base drift', the practice of starting the new target from the actual (higher) money stock obtaining at the end of each quarter, rather than from the previously desired objective position (M. Friedman, 1982; Broaddus and Goodfriend, 1984 and Wang, 1980). The Bank of Japan did not provide a public announcement of the future path of M2 until 1978, and even then these have continued to be termed 'forecasts' rather than targets, (Tamura, 1987). In the United Kingdom, the authorities had been required to accept ceilings on Domestic Credit Expansion by the IMF in the course of dealing with the exchange rate crisis of 1976: while the associated adoption of published monetary objectives by the UK government was an independent decision, it is doubtful whether they would have taken that step without the external pressures. Moreover, whereas the Prime Minister (Callaghan) (1976) and Chancellor (Healey) did appreciate that the pursuit of some level of employment, or output growth, beyond that consistent with equilibrium would lead to accelerating, and unacceptable, inflation, it was doubtful how far the Labour Party as a whole was willing to absorb that argument, or still believed that some refurbished incomes policy could reconcile both nominal and real objectives. The Bank of England's wavering attitude to the proper balance between monetary targets and incomes policies is apparent in Lord Richardson's Mais Lecture (1978).

Be that as it may, the second half of the 1970s saw only limited further improvements in the reduction of inflation, following those achieved in the post-1973 deflation. Nominal interest rates remained in many countries below the concurrent rate of inflation, and even reached the ridiculously low figure of 5% in the autumn of 1977 in the United Kingdom as the authorities strove to maintain the competitive advantage for their manufacturing industry of the low exchange rate occasioned by the crisis in 1976 – a scenario that was to be replayed with a different cast in 1987/8. Inflationary expectations remained entrenched.

The overthrow of the Shah of Iran, causing fears of a shortage of oil, then led to the second oil shock in 1979, with crude oil prices more than doubling, to about $29 a barrel, by the beginning of 1980. Besides the direct effect of this on prices, the apparent weakness of President Carter led to growing fears about American policies more generally, and for the longer-term outlook for US inflation. The dollar had weakened sharply in 1978, and remained weak, despite official support in 1979: moreover, during 1979, there was a remarkable surge in the prices of precious metals, gold and silver, which, following the Russian intervention in Afghanistan, reached an extraordinary peak in early 1980.

This was the backdrop to the newly appointed Chairman of the Federal Reserve Board Paul Volcker's announcement of a new approach to monetary control on Saturday, 6 October 1979. Previously, the Fed had operated by controlling the level of the Fed Funds rate. While they could hit their chosen rate virtually exactly, various pressures, such as the natural tendency to limit changes under conditions of uncertainty, and the political unpopularity of upward movements in interest rates, had limited the flexibility with which the Fed felt able to vary such rates. From 6 October the Fed moved to control non-borrowed reserves – a modified form of MBC, see Section III below – allowing interest rates to vary, within wide and unpublished limits, as market forces might dictate. This single step transformed monetary conditions around the world, and was quite largely responsible, along with concurrent shifts to more deflationary policies in other major countries, for the shift from the generally inflationary conditions of the 1970s to the generally deflationary conditions of the 1980s.

Meanwhile in the United Kingdom the General Election of May 1979 had led to a Conservative victory. The new Conservative leaders had interpreted the inflationary upsurge of 1974/5 as being the direct consequence of the explosive increase in the broad money stock, £M3, in 1972/3. From the outset, in his first Budget on 12 June 1979, the Chancellor, Sir Geoffrey Howe, reaffirmed the government's commitment to controlling the growth of the monetary aggregates as the centrepiece of monetary policy (Howe 1979). At the same time, however, he presided over measures that would make such control more problematical. First, he raised the general level of VAT sharply, from 8 to 15%, thereby at a stroke increasing the margin between the current rate of increase of prices and of nominal expenditures on the one hand, and the target rate of monetary growth on the other. Second, he set in motion the removal of exchange controls, which was fully effected in October 1979; this allowed such obvious possibilities of disintermediation from the direct control over monetary growth then in operation, the 'Corset' – for an account see Bank of England (1982a) – that there was no alternative but its speedy abandonment, which occurred in June 1980.

'Concurrent and retrospective policy analyses of this 1979–82 period indicate that there were significant moves towards stricter monetary control in other countries at the same time. (See BIS, 1983; for Italy, see Barbato, 1987). Some of this alleged pervasive movement towards greater monetary discipline may have come from the influence that U.S. monetary policy had on the rest of the world, but some of it simply may have emerged simultaneously as an idea whose time had come' (Laney, 1985).

(ii) 1979–1982: The High-water Mark of National Monetarism

In the face of the upsurge of prices, and of nominal incomes, in 1979, with the RPI year-on-year reaching a peak of 21·9% in May 1980, the Bank of England ran into immediate problems in trying to hold £M3 down to the re-affirmed target of 7–11%. Bank lending rates were increased to 17% in November. Despite such operational problems, the Chancellor adopted a Medium Term Financial Strategy, announced in the March 1980 Budget, in which a pre-set declining target path for £M3 was made the centrepiece of the government's strategy, and whereby the fiscal policy decision, on the size of the Budget deficit, the Public Sector Borrowing Requirement (PSBR), was subordinated to the need to achieve the monetary target at acceptable levels of interest rates.[4] Thus 'there would be no question of departing from the money supply policy, which is essential to the success of any anti-inflationary strategy' (Treasury, 1980–81, page 19, para. 16).

Given the extent of instability already evident in UK demand-for-money studies (e.g. Hacche, 1974), there were grounds for concern whether the relationships between (any particular definition of) monetary growth and nominal incomes were too fragile a basis for such a long-term commitment. A number of commentators, e.g. the Treasury and Civil Service Committee (1981), expressed such doubts. Perhaps because of differing views about the existing evidence, more likely because of a belief that it was worth taking risks in order to establish a convincing picture of credible commitment, such worries were brushed aside by the government. Such commitment was welcomed by a number of influential commentators (e.g. Brittan, 1980), who believed that it could so alter expectations as to allow a decline in inflation with less

---

[4] The association between monetary and fiscal policy can be most easily seen via the credit counterparts approach. Assume that, with flexible exchange rates, the expected change in banks' net foreign assets is zero, and also ignore any possible change in banks' non-deposit liabilities. Then, the following accounting identities will hold: $\Delta D = \Delta A$; $\Delta A = \Delta BLPub + \Delta BLPS$; $\Delta BLPub = PSBR - DS, NBPS$; where D is £M3, A banks' holdings of domestic assets, $BLPub$ bank lending to the public sector, $BLPS$ bank lending to private sector, $DS, NBPS$ are (net) public sector debt sales to the non-bank private sector.

With both $BLPS$ and $DS, NBPS$ being functions of interest rates and a vector of other assets, so that $\Delta BLPS = F(i, X)$, then given X, a desire to achieve both the target for ΔD, and some preferred level of i, constrains the size of the PSBR. 'Too high a PSBR requires either that the Government borrow heavily from the Banks – which adds directly to the money supply; or, failing this, that it borrows from individuals and institutions, but at ever-increasing rates of interest, which places an unacceptable squeeze on the private sector. From these two facts comes one conclusion, and one conclusion only – that the PSBR is too large' (Lawson, 1980). Also see Treasury (FSBR Red Book) (1980–81, page 16, para. 4). For a more sceptical view of the strength of the *behavioural* relationships involved, see Treasury and Civil Service Committee (1981), and Dow and Saville (1988). Indeed despite these accounting identities, the strength of the relationship between public sector deficits and interest rates, and between public sector deficits and the growth of monetary aggregates, has usually been found to be weak when the data are tested, see Dwyer (1985). This finding caused this aspect of the MTFS to be criticised both by British Keynesians, e.g. Kaldor (1982), and by US monetarists, e.g. Friedman in his evidence to the above Committee.

associated unemployment. The *locus classicus* wherein the authorities' strategy was outlined was the speech given in Zurich on 14 January 1981 by Lawson, then the Financial Secretary (Lawson, 1981; also see Lawson, 1980, 1982, 1985), who is generally held to be the architect of the MTFS.

In that summer, June 1980, the 'Corset' control ended. An immediate upsurge in bank deposits, and in bank lending, had been forecast, as re-intermediation became possible. In the event the upsurge was over twice what had been expected, and the growth of £M3 shot through its upper limit, causing considerable embarrassment and annoyance (mostly aimed at the Bank) in the Government, especially coming so shortly after its prior public commitment. Interest rates were kept at the high level of 16%, and there was intensive consideration of the merits of moving to monetary base control (MBC).

At the same time (in 1980), however, the combination of the United Kingdom's new found role as a major oil producer, the high level of interest rates, and the credibility of Mrs Thatcher's anti-inflation commitment, led to a dramatic rise in the United Kingdom's nominal, and even more in its real, exchange rate,[5] see Buiter and Miller (1982, 1983).

Despite the embarrassment of accepting a large overshoot in the first year of the MTFS, a further tightening of monetary policy, in the form of higher interest rates, beyond 16%, at such a time was unacceptable, and, indeed, rates were reduced to 14% in November 1980.[6] Even so, the deflationary pressure from the increased real exchange rate was intense, with industrial production falling by 10% (1980 Q4 on 1979 Q4) and unemployment rising by over a half, from 1·3 to 2·2 million during 1980 (January/January).

Moreover, during the autumn of 1980 Alan Walters took up position as economic adviser to the P.M. He doubted, on analytical grounds, whether £M3 was the most appropriate monetary aggregate to target, and noted that the stance of monetary policy appeared much tighter if one looked at narrower aggregates, M1 or M0, instead (Walters, 1986). A colleague from Johns Hopkins, Prof. J. Niehans, was encouraged to do an academic study of this issue. His paper, widely circulated though not subsequently published in a journal (Niehans, 1981), was influential.

Nevertheless, if monetary and nominal income growth were to be reduced in line with the target, without any further upwards ratchet in interest and exchange rates, it was thought that the PSBR had to be kept tight. The continuing commitment of the Chancellor to the MTFS, and his refusal to allow even the automatic stabilisers to bring about an increase in the PSBR at a time of severe cyclical downturn, brought down upon his head the outrage of the (Keynesian) economic establishment in the United Kingdom, as the famous letter organised by Hahn and Nield from the 364 economists attests (*The Times*, March 31 1981; also see Healy, 1987). The publication date

[5] It proved remarkably difficult to sort out the proportional responsibility of these different factors, and none of the attempts appears really convincing, see Bean (1987) and Niehans (1981) among others.

[6] The Bank of England's Minimum Lending Rate, MLR, was suspended in August 1981: thereafter interest rates in the United Kingdom refer to the London Clearing Bank base rates, unless otherwise specified.

of the letter coincided fairly closely with the low point in the cycle. A combination of world-wide deflation and, beyond that, the rise in the UK exchange rate was helping to bring about a sharp decline in import prices,[7] which began to feed through into declining levels for the RPI and for nominal wage increases. Moreover the latter did appear sensitive to movements in (short-term) unemployment (Hall and Henry, 1987; Layard and Nickell, 1986). It is also arguable that the 1981 Budget decision, whether or not strictly necessary within the MTFS framework, provided a dramatic manifestation of the government's shift to counter-inflationary commitment away from Keynesian demand management, and hence helped to break the inflationary psychology of the time.

During the first half of fiscal 1981, a Civil Service strike led to delays in the receipt of certain taxes, so the course of monetary growth was distorted. With the rate of growth of nominal incomes declining quite sharply, while monetary growth remained quite strong, with £M3 growing by about 14·5% in 1981/2, the pressures imposed on the system by the MTFS were somewhat relieved, and interest rates, having been raised sharply in the autumn of 1981 to counteract downward pressure on the pound, were steadily reduced in 1982 to a trough of 9% in November.

Meanwhile, in the United States the authorities did not flinch from allowing interest rates to adjust flexibly in response to market pressures emanating from the revised operating procedures, whereby they sought to achieve a chosen level for the non-borrowed reserve base (see further below in Section III). It was, however, a bumpy ride. The volatility of interest rates (both short and long term) increased by a factor of about five to eight times as compared with the pre-October 1979 period (Dickens, 1987; Walsh, 1982; Evans, 1984: though for qualifications see Rosenblum and Storin, 1983). This was not entirely the result of the change in operating procedures, since the (ill-considered) imposition and subsequent withdrawal of direct controls on personal credit in spring 1980 led to sharp fluctuations in monetary growth and in interest rates.

Some considerable increase in the volatility of short-term interest rates had always been viewed as a likely concomitant of a move towards MBC. Simulations of constant monetary growth rules have tended to indicate extreme interest rates volatility, e.g. Anderson and Enzler (1987). What was more surprising was that this was accompanied by an increase in the volatility of monthly and quarterly (i.e. short term) rates of monetary growth and in long term interest rates, (see further Section III). Despite these greater short-term fluctuations, the Fed did get close to the *annual* targets for monetary growth (M1) that it had set.

Certainly the Fed in general, and its Chairman Paul Volcker in particular, established credibility for their anti-inflation commitment. Such credibility was probably based more on their demonstrated willingness to accept a painfully

---

[7] Papers arguing that the reduction in inflation in the 1980s has been largely due to a fall in commodity prices, not to the (direct) effect of monetary restriction, (Beckerman 1985), can be misleading in so far as such declines are themselves the indirect consequence of monetary tightness, (see Lawson, 1986).

high level of (real) interest rates and a sharp downturn in output, rather than on the achievement of a particular monetary target (Solomon, 1984), as may also have been true in Switzerland (Bomhoff, 1983, 1985) and in the United Kingdom. Even so Central Bankers appreciated the function of a monetary target in providing them with 'a place to stand' in warding off calls for a premature easing of policy, (Bouey, 1982a). Also Fforde (1983) commented that, 'it would scarcely have been possible to mount and carry through, over several years and without resort to direct controls of all kinds, so determined a counter-inflationary policy if it had not been for the initial "political economy" of the firm monetary target'.

Much of the pain of the monetary deflation fell, however, on producers of raw materials – except where protected, e.g. European agriculture – for whom the combination of falling output prices and sharply rising interest rates proved devastating. The summer of 1982 saw the conflation of the onset of the LDC debt crisis, growing success and credibility in the domestic (United States) struggle against inflation, and a growing difficulty in interpreting (or controlling) the increasingly wayward path of M1. The consequence was that the operating procedure, of targeting *non-borrowed* reserves, was (quietly) shelved, and replaced by one of targeting *borrowed* reserves (see Section III), which had the effect of accommodating unforeseen shifts in the demand for money, and allowed the authorities to reintroduce more stability into interest rate movements (see Axilrod 1985).

For an account of how Central Bankers, not only in the United States and United Kingdom but also in a selection of other major countries, viewed the conduct of monetary targets at about this time (1982) see Meek (1983). For further details on the policy and experience of the Bank of Japan, see Suzuki (1986), and Hamada and Hayashi (1985); a discussion of the Bundesbank's practices and experience is provided by Dudler (1984); a useful chronology and account of monetary policy in Italy is provided by Barbato (1987); for France refer to the annual reports of the Conseil National du Crédit. For a more general survey of several countries' experience, see Argy (1988), Hoskins (1985) and Johnson (1983).

(iii) 1982–5: The Return to Pragmatism

Apart from 1972/3, the years of the Barber 'boom' and monetary surge, the path of velocity of £M3 in the United Kingdom remained steadily upwards, i.e. nominal incomes growing faster than £M3, from the 1960s through till 1979. This historical trend, quite naturally, provided the main basis for choosing the target rates of growth of £M3 in June 1979 and March 1980. Initially the overshoots in 1980/1 and 1981/2 led to fears that there was a resulting excess 'overhang' of money which would lead to a subsequent re-emergence of inflation.

On the other hand more immediate measures of inflationary pressure, e.g. the exchange rate, asset prices, wage increases, various measures of inflation itself, e.g. RPI or GDP deflator – let alone real variables such as output and unemployment – were indicating the continuing presence of deflation. Initially, up till March 1982, an uneasy compromise resulted. The target for £M3 was extended on the assumption that the historic trend in velocity would be re-established, but no attempt was made to claw back prior overshoots, despite initial hopes/intentions to do so (Lawson, 1982; Treasury, 1981–2, page 16, para. 11). Meanwhile, pressure was maintained on the Bank of England to achieve the target growth rate, but interest rates were not allowed to vary without limit in pursuit of that target.

But as time went by, it became increasingly difficult for the authorities to believe that they fully understood, or could predict, the path of velocity, and/or the demand for money (see Section II). This erosion of confidence in their ability to interpret the signals given by their prior chosen main target and indicator, £M3, led the authorities to extend the range of monetary and other variables, including notably the exchange rate, that they would consult in assessing the stance of policy,[8] and hence in deciding on how to vary interest rates. Thus, in the March 1982 Budget, (see Treasury, 1982–83), targets were set for two additional monetary aggregates, M1, a narrow definition, and PSL2, (Private Sector Liquidity, Second Definition) an even broader aggregate than £M3 (for an account of UK monetary statistics, see Bank of England, 1982 b, 1987). Outside commentators complained that this would give the authorities a greater chance to hit at least one target; insiders worried that the markets would concentrate on whichever indicator/target was currently doing worst.

Meanwhile, the demand by the private sector for bank loans continued to grow at persistently high levels, due initially to the needs of industry to overcome the financial squeeze in 1980/1, and then increasingly to the (apparently almost insatiable) demand for mortgage finance from the personal sector. Such demand for bank loans appeared to be, both from casual and econometric evidence (Goodhart, 1984; Moore and Threadgold, 1985), highly interest *inelastic*. Even as early as the autumn of 1980, the government shrunk from the option of pushing up interest rates high enough, (and what level would that be?) to close off such lending directly. In order then to prevent such rapid increases in bank lending coming through in a commensurate increase in bank deposits, the authorities had to reduce bank lending to the public sector, (see footnote 4); they did so by selling more public sector debt to the non-bank private sector than necessary to finance the PSBR, i.e. 'over-funding'. They achieved this in part by a number of innovations which made public sector debt more attractive to the private sector, e.g. part-paid issues, convertibles, index-linked issues, in part by an assiduous concern with maximising sales in the light of existing market conditions. At no time did the authorities seek to force some prearranged quantum of gilts upon an unwilling market. Moreover, while

[8] There was some subsequent reinterpretation of the degree to which the government had tied itself to the single target, £M3, (Lawson, 1982), together with the beguiling concept, (later formalised in some of the academic literature on policy games, see for example Persson (1988) and Driffill (1988)), that the more committed the authorities appeared to be to monetarism in theory, the more discretionary they could be in practice. Thus, 'If, on the other hand, the discretion is being exercised by those whose commitment to the policy, and to the overriding need to maintain financial discipline is beyond doubt, then there is no cause for such misgivings' (Lawson, 1982, page 5).

overfunding may have *resulted* in some twist to the yield curve, (though no rigorous evidence to that effect is available), it was not brought about by the authorities acting directly on the yield curve for that purpose.

In practice, the Bank of England was remarkably successful in this exercise. But with bank *credit* continuing to grow at a very rapid pace, some commentators wondered whether mopping up bank deposits by selling a larger volume of gilts, public sector bonds, was a somewhat contrived, even artificial, way of holding monetary growth nearer to its target level. With growing uncertainty about the central relevance of £M3, and with its control in the years 1982–5 more subject to the influence of 'over-funding' than of interest rate changes, this then left the question of what factors determined the choice of short-term interest rates during this period. This latter became increasingly pragmatic, involving a combined assessment of a range of monetary indicators, of direct measures of domestic inflation, even on occasions with a glance at real variables, but increasingly attention became drawn in practice to exchange rate fluctuations. It was no accident that the main occasions from 1981 through to 1986 on which interest rates were jerked upwards, (in October 1981, January 1983, July 1984, January 1985 and January 1986), all coincided with periods of pound weakness on the forex market.

Whereas some aspects of this story are peculiar, even unique, to the United Kingdom, e.g. the use of 'over-funding' to seek to attain a broad monetary target, other aspects were also reflected abroad. In particular the timing, and scale, of the bend in the trend in the growth of the key monetary aggregate (M1) in the United States and in Canada coincides very closely with United Kingdom experience, even though the coverage of the monetary aggregate concerned differed. Possible causes for this are discussed further in Section II.

The consequences, and reactions, were – not surprisingly – much the same in the United States and Canada, as in the United Kingdom. Until 1982, (see Lindsey, 1986), the United States authorities kept M1 as the main target, viewing disturbances to the demand for money function as possibly temporary, or owing to transitory shocks such as the introduction of NOW accounts nation-wide in 1981, (see the series of papers by Wenninger and associates in the 1980s, e.g. Radecki and Wenninger, 1985). Then, in the face of the continuing unpredictability of velocity, (while some considerable success and credibility had been achieved in the containment of inflation), the Fed moved, at broadly the same speed as in the United Kingdom, down the road of widening the range of monetary targets/indicators, and returning to a more discretionary and pragmatic mode of determining money market rates. In Canada the switch from the regime of monetary targeting to discretionary interest rate adjustment appeared rather more abrupt (see Bouey, 1982*b*; Freedman, 1983); as also in Australia, (Keating, 1985; Johnston, 1985).

Moreover, velocity tended to fall, although not perhaps as dramatically, and there were (unpredicted) increases in the demand for money, in certain other countries around the same time, for example Japan (see Bank of Japan, 1988*a*, Chart 15) and Australia (Stevens *et al.*, 1987).

This experience, of unstable velocities, was not, however, universal: in particular in West Germany, and in France, there were no clear signs of any break in the trend of velocity at this juncture. Consequently the Bundesbank exhibited greater persistence with targetry than other Central Banks, though, even so with some greater flexibility in operating methods, (see Schlesinger, 1984, 1988; and Deutsche Bundesbank, 1985).

Elsewhere, apart from West Germany, e.g. in Japan, Australia, the achievement of an intermediate monetary target had not been elevated to be the centre-piece of monetary policy in quite such a committed manner. Consequently the subsequent withdrawal towards a more discretionary policy mode was also achieved with less public drama.

(iv) 1985 Onwards: Increasing Concern with Exchange Rate Regimes

The misalignment of the pound during the years 1980–2 had had a devastating impact on the UK manufacturing sector, but had not impinged seriously on the Western world more widely. The subsequent misalignment of the United States dollar, however, reaching its apogee in early 1985, greatly affected all the major countries. This latter experience led to growing doubts among policy-makers whether it really was the case that the forex market did adjust prices efficiently, (or at least more efficiently than policy makers could) and rapidly into line with some 'fundamental equilibrium'. 'Governments have to come to terms with the behaviour of the foreign exchange market. Left entirely to its own devices, we have seen in recent years how destabilising and destructive that behaviour can at times be', (Lawson, 1988).

The combination of growing doubts about the predictability of domestic velocity, and increasing concern about medium-term forex misalignments, led to a tendency for medium-sized countries, e.g. Sweden, Canada, the United Kingdom and Australia, to conduct their own monetary policy in practice[9] largely with a view to stabilising their exchange rate, in some cases bilaterally with a larger neighbour, the United States or West Germany, (see Crow, 1988) but on occasions against a basket of currencies (for Australia, see Hogan, 1986): for a more general assessment, see Atkinson and Chouraqui (1987).

This option was not really open to the three main economies, the United States, Japan and West Germany. In this latter case academic interest turned to the possibility of applying co-operative monetary policies (among the three majors) for the joint purpose of stabilising both international exchange rates and world inflation. Suggestions to this end were put forward by Williamson (1983); Edison et al. (1987); McKinnon (1984) and McKinnon and Ohno (1988), among others. For a commentary and a critique, see Frenkel and Goldstein (1988). Although a series of meetings of Finance Ministers, starting with that at the Plaza in New York in September 1985, was held with the aim of establishing whether there was scope for enhanced international co-ordination, it is debatable how much actual difference such meetings have made to the policy steps the protagonists would have adopted independently anyhow, (see Feldstein, 1988). This should not be read as implying that exchange rate

[9] In principle, however, some of these countries e.g. United Kingdom, France retained domestic monetary targets as their formally declared intermediate objective.

movements had no influence on the domestic monetary policy decisions in Germany and Japan – clearly the German and Japanese authorities adjusted the fervour with which they pursued their domestic monetary targets in the light of external developments – but rather that such adjustments were autonomously decided, and not undertaken in order to preserve international co-operation and amity.

Be that as it may, doubts about the central significance of £M3, and concern whether 'over-funding' was leading to some artificial distortions in both relative interest rates and in the growth of the aggregates, led the Chancellor to aim at 'full-funding' – but not over-funding of the PSBR – and to down-grade £M3 as a target variable during the course of 1985 (Lawson, 1985). The virtual abandonment, by 1985, of the monetary variable chosen to be the centre-piece of policy in 1979/80 represented a considerable volte-face. It was, however, too much for the Chancellor, who in 1980/1 had opposed virtually any intervention to check the giddy rise of pound, to take the further step of linking monetary policy formally to exchange rate developments (see Lawson, 1986, 1988), and also politically difficult for him to do so in the context of the Prime Minister's opposition to the United Kingdom's joining the Exchange Rate Mechanism (ERM) of the European Monetary System (EMS).

In any case financial innovations, that were held to be largely responsible for the breakdown in the statistical relationships between the various monetary aggregates on the one hand and nominal incomes and interest rates on the other, (see Section II and Leigh-Pemberton, 1986), appeared to be causing relatively *less* disturbance to the relationship between the monetary base (Mo) and nominal incomes in the United Kingdom (Johnston, 1984): nevertheless, technological and social changes, e.g. the spread of automated teller machines (ATMs), electronic funds transfers, EFT-POS (point of sale, or place of work, etc.), home banking, etc. threatened potential instability here too (Hall *et al.*, 1988). Such instability has, moreover, occurred recently in West Germany, leading the Bundesbank to shift from their prior Central Bank Money to an M3 target, (Deutsche Bundesbank, 1988; Holtham *et al.*, 1988).

Moreover, Mo is overwhelmingly (99%) represented by currency outstanding, in the hands of the public (84%) or in banks' vaults/tills (15%). Such currency is provided automatically on demand by the Bank of England. While there *are* reasons why one might believe, (see Section IV (*ii*)), that monetary/credit shocks would have subsequent effects on the economy, most outside commentators in the United Kingdom reckoned that movements in Mo were no more than a concurrent measure, with additional noise, of consumer expenditures. The Chancellor disagreed, and he emphasised that he regarded Mo as an '*advance* indicator' of money GDP, (Lawson, 1986, p. 12); the econometric basis for this claim is uncertain, (and is not to be found in Johnston, 1984).

Nonetheless, perhaps out of a belief in its economic significance, perhaps out of a presentational desire to stick with *some* monetary target aggregate, (and one for which technological/social changes were still leading to comparatively low growth figures), the Chancellor and Treasury have since maintained an annual target for Mo as *the* monetary target[10] for the conduct of monetary policy. In practice, however, interest rate adjustments during the course of 1986 appeared to depend on the same pragmatic blend of discretionary response to monetary developments, (more generally than just Mo), on current domestic inflationary indicators, and on exchange rate developments, as already described.

Then, sometime in the early spring (March?) in 1987, policy appeared to shift, in part perhaps influenced by the understandings in February reached between Finance Ministers at the Louvre meeting, though without any formal, public announcement – indeed the monetary target set out in the Budget Red Book (Treasury, 1987) continued to be expressed in terms of a growth rate for Mo. However, from March 1987 to March 1988 the value of the pound remained held in a narrow trading range against the Dm, and whenever the pound tended to rise above 3·00 Dm[11] overt policy action, either in the form of intervention or reductions in interest rates, was taken to prevent it breaking that limit. There was still room for intra-marginal interest rate adjustments, e.g. the upwards hike in August 1987 owing to general concern with inflation, and the post-October-crash (internationally concerted) reductions. Even so, the parameters within which such discretion could operate appeared to have become more closely restricted by this new policy of 'shadowing' the Dm in the forex market.

Early in 1988 this caused a problem. Boom conditions in the United Kingdom gave rise to fears about incipient worsening inflation, such that higher interest rates appeared domestically prudent. But there was already a yield differential *vis-à-vis* German interest rates that made capital inflows profitable, so long as the expectation remained that the peg to the Dm would remain in place. The scale of capital inflows put upwards pressure on the sterling sufficient to force large intervention by the Bank of England to maintain the peg, and this in turn tended to expand the money stock even faster.

This gave rise to a policy dilemma, (a dilemma condition that Walters (1986) had warned would be endemic in such instances), to hold the external peg and suffer worse short-term inflationary pressures, or to abandon the peg and lose the medium-term (counter-inflationary) support of maintaining a Dm peg. There were reports in the newspapers of high-level ministerial conflict over which choice to make; in the event the second was adopted. Thereafter, for some three and a half months, policy seemed to move on to a new tack, of varying the balance between the exchange rate and interest rates so as to maintain a constant pressure upon nominal incomes. The (econometric) finding of HMT's forecasting model, whereby a 4% appreciation of the sterling, e.g. from 3·00 Dm to 3·12 Dm, would have its deflationary effect on nominal incomes offset by a 1% reduction, e.g. from 9·5% to 8·5%, decline in short-term interest rates, found its way into the Press. Whether or not this was

---

[10] N.B. There was no suggestion, however, in this latter period that the authorities should also shift their control mechanism, and adopt MBC. Indeed this latter option was publicly dismissed, (Lawson, 1983).

[11] Because £ remained generally strong during this period, the associated (unpublished) lower limit could not be so easily ascertained.

an accurate report, from March until July 1988, it was noted that every five/seven pfennig appreciation (depreciation) in the £/Dm Spot exchange rate was counterbalanced by a 1/2% cut (hike) in interest rates.

In turn this period, of appearing to balance interest rate adjustments against exchange rate adjustments, so as to achieve a constant pressure (of demand) on nominal incomes, seemed to conclude in early July. A series of indicators revealed continuing strong output, worsening inflationary pressure and a weakening balance of payments. The authorities then raised interest rates, (though initially in steps of only 1/2% at a time), quite sharply through the course of the summer: the strength of the United States dollar and some appalling United Kingdom trade figures enabled the authorities to do so without incurring any further appreciation of pound, which became increasingly subject to weakness.

With national monetarism, plus flexible exchange rates, having effectively broken down in the first half of the 1980s, the Chancellor appeared to be looking for an alternative (coherent) strategy of international monetary co-operation and co-ordination, involving more or less formal linkages within regions, e.g. the ERM in Europe, and closer co-operation between the G3 (the Group of Three, United States, Germany and Japan). In the event in early 1988 this objective conflicted with the government's overriding commitment to contain domestic inflation causing a policy dilemma. The latter objective took priority, (as it also has in similar dilemmas in West Germany), but exactly how the conduct of monetary policy can best be calibrated under present conditions to achieve this objective remains a subject for debate.

II. THE UNSTEADY RELATIONSHIP BETWEEN MONEY AND NOMINAL INCOMES

(i) *The Demand for Money*

Studies of the demand for money usually start from a presumption that there exists a long-term equilibrium relationship between private sector money holdings and certain other aggregate macro-economic variables, such as the price level, real incomes (or expenditures), (some set of) interest rates and, perhaps, wealth and the rate of inflation. The relevant variables, to appear as arguments in this long-run (equilibrium) relationship, are normally initially chosen on the basis of a priori theory, whether deriving from Keynes' suggested motives for holding money (i.e. transactions, precautionary, speculative), from a Tobin-Baumol inventory theoretic analysis, or from Friedman's more general portfolio choice approach, (Friedman, 1956). In most earlier studies the variables, considered to be relevant in the long-term equilibrium relationship, were then embedded in a short-run demand-for-money function, via some, often *ad hoc*, partial adjustment mechanism; and then tested directly against the data. Indeed this is still the most usual approach in the United States; for recent surveys see Roley (1985) and Judd and Scadding (1982).

More recently econometricians have sought to examine and test for the presence of such a long-run equilibrium relationship between variables directly, (*before* embedding them in equations which also explore short-run dynamic adjustments), by testing whether such variables are co-integrated. If such a long-run relationship does exist between variables X and Y, which may well both be non-stationary and trended in levels, but stationary in differenced form, i.e. they are both $I(1)$ series, then in the simple linear relationship between the series in levels,

$$Z_t = X_t - aY_t,$$

Z_t (the residual from an OLS regression of X on Y) will be stationary, (i.e. an $I(0)$ series), and this can be easily tested (see Engle and Granger, 1987), though problems may still arise since the co-integrating vector need not be unique. It is, however, minimal information to know that X and Y are co-integrated. One does not know why and in what relationship that appears; in a multi-equation context it would not even tell one which linear combinations of which co-integrated variables constituted the long-run relationship of interest. So it is necessary to proceed, as Hendry argues, (e.g. 1985, 1988), to model jointly the long-run and the short-run to establish in which equations the error corrections appear and hence to identify them.

In more behavioural terms, if an equilibrium long-run relationship exists between variables X and Y, say of the linear form $X = aY$, then any deviation from this relationship will induce pressures to drive either X, or Y, or both, back towards the equilibrium. The implication of this is that equations to examine short-run adjustment should include an error-correction mechanism, along the lines proposed by Granger in more theoretical work, (e.g. 1981), and by Hendry in a series of more applied studies, (e.g. 1979, 1985, 1988).

This approach involves no pre-conditions, either about the nature of the shocks that may disturb the long-run equilibrium relationship, or about whether the resumption of the equilibrium involves a readjustment primarily in X or Y, or whether they both adjust. Thus, in the context of the relationship between money holdings and nominal incomes, the existence, if indeed it does still exist, (see further below) of a long-run relationship between them (i.e. a predictable and stable velocity) implies no prior conditions on whether the shocks that disturb the relationship occur primarily to money holdings or to nominal incomes, or whether the subsequent return to equilibrium occurs via an adjustment in money holdings or in nominal incomes. In particular, the money stock may well be largely endogenously determined, as economists such as Moore (1988*a,b*) and Kaldor (1982) have argued, and it can still be the case that shocks to the money stock, which disturb the long-term equilibrium, may lead to subsequent adjustments in nominal incomes. The latter is an empirical question, which does *not* depend on the money stock being exogenous with respect to nominal incomes.

There is quite a close connection, though it has not been widely recognised, between the co-integration error correction mechanism and the buffer stock approach to monetary analysis (see Laidler, 1983*b*, 1986). Like the former, the latter depends on the existence of a stable long-term relationship between money holdings and nominal incomes. Various shocks, especially those affecting bank credit expansion, e.g. on the occasion of deregulation, then drive actual money balances away from their long-term equilibrium level, a divergence that people are willing to tolerate temporarily because money balances are particularly well suited to act as a buffer to such shocks. But this divergence (from long-term equilibrium) then sets up forces that will affect both monetary variables, (i.e. the demand both for loans and deposits), *and* nominal expenditures. Models along this line began with 1976 Reserve Bank of Australia model, (Jonson *et al.*, 1977), and (generally small) models have since been constructed for several countries, including the United States (Laidler and Bentley, 1983), the Netherlands (Knoester and Van Sinderen, 1982) and the United Kingdom (Davidson, 1987; Davidson and Ireland, 1987). The literature on buffer stock money is now becoming large: for recent contributions see Cuthbertson and Taylor (1987) and Muscatelli (1988). Again this approach has not been widely adopted in the United States, with certain exceptions, e.g. Carr and Darby (1981) and Judd and Scadding (1981), in part because critics such as Milbourne (1987) have queried the microfoundations of the approach, and in part because the concept that agents may allow themselves to be driven temporarily off their demand function is alien to the dominant United States model of (relatively) perfect clearing markets.

Be that as it may, early empirical work, (see Goldfeld, 1973, for the United States; Laidler and Parkin, 1970, and Goodhart and Crockett, 1970, for the United Kingdom) soon established that money holdings appeared to adjust to the arguments in the long run relationship rather slowly, i.e. with long lags. In most United States literature such lags were modelled by the adoption of a partial adjustment mechanism applied either to real or to nominal money balances, (see Roley, 1985 and the Comment thereon by Hafer, 1985). In the United Kingdom, again under the influence of David Hendry, the recent tendency in such econometric work has been to put as few prior restrictions on the form of the dynamic adjustment model as possible, but to test down from very general models to more 'parsimonious' equations, using restrictions, e.g. excluding variables, that are data consistent. So there is quite a marked disparity between the Granger–Engle–Hendry approach (i.e. start by examining the stationarity characteristics of the time series; next test for co-integration; then embed the resulting error correction variable(s) into a general short-term adjustment model, which is tested down to a more parsimonious version), and the more common single equation, partial adjustment, standard demand for money function.

Either approach, however, is liable to leave one with a 'preferred' equation including lags of the monetary aggregate serving as dependent variable and, possibly, lagged values of the other arguments, which generally imply a lengthy adjustment period. This has been criticised on several scores. First, it would seem to suggest that, should there be 'exogenous' shocks to the money stock, certain other variables, e.g. interest rates, would have to overshoot. Second, the length of adjustment seems to be too long to be readily accounted for by costs of adjustment, see Laidler (1985) and Goodfriend (1985). Third, it is not generally clear whether these lags, and the error correction feedback mechanism, are consistent with rational expectations. Cuthbertson (1988*a*),

Cuthbertson and Taylor (1987), Lane (1984) and Dutkowsky and Foote (1988), among others, have explored a two stage approach, whereby a 'model consistent' estimate of expectations is constructed in stage one, and these forward-looking variables are then entered into a demand-for-money function, in conjunction with backwards-looking variables including error-correction mechanisms.

Hendry (1988) has argued that, should the expectations generating process shift during the data period, it should be possible to discriminate between feedback and 'feedforward' mechanisms (also see Hendry and Neale, 1988). While he clearly demonstrates that interest rates and real output movements are so hard to predict, being close to random walks, that there can be little power to feed-forward mechanisms, even he expresses surprise that apparently the data suggest that agents 'ignore the predictability of inflation in adjusting their M1 balances' (p. 146). Cuthbertson (1988 b) has responded by arguing that Hendry's assessment, and claimed refutation, of the Lucas critique is weakened by the fact that, in a finite sample, the marginal model for the forward looking variables is likely to be highly inefficient, but if such marginal models, including in this case Cuthbertson's own equations, are so inefficient how can any *confident* forward-looking expectation be established?

But this is not a survey of demand-for-money studies, even less of their econometric technicalities. Policy makers were, in the main, less concerned with the academic details of the studies than with the question of whether the relationships uncovered were sufficiently robust to serve as a basis for conducting monetary policy. As already noted, the early work on such relationships, undertaken in the years until 1973, did in the main appear to demonstrate, *circa* the end of the 1960s, that the demand for money was a predictable function of a few variables. That predictability then suffered some knocks, however, during the disturbed years in the early mid-1970s, notably with 'the case of the missing money' (Goldfeld, 1976) in the United States.

Nowhere else, however, did the prior stability of the (short-run) demand for money function exhibit such a comprehensive collapse as in the case of £M3 in the United Kingdom in 1972/3. A surge in bank lending to the private sector (and a large public sector borrowing requirement) was funded by a massive increase in wholesale bank deposits, as the banks bid aggressively for funds. This drove £M3 far beyond the level that would have been predicted on the basis of previously calculated equations: even when attempts (Hacche, 1974; Smith, 1978, 1980) were made to account for the banks' new liability management practices, the refitted equations could not account satisfactorily for the monetary surge in 1972/3 (for an exception, see Taylor, 1987). The consensus remains that the demand-for-money function for £M3 broke down in 1972/3, and has remained unstable ever since; (this breakdown is most evident in the case of company sector holdings of £M3; indeed Lubrano *et al.* (1986) report that the *long-term* relationship for the *personal* sector remained fairly stable, at least until 1981). At one time a study by Grice *et al.* (1981) (also Grice and Bennett, 1984), did suggest that a stable function for £M3 could be obtained by relating £M3 to a measure of gross financial wealth and an estimate of expected returns on gilts (i.e. government bonds), but not only did this formulation entail some inherent problems (e.g. in taking bank lending as exogenously determined), but its out-of-sample forecasting properties soon disappointed. For a recent survey, see Holtham *et al.* (1988).

This might provoke the question why this breakdown did *not* discourage United Kingdom policy makers from placing so much reliance on £M3. The crucial reason is that the subsequent upsurge in prices and nominal incomes in 1974/5 appeared to confirm the monetarists' historical/policy claim that major monetary shocks caused *subsequent* nominal income changes. Thus the breakdown of the (*short-run*) demand for money function in the United Kingdom signalled to many monetarist economists (and policy makers) here that we had been running these regressions the wrong way around, rather than that the *long-run* money/nominal income nexus was fragile and unreliable.

First steps at transforming the equation to make £M3 into an independent, right-hand-side variable were taken Artis and Lewis (1976), but initially they took the level of interest rates, rather than nominal incomes as their dependent variable, (also see Andersen, 1985). Subsequently Mills (1983 *b*) examined the extent to which various measures of the United Kingdom money stock appeared to be able to predict movements in nominal incomes, once the pattern of auto-regression in nominal incomes had been taken into consideration, and concluded that £M3 represented the best guide; for a broadly similar study on West Germany, see Geisler (1986).

The United Kingdom experience in the mid 1970s was, however, unusual. In several other countries the earlier fitted equations had had some predictive problems in the mid 1970s, but these had been quite minor, relative to the shock in the United Kingdom, and normal econometric running repairs had encouraged Central Banks in most major countries to base the technical choice of their chosen money stock target numbers on their preferred demand-for-money function.

As recorded earlier in Section I, policy shifted in late 1979 onto a much more deflationary tack, initiated by the major change in the monetary control regime in the United States. From that point onwards, velocity trends shifted, and the monetary aggregates grew more rapidly relative to nominal incomes than in the past. This experience occurred at roughly the same time, though to different degrees, in most Western countries, and in Japan (Ueda, 1988).

Lucas (1976) had earlier demonstrated why a regime change might well lead to instability and parameter shifts in previously estimated 'structural' equations. The adoption of new operating procedures in the United States on 6 October 1979 represented a major policy regime change. American economists soon noted that the prediction errors in the demand for money functions could have resulted from such regime changes (Judd and Scadding 1982). Indeed, Gordon (1984) called for the abandonment of efforts to estimate *short-term* demand-for-money functions, since the appropriate form of short-run relationships that may be estimated between the monetary base, the money stock, interest rates and nominal incomes may depend more on the (changing) form of the policy regime than on the (changing) nature of behavioural responses of the private sector.

Even though a number of economists, especially in the United States, have continued to argue that (at least some definitions, especially the monetary base, of) the money stock still exhibits a well-behaved demand-for-money function,[12] the extent of predictive failure subsequently went beyond the ability of most (US) economists to explain in terms of regime change, or of (UK) economists to explain in terms of a buffer-stock (disequilibrium) response to monetary shocks. The inherent problem with these approaches has been that they seek to, and can only, explain *short-term* deviations of velocity. Thus a monetary surge, caused, say, by the abolition of the 'Corset' control in the United Kingdom in 1980, will lead to a temporary fall in velocity; or alternatively the changed monetary regime, as in the United States in 1979, could lead people to expect an initial monetary overshoot, relative to the target, to provoke a future rise in interest rates, as the authorities react, and hence cause the private sector to wish to hold more, not less, monetary balances on speculative grounds (see Vaciago, 1985).

So, there are quite a number of (partly related) grounds for explaining short-term fluctuations in velocity, and short-term instability in the demand-for-money function. But such approaches, (notably including the buffer stock/disequilibrium models), generally incorporate an assumption of a stable *long-run* equilibrium relationship between money holdings and nominal incomes. Indeed it is the divergence of the short-run, (credit-counterpart determined), money stock from the stable long-run desired level that drives expenditures in these models. In more policy-oriented terms, economic advisers in the United Kingdom were waiting with trepidation for the built-up 'overhang', or excess money balances, to spill over into higher expenditures in 1981, 1982, 1983, 1984. Eventually they tired of waiting, and accepted that there must have been some change to the underlying *long-term* demand for money (though see Artis and Lewis, 1984, and Budd and Holly, 1986, for a graphical illustration of its prior stability). Similarly in the United States and Canada, the change in the trend since 1979 has gone on too long to explain as a purely short-run phenomenon. For an illustration of the long run changes in velocity in the various countries discussed in this paper, see the charts below.

Put in more formal terms, both Engle and Granger (1987) and Miller (1988) have demonstrated that, over the last couple of decades in the United States, the various monetary aggregates have *not* been co-integrated with nominal incomes, with the possible exception of M2, i.e. velocity has been generally non-stationary. The latest empirical studies undertaken within the Federal Reserve Board now also lead to a preference for M2, over M1, as a monetary target, (Moore *et al.*, 1988); the same preference also currently holds in

---

[12] For a recent example see Rasche (1988) who states that 'The research cited here suggests strongly that a very simple demand function specification can account for a large portion of the observed variation in all of these [monetary] aggregates, and that with only two exceptions this function appears very robust over the entire post accord period. The two exceptions are the monetary base and M1 for which there is a significant change in the constant term of the first difference specification around the beginning of 1981' (p. 58). Also see Hamburger (1983) and Baba *et al.* (1987).

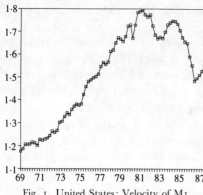

Fig. 1. United States: Velocity of M1.

Fig. 2. United Kingdom: Velocity of M3.

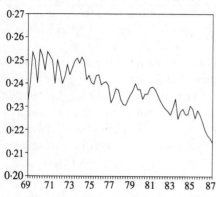

Fig. 3. West Germany: Velocity of CBM.

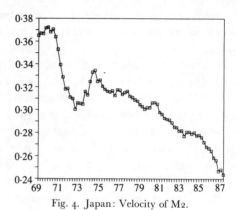

Fig. 4. Japan: Velocity of M2.

Fig. 5. France: Velocity of M2. □, 1969 unadjusted; ◇, 1977 Q4–1987M2;
+ 1970–1977 Q3 M2 R.

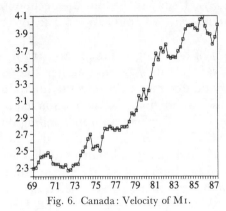

Fig. 6. Canada: Velocity of M1.

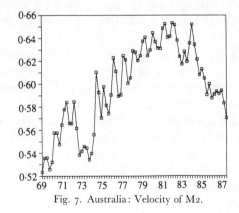

Fig. 7. Australia: Velocity of M2.

Canada, (Crow, 1988). This longer term departure of velocity for US M1 from prior trends has been nicely illustrated by B. Friedman (1988a); also see Wenninger (1988).

In such circumstances a number of United States economists have advocated running demand-for-money equations in first difference form (without error-correction-mechanism), see Cover and Keeler (1987), but, while this may allow accurate short-term forecasting, it enables velocity to wander without limit over time. See Roley (1985, pp. 620–1) for a review of economists who have proposed that the equation be specified in such a first differenced format.

Replications for the United Kingdom of the Engle–Granger tests of co-integration between monetary aggregates and nominal incomes during recent decades are currently being undertaken (Ireland and Wren-Lewis, 1988, and Hall *et al.*, 1988) – for an earlier exercise covering a longer data period see Hendry and Ericsson (1983). Although these results are still provisional, the general finding in the United Kingdom is that the monetary aggregates are *not* currently simply co-integrated with nominal incomes: however, the addition of certain other variables, e.g. wealth, can allow co-integration to be restored. Be that as it may, bends in the trend of velocity of monetary aggregates have appeared in several countries during the 1980s, often in that aggregate chosen to be *the* national intermediate target, and have often proved difficult to explain, (though Mayer (1988) has argued that the extent of such 'breaks' has often been exaggerated).

(ii) Some Explanations of the Shifting Path of Velocity

So, why did the trend bend? There are a variety of suggested answers, none of them fully satisfactory, though all of them may possess some validity. First, it may be that econometricians had previously failed to estimate the effect of certain interest rate relativities correctly. As already noted, the period 1979–82 was marked by extreme interest rate volatility in the United States. One would expect an increase in the variance of key asset prices, around a given mean level, to raise the (speculative and precautionary) demand for money (Tobin, 1958; Buiter and Armstrong, 1978; Walsh, 1984). There is some econometric evidence to this effect, e.g. Baba *et al.* (1987), Ueda (1988), but the decline in velocity continued after 1982 whereas interest rate volatility reverted to lower levels.

Second, the 1980s represented a period of declining inflation, and (rather more slowly) declining nominal interest rates. It may be that earlier studies underestimated the elasticity of response of desired money balances to inflation and/or nominal interest rates. In those cases where financial innovation led to the payment of interest rates that were either *fixed* or had an upper ceiling on certain monetary aggregates – as with NOW accounts in the United States until January 1986 – it is possible that the elasticity of such balances to changes in market interest rates increased (Heller, 1988; Simpson, 1984). The question of whether financial innovations led to an increase in interest elasticity, or not, has provoked a sizeable literature in the United States, see Hafer and Hein (1984), Brayton *et al.* (1983), Akhtar (1983), Wenninger (1986), Darby *et al.* (1987) etc. Greenspan (1988) appears confident that 'the aggregates have become more responsive to interest rate changes in the 1980s'. The same is apparently also the case in Japan, (Bank of Japan 1988 *b,c*).

If such elasticities should be higher than previously thought, this would then intensify certain consequential problems for monetary targetry, commonly described as 'the re-entry problem' (see Simpson, 1984; Blundell-Wignall and Thorp, 1987; and Budd and Holly, 1986). The difficulty is that a successful counter-inflationary policy would entail lower inflation and nominal interest rates; this would so raise the demand for money that either the resulting target values would *look* lax, or, if a continuing hold was kept on the target numbers, then the intermediate target objective could prove unduly restrictive.

Third, the increase in competitive pressures in the financial system, among banks, and between banks and other financial intermediaries, in the 1980s has led to a paring of spreads between lending and deposit rates, with interest rates on deposits being made more attractive, while the cost of borrowing to the personal sector, e.g. on mortgages, has been reduced in a number of countries, notably in the United Kingdom. The private sector, both the company and the personal sectors, has increased both its indebtedness to, and claims upon, the banking sector enormously. Although the micro level data make it hard to estimate whether the borrowers are the same, or different, entities as the depositors, (note, though, that more assured access to bank borrowing facilities could have been expected to reduce precautionary holdings of deposits), there is no question but that the scale of bank intermediation has increased dramatically; for an analysis of the UK personal sector, see R. B. Johnston (1985), and for the UK company sector, see Chowdhury *et al.* (1986). The best measure of the cost of intermediating through (some part of) the financial system is the spread charged therein, (see Miller and Sprenkle, 1980; Johnston, 1983). As Miller and Sprenkle argued, the scale of intermediation may respond elastically to reductions in the spread.

A further factor tending to raise the demand for liquid assets, in general, will have been the massive increase in the value of non-human wealth, e.g. equities and houses, during the bull market of the early eighties (up till 1987/8) and an associated upsurge in the volume of financial transactions, see Ueda (1988) and Grice and Bennett (1984), though Wenninger and Radecki (1986) doubt whether the growth of financial transactions had much effect on M1's growth in the United States.

This first set of suggestions all point to the possibility that the response of desired money balances to certain interest rate relativities may have been underestimated. The second set of suggestions, *not* in any way mutually exclusive with the first, cover the possibility that the characteristics of bank liabilities and assets were upgraded by financial innovation making them more attractive to hold (Hester, 1981; Akhtar, 1983; Artus, 1987; Tamura, 1987; Leigh-Pemberton, 1986; de Cecco, 1987). The term, financial innovation, tends to make most people think of exotic new instruments, e.g. options, futures, options on futures, forward rate agreements, swaps, etc. but the financial innovations of key importance for the conduct of monetary policy have been rather more prosaic. The controls imposed by the authorities, both 'prudential' and direct credit controls, and in several countries the oligopolistic nature of the banking industry, had restricted the range and variety of lending facilities and the payment of interest on deposits, available to the private sector, *retail* customer, (the effect of financial liberalisation in stimulating the growth of the money stock has been a regular theme recently of the Bank of Japan, e.g. (1988 *a,b*)), – the *wholesale* customer had benefited from the 1960s onwards from the bench-mark competition provided by the euro-currency markets.

Anyhow, the extension of variable rate lending in mortgage form made relatively much cheaper credit available to personal sector borrowers in the United Kingdom. The rapid expansion of bank credit to the private sector in most countries throughout the 1980s, in part a supply-side shock, required the banks to act more aggressively to fund the additional demand for loans and the continuing process of de-regulation allowed them to do so. This need for funds, the increasing competition in the industry and the trend towards de-regulation[13] then combined to induce banks to pay higher – than previously – often market-related, interest rates on categories of deposit that had previously, by custom or by regulation, borne zero interest, e.g. checkable, sight deposits, or where the rates had been administratively pegged.

The payment of market related interest rates on certain categories of checkable deposits naturally made them much more attractive to hold. Assets jointly held in a portfolio will provide, at the margin, the same utility. If one asset offers the same rate of interest as another safe, but non-monetary asset, but also provides certain extra liquidity or transaction services, then both assets will only be held simultaneously if the demand for the transactions/liquidity services of the first asset is completely satiated. So the provision of market related interest rates on a wider range of bank deposits would lead to a surge in demand for them, until the demand for their extra liquidity services became

---

[13] A dramatic switch occurred in New Zealand in 1984/5, see Spencer and Carey (1988) and RBNZ (1986).

approximately satisfied, and, at the margin, such deposits were held as interest-bearing safe assets, rather than as 'money'.

In that case the rate of growth of the monetary aggregates will have overstated, possibly considerably, the rate of growth of true 'money', since the money-like characteristics of the interest-bearing deposits will have declined. This is the argument, and analysis, preferred by those who advocate the use of a Divisia index, whereby the 'moneyness' of a deposit is represented by the divergence between its own rate and that on a non-monetary safe asset. There is now quite a large literature on this topic, see Barnett *et al.* (1984), Barnett (1982); for the United Kingdom, Mills (1983*a*). The use of a Divisia-index to measure money can go some way to explain recent trends in velocity, in so far as the innovation process is reflected in shifts in relative interest rates. While in principle this approach would seem to have much to recommend it in a period of rapid shifts in deposit characteristics, in practice the use of such monetary indices in the United States would have provided 'little clear improvement in terms of either demand equation or reduced-form equation performance' in the 1980s, (Lindsey and Spindt, 1986). And, despite much of the academic research on it having been done under the aegis of Central Banks, senior officials have been reluctant to give the concept much public prominence or any policy role.

Competition may well drive banks towards offering a fully market-related interest rate for deposits, while at the same time charging full economic costs for their payments and transactions services. If so, the above analysis would suggest that deposit holdings would increase until the demand for liquidity was satiated, and would be perfectly substitutable for non-monetary assets of the same maturity. If so, what, if anything, would remain of the distinction between money and other assets of a similar maturity? Is one particular characteristic of money, as Tobin (1963) has earlier suggested, that the interest payable on it is externally restricted? And could the distinction between monetary and non-monetary assets become further blurred by an extension in the range of assets that can be monetised, and/or the range of intermediaries offering, perhaps limited, payments services on the back of electronic technology? It might seem that, with the extension of market related interest rates to a wider range of deposits, the only essential 'money' left might be currency outstanding, or the monetary base, (see Solomon, 1981). But the demand for such currency is affected by cross-border holdings (e.g. for DM in Eastern Europe, and for $ around the world, (Greenspan, 1988 and Board of Governors, 1988, Appendix on Monetary Base), and by the 'black economy' (Thomas, 1988); thus surveys of currency holdings can only account for a fraction of the amount outstanding, (see Avery *et al.*, 1987 and Porter and Bayer, 1983); (though econometric studies for the United Kingdom (Johnston, 1984) and for the United States (Dotsey, 1988) have continued to show generally stable demand for currency functions, unlike West Germany where the demand for currency function has recently become unstable, (see Deutsche Bundesbank, 1988; Holtham *et al.*, 1988). Moreover, techniques are available whereby interest *could* be paid even now on currency, (McCulloch, 1986), though they are unlikely to be adopted, since seigniorage represents an attractive and simple source of taxation. While such receipts are small in most developed, non-inflationary countries (Buiter, 1985), they are large enough in several southern European countries to cause certain problems in the process of convergence to a unified, non-inflationary European Monetary System, (see for example Grilli, 1988).

III. MONETARY CONTROL METHODS

The advent of liability management weakened the ability of the authorities to use their traditional mechanism, of interest rate adjustment, to control monetary growth, because the banks would compete with the Central Bank for funds, leading to an upwards spiral in interest rates, so long as they could continue to intermediate profitably, i.e. to lend out such funds to borrowers at a margin above (wholesale) deposit rates (Moore, 1989). And the demand for bank loans has proven notably interest inelastic. Moreover there had always been certain other difficulties in using this approach.

Even before the adoption of liability management, the interest elasticity of demand for bank deposits was subject to considerable uncertainty, so the authorities could not calibrate at all exactly how much interest rates had to change to bring about a desired adjustment in the money stock. Moreover, the authorities only had occasional, once a month or once a quarter in most countries, snapshots of the money stock, which were frequently distorted by temporary disturbances, e.g. a large new issue, or a take-over bid, or a strike, or even bad weather disrupting the normal course of bank clearing: so it was always hard to distinguish temporary from more permanent monetary movements. Given such uncertainty, and the 'political' dislike of raising interest rates – interestingly enough more clearly apparent in the United States where the Fed is independent of the Executive than in the United Kingdom where it is not – there was a natural tendency for interest rate adjustments to be (or to be perceived to be) 'too little and too late', as was recognised in the Green Paper on *Monetary Control* (Treasury and Bank of England, 1980), also see Friedman (1982, 1984 b).

There were, therefore, inherent reasons to suspect that Central Banks' traditional methods, of interest rate adjustments, would not operate satisfactorily to achieve adequate monetary control, and that such deficiencies would be particularly marked at times of severe inflationary pressures, when lags in the process of interest rate adjustment would induce the authorities temporarily to accommodate each inflationary shock to the demand for money until they had both managed to observe it *and* come to a decision to offset it. With monetary control becoming the centre-piece of many governments' policies at the end of the 1970s, it was therefore inevitable that intensive consideration would be given to an alternative method of monetary control, namely monetary base control, or MBC.

Banks need to maintain high-powered cash reserves (R) in order to honour their commitment to maintain the convertibility of their deposits (D) into currency (C). If the ratio which they maintain of such reserves to deposits is stable, and if the general public maintains a stable currency/deposit ratio, then the multiplier linking the money stock (M) to the high-powered reserve base (H) will also remain stable via the identity $M = H\,(C/D + 1)/(C/D + R/D)$. Empirical work tended to demonstrate that these ratios were generally stable and quite closely predictable for the United States; Johannes and Rasche (1979, 1981); Balbach (1981); Hafer *et al.* (1983); Rasche and Johannes (1987); Dewald and Lai (1987); and also for West Germany, van Hagen (1988); but less so in the United Kingdom in recent years, Capie and Wood (1986); or in Australia, Macfarlane (1984). So the argument was straight-forward. The Central Bank can control H, which incidentally represents its own liabilities, by open market operations. Given the predicted values for the two key ratios, (which might, indeed, be sensitive to interest rates, but one could attempt to measure such sensitivity), the authorities could set H in a manner that would deliver any desired M. Of course, the determination of a quantity M implies the determination of a dual: In the short term, while the general level of prices is slowly adjusting, this would be reflected in changes of flexible asset prices, in particular of nominal interest rates. But it was the excessively sluggish adjustment of nominal interest rates that was (it was claimed) part of the problem with the traditional mechanism, and much more variable short-term interest rates would be an acceptable price to pay for better monetary control, especially since longer term asset prices might show *greater* stability than in the past because inflationary expectations would be stabilised.

After a pre-emptive counter-attack by the Bank of England on these arguments, (Foot *et al.*, 1979), the government established a Bank–Treasury working party to study the issue, and their report, in effect, was published in the Green Paper on *Monetary Control* (Treasury and Bank of England, 1980). In this, the working party accepted much of the case against MBC. Briefly it runs as follows. The historical stability of the banks' reserve ratio had depended on the willingness of the authorities always to supply extra cash on demand at an interest rate chosen by the authorities. If the authorities should shift the operational form of the system, by refusing banks' access to cash freely at any price, the banks' desired reserve ratio might experience a major shift, and could then become much more variable. There would be a long transition period, from regime to regime, in which it would be hard to select an appropriate level of base money, and the variability of the banks' reserve/deposit ratio under the new system could be so large as to prevent any improvement in monetary control, while at the same time losing grip on interest rates.

The above arguments referred essentially to a system of MBC operated without any mandatory controls on required bank reserves. If, however, the banks were required to hold a mandatorily required reserve ratio, then there would be a (somewhat) firmer fulcrum, with a more stable reserve/deposit ratio. But this alternative option ran into some technical problems over the accounting base for the required reserves, which has plagued the Americans in practice. If the required reserves were to be based on a previous, known deposit base, a lagged accounting rule, then there would be nothing the banks could do by their own actions, e.g. by running down current assets, to lessen their need for reserves. Under such circumstances the authorities really have no alternative to giving them the reserves the banks require, as in the case, for example, in West Germany, see Kloten (1987); they can only choose the interest rate, or penalty, for providing the required reserves, (for an authoritative account of the operational practices of the Bundesbank, see the Deutsche Bundesbank, 1987). But this would then just be a throw-back to the traditional system (see M. Friedman, 1982). Owing to the difficulty of estimating deposit levels except at the close of business, operational lags, etc., moving to a current accounting basis does not really avoid this prior difficulty.

A more radical solution to this problem, advocated in a few quarters, (see Laurent, 1979; and Kopecky, 1984, and reply by Laurent, 1984), was to move to a system of forward accounting, whereby the permissible volume of deposits at future date $t + x$ would be dependent on the volume of reserves held at time t. An inherent problem with this approach, as with the even more radical suggestion, (Duck and Sheppard, 1978), of selling the commercial banks' (non-monetary) permits to expand deposits, is that it would have the effect of artificially raising the cost of *banks'* intermediation, when restrictive pressure was applied, relative to costs via other financial channels and would thus promote large-scale ('cosmetic') disintermediation.

Since the arguments, pro and con, in the United Kingdom depended largely on claims about how banks, and other agents, in the financial system might behave in the *hypothetical* conditions of a change in the regime to (some version of) MBC, it was not really possible to *demonstrate* the superiority of one set of arguments over the other. The protagonists on either side in the United Kingdom, who met to discuss it under official auspices, in the improbable venue of Church House in Westminster on 29 September 1980, stuck generally to their prejudices. One argument that did, however, sway some of those in positions of power and influence was that it would be difficult to steer the system clearly through the transitional learning period: thus 'we in the UK have very little idea of the size of cash balances the banks would wish to hold if we were to move to a system of monetary base control', (Lawson, 1981); moreover the ratio of £M3 to base money was not stable or predictable, so there was 'little or no point in trying to use the MBC system to control £M3', (Walters, 1986, p. 123). These considerations, combined with the convinced opposition to MBC from the Bank of England, the commercial bankers and the City of London, persuaded the monetarists not to push more strongly for MBC, although remaining unpersuaded of the contrary case, in the early years of the MTFS, e.g. in 1980/1/2. Thereafter, the progressive withdrawal from monetary targetry has relegated the associated/subsidiary issue of MBC to the very back of the policy burner.

In the United States the constraints on a flexible use of traditional interest rate adjustments were even more severe than in the United Kingdom. Accordingly the authorities *did* decide to shift their operating procedures, on 6 October 1979, into a form with a number of the characteristics of MBC. The approach adopted, to control *non-borrowed reserves*, was ingenious. Although the accounting system remained on a lagged basis, so the banks *had* to obtain a *given* total of required reserves, they could do so by *borrowing* reserves from the Fed, given the volume of non-borrowed reserves. The US system of borrowing at the discount window is such that additional borrowing would be stimulated by a rise in the margin between market rates and the (administratively pegged) discount rate, though the relationship involved some inter-temporal complexities, (see Goodfriend, 1983). Hence an expansionary monetary shock impinging on an unchanged non-borrowed-reserve total would lead to a quasi-automatic market increase in interest rates until enough extra borrowing was induced to allow the banks to satisfy their required ratio, (Axilrod and Lindsey, 1981; Federal Reserve Staff Studies, 1981). Thus interest rates would adjust much more rapidly and flexibly in the face of monetary shocks, but would not spiral away without limit: as a further safety measure the Fed set (unpublished) interest rate bands, whereby at the upper (lower) limit it would intervene directly to inject (withdraw) reserves to prevent excessively wild interest rate movements.

In the event, however, these bands were set quite widely and often adjusted into line with market movements, so they only rarely came into play, (Sternlight and Axilrod, 1982). The change in policy immediately, and dramatically, increased both the level and volatility of market interest rates, with volatility in the period 1979/82 being some 4/5 greater than before 1979, (see Evans, 1981, 1984; Walsh, 1982; Mascaro and Meltzer, 1983). The effect of such high, and variable, interest rates, and the determination of Paul Volcker to continue with the medicine, undoubtedly played a major role both in shifting the US and world economy from a generally inflationary to a generally deflationary tack, and in stemming inflationary expectations and psychology.

A number of technical operating problems did, however, arise (see the papers presented at the Conference on 'Current Issues in the Conduct of U.S. Monetary Policy', republished in the *Journal of Money, Credit and Banking* November 1982). First, although the Fed did broadly achieve its annual M1 targets, the shorter-term, quarter to quarter, time path of M1 became even more variable than before 1979. Second, whereas some greater variability of short-term interest rates had been expected (though no one was sure in advance of the scale of the increase; see Walsh (1982) for a comparison of the outcome with earlier studies), the concomitant increase in volatility of longer-term bond yields had not been predicted (Volcker, 1978; Spindt and Tarhan, 1987). Monetarists ascribed both failings to a lack of zeal in the Fed, and to the modifications from full MBC outlined above, and advocated such measures as a shift to current accounting, (adopted in 1984), and closure of, or greater penalties from using, the discount window, and/or a shift from using non-borrowed reserves to a total reserves or monetary base operating target, viz. Poole (1982), Friedman (1982, 1984*a,b*), Mascaro and Meltzer (1983), McCallum (1985), Rasche (1985), Brunner and Meltzer (1983), Rasche and Meltzer (1982). The Fed often advanced particular conjunctural explanations for each short-term surge, or fall, in M1, (see the studies by Wenninger and associates from 1981 onwards, e.g. Radecki and Wenninger, 1985), and Bryant (1982) provided econometric evidence to support the claim that little, or no, improvement in monetary control could have been obtained by changing the operational basis, e.g. to a total reserves target, (see Lindsey *et al.*, 1984, and Tinsley, *et al.*, 1982). Others regarded such fluctuations as the inevitable result of trying (too hard) to impose short term control on a monetary system wherein there were lengthy lags in the adjustment of the demand of both deposits and advances to interest rates (instrument instability), (e.g. White, 1976; Radecki, 1982; Cosimano and Jansen, 1987, but see Lane, 1984 and McCallum, 1985 for an attempted rebuttal).

Be that as it may, the adoption of this operating procedure led to a very bumpy ride over the period 1979–82.[14] In the summer of 1982, a combination of falling inflation in the United States, and the onset of the LDC debt crisis, (in some large part triggered by the change in US monetary policy, see Congdon, 1988), induced the Fed to move away from MBC. This took the form of shifting from a target for *non-borrowed reserves* to a target for *borrowed* reserves (see Wallich, 1984*a*). At a superficial glance this still sounds like a reserve base objective. However, as already noted, the demand for borrowed reserves is a function of the margin between market interest rates and the discount rate, so a target for borrowed reserves implicitly represents an interest rate objective, and also implies that monetary shocks would be accommodated by accompanying movements in non-borrowed reserves at given borrowed reserve/interest rate levels. As in the United Kingdom and elsewhere, the withdrawal from monetary targetry in the United States has meant that this area of argument has gone quiet there too, though not as moribund as here. Moreover, the success of both the Japanese (see Dotsey, 1986) and Germans in achieving more stable growth (than in the United States), both for the monetary aggregates and for nominal incomes while still using interbank market interest rates as their policy instrument, (Fukui, 1986; Suzuki, 1988 for Japan; Deutsche Bundesbank, 1987 for Germany), suggests that it has not been operating procedures that have distinguished the differing macro-economic outcomes of monetary policy.

For a recent account of such procedures, see Suzuki *et al.* (1988) for Japan; Willms and Dudler (1983), Kloten (1987) for West Germany; Conseil National du Crédit (1986) for France; Dotsey (1987), Macfarlane (1984) and Reserve Bank of Australia (1985) for Australia.

(i) Subsequent UK History

Although the UK government did not seek to impose MBC in 1980/1 on a banking community that deeply opposed the idea, one of the features of MBC that had attracted the government was that it removed the determination of nominal interest rates from the hands of the authorities, and gave it to the market. At that time it was one of the tenets of the Conservative government

---

[14] For an analysis of some of the consequences of greater interest rates volatility, see B. Friedman (1982) for its effects in United States capital markets; Enzler and Johnson (1981) for its effects on output and prices; Black (1982) for its effects on exchange rates; Walsh (1984) for its effects on the demand for money.

that prices were set much more efficiently in markets, than by the decision of some group of policy makers. So, even though the government did not insist on MBC, they wanted to introduce a system which gave more scope to the market, and equivalently less to the Bank of England, to set interest rates.

Previously, the Bank of England had organised the pattern of the weekly Treasury Bill issue, so as to leave the market normally slightly short of its desired cash reserve levels (Bank of England, 1984b, Chapter 6). Since the market would have then regularly to sell paper to the Bank to obtain cash, it would facilitate the Bank's control over the price the market would receive for such paper, i.e. over nominal interest rates. In mid-1981, the government and the Bank agreed that this practice would henceforth cease. The Bank would aim, at its weekly Treasury Bill tender, to leave the market in balance. On those days – expected to be in the majority – when the market was roughly in balance the Bank could withdraw from the market, leaving rates to be determined in the free market. The authorities remained, however, concerned not to allow freedom to become entirely untrammelled, and thus stated that they would set (unpublished) bands, which would represent those levels of interest rates beyond which the authorities would intervene to prevent further market-driven movement of interest rates.

In the event, however, this system never came into operation, and the concept of market freedom within unpublished bands proved chimerical. The reason was as follows. During the years 1981–5, the authorities continued to aim to achieve a target for £M3. But at the same time the authorities had lost faith in their ability to achieve such a target by an (acceptable) adjustment in the level of nominal interest rates, and were beginning to vary interest rates in the light of the (pragmatic) blend of concern with monetary conditions, domestic indicators of inflation and exchange rates, described earlier. Meanwhile, with interest rates thus determined, bank lending to the private sector continued to grow at around 20% p.a., compared to a target for £M3 nearer 10% p.a. The authorities, the Bank taking the lead, sought to resolve this conundrum by offsetting the faster rate of growth of bank lending to the private sector by inducing a fall in bank lending to the public sector. They did this by selling more public sector debt to the *non-bank* private sector than needed to fund the PSBR, thus making the banks *systematically short of cash* in their transactions with the government via the Bank. The commercial banks then relaxed their cash shortage by allowing their short-dated public sector debt to run-off, or by selling their longer dated public sector debt. But this effectively forced the Bank again to determine the interest rate level at which it would resolve the systematic cash shortage by buying in the banks' paper, (see Bank of England, 1984a).

This policy was remarkably successful in reconciling continuing extremely rapid bank credit creation with a much lower monetary target. By about 1981, however, a technical problem ensued. The commercial banks effectively ran out of public sector debt to sell back, or run off. This problem was then resolved by the Bank of England buying private sector commercial bills from the commercial banks. This resolved the problem, but only temporarily till the bills matured, when the whole process had to be rolled over. So, on each occasion of overfunding, the 'bill mountain' steadily grew, leading in time to an almost farcical situation of vast quantities of bills maturing on each day, huge resulting cash shortages in the banking system and the Bank needing to purchase 'wheelbarrows' full of further commercial bills from the market to balance the books. This raised numerous questions. The authorities were selling long dated securities, and buying back short-dated bills. Did this make commercial sense?[15] In order to generate the wheelbarrow loads of commercial bills they needed to buy (to square the books),[16] interest rates on commercial bills were reduced below interest rates on alternative assets. This led to some arbitrage opportunities. Indeed, the authorities aimed to induce borrowers to shift to bill finance out of loan finance. But it was claimed that the need to generate the vast additional amounts of bills at times caused bill rates to fall to a level that could encourage various undesirable forms of 'hard' arbitrage, which could inflate both bank lending and deposits. More generally, did a programme of selling longer-dated debt and buying shorter-dated bills tilt the yield curve in a way that would encourage private sector borrowers to seek funds from banks rather than from capital markets, which was one cause of the original problem? More fundamentally yet, was a technique that allowed bank credit expansion to continue roaring ahead, but restrained the growth of bank deposits, achieving any proper purpose, or was it just another 'cosmetic' device?

It has never been easy to answer these questions, and they continued to raise nagging doubts at the time. As the emphasis given to controlling £M3 lapsed, (and such control was largely achieved by over-funding), so the Chancellor decided in mid 1985 to abandon the policy of over-funding, to shift to a policy of fully funding the (rapidly falling) PSBR outside the banking system (Lawson, 1985); a similar full-fund policy was also adopted in Australia (Johnston, 1985) and New Zealand (Reserve Bank, 1987a). Quite how this (full-fund) policy might be operated now that the public sector has moved into increasing surplus[17] remains to be seen. In the event, the abandonment of over-funding did have the predicted effect of bringing about a jump increase in the growth rate of £M3, broadly into line with that of bank lending, at about 20% p.a. in 1987/8, compared with a growth of nominal incomes of about half as much.

Whereas the government, which had claimed in 1980/1 that £M3 was the absolute centre-piece of policy, treated such expansion with apparent unconcern, the Bank remained concerned that, though the messages from the

[15] In fact the yield curve was downwards sloping for much of the period, and the authorities may well have made a commercial profit from the exercise.

[16] By this time the authorities' effective money market dealing was almost entirely in commercial bills. Treasury bills could have been completely phased out. The only reason for continuing with a residual TB market, and weekly tender, was the educational function of keeping market-makers familiar with an instrument which might some day regain an important role.

[17] In the introduction, we described how the adoption of the MTFS led the fiscal decision on the size of the PSBR to be subordinated to the requirements of monetary policy. With the progressive abandonment of monetary targetry, the influence of such monetary considerations on the fiscal decision weakened. Indeed, exactly what balance of Keynesian, monetarist, long-term structural, or yet other concepts and ideas, either does, or should, now influence the choice of the size of public sector deficit/surplus in the United Kingdom remains unclear, but to follow that murky issue further would take us outside the scope of this paper.

broad monetary aggregates might be hard to decipher, it was wrong to ignore them entirely.

IV. MONETARY TRANSMISSION MECHANISMS

(i) *The Effect of Interest Rates on the Domestic Economy*

The unification of financial markets, especially following the abolition of exchange controls, has lessened the efficacy of direct *credit controls*, or other constraints on intermediation, imposed on one segment of that (international) market. In any case the conventional wisdom is that such direct controls on financial markets are generally undesirable. This has left the authorities' discretionary determination of (short-term) market interest rates as the chief, virtually the sole, instrument of monetary policy[18] (see Leigh-Pemberton, 1987).

The main effect of interest rate adjustment probably works through its influence on external capital flows and exchange rates, but space limitation precludes us from considering that here. Instead, in the remainder of this sub-section, we shall review briefly how interest rate adjustments are perceived to affect domestic nominal expenditures and incomes. This topic, however, is, perhaps, more a part of general applied macro-economics; although it is a subject of major concern to monetary policy makers, it is one where they turn mainly to specialist economic advisers for advice and assistance, rather than a subject where they feel responsible for reaching, and defending, a conclusion themselves. Accordingly I shall refer briefly to some general surveys, rather than more specialised papers.

A suitable starting point is the OECD paper by Chouraqui *et al.* (1988) on 'The Effects of Monetary Policy on the Real Sector: An Overview of Empirical Evidence for Selected OECD Economies', which explores the evidence from some thirty large-scale national and international macro models. For a recent study concentrating on the effect of changes in interest rates in UK macroeconomic models, see Easton (1985), and for a review of such effects in the United States, see Akhtar and Harris (1987).

Chouraqui *et al.* begin by noting that an initial decline in interest rates, associated with a rise in the monetary base, *can* lead to such flexible adjustments in inflationary expectations and in prices that any systematic, or anticipated, monetary policy becomes impotent to affect real output, following the arguments of the new classical economics, of which Sargent and Wallace (1975) represents the prototype. They then examine the evidence whether rational expectation, structurally neutral (RESN) conditions appeared to hold in practice. One of the tests of this, following Barro (1977; 1978), is whether

---

[18] Some economists worry over the question whether, and how, the Central Bank can set interest rates, e.g. Dow and Saville (1988). In practice, on a day-to-day basis the Central Bank's monopoly control over the high powered monetary base enables the Central Bank to dictate the price, the short-term interest rate, at which it will provide the banking system with the cash that it requires, (see Bank of England, 1984*b*, Ch. 6). In the medium and longer term, however, the Central Bank's ability to determine the nominal, and even more so the real, interest rate is constrained by a wide range of both political and economic considerations.

real output reacts to *unanticipated* monetary changes, but not to *anticipated* monetary movements. They survey some *seventy* empirical studies of this question, covering seven countries (Table 13), and note that 'the number of studies claiming refutation of the proposition that only unanticipated monetary policy matters is running ahead of corroborative ones' (p. 27). For this, and other reasons, e.g. 'the apparent dependence of the current price level on its own past values' (p. 24) and that 'Evidence from survey data on expectations does not generally support the idea that expectations are formed rationally', (referring to Holden *et al.* (1985) for a comprehensive survey of studies of data on expectations surveys), they reach the conclusion that 'On the whole, the evidence on models which combined market clearing and rational expectations is not favourable to their relevance in current circumstances. Market clearing and rational expectations have little or no empirical foundation, the weight of evidence providing more support for a macroeconomic framework in which prices adjust slowly.'

Be that as it may – and it is not a function of this survey to attempt further adjudication – the major macro-economic models to which policy makers turn for a quantification of the effect of interest rates changes do incorporate a sluggish adjustment of prices and of future inflationary expectations. Although this does imply that administered interest rate adjustments, whether anticipated or not, would not be impotent, the effect of such changes on the various categories of (domestic) expenditures, e.g. business fixed investment, residential investment, consumption, inventory investment, varies quite widely not only between countries, but even more markedly between models. Even so, Chouraqui *et al.* comment that 'One thing that does emerge from recent evidence compared with studies of earlier vintage is the finding of significant interest rate effects' (on domestic expenditures) (p. 13), perhaps because the recent high level of real interest rates has made agents more conscious of interest costs and because the more competitive and more nearly perfect financial markets spread their effects more widely. Even so, 'The diversity in the size of the reported multipliers and the widely varying structure of the models, the parameters of which are often subject to large revisions, means that the short-run response of real sector variables to changes in financial conditions cannot be known with any degree of confidence' (p. 22).

Even though both the strength of the effect of interest rates on domestic expenditures, and the time lags involved, are uncertain, at least the direction of effect appears unambiguous.

But in the *short* run the relationship between increases in interest rates and in price levels can be ambiguous, in part because interest rates represent a business cost – and pricing may be of the cost-plus form – and in part because of the curious manner in which mortgage interest rates enter into the RPI in the United Kingdom (also see Reserve Bank of New Zealand, 1987a). As already noted, however, the main impact of changes in interest rates is, however, perceived to work through its effect on international capital flows, and hence on the exchange rate. 'More immediate, and more powerful, channels through which interest rate changes influence demand work through induced movements in real competitiveness', (Miles and Wilcox, 1988). If this latter channel is allowed to work freely, any short run adverse domestic effect on inflation of higher interest rates should be more than countered by an appreciation in the exchange rate.

(ii) Other Possible Channels

An unhelpful dichotomy, between the theory and the reality of Central Bank operations, was introduced into macro-economics by the IS/LM codification of Keynes' *General Theory* (1936), and has been continued by Friedman (1970, 1971) among others. When either of these two great economists would discuss practical policy matters concerning the level of short-term interest rates, they had no doubts that these were normally determined by the authorities, and could be changed by them, and were not freely determined in the market, (putting the US experience 1979–82 on one side). Whether, or not, this was the most appropriate operating procedure is another question; this was how it has worked in practice.

But when they came to their more theoretical papers, they often reverted to the assumption that the Central Bank sets the nominal money stock, or alternatively fixes the level of the monetary base. If then the goods and labour markets were somewhat sticky, so that the general level of prices did not adjust immediately, the demand and supply of money would be equilibrated in the short run, in this theoretical framework, by market-led adjustments in nominal interest rates. With equilibrium between the demand and supply of money being thus restored by adjustments in nominal interest rates, subsequent effects on nominal incomes/expenditures would seem to *have to work* entirely via such interest rate movements, (see, for example, Crow, 1988 for a restatement of this 'mainline' view), unless one made some auxiliary assumption, e.g. using the buffer stock/disequilibrium money type approach, that the equilibrium achieved in the money market was less than perfect.

All that remains a subject of continuing debate. If, however, one sticks to the real world in which the authorities set the level of nominal interest rates, then the question of the additional effects on the economy, beyond that working via adjustments in interest rates, of monetary and credit shocks is much easier to comprehend. With a given, discretionarily determined, level of short-term interest rates, there can, of course, be all kinds of shocks to the credit and money markets, which will cause the aggregates to change, without there being any (necessary) change in short-term money market rates. How much do these latter changes in the aggregates matter? Moreover, in Section III, we noted how 'over-funding' could divorce bank credit shocks from monetary changes. Although money and (bank) credit usually vary together, they need not do so, and as Brunner and Meltzer have continued to argue (1972 a, b, 1988), they are not the same thing: on this same subject also see Greenfield and Yeager (1986) and Kohn (1988). Which matters most?

In a world characterised by *perfect* markets, expenditure decisions would be determined by the budget constraint in the form of the present value of human and non-human wealth, the current and expected future levels of prices, etc. It is not clear why monetary, or various credit, aggregates should then play a strategic role. Thus Gertler (1988) comments that 'Most of macroeconomic theory presumes that the financial system functions smoothly – and smoothly enough to justify abstracting from financial considerations.... The currently popular real business cycle paradigm proceeds under the working hypothesis that financial structure is irrelevant.'[19] Indeed in a world of perfect markets, which presumably implies costless information, complete trust, etc., it is dubious whether there is any need for money in its role as a means of exchange, (without the introduction of *ad hoc* imperfections, such as a cash in advance constraint, which would be inconsistent with the conditions otherwise allowing perfect markets to exist), though there would still be a need for inter-temporal stores of value (the literature on all this is, of course, vast; for a formal treatment see Gale, 1982, 1983).

Accordingly, a key function of credit/monetary expansion, given the level of interest rates, may be in allowing certain market imperfections, owing to imperfect, or asymmetric, information to be overcome (Kohn and Tsiang, 1988). There has been considerable theoretical interest in the question of whether credit rationing may exist when the financial system is in 'equilibrium', e.g. Jaffee and Russell (1976), Stiglitz and Weiss (1981), Gale and Hellwig (1985) (as well as when such rationing occurs as a result of slow, or restricted, adjustment of interest rates; see Fry, 1988; McKinnon, 1973; Shaw, 1973). Such studies, in which Stiglitz has been a major contributor, have extended to both theoretical and empirical analyses of how changes in credit conditions can affect the economy (Blinder, 1987; Gertler, 1988; Gertler and Hubbard, 1988; Bernanke and Gertler, 1987; Greenwald and Stiglitz, 1988; Woodford in Kohn and Tsiang, 1988, etc., etc.).

A practical current example of this in the United Kingdom has been the move of banks into mortgage lending,[20] the greater competition between banks and building societies in (mortgage-backed) personal lending, and the surge in such lending following the end of the Building Societies' cartel (Meen, 1985). The effect of this can be seen in Table 2 below. This has raised the question of what effect this supply-side shock has had on the real economy, e.g. consumer demand, house construction, housing prices, etc. (see Drayson, 1985).

During the early 1980s, the effect of this credit surge on the broad money supply was offset by the policy of over-funding. As noted in Section I, this involved offering terms on gilt-edged securities that would shift wealth holders out of bank deposits into gilts. Whereas it is comparatively easy to see how certain market imperfections may be assuaged by relaxations in credit market conditions, (or vice versa following the imposition of credit controls), it is

[19] In this same paper, p. 10, Gertler commented that, 'the methodological revolution in macroeconomics in the 1970s also helped shift attention away from financial factors, in a less direct but probably more substantial way. The resulting emphasis on developing macroeconomic models explicitly from individual optimization posed an obstacle. At the time, the only available and tractable model suitable for pursuing this methodological approach – the stochastic competitive equilibrium growth model, developed by Brock and Mirman (1972) and others – was essentially an Arrow–Debreu model, and thus had the property that financial structure was irrelevant.'

[20] For practical examples concerning the United States, see Wojnilower (1980).

Table 2

	1976	1977	1978	1979	1980	1981	1982	1983	1984	1985	1986	1987
Increase in lending (%)	15·9	17·7	19·6	20·1	17·8	21·1	24·1	21·1	18·6	17·8	18·7	18·2
to persons (£ bn)	4·1	5·3	6·9	8·5	9·0	12·6	18·0	19·5	20·7	24·8	29·4	33·8
Of which												
Building societies (£ bn)	3·6	4·1	5·1	5·3	5·7	6·3	8·1	10·9	14·5	14·6	19·4	15·3
Banks (£ bn)	0·5	1·2	1·8	3·2	3·3	6·3	9·8	8·6	6·2	10·2	10·0	18·5
Of which latter,												
mortgage-based (£ bn)	0·1	0·1	0·3	0·6	0·5	2·3	5·1	3·5	2·0	4·2	4·7	10·0

somewhat harder to see why expenditures should respond directly to portfolio shifts between monetary deposits and other assets, *except* in response to the shift in wealth and in the pattern of interest rates thereby generated. Now that proviso is, of course, of vital importance. Friedman has argued that the linkage between (some definition of) the monetary aggregates and nominal incomes and expenditures has been sufficiently stable and strong that no significant extra explanatory power would be achieved by considering the nature of the credit counterparts to that expansion. For example, in the context of the policy-oriented discussion of over-funding, it is arguable that, had that been continued after 1985, with £M3 correspondingly lower, there would have been less money directed towards UK housing, property and equity markets, so that non-human wealth, expenditures and nominal incomes would all now have been lower.

All this is now a subject of both theoretical and empirical debate. In his survey paper, Gertler (1988) notes that earlier 'the theory of liquidity preference and the time series work of Friedman and Schwartz (1963 and 1982) provided motivation for the preoccupation with money'. Moreover 'the widespread use of vector autoregressions to analyse time series shifted the focus back to money as the key financial aggregate', e.g. Sims (1972). But now, Gertler claims, there is a revival of interest in studying the financial, and especially the credit-related, aspects of the business cycle, both at the theoretical level, e.g. Williamson (1987), and at the empirical level, e.g. Bernanke (1983), Gertler and Hubbard (1988), Hamilton (1987), (but for doubts about the empirical relevance of the credit view, see King, 1986).

Although B. Friedman had reported (1980a, 1982) that a credit aggregate could be found in the United States which gave just as stable a relationship with nominal incomes, as did M1 for example, the weight of argument in the 1970s persuaded most Central Bankers that it was, indeed, the (most appropriate definition of the) money stock that should be the centre of policy, rather than some more pragmatic blend of concern with interest rates, monetary *and* credit expansion, asset prices, etc. Now, of course, that earlier, (always somewhat fragile), confidence in the stability (predictability) of the velocity of money has gone, and Central Bankers' traditional (see M. Friedman, 1982) concern with credit (rather than, or as well as, money) has resurfaced; even though the stability of the credit aggregate relationship has fared no better econometrically (B. Friedman, 1988 a).

But in this somewhat confused state (of economic argumentation), what exactly, besides the level of nominal (and real) interest rates does/should a policy-maker look at, and how does one arrive at a policy judgement?[21]

To conclude and summarise, the (pure Keynesian) route for assessing the effect of money upon the economy, using the IS–LM paradigm, usually has money market interest rates determined by the interaction of the demand for, and (Central Bank) determined supply of, the (high-powered) money base; then short-term interest rates affect longer-term rates, equity yields, etc. and hence, via Tobinesque q effects and standard interest elasticities, then affect expenditures; and thereby influence nominal expenditures. This approach ignores the effects of credit and monetary shocks, at given levels of interest rates, in relaxing certain market imperfections, as even erstwhile committed Keynesians now accept, e.g. Dow and Saville (1988). *Per contra*, the monetarist approach wrapped up all the various channels of possible influence in its concentration on the direct (econometric) relationship between money and nominal incomes. The weakening in the predictability of such relationships has now made policy makers reluctant to continue to base policy on any further revised and warmed-up econometric findings in this field.

Instead, policy makers are tending to look directly at domestic indicators of nominal incomes, and of inflation, and to vary nominal interest rates in the light of these, while continuing to cast a rather anxious glance at both credit and monetary aggregates, and also at asset prices (e.g. equities and houses mainly). This is sometimes partially formalised into a 'check-list' approach, (Johnston, 1985; Reserve Bank of New Zealand, 1987 b), whereby Central Bankers record the list of indicators which they take into account. Supporters would describe it as sensible pragmatism; detractors as a reversion to a muddled discretion, which, once again, allows the authorities more rope than is good for them, or us.

V. CONCLUSIONS

During the course of the 1970s, economists and policy makers came to view the economic system as based on a number of long-term equilibrium conditions. Among the most important were: (*i*) the natural (equilibrium) level of output and unemployment; (*ii*) the long-run relationship between the money stock and nominal incomes, a predictable long-term velocity; and (*iii*) the long-run relationship between prices of tradeable goods among pairs of countries and their bilateral exchange rate, purchasing power parity.

A whole variety of shocks, on the demand or supply side, induced by natural

[21] A good example of such uncertainty can be found in policy makers' reaction to the crash of 19 October 1987. It was argued that the fall in asset prices might have a deflationary effect for various reasons. First, it might cause insolvencies and a contagious collapse in the financial system; second, and related to the first, it might cause a weakening in 'confidence' and hence in both business and personal expenditure; third, through the wealth effect, it would cause some reduction in consumers' expenditures. With the benefit of hindsight the (rather slight) effect of the last factor appears to have been well captured by the models. But was the subsequent absence of the first two effects due to a (correctly) expansionary monetary policy then adopted by the authorities, or were the fears always exaggerated?

causes or by human agents, could divert the economy temporarily from its
long-run equilibrium, but market forces would tend to restore the economy to
that equilibrium. The speed with which market forces would operate to restore
the economy to its full equilibrium would depend on the extent of market
imperfection, and consequential price sluggishness, and there was, and remains,
considerable debate on how extensive such imperfections might be. Nevertheless, given that agents could anchor their longer-term expectations on the
restoration of such fundamental equilibria (a tranversality condition) and
dependent on the assumed extent of shorter run price stickiness, it should, in
principle, be possible to trace out the (rationally expected) intervening future
path for the economy in response to current shocks. In this context it was hard
to see any useful role for the authorities apart from setting a medium-term
target (rule) for monetary growth, so as to anchor long term expectations of
price inflation, and also acting to eliminate current market imperfections
(supply side economics).

The main problem with this view of the economic system is that experience
in the 1980s has demonstrated that there appears to be little tendency for the
economy to revert with any perceptible speed to a (unique) equilibrium.
Unemployment in the United Kingdom rose sharply at the start of the 1980s,
and remained high – only falling markedly in 1987/8 – without apparently
causing much sustained downwards pressure on wages and prices. More
important for our own story, previously predictable long-term relationships
between the money stock and nominal incomes appeared to fall apart, while
exchange rates proved capable of diverging both massively and for long periods
from PPP.

Under these circumstances the anchor given to forward expectations by such
long-term equilibrium conditions, or by the (in the event temporary) adoption
of monetary targets by the authorities in the early 1980s, was not firmly set.
During this last decade speculation based on an expectation of a (rapid)
reversion of velocity or exchange rates to their prior norm would not have been
generally financially rewarding, and indeed speculation based on such longer-
term fundamentals was rarely visible.

If the natural forces driving the economy back to a (unique) equilibrium are,
in practice, much weaker than earlier expected – or even at times non-existent,
or offset by other market considerations – then there is much more room for
intervention, and much more need for discretion, by the authorities, since they
cannot just sit back and leave affairs to rational agents operating in efficient
markets.

In the main, policy makers, even some of those most captivated by the earlier
vision, such as Lawson, have accepted that practical lesson. We do not live in
a world in which one can confidently rely on market forces to restore the
economy to a stable (unique) equilibrium, so long as the authorities themselves
do not rock the boat. In this context, the authorities have reverted to
discretionary intervention. Their current main problem is how to operate so as
to balance the (occasionally conflicting) objectives of external and internal
price stability, but that is another, continuing story.

Many macro-theorists are apparently loath to accept any dilution of their earlier image of the economy, partly because it raises questions about the adequacy of their models, and the meaning of such accepted concepts as rational expectations. As noted in the introduction, this has led to an increasing divide between state-of-the-art macro-theory and practical policy analysis. On this my own sympathies are firmly on the side of the policy maker, who has to cope with reality, and cannot retreat to the more tractable and elegant models of the theorist.

REFERENCES

Aftalion, Florin (1983). 'The political economy of French monetary policy.' In *The Political Economy of Monetary Policy: National and International Aspects* (ed. D. Hodgman). Boston: Federal Reserve Bank of Boston, pp. 7–25, and 'Discussion' of above by Robert Raymond, pp. 26–33.

Akhtar, M. Akbar (1983). 'Financial innovations and their implications for monetary policy: an international perspective.' *Bank for International Settlements Economic Papers*, no. 9.

—— and Harris, Ethan S. (1987). 'Monetary policy influence on the economy – an empirical analysis.' *Federal Reserve Bank of New York Quarterly Review*, Winter, pp. 19–32.

Andersen, Palle S. (1985). 'The stability of money demand functions: an alternative approach.' BIS Economic Papers, no. 14.

Anderson, Robert and Enzler, Jared J. (1987). 'Toward realistic policy design: policy reaction functions that rely on economic forecasts.' Chapter 10 in *Macroeconomics and Finance* (ed. R. Dornbusch, S. Fischer and J. Bossons), pp. 291–330. Cambridge, Mass.: MIT Press.

Argy, Victor (1988). 'Money growth targeting – the international experience.' Centre for Studies in Money, Banking and Finance, Macquarie University, Working Paper no. 8806A (August).

Artis, Michael J. and Lewis, Mervyn, K. (1976). 'The demand for money in the United Kingdom, 1963–73.' *Manchester School*, vol. 44, no. 2, pp. 147–81.

—— and —— (1984). 'How unstable is the demand for money in the United Kingdom?' *Economica*, vol. 51, pp. 473–6.

Artus, Patrick (1987). 'La politique monétaire en France dans un contexte d'innovation financière de déréglementation et de plus grande mobilité des capitaux.' Banque de France, Direction Générale des Études, Working Paper 87–36/2 (March).

Atkinson, Paul and Chouraqui, Jean-Claude (1987). 'Implications of financial innovation and exchange rate variability on the conduct of monetary policy.' *Journal of Foreign Exchange and International Finance*, vol. 1, no. 1, pp. 64–84.

Avery, Robert B. *et al.* (1987). 'Changes in the use of transaction accounts and cash from 1984 to 1986.' *Federal Reserve Bulletin*, vol. 73, pp. 179–96.

Axilrod, Stephen H. (1985). 'US monetary policy in recent years: an overview.' *Federal Reserve Bulletin*, vol. 71, no. 1, pp. 14–24.

—— and Lindsey, David, E. (1981). 'Federal Reserve System implementation of monetary policy: analytical foundations of the new approach.' *American Economic Review*, vol. 71, no. 2, pp. 246–52.

Baba, Yoshihisa, Hendry, David F. and Starr, Ross M. (1987). 'U.S. money demand, 1960–1984.' Nuffield College Oxford, Discussion Paper no. 27.

Balbach, Anatol B. (1981). 'How controllable is money growth?' *Federal Reserve Bank of St Louis Review*, vol. 63 (April), pp. 3–12.

Bank of England (1982a). 'The supplementary special deposits scheme.' *Bank of England Quarterly Bulletin*, vol. 22, no. 1, pp. 74–85.

—— (1982b). 'Composition of monetary and liquidity aggregates, and associated statistics.' *Bank of England Quarterly Bulletin*, vol. 22, no. 4, pp. 530–7.

—— (1984a). 'Funding the public sector borrowing requirement: 1952–83.' *Bank of England Quarterly Bulletin*, vol. 24, no. 4, pp. 482–92.

—— (1984b). *The Development and Operation of Monetary Policy, 1960–1983.* Oxford: Clarendon Press.

—— (1987). 'Measures of broad money.' *Bank of England Quarterly Bulletin*, vol. 27, no. 2, pp. 212–19.

—— (1988). 'Bank of England operations in the sterling money market.' *Bank of England Quarterly Bulletin*, vol. 28, no. 3, pp. 391–409.

Bank for International Settlements (1983). *Fifty-third Annual Report*. Basle, pp. 68–78.

—— (1986). *Recent Innovations in International Banking.* Report of a Committee of Central Bankers chaired by Samuel Cross, Basle: BIS.

Bank of Japan, Research and Statistics Department (1985). 'Characteristics of interest rate fluctuations amidst deregulation and internationalization of financing.' Special Paper no. 126, (October).

—— (1988a). *Quarterly Economic Outlook*, Special Paper no. 163, (Spring).

—— (1988b). 'On the recent behaviour of the money supply.' (In Japanese). *Monthly Review*.

—— (1988c). *Annual Review of Monetary and Economic Developments in Fiscal 1987*, (June).

Banque de France, Direction Générale des Études (1987). 'L'évolution des instruments de la politique monétaire en France et la nouveau dispositif de contrôle monétaire.' Note no. 87. 24/2 (March).

Barbato, Michele (1987). 'The evolution of monetary policy and its impact on banks.' *Review of Economic Conditions in Italy*, no. 2, pp. 165–208.

Barnett, William A. (1982). 'The optimal level of monetary aggregation.' *Journal of Money, Credit and Banking*, vol. 14, no. 4, part 2, pp. 687–710.

——, Offenbacher, Edward K. and Spindt, Paul A. (1984). 'The new Divisia monetary aggregates.' *Journal of Political Economy*, vol. 92, no. 6, pp. 1049–85.

Barro, Robert J. (1977). 'Unanticipated money growth and unemployment in the United States.' *American Economic Review*, vol. 67, no. 2, pp. 101–15.

—— (1978). 'Unanticipated money, output and the price level in the United States.' *Journal of Political Economy*, vol. 86, no. 4, pp. 549–80.

—— (1986). 'Recent developments in the theory of rules versus discretion.' ECONOMIC JOURNAL, vol. 96, Supplement, pp. 23–37.

—— and Gordon, David B. (1983a). 'Rules, discretion and reputation in a model of monetary policy.' *Journal of Monetary Economics*, vol. 12, no. 1, pp. 101–21.

—— and —— (1983b). 'A positive theory of monetary policy in a natural rate model.' *Journal of Political Economy*, vol. 91, no. 4, pp. 589–610.

Bean, Charles (1987). 'The impact of North Sea oil.' Chapter 3 in *The Performance of the British Economy* (ed. R. Dornbusch and R. Layard). Oxford: Clarendon Press.

Beckerman, Wilfred (1985). 'How the battle against inflation was really won.' *Lloyds Bank Review*, January, pp. 1–12.

Bernanke, Ben S. (1983). 'Non-monetary effects of the financial crisis in the propagation of the Great Depression.' *American Economic Review*, vol. 73 (June), pp. 257–76.

—— and Gertler, Mark (ed.) (1987). 'Banking and macroeconomic equilibrium.' In *New Approaches to Monetary Economics*, (ed. W. A. Barnett and K. Singleton). New York: Cambridge University Press.

Black, Stanley, W. (1982). 'The effects of alternative monetary control procedures on exchange rates and output.' *Journal of Money, Credit and Banking*, vol. 14, no. 4, part 2, pp. 746–60.

Blinder, Alan S. (1987). 'Credit rationing and effective supply failures.' ECONOMIC JOURNAL, vol. 97, no. 386, pp. 327–52.

Blundell-Wignall, Adrian and Thorp, Susan (1987). 'Money demand, own interest rates and deregulation.' Reserve Bank of Australia Research Discussion Paper, no. 8703 (May).

Board of Governors of the Federal Reserve System (1988). 'Monetary policy report to Congress pursuant to the full employment and balanced growth [Humphrey-Hawkins] Act of 1978.' Federal Reserve Board Press Release, July 13.

Bomhoff, Edward J., (1983). *Monetary Uncertainty*. Amsterdam: North-Holland.

—— (1985). 'Monetary targeting in West Germany, Holland and Switzerland.' *Contemporary Policy Issues*, vol. II (Fall), pp. 85–98.

Bordes, Christian and Strauss-Kahn, Marc-Olivier (1988). 'Dispositifs de contrôle monétaire en France et chocs sur la vitesse dans un environment en mutation.' *Économies et Sociétés*, no. 1, pp. 105–54.

Bouey, Gerald K. (1982a). 'Monetary policy – finding a place to stand.' Paper presented at the Per Jacobsson Lecture, 5 September, mimeo, Bank of Canada.

—— (1982b). 'Recovering from inflation.' Notes for Remarks to the Canadian Club, Toronto, Ontario, 29 November, reprinted in the *Bank of Canada Review*, December.

Brayton, Flint, Farr, Terry and Porter, Richard, (1983). 'Alternative money demand specifications and recent growth in M1.' Processed, Board of Governors of the Federal Reserve System (May).

Brittan, Samuel, (1980). 'A coherent budget at last.' *Financial Times*, 27 March, p. 24.

Broaddus, Alfred and Goodfriend, Marvin (1984). 'Base drift and the longer run growth of M1: experience from a decade of monetary targeting.' *Federal Reserve Bank of Richmond Economic Review*, vol. 70, no. 6, pp. 3–14.

Brock, William, A. and Mirman, Leonard J. (1972). 'Optimal economic growth and uncertainty: the discounted cases.' *Journal of Economic Theory*, vol. 4, pp. 479–513.

Brunner, Karl and Meltzer, Allan H. (1972a). 'Money, debt, and economic activity.' *Journal of Political Economy*, vol. 80, no. 5, pp. 951–77.

—— and —— (1972b). 'A monetarist framework for aggregative analysis.' *Proceedings of the First Konstanzer Seminar*, *Kredit und Kapital*, Beideft 1, Berlin.

—— and —— (1983). 'Strategies and tactics for monetary control.' In *Money, Monetary Policy, and Financial Institutions*, (eds. K. Brunner and A. H. Meltzer), Carnegie-Rochester Conference Series on Public Policy, vol. 19, Amsterdam: North Holland.

—— and —— (1988). 'Money and credit in the monetary transmission process', *American Economic Review*, vol. 78, no. 2, pp. 446–51.

Bryant, Ralph C. (1982). 'Federal Reserve control of the money stock.' *Journal of Money, Credit and Banking*, vol. 14, no. 4, part 2, pp. 597–625.

Budd, Alan and Holly, Sean (1986). 'Does broad money matter?' from *The London Business School Economic Outlook*, vol. 10, no. 9, pp. 16–22.

Buiter, Willem H. (1985). 'A guide to public sector debt and deficits.' *Economic Policy*, vol. 1, (November), pp. 14–79.

—— and Armstrong, Clive A. (1978). 'A didactic note on the transaction demand for money and behavior towards risk.' *Journal of Money, Credit and Banking*, vol. 10 (November), pp. 529–38.

—— and Miller, Marcus H. (1982). 'Real exchange-rate overshooting and the output cost of bringing down inflation.' *European Economic Review*, vol. 18, no. (1–2), pp. 85–123.

—— and —— (1983). 'Changing the rules – economic consequences of the Thatcher regime.' *Brookings Papers on Economic Activity*, no. 2, pp. 305–79.

Burdekin, Richard C. K. (1986). 'Cross-country evidence on the relationship between central banks and governments.' Federal Reserve Bank of Dallas Research Paper no. 8603.

Burger, Albert E., Kalish, Lionel III and Babb Christopher T. (1971). 'Money stock control and its implications for monetary policy.' *Federal Reserve Bank of St Louis Review*, vol. 33, pp. 6–22.

Callaghan, James, (1976). Speech to Labour Party Conference, 28 September, as reported in *The Times*, 29 September, p. 1.

Calvo, Guillermo A. (1978). 'On the time consistency of optimal policy in a monetary economy.' *Econometrica*, vol. 46, (November), pp. 1411–28.

Capie, Forrest, H. and Wood, Geoffrey E. (1986). 'The long run behaviour of velocity in the UK.' Centre for Banking and International Finance, Centre for the Study of Monetary History, The City University, Discussion Paper no. 23, (May).

Carr, Jack and Darby, Michael, (1981). 'The role of money supply shocks in the short-run demand for money.' *Journal of Monetary Economics*, vol. 8 (September), pp. 183–200.

Cosse, Marcello de (ed.) (1987). *Changing Money: Financial Innovation in Developed Countries*. Oxford: Basil Blackwell.

Chouraqui, Jean-Claude, Driscoll, Michael and Strauss-Kahn, Marc-Olivier, (1988). 'The effects of monetary policy on the real sector: an overview of empirical evidence for selected OECD economies.' *OECD Working Papers* no. 51, (April).

Chowdhury, Gopa, Green, Christopher J. and Miles, David K. (1986). 'An empirical model of company short-term financial decisions: evidence from company accounts data.' *Bank of England Discussion Paper* no. 26.

Clinton, Kevin and Chouraqui, Jean-Claude (1987). 'Monetary policy in the second half of the 1980s: how much room for manoeuvre?' OCED Department of Economics and Statistics Working Papers no. 39 (February).

Congdon, Tim (1988). *The Debt Threat*. Oxford: Basil Blackwell.

Conseil National du Crédit, (1986). *Rapport Annuel*. Paris: Banque de France.

—— (1987). *Rapport Annuel*. Édition provisoire. Paris: Banque de France.

Cosimano, Thomas F. and Jansen Dennis W. (1987). 'The relation between money growth variability and the variability of money about target.' *Economics Letters*, vol. 25, pp. 355–8.

Cover, James P. and Keeler, James P. (1987). 'Estimating money demand in log-first-difference form.' *Southern Economic Journal*, vol. 53, no. 3, pp. 751–67.

Crow, John, W. (1988). 'The work of Canadian monetary policy.' Paper presented at the Eric S. Hanson Lecture, University of Alberta, 18 January, mimeo, Bank of Canada.

Cuthbertson, Keith (1988*a*). 'The demand for M1: a forward-looking buffer stock model.' *Oxford Economic Papers*, vol. 40, pp. 110–81.

—— (1988*b*). 'The encompassing implications of feedforward versus feedback mechanisms: a comment.' Mimeo, Newcastle University (July).

—— and Taylor, Mark P. (1987). 'Buffer-stock money: an appraisal.' Chapter 5 in *The Operation and Regulation of Financial Markets*, (ed. C. Goodhart, D. Currie and D. Llewellyn). London: Macmillan.

Darby, Michael, *et al.* (1987). 'Recent behavior of the velocity of money.' *Contemporary Policy Issues*, vol. 5 (January), pp. 1–32.

Davidson, James E. H. (1987). 'Disequilibrium money: some further results with a monetary model of the UK.' Chapter 6 in *The Operation and Regulation of Financial Markets* (ed. C. Goodhart, D. Currie and D. Llewellyn). London: Macmillan.

—— and Ireland, Jonathan, (1987). 'Buffer stock models of the monetary sector.' *National Institute Economic Review*, 121 (August), pp. 67–71.

Deutsche Bundesbank (1985). 'The longer-term trend and control of the money stock.' *Monthly Report*, vol. 37, no. 1 (January), pp. 13–26.

—— (1987). *The Deutsche Bundesbank: its monetary policy instruments and functions*. Special Series, no. 7.

—— (1988). 'Methodological notes on the monetary target variable "M3".' *Monthly Report*, vol. 40, no. 3, pp. 18–21.

Dewald, William G. and Lai Tsung-Hui, (1987). 'Factors affecting monetary growth: ARIMA forecasts of monetary base and multiplier.' *Kredit und Kapital*, vol. 20, no. 3, pp. 303–16.

Dickens, Rodney R. (1987). 'International comparison of asset market volatility: a further application of the ARCH model.' *Bank of England Technical Paper* no. 15 (February).

Dotsey, Michael (1986). 'Japanese monetary policy: a comparative analysis.' *Bank of Japan Monetary and Economic Studies*, vol. 4, no. 2, pp. 105–27.

—— (1987). 'The Australian money market and the operations of the Reserve Bank of Australia: a comparative analysis.' *Federal Reserve Bank of Richmond Economic Review* (September–October) pp. 19–31.

—— (1988). 'The demand for currency in the United States.' *Journal of Money, Credit and Banking*, vol. 20, no. 1, pp. 22–40.

Dow, Christopher and Saville, Iain (1988). *A Critique of Monetary Policy*. Oxford: Clarendon Press.

Drayson, Stephen J. (1985). 'The housing finance market: recent growth in perspective.' *Bank of England Quarterly Bulletin*, vol. 25, no. 1, pp. 80–91.

Driffill, John (1988). 'Macroeconomic policy games with incomplete information.' *European Economic Review*, vol. 32, pp. 533–41.

Duck, Nigel W. and Sheppard, David K. (1978). 'A proposal for the control of the UK money supply.' ECONOMIC JOURNAL, vol. 88, no. 349, pp. 1–17.

Dudler, Hermann-Josef (1984). *Geldpolitik und ihre Theoretischen Grundlagen*. Frankfurt am Main: Fritz Knapp Verlag.

—— (1986). 'Geldmengenpolitik und Finanzinnovationen.' *Kredit und Kapital*, Heft 4, pp. 472–95.

—— (1987). 'Financial innovation in Germany.' Chapter 7 in *Changing Money* (ed. de Cecco). Oxford: Basil Blackwell.

Dutkowsky, Donald H. and Foote, William G. (1988). 'The demand for money: a rational expectations approach.' *Review of Economics and Statistics*, vol. 70, no. 1, pp. 83–92.

Dwyer, Gerald P. Jr. (1985). 'Federal Deficits, Interest Rates and Monetary Policy.' *Journal of Money, Credit and Banking*, vol. 17, no. 4, part 2, pp. 655–81.

Easton, W. W. (1985). 'The importance of interest rates in five macroeconomic models.' *Bank of England Discussion Papers* no. 24 (October).

Edison, Hali J., Miller, Marcus, H. and Williamson, John (1987). 'On evaluating and extending the target zone proposal.' *Journal of Policy Modelling*, vol. 9, no. 1, pp. 199–224.

Engle, Robert F. and Granger, Clive, W. J. (1987). 'Cointegration and error correction: representation, estimation and testing.' *Econometrica*, vol. 55, no. 2, pp. 251–76.

Enzler, Jared J. and Johnson, Lewis (1981). 'Cycles resulting from money stock targeting.' In *New Monetary Control Procedures*, Federal Reserve Staff Study, vol. 1, Board of Governors of the Federal Reserve System: Washington DC.

Evans, Paul (1981). 'Why have interest rates been so volatile?' *Federal Reserve Bank of San Francisco Economic Review*, (Summer), pp. 7–20.

—— (1984). 'The effects on output of money growth and interest rate volatility in the United States.' *Journal of Political Economy*, vol. 92, no. 2, pp. 204–20.

Fay, Stephen (1987). *Portrait of an Old Lady*. Harmondsworth: Viking.

Federal Reserve Staff Studies (1981). *New Monetary Control Procedures*. (2 vols), Washington: Board of Governors of the Federal Reserve System.

Feldstein, Martin (1988). 'Rethinking international economic coordination.' *Oxford Economic Papers*, vol. 40, no. 2, pp. 205–19.

Fforde, John S. (1983). 'Setting monetary objectives.' In *Central Bank Views on Monetary Targetting*. (ed. P. Meek). Federal Reserve Bank of New York, 1983; also reprinted in Bank of England (ed.). *The Development and Operation of Monetary Policy*. Oxford: Clarendon Press (1984).

Filc, Wolfgang; Hubl Lothar and Pohl Rudiger (eds.), (1988). *Herausforderungen der Wirtschaftspolitik*. Berlin: Duncker and Humblot.

Fischer, Stanley (1988). 'Recent developments in macroeconomics.' ECONOMIC JOURNAL, vol. 98, no. 391, pp. 294–339.

Foot, Michael D. K. W. (1981). 'Monetary targets: their nature and record in the major economies.' In *Monetary Targets*, (ed. B. Griffiths and G. E. Wood). London: Macmillan.

——, Goodhart, Charles A. E. and Hotson, Anthony C. (1979). 'Monetary base control.' *Bank of England Quarterly Bulletin*, vol. 19, no. 2, pp. 149–59.

Freedman, Charles (1983). 'Financial innovation in Canada: causes and consequences.' *American Economic Review*, vol. 73, no. 2, pp. 101–6.

Frenkel, Jacob, A. and Goldstein, Morris (1988). 'Exchange rate volatility and misalignment: evaluating some proposals for reform.' Paper presented at Federal Reserve Bank of Kansas City Conference on Financial Market Volatility. August 17–9.

Frey, Bruno and Schneider, Friedric (1981). 'Central bank behavior: a positive empirical analysis.' *Journal of Monetary Economics*, vol. 7. pp. 291–316.

Friedman, Benjamin M. (1980a). 'Debt and economic activity in the United States.' In *The Changing Roles of Debt and Equity in Financing U.S. Capital Formation.* (ed. B. M. Friedman). Chicago: University of Chicago Press, pp. 91–110.

—— (1980b). 'Postwar changes in the American financial markets.' In *The American Economy in Transition.* (ed. M. Feldstein). Chicago: University of Chicago Press, pp. 9–78.

—— (1982). 'Federal Reserve policy, interest rate volatility, and the U.S. capital raising mechanism.' *Journal of Money, Credit and Banking,* vol. 14, no. 4, part 2, pp. 721–45.

—— (1988a). 'Monetary policy without quantity variables.' *American Economic Review Proceedings,* vol. 78, no. 2, pp. 440–5.

—— (1988b). 'Targets and instruments of monetary policy.' National Bureau of Economic Research Working Paper no. 2668, (July).

Friedman, Milton (1956). 'The quantity theory of money – a restatement.' In *Studies in the Quantity Theory of Money* (ed. M. Friedman). Chicago: University of Chicago Press.

—— (1968). 'The role of monetary policy.' *American Economic Review,* vol. 58 (March), pp. 1–17.

—— (1970). 'A theoretical framework for monetary analysis.' *Journal of Political Economy,* vol. 78, (March/April), pp. 193–228.

—— (1971). 'A monetary theory of nominal income.' *Journal of Political Economy,* vol. 79, (March–April), pp. 323–37.

—— (1982). 'Monetary theory: policy and practice.' *Journal of Money, Credit and Banking,* vol. 14, no. 1, pp. 98–118.

—— (1984a). 'Monetary policy of the 1980s.' Chapter 2 in *To Promote Prosperity,* (ed. J. Moore). Stanford: Hoover Institute Press.

—— (1984b). 'Lessons from the 1979–82 monetary policy experiment.' *American Economic Review,* vol. 74, no. 2, pp. 397–400.

—— and Schwartz, Anna J. (1963). *A Monetary History of the United States, 1867–1960.* Princeton: Princeton University Press for NBER.

—— and —— (1982). *Monetary Trends in the United States and the United Kingdom.* Chicago: University of Chicago Press.

Fry, Maxwell J. (1988). *Money, Interest, and Banking in Economic Development.* Baltimore: Johns Hopkins University Press.

Fukui, Toshihiko, (1986). 'Recent developments of the short-term money market in Japan and changes in monetary control techniques and procedures by the Bank of Japan.' Bank of Japan, Research and Statistics Department, Special Paper, no. 130, (January).

Gale, Douglas (1982). *Money: In Equilibrium.* Cambridge University Press.

—— (1983). *Money: In Disequilibrium.* Cambridge University Press.

—— and Hellwig, Martin (1985). 'Incentive-compatible debt contracts: the one-period problem.' *The Review of Economic Studies,* vol. 52, no. 4, pp. 647–64.

Geisler, Klaus-Dieter (1986). 'Sur "Kausalitat". von Geldmenge und Sozialprodukt.' *Kredit und Kapital,* Heft 3, pp. 325–39.

Germany, J. David and Morton, John E. (1985). 'Financial innovation and deregulation in foreign industrial countries.' *Federal Reserve Bulletin,* vol. 71, no. 10, pp. 743–53.

Gertler, Mark (1988). 'Financial structure and aggregate economic activity: an overview.' NBER Working Paper no. 2559, (April), subsequently published in the *Journal of Money, Credit and Banking,* vol. 20, no. 3, part 2, (August), pp. 559–89.

—— and Hubbard, Glenn R. (1988). 'Financial factors and business fluctuations.' Paper presented at Federal Reserve Bank of Kansas City Conference on Financial Volatility, Jackson Hole, Wyoming, August 17–19.

Goldfeld, Stephen, M. (1973). 'The demand for money revisited.' *Brookings Papers on Economic Activity,* no. 13, pp. 577–638.

—— (1976). 'The case of the missing money.' *Brookings Papers on Economic Activity,* no. 3, pp. 683–730.

Goodfriend, Marvin (1983). 'Discount window borrowing, monetary policy, and the post-October 6, 1979, Federal Reserve operating procedure.' *Journal of Monetary Economics,* vol. 12, pp. 343–56.

—— (1985). 'Reinterpreting money demand regressions.' In *Understanding Monetary Regimes,* (ed. K. Brunner and A. H. Meltzer). Carnegie-Rochester Conference Series on Public Policy, vol. 22, Amsterdam: North Holland.

Goodhart, Charles (1984). *Monetary Theory and Practice.* London: Macmillan.

—— and Crockett, Andrew D. (1970). 'The importance of money.' *Bank of England Quarterly Bulletin,* vol. 10, no. 2, pp. 159–98.

Gordon, Robert J. (1984). 'The short run demand for money: a reconsideration.' *Journal of Money, Credit and Banking,* vol. 16, part 1, pp. 403–34.

Granger, Clive, W. J. (1981). 'Some properties of time series data and their use in econometric model specification.' *Journal of Econometrics,* vol. 16, no. 1.

Greenfield, Robert L. and Yeager, Leland B. (1986). 'Money and credit confused: an appraisal of economic doctrine and Federal Reserve procedure.' *Southern Economic Journal,* vol. 53, no. 2, pp. 364–73.

Greenspan, Alan (1988). 'Statement before the US Senate Committee on Banking, Housing and Urban Affairs', Press Release, Federal Reserve Board, July 13.

Greenwald, Bruce C. and Stiglitz, Joseph E. (1988). 'Imperfect information, finance constraints, and business fluctuations' and 'Money, imperfect information, and economic fluctuations.' Chapters 7 and 8. In *Finance Constraints, Expectations, and Macroeconomics*. (ed. M. Kohn and S-C. Tsiang). Oxford: Clarendon Press.

Greider, William (1988). *Secrets of the Temple*. New York: Simon and Schuster.

Grice, Joe, Bennett, Alan and Cumming, Norman (1981). 'The demand for sterling £M3 and other aggregates in the United Kingdom.' *Treasury Working Paper*, no. 20 (August).

—— and —— (1984). 'Wealth and the demand for £M3 in the United Kingdom, 1963–1978.' *Manchester School*, vol. 52, no. 3, pp. 239–71.

Grilli, Vittorio (1988). 'Exchange rates and seigniorage.' Unpublished manuscript.

Hacche, Graham (1974). 'The demand for money in the United Kingdom: experience since 1971'. *Bank of England Quarterly Bulletin*, vol. 14, no. 3, pp. 284–305.

Hafer, R. W. (1985). 'Comment on "Money Demand Predictability".' *Journal of Money, Credit, and Banking*, vol. 17, no. 4, part 2, pp. 642–6.

—— and Hein, Scott E. (1984). 'Financial innovations and the interest elasticity of money demand: some historical evidence.' *Journal of Money, Credit and Banking*, vol. 16, no. 2, pp. 247–52.

——, —— and Kool, Clemens J. M. (1983). 'Forecasting the money multiplier: implications for money stock control and economic activity.' *Federal Reserve Bank of St Louis Review*. (October), pp. 22–33.

van Hagen, Jurgen, (1988). 'Alternative operating regimes for money stock control in West Germany: an empirical evaluation.' *Weltwirtschaftsliches Archiv*. vol. 124, no. 1, pp. 89–107.

Hall, Steven and Henry, Brian (1987). 'Wage models.' *National Institute Economic Review*, no. 119, (February).

——, —— and Wilcox, Joe, (1988). 'The long run determination of the UK monetary aggregates.' Bank of England, mimeo (April).

Hall, Robert E. (1986). 'Optimal monetary institutions and policy.' Chapter 6. In *Alternative Monetary Regimes*. (ed. C. D. Campbell and W. R. Dougan). Baltimore: Johns Hopkins University Press.

Hamada, Koichi and Hayashi, Fumio (1985). 'Monetary policy in postwar Japan', In *Monetary Policy in Our Times*. (ed. A. Ando, H. Eguchi, R. Farmer and Y. Suzuki). Cambridge, Mass.: MIT Press.

Hamburger, Michael J. (1983). 'Recent velocity behavior, the demand for money and monetary policy.' Conference on Monetary Targetting and Velocity, Federal Reserve Bank of San Francisco.

Hamilton, James (1987). 'Monetary factors in the Great Depression.' *Journal of Monetary Economics*, vol. 19, no. 2, pp. 145–70.

Havrilesky, Thomas (1988). 'Monetary policy signalling from the administration to the Federal Reserve.' *Journal of Money, Credit and Banking*, vol. 20, no. 1, pp. 83–101.

Healy, Nigel M. (1987). 'The UK 1979–82 "Monetarist Experiment": why economists will still disagree.' *Banca Nazionale del Lavoro Quarterly Review*, no. 163, (December), pp. 471–99.

Heller, H. Robert (1988). 'Implementing Monetary Policy.' *Federal Reserve Bulletin*, vol. 74, no. 7, pp. 419–29.

Hendry, David, F. (1979). 'Predictive failure and econometric modelling in macroeconomics: the transactions demand for money.' Chapter 9 In *Economic Modelling*. (ed. P. Ormerod). London: Heinemann.

—— (1985). 'Monetary economic myth and econometric reality.' *Oxford Review of Economic Policy*, vol. 1, no. 1, pp. 72–84.

—— (1988). 'The encompassing implications of feedback versus feedforward mechanisms in econometrics.' *Oxford Economic Papers*, vol. 40, pp. 132–49.

—— and Ericsson, Neil R. (1983). 'Assertion without empirical basis: an econometric appraisal of "Monetary Trends in...the United Kingdom" by Milton Friedman and Anna Schwartz.' Bank of England Panel of Academic Consultants, Panel Paper, no. 22, (October).

—— and Neale, Adrian J. (1988). 'Interpreting long-run equilibrium solutions in conventional macro models: a comment.' ECONOMIC JOURNAL, vol. 98, no. 392, pp. 808–17.

Hester, Donald D. (1981). 'Innovations and monetary control.' *Brookings Papers on Economic Activity*, no. 1, pp. 141–89.

Hodgman, Donald R. (1983). *The Political Economy of Monetary Policy: National and International Aspects*. Federal Reserve Bank of Boston.

Hogan, Lindsay I. (1986). 'A comparison of alternative exchange rate forecasting models.' *Economic Record*, vol. 62, no. 177, pp. 215–23.

Holden, K., Peel, D. and Thompson, J. (1985). *Expectations: Theory and Evidence*. London: Macmillan.

Holtham, Gerald, Keating, Giles and Spencer, Peter (1988). 'Developments in the demand for liquid assets in Germany and the UK.' Paper presented at the Conference on Monetary Aggregates and Financial Sector Behavior in Interdependent Economies, Board or Governors of the Federal Reserve System, Washington D.C., May 26–7.

Hoskins, W. Lee (1985). 'Foreign experiences with monetary targeting: a practitioner's perspective.' *Contemporary Policy Issues*, vol. III, pages 71–83.

Howe, Sir Geoffrey (1979). 'Budget Statement.' *Hansard*, vol. 968, London: HMSO, pp. 241–4.

—— (1981). 'The fight against inflation.' The Third Mais Lecture, City University Business School pamphlet (May).

Ireland, Jonathan and Wren-Lewis, Simon, (1988). 'Buffer stock money and the company sector.' Paper presented at the Money Study Group Conference, Oxford, September 23rd.

Isard, Peter and Rojas-Suarez, Liliana (1986). 'Velocity of money and the practice of monetary targeting: experience, theory, and the policy debate.' Chapter 3 in *Staff Studies for the World Economic Outlook*, International Monetary Fund: Washington, D.C. (July), pp. 73–112.

Jaffee, Dwight M. and Russell, Thomas (1976). 'Imperfect information and credit rationing.' *Quarterly Journal of Economics*, vol. 90, no. 4, pp. 651–66.

Johannes, James, M. and Rasche, Robert H. (1979). 'Predicting the money multiplier.' *Journal of Monetary Economics*, vol. 5, pp. 301–25.

—— (1981). 'Can the reserves approach to monetary control really work?' *Journal of Money, Credit and Banking*, vol. 13, (August), pp. 298–313.

Johnson, Karen H., (1983). 'Foreign experience with targets for monetary growth.' *Federal Reserve Bulletin*, vol. 69, (October), pp. 745–54.

Johnston, Robert A. (1985). 'Monetary policy – the changing environment.' T. A. Coghlan Memorial Lecture, University of NSW (May), reprinted in *Reserve Bank of Australia Bulletin*, (June).

Johnston, R. Barry (1983). *The Economics of the Euro-Market*, London: Macmillan.

—— (1984). 'The demand for non interest bearing money in the United Kingdom.' *Treasury Working Paper*, no. 28.

—— (1985). 'The demand for liquidity aggregates by the UK personal sector.' *Treasury Working Paper*, no. 36.

Jonson, Peter D., Moses, E. R. and Wymer, Cliff R. (1977). 'The RBA76 model of the Australian economy.' In *Conference in Applied Economic Research*, Reserve Bank of Australia, (December).

—— and Rankin, R. W., (1986). 'On some recent developments in monetary economics.' *Economic Record*, vol. 62, no. 179, pp. 257–267.

Judd, John P. and Scadding, John, L. (1981). 'The search for a stable money demand function: a survey of the post-1973 literature.' *Journal of Economic Literature*, vol. 20 (September), pp. 993–1023.

—— and —— (1982). 'Liability management, bank loans, and deposit "market" disequilibrium.' *San Francisco Federal Reserve Bank Review*, (Summer), pp. 21–44.

—— and Motly, Brian (1984). 'The "Great Velocity Decline" of 1982–83: a comparative analysis of M1 and M2.' *Federal Reserve Bank of San Francisco Economic Review*, (Summer), pp. 56–74.

Kaldor, Nicholas (1982). *The Scourge of Monetarism*, Oxford: Oxford University Press.

Keating, Paul (1985). 'Statement by the Treasurer, The Hon. Paul Keating, M.P.', Press Release, Canberra (January), reprinted in *Reserve Bank of Australia Bulletin* (February) pp. 507–9.

Keynes, J. Maynard (1936). *The General Theory of Employment Interest and Money*, reprinted 1973 for the Royal Economic Society. London: Macmillan.

King, Robert G. and Plosser, Charles I. (1984). 'Money, credit and prices in a real business cycle.' *American Economic Review*, vol. 74, (June), pp. 363–80.

King, Stephen R. (1986). 'Monetary transmission: through bank loans and bank liabilities?' *Journal of Money, Credit and Banking*, vol. 18, no. 3, pp. 290–303.

Kloten, Norbert (1987). 'The control of monetary aggregates in West Germany under changing conditions: the impact of innovations, the internationalisation of financial markets and the EMS.' Paper presented at the Second Surrey Monetary Conference on Financial Innovation, Deregulation and the Control of Monetary Aggregates, University of Surrey, Guildford, 8–10 April.

Knoester, Arthonic and van Sinderen, Jarig (1982). 'Economic policy and unemployment.' In *Unemployment: A Dutch Perspective*, (ed. A. Maddison and B. S. Wilpstra). The Hague.

Kohn, Meir (1988). 'The finance constraint theory of money: a progress report.' Dartmouth College Working Paper, (August).

—— and Tsiang Sho-Chieh (1988). *Financial Constraints, Expectations, and Macroeconomics*. Oxford: Clarendon Press.

Kopecky, Kenneth J. (1984). 'Monetary control under reverse lag and contemporaneous reserve accounting: a comparison' and 'A reply.' by Robert D. Laurent, *Journal of Money, Credit and Banking*, vol. 16, no. 1, pp. 81–92.

Kydland, Finn E. and Prescott, Edward C. (1977). 'Rules rather than discretion: the inconsistency of optimal plans.' *Journal of Political Economy*, vol. 85 (June), pp. 473–91.

—— and —— (1982). 'Time to build and aggregate fluctuations.' *Econometrica*, vol. 50 (November), pp. 1345–70.

Laidler, David E. W. (1983a). *Monetarist Perspectives*. Oxford: Philip Allan.

—— (1983b). 'The buffer stock notion in monetary economics.' ECONOMIC JOURNAL, *Supplement*, vol. 94, pp. 17–34.

132   CHARLES GOODHART

—— (1985). 'Comment on "Money Demand Predictability"', *Journal of Money, Credit and Banking*, vol. 17., no. 4, part 2, pp. 647–53.

—— (1986). 'What do we really know about monetary policy?' *Australian Economic Papers*, vol. 25, no. 46, pp. 1–16.

—— (1988a). 'Taking money seriously.' University of Western Ontario Department of Economics Research Report, no. 9904.

—— (1988b). 'Monetarism, microfoundations and the theory of monetary policy.' Working Paper, Centre for the Study of International Economic Relations, Working Paper, no. 8807c. Paper presented at a Conference on Monetary Policy at the Free University of Berlin, August 31–Sept. 2.

—— and Bentley, Brian (1983). 'A small macro-model of the post-war United States 1953–72.' *Manchester School*, vol. 51 (December), pp. 317–40.

—— and Parkin, Michael J. (1970). 'The demand for money in the United Kingdom, 1956–1967: some preliminary estimates', *Manchester School*, vol. 38, no. 3, pp. 187–208.

Lamfalussy, Alexandre (1981). '"Rules vs. Discretion": an essay on monetary policy in an inflationary environment.' BIS Economic Papers, no. 3.

Lane, Timothy, D. (1984). 'Instrument instability and short-term monetary control.' *Journal of Monetary Economics*, vol. 14, pp. 209–24.

Laney, Leroy O. (1985). 'An international comparison of experiences with monetary targeting: a reaction function approach.' *Contemporary Policy Issues*, vol. III, (Fall), pp. 99–112.

Laurent, Robert D. (1979). 'Reserve requirements: are they lagged in the wrong direction?' *Journal of Money, Credit and Banking*, vol. 11, (August), pp. 301–10.

Lawson, Nigel (1980). 'Britain's policy and Britain's place in the international financial community.' Speech at the Financial Times 1980 Euromarket Conference, 21st January, H.M. Treasury Press Release.

—— (1981). 'Thatcherism in practice: a progress report.' Speech to the Zurich Society of Economics, 14 January, H.M. Treasury Press Release.

—— (1982). 'Financial discipline restored.' Conservative Political Centre Pamphlet. (May).

—— (1983). 'Mansion House Speech.' H.M. Treasury Press Release, October.

—— (1984). 'The British Experiment.' The Fifth Mais Lecture, City University Business School pamphlet, (June).

—— (1985). 'Mansion House Speech.' H.M. Treasury Press release, Oct. 17.

—— (1986). 'Monetary policy.' Lombard Association Speech, H.M. Treasury Press Release, April 16.

—— (1988). 'The State of the Market.' Speech to the Institute of Economic Affairs, H.M. Treasury Press Release, 21 July.

Layard, Richard and Nickell, Stephen, (1986). 'Unemployment in Britain.' *Economica*, vol. 33, supplement, pp. 121–70.

Leigh-Pemberton, Robin (1986). 'Financial change and broad money.' Loughborough University Banking Centre Lecture in Finance, *Bank of England Quarterly Bulletin*, vol. 26, no. 4, pp. 499–507.

—— (1987). 'The instruments of monetary policy.' Seventh Mais Lecture at the City University Business School, May 13th *Bank of England Quarterly Bulletin*, vol 27, no. 3, pp. 365–70.

Lewis, Mervyn, K. and Davis, Kevin T. (1987). *Domestic International Banking*, Oxford: Philip Allan.

Lindsey, David E. (1986). 'The monetary regime of the Federal Reserve System.' Chapter 5. In *Alternative Monetary Regimes*. (ed. C. D. Campbell and W. R. Dougan). Baltimore: Johns Hopkins University Press.

——, Farr, Helen T. Gillum, Gary P. Kopecky, Kenneth J. and Porter, Richard D. (1984). 'Short-run monetary control.' *Journal of Monetary Economics*, vol. 13, pp. 87–111.

—— and Spindt, Paul (1986). 'An evaluation of monetary indices.' Federal Reserve Board, Division of Research and Statistics, Special Studies Paper, no. 195.

Long, John B, Jr. and Plosser, Charles I. (1983). 'Real business cycles.' *Journal of Political Economy*, vol. 91, (February), pp. 39–69.

Lubrano, M., Pierse, R. G. and Richard, J. F. (1986). 'Stability of a UK money demand equation: a Bayesian approach to testing exogeneity.' *Review of Economic Studies*, vol. 53, pp. 603–34.

Lucas, Robert E., Jr. (1972). 'Expectations and the neutrality of money.' *Journal of Economic Theory*, vol. 4 (April), pp. 103–24.

—— (1976). 'Econometric policy evaluation: a critique', In *The Phillips Curve and Labor Markets*, (ed. K. Brunner and A. H. Meltzer). Carnegie-Rochester Conference Series on Public Policy, vol. 1, Amsterdam: North Holland, pp. 19–46.

McCallum, Bennett, T. (1985). 'On consequences and criticisms of monetary targeting.' *Journal of Money, Credit and Banking*, vol. 17, no. 4, part 2, pp. 570–97.

—— (1987). 'The case for rules in the conduct of monetary policy: a concrete example.' *Weltwirtschaftliches Archiv*, Bd. 123, pp. 415–28.

—— (1988). 'Postwar developments in business cycle theory: a moderately classical perspective', *Journal of Money, Credit and Banking*, vol. 20, no. 3, part 2, pp. 459–71.

McCulloch, J. Huston (1986). 'Beyond the historical gold standard.' In *Alternative Monetary Regimes*. (ed. C. D. Campbell and W. R. Dougan). Baltimore: Johns Hopkins University Press, pp. 73–81.

McKinnon, Ronald, I. (1973). *Money and Capital in Economic Development*. Washington, D.C.: Brookings Institute.
—— (1984). *An International Standard for Monetary Stabilisation*, Washington: Institute for International Economics.
—— and Ohno, Kenichi (1988). 'Purchasing Power Parity as a Monetary Standard,' Paper presented at a Conference on the Future of the International Monetary System, Toronto: York University.
Macfarlane, Ian J. (1984). 'Methods of monetary control in Australia.' Paper presented at the New Zealand Association of Economists Annual Conference, Massey University (August).
Mankiw, N. Gregory (1988). 'Recent developments in macroeconomics: a very quick refresher course', *Journal of Money, Credit and Banking*, vol. 20, no. 3, part 2, pp. 436–49.
Mascaro, Angelo and Meltzer, Allan, H. (1983). 'Long-and short-term interest rates in a risky world.' *Journal of Monetary Economics*, vol. 12, (November), pp. 485–518.
Mayer, Thomas (1987). 'The debate about monetarist policy recommendations.' *Kredit and Kapital*, vol. 20, pp. 281–302.
—— (1988). 'Monetarism in a world without "money".' University of California, Davis, Research Program in Applied Macroeconomics and Macro Policy, Working Paper, no. 56.
Meek, Paul, (ed.) (1983). *Central Bank Views on Monetary Targeting*. Federal Reserve Bank of New York.
Meen, Geoffrey P. (1985). 'An econometric analysis of mortgage rationing.' U.K. Government Economic Service Working Paper, no. 79.
Milbourne, Ross (1987). 'Re-examining the buffer-stock model of money.' Economic Journal, *Conference Supplement*, vol. 97, pp. 130–42.
Miles, David K. and Wilcox, Joseph B. (1988). 'The transmission mechanism.' Bank of England, mimeo.
Miller, Marcus H. and Sprenkle, Case M. (1980). 'The precautionary demand for narrow and broad money.' *Economica*, vol. 47, no. 188, pp. 407–22.
Miller, Stephen M. (1988). 'Long-run and short-run money demands: an application of co-integration and error-correction modelling.' mimeo, (June).
Mills, Terry, C. (1983a). 'Composite monetary indicators for the United Kingdom; construction and empirical analyses.' *Bank of England Discussion Papers, Technical Series*, no. 3.
—— (1983b). 'The information content of the UK monetary components and aggregates.' *Bulletin of Economic Research*, vol. 35, no. 1, pp. 25–46.
Moore, George, R., Porter, Richard D. and Small, David H. (1988). 'Modeling the disaggregated demands for M2 and M1 in the 1980's: the US experience.' Paper presented on May 26 to the Federal Reserve Board Conference on Monetary Aggregates and Financial Sector Behavior in Interdependent Economies.
Moore, Basil, J. (1988a). 'The endogenous money supply.' *Journal of Post Keynesian Economics*, vol. 10, no. 3, pp. 372–85.
—— (1988b). *Horizontalists and Verticalists: The Macroeconomics of Credit Money*. Cambridge University Press.
—— (1989). 'A simple model of bank intermediation.' *Journal of Post Keynesian Economics*, forthcoming.
—— and Threadgold, Andrew (1985). 'Corporate bank borrowing in the U.K., 1965–1981, *Economica*, vol. 52, (February), pp. 65–78.
Moran, Michael (1984). *The Politics of Banking*. London: Macmillan.
Muscatelli, V. A. (1988). 'Alternative models of buffer stock money: an empirical investigation.' *Scottish Journal of Political Economy*, vol. 35, no. 1, pp. 1–21.
Niehans, Jurg (1981). 'The appreciation of sterling – causes, effects, policies.' Money Study Group Discussion Paper, mimeo (February).
Pavel, C. (1986). 'Securitization.' *Federal Reserve Bank of Chicago Economic Perspectives*, vol. 10, no. 4, pp. 16–31.
Persson, Torsten (1988). 'Credibility of macroeconomic policy: an introduction and a broad survey.' *European Economic Review*, vol. 32, pp. 519–32.
Phelps, Edmund S. (1968). 'Money wage dynamics and labor market equilibrium', *Journal of Political Economy*, vol. 76, (August), pp. 678–711.
Poole, William (1982). 'Federal Reserve operating procedures: a survey and evaluation of the historical record since October 1979.' *Journal of Money, Credit and Banking*, vol. 14, no 4, part 2, pp. 576–96.
Porter, Richard D. and Amanda Bayer (1983). 'A monetary perspective on underground economic activity in the United States.' *Federal Reserve Bulletin*, vol. 70, pp. 177–89.
Radecki, Lawrence (1982). 'Short-run monetary control: an analysis of some possible dangers.' *Federal Reserve Bank of New York Quarterly Review*. vol. 7, (Spring), pp. 1–10.
—— and Wenninger, John (1985). 'Recent instability in M1's velocity.' *Federal Reserve Bank of New York Quarterly Review*, (Autumn), pp. 16–22.
Rasche, Robert H. (1985). 'Interest rate volatility and alternative monetary control procedures.' *Federal Reserve Bank of San Francisco, Economic Review*. (Summer), pp. 46–63.
—— (1988). 'Demand functions for U.S. money and credit measures.' Paper presented at the Conference on 'Monetary Aggregates and Financial Sector Behavior in Interdependent Economies,' mimeo, Federal Reserve Board, Washington D.C., May 26/27.

—— and Meltzer Allan H. (1982). 'Is the Federal Reserve's monetary control policy misdirected?' arguing for the affirmative in the JMCB Debate, April 30, 1981, reprinted in the *Journal of Money, Credit and Banking*, vol. 14, no. 1, pp. 119–47.

—— and Johannes, James M. (1987). *Controlling the Growth of Monetary Aggregates*. Kluwer Academic Publishers.

Reserve Bank of Australia (1985). 'The Reserve Bank's domestic market operations.' mimeo, Sydney (May).

Reserve Bank of New Zealand (1986). *Financial Policy Reform*. Wellington, New Zealand: RBNZ.

—— (1987a). 'A layman's guide to monetary policy in the New Zealand context.' *Reserve Bank Bulletin*, vol. 50 (June), pp. 104–10.

—— (1987b). 'Post-election briefing paper to the Minister of Finance.' Special Paper, Wellington (August).

Richardson, Gordon (1978). 'Reflections on the conduct of monetary policy.' *Bank of England Quarterly Bulletin*, vol. 18, no. 1, pp. 51–8.

Roley, V. Vance (1985). 'Money demand predictability.' *Journal of Money, Credit and Banking*, vol. 17, no. 4, part 2, pp. 615–41.

—— (1986). 'Market perceptions of U.S. monetary policy since 1982.' *Federal Reserve Bank of Kansas City Economic Review*, (May), pp. 27–40.

Rosenblum, Harvey and Storin, Steven (1983). 'Interest rate volatility in historical perspective.' *Federal Reserve Bank of Chicago, Economic Review*, vol. 7 (January, February) pp. 10–9.

Roth, Howard L. (1986). 'Leading indicators of inflation.' *Federal Reserve Bank of Kansas City Economic Review*, (November), pp. 3–20.

Sargent, Thomas J. and Wallace, Neil (1975). '"Rational" expectations, the optimal monetary instrument, and the optimal money supply rule.' *Journal of Political Economy*, vol. 83, no. 2, pp. 241–54.

Schlesinger, Helmut, (1984). 'Zehn Jahre Geldpolitik mit einem Geldmengenziel.' In *Öffentliche Finanzen und Monetäre Ökonomie*. (ed. W. Gebauer). Frankfurt am Main: Fritz Knapp Verlag, pp. 123–47.

—— (1988). 'Kontinuität in den Zielen, Wandel in den Methoden.' *Herausforderungen der Wirtschaftspolitik*. (eds. W. Filc, L. Hubl and R. Pohl), Berlin: Duncker & Humblot, pp. 197–210.

Shaw, Edward S. (1973). *Financial Deepening in Economic Development*, New York: Oxford University Press.

Simpson, Thomas, D. (1984). 'Changes in the financial system: implications for monetary policy.' *Brookings Papers on Economic Activity*, no. 1, pp. 249–65.

Sims, Christopher A. (1972). 'Money, income and causality.' *American Economic Review*, vol. 62, no. 4, pp. 540–52.

Smith, David (1978). 'The demand for alternative monies in the UK, 1924–77', *National Westminster Bank Quarterly Review*, November 1978, pp. 35–49.

—— (1980). 'The monetary conundrum', *London Business School Economic Outlook*, vol. 5, no. 2, pp. 1–2.

Solomon, Anthony M. (1981). 'Financial innovation and monetary policy.' Paper presented before the joint luncheon of the American Economic and American Finance Associations, December 28, mimeo, (Federal Reserve Bank of New York).

—— (1984). 'Some problems and prospects for monetary policy in 1985', Remarks before the Money Marketeers of New York University, November 20th, mimeo, Federal Reserve Bank of New York.

Spencer, Grant and Carey, David (1988). 'Financial policy reform: the New Zealand experience.' Reserve Bank of New Zealand Discussion Paper, no. G88/1 (April).

Spindt, Paul A. and Tarhan, Vefa (1987). 'The Federal Reserve's new operating procedures: a post mortem.' *Journal of Monetary Economics*, vol. 19, pp. 107–23.

Sternlight, Peter, D. and Axilrod, Stephen, H. (1982). 'Is the Federal Reserve's monetary control policy misdirected?' arguing for the negative in the JMCB Debate, April 30, 1981, reprinted in the *Journal of Money, Credit and Banking*, vol. 14, no. 1 pp. 119–47.

Stevens, Glenn, Thorp, Susan and Anderson, John (1987). 'The Australian demand function for money: another look at stability.' Reserve Bank of Australia Research Discussion Paper, no. 8701.

Stiglitz, Joseph, E. and Weiss, Andrew (1981). 'Credit rationing in markets with imperfect information.' *American Economic Review*, vol 71, no. 3, pp. 393–410.

Summers, Lawrence H. (1986). 'Do we really know that financial markets are efficient?' In *Recent Developments in Corporate Finance*. (ed. J. Edwards *et al*). Cambridge University Press.

—— (1988). 'Comment' on B. T. McCallum (1988). *Journal of Money, Credit and Banking*, vol. 20, no. 3, part 2, pp. 472–6.

Suzuki, Yoshio (1986). *Money, Finance and Macroeconomic Performance in Contemporary Japan*. New Haven: Yale University Press.

—— (1988). 'Monetary policy in Japan-price stability and stable growth under the floating exchange rate regime.' Paper presented at the PACE/FMG Conference on Japanese Financial Growth in London, October.

Suzuki, Yoshio, Kuroda, Akio and Shirankawa, Hiroimichi (1988). 'Monetary control mechanism in Japan.' Paper presented at the Conference on Monetary Aggregates and Financial Sector Behavior in Interdependent Economies, at the Federal Reserve Board, Washington, D.C. (May).

Tamura, Tatsuya (1987). 'Monetary control in Japan.' Paper presented at the Second Surrey Monetary

Conference on Financial Innovation, Deregulation and the Control of Monetary Aggregates, University of Surrey, Guildford, April 8–10.

Taylor, Mark P. (1987). 'Financial innovation, inflation and the stability of the demand for broad money in the United Kingdom.' *Bulletin of Economic Research*, vol. 39, no. 3, pp. 225–33.

Thatcher, Margaret (1988). Parliamentary answers at Question Time on March 10th, as reported in *The Times*, March 11, 1988, p. 2.

Thomas, James, J. (1988). 'The politics of the black economy.' *Work, Employment and Society*, vol. 2, (June), pp. 169–90.

Tinsley, Peter A., Farr, Helen, T., Fries, Gerhard, Garrett, Bonnie and Muehlen, Peter Von Zur (1982). 'Policy robustness: specification and simulation of a monthly money market model.' *Journal of Money, Credit and Banking*, vol. 14, no. 4, part 2, pp. 829–56.

Tobin, James (1958). 'Liquidity preference as behavior towards risk.' *Review of Economic Studies*, vol. 25 (February), pp. 65–86.

—— (1963). 'Commercial banks as creators of "money".' Chapter 22 In *Banking and Monetary Studies*. (ed. D. Carson). Homewood, Illinois: Richard Irwin Inc.

—— (1983). 'Monetary policy: rules, targets and shocks.' *Journal of Money, Credit and Banking*, vol. 15, no. 4, pp. 506–18.

Treasury, Her Majesty's *Financial Statement and Budget Report*, (FSBR Red Book). London: HMSO (annually).

—— and Bank of England (1980). *Monetary Control*. London: HMSO, Cmnd. 7858.

Treasury and Civil Service Committee (1981). *Monetary Policy: Report*. London: HMSO.

Trehan, Bharat (1988). 'The practice of monetary targeting: a case study of the West German experience.' *Federal Reserve Bank of San Francisco, Economic Review*, pp. 30–44.

Ueda, Kazuo (1988). 'Financial deregulation and the demand for money in Japan.' Paper presented at the Conference on Monetary Aggregates and Financial Sector Behavior in Interdependent Economics, at the Federal Reserve Board, Washington D.C., May 26/27.

Vaciago, Giacomo (1985). 'Financial innovation and monetary policy: Italy *versus* the United States.' *Banca Nazionale del Lavoro Quarterly Review*, no. 155, pp. 309–26.

Volcker, Paul A. (1978). 'The role of monetary targets in an age of inflation.' *Journal of Monetary Economics*, vol. 4, pp. 329–39.

Wallich, Henry, C. (1984a). 'Recent techniques of monetary policy.' *Federal Reserve Bank of Kansas City Economic Review*, (May) pp. 21–30.

—— (1984b). 'A broad view of deregulation.' Remarks at the Conference on Pacific Basin Financial Reform organised by the Federal Reserve Bank of San Francisco, Dec 2nd, mimeo.

Walsh, Carl E. (1982). 'The Federal Reserve's operating procedures and interest rate fluctuations.' *Federal Reserve Bank of Kansas City Economic Review*, pp. 8–18.

—— (1984). 'Interest rate volatility and monetary policy.' *Journal of Money, Credit and Banking*, vol. 16, no. 2, pp. 133–50.

Walters, Alan (1986). *Britain's Economic Renaissance*, New York: Oxford University Press.

Wang, Richard W. (1980). 'The FOMC in 1979: introducing reserve targetting.' *Federal Reserve Bank of St. Louis Review*, vol. 62, no. 3, pp. 2–25.

Wenninger, John (1986). 'Responsiveness of interest rate spreads and deposit flows to changes in market rates.' *Federal Reserve Bank of New York Quarterly Review*, (Autumn), pp. 1–10.

—— (1988). 'Money demand – some long-run properties.' *Federal Reserve Bank of New York Quarterly Review*, (Spring), pp. 23–40.

—— and Radecki, Lawrence J. (1986). 'Financial transactions and the demand for M1.' *Federal Reserve Bank of New York Quarterly Review*, Summer, pp. 24–9.

White, Lawrence H. (1984). *Free Banking In Britain*, New York: Cambridge University Press.

White, William, R. (1976). 'The demand for money in Canada and the control of monetary aggregates.' Bank of Canada, mimeo.

Williamson, John, (1983). *The Exchange Rate System*, Washington: Institute for International Economics (revised).

Williamson, Stephen D. (1987). 'Financial intermediation, business failures, and real business cycles. *Journal of Political Economy*, vol. 95, no. 6, pp. 1196–216.

Willms, Manfred, (1983). 'The monetary decision process in the Federal Republic of Germany.' In *The Political Economy of Monetary Policy: National and International Aspects*. (ed. D. R. Hodgman). Federal Reserve Bank of Boston, pp. 34–58, also the 'Discussion' by H-J. Dudler, pp. 59–64.

Wojnilower, Albert M. (1980). 'The central role of credit crunches in recent financial history.' *Brookings Papers on Economic Activity*, no. 2, pp. 277–339.

Woodford, Michael (1988). 'Expectations, finance and aggregate instability.' Chapter 12. In *Finance Constraints, Expectations, and Macroeconomics*. (ed. M. Kohn and S-C. Tsiang). Oxford: Clarendon Press, pp. 230–61.

Wooley, John (1984). *Monetary Politics: The Federal Reserve and the Politics of Monetary Policy*, New York: Cambridge University Press.

4

UNEMPLOYMENT: A SURVEY*

Stephen Nickell

The unemployment rate is one of the most intensively discussed and analysed of all economic statistics. Along with the rate of growth of output and the rate of inflation, it is considered to be a key indicator of economic health. And for good reason. High unemployment reduces current output and aggregate income. It increases the inequality of the income distribution, since the unemployed lose more than the employed. It erodes a nation's human capital. Finally, it involves psychic costs, for people need to be needed. Though unemployment increases leisure, in many cases the value of this is partly or wholly offset by the pain of rejection.

What is unemployment? The unemployed consist of those individuals who are not currently working, yet are actively seeking work. The labour force consists of the unemployed and those in employment. The unemployment rate is the proportion of the labour force who are unemployed. To provide some factual background, we present in Figs. 1 and 2 a time series of the unemployment rate in the United States, the United Kingdom, Japan and West Germany along with that for the OECD as a whole. A number of features stand out. In the United States, there is a clearly defined cyclical pattern around a relatively stable trend. In the United Kingdom and West Germany, on the other hand, movements after the mid 1960s are dominated by a series of upward jumps followed by more or less partial recoveries. It is also clear that there are wide variations in the level of unemployment, both across countries and across decades. This latter fact is emphasised in Table 1, where we report recent unemployment patterns in a wide variety of OECD countries.

It is clear from these facts that theories of unemployment must address two questions. First, why does unemployment fluctuate in a fairly regular short-term fashion? Second, why do the broad levels of unemployment differ so dramatically across countries, and in some countries, across successive decades? It is probably true to say that more theorising about unemployment has been addressed to the former of these two questions than to the latter. Since most new theory is produced in the United States and the pattern of United States unemployment is dominated by cycles, this is perhaps not so surprising. However, this is only a matter of emphasis. Most theories of unemployment will explain both fluctuations and levels, and any deep separation of these two issues tends to be artificial.

Not surprisingly, a good deal of this survey is concerned with macroeconomic issues because unemployment is a general equilibrium phenomenon. The

* This chapter was first published in the ECONOMIC JOURNAL, vol 100, June 1990. The work was funded by the Economic and Social Research Council and the Esmee Fairburn Charitable Trust. I should like to thank Annalisa Cristini and Paul Kong for their assistance and George Alogoskoufis, Richard Layard, John Muellbauer, Andrew Oswald, Chris Pissarides and three referees for helpful comments on an earlier draft.

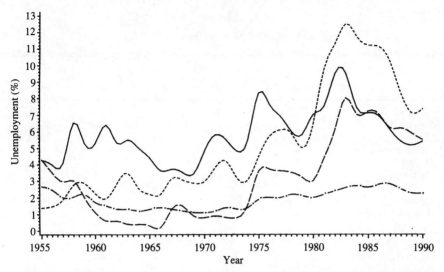

Fig. 1. Percentage of unemployment from 1955 to 1990. ——, United States; ----, United Kingdom; ————, Japan; ———, West Germany. (Source: as in Table 1.)

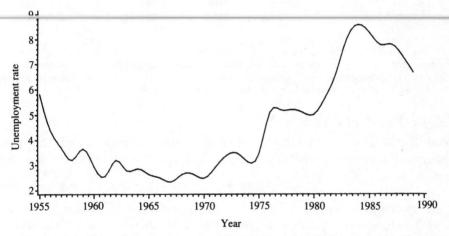

Fig. 2. OECD unemployment rate. Source: OECD *Labour Force Statistics* and *Main Economic Indicators*. The rate presented is the OECD labour force weighted average of the individual country rates (i.e. the OECD aggregate rate).

overlap with the macroeconomic survey in this series (Fischer, 1988) has, however, been kept to a minimum although there are, of necessity, some common discussions. In the first section, we look at competitive models and this is followed by a consideration of imperfect competition in the product market. The third section deals with imperfectly competitive labour markets and in the final section we discuss the macroeconomics of unemployment and cross-country comparisons.

I. COMPETITIVE MODELS OF UNEMPLOYMENT

In order to provide a consistent thread running through this survey, it helps to have a simple model to which we can refer.

Table 1

Unemployment in OECD Countries: 1960–90 (%)

		1960–8	1969–73	1974–9	1980–5	1986–90
BE	(Belgium)	2·35	2·38	6·32	11·28	10·27
DK	(Denmark)	1·46	0·95	6·02	10·00	9·33
FR	(France)	1·69	2·52	4·52	8·32	10·2
GE	(W. Germany)	0·71	0·84	3·20	5·95	6·04
IR	(Ireland)	4·98	5·76	6·77	11·64	15·50
IT	(Italy)	3·64	3·95	4·37	6·15	7·63
NL	(Netherlands)	1·14	2·05	5·05	10·05	9·46
SP	(Spain)	2·42	2·74	5·27	16·58	19·00
UK	(United Kingdom)	2·62	3·39	5·04	10·48	8·80
AL	(Australia)	2·17	2·04	5·02	7·64	7·40
NZ	(New Zealand)	0·16	0·28	0·67	4·17	6·06
CA	(Canada)	4·71	5·56	7·17	9·88	8·26
US	(United States)	4·74	4·86	6·68	8·00	5·79
JA	(Japan)	1·36	1·22	1·93	2·42	2·52
AU	(Austria)	1·96	1·40	1·78	3·23	3·33
FN	(Finland)	1·83	2·34	4·53	5·60	5·10
NW	(Norway)	2·01	1·66	1·82	2·55	3·11
SW	(Sweden)	1·64	2·22	1·88	2·83	1·89
SZ	(Switzerland)	0·06	0·01	1·08	1·92	2·37

These are OECD standardised rates, with the exception of Italy which is taken from the statistics prepared by the United States Department of Labor. Rates for,1989–90 are generated from OECD forecasts.

A Simple Theoretical Framework

Labour supply. There are a large number of identical households which supply labour and consume goods. Their aggregate labour supply takes the *log-linear* form

$$n^s = \beta_{01} + \beta_1(w-p) - \beta_1(w-p)^* - z, \tag{1}$$

where n = employment, w = wage, p = aggregate price, $(w-p)$ = real wage, $(w-p)^*$ = long run equilibrium real wage, z = other factors which tend to reduce labour supply. This is a simplified version of the standard life-cycle model as set out, for example, in Lucas and Rapping (1969) and, more formally, in Sargent (1979). The idea is that labour supply is increasing in the current real wage as it fluctuates relative to its long run equilibrium level. The substitution effect thus dominates in the short run as individuals concentrate their work effort in periods when the real wage is high relative to its average level. In the long run, labour supply is completely inelastic. The implications of this simplifying assumption are discussed later.

The z variables are particularly important. Aside from tastes and the like, they would particularly include the generosity of the unemployment benefit system as measured by the benefit to income ratio. As benefits rise, the supply of labour at any given wage will tend to fall. It is also worth remarking that in the standard life-cycle model, the (negative of the) real interest rate will appear in z. When the real interest rate rises, future real wages fall in present value terms relative to the current wage, and hence current labour supply increases.

Since we wish to focus on unemployment, we may transform (1) into an unemployment equation by supposing that the labour force is constant. The unemployed are those moving from job to job, plus those for whom the current wage is higher than their reservation wage.[1] So if l is the log labour force, then the unemployment rate corresponding to labour supply, u^s, is given by

$$u^s = l - n^s$$

or, from (1),
$$u^s = \beta_0 - \beta_1(w-p) + \beta_1(w-p)* + z, \qquad (2)$$

where $\beta_0 = l - \beta_{01}$.

Goods demand. There are $i = 1 \ldots F$ goods which are imperfect substitutes. Household utilities are symmetric in these and total demand for the ith good, Y_i, is given by

$$Y_i = (P_i/P)^{-\theta} Y/F \quad (i = 1 \ldots F), \qquad (3)$$

where $a_0 = \log(\gamma) - \log(1-\gamma)$. In order to concentrate on unemployment, we redefine demand in terms of deviations from full capacity output, $\bar{y}$. The latter is defined as

$$Y = \frac{\gamma}{1-\gamma} M/P, \qquad (4)$$

where M is the stock of money.[2]

Firms. There are $i = 1 \ldots F$ firms with identical technologies which have the constant returns form

$$Y_i = N_i^{\alpha} K_i^{(1-\alpha)} \exp(\epsilon_p), \qquad (5)$$

where N_i = employment, K_i = capital stock (fixed), ϵ_p = technology shock (mean zero).

If the firms behave competitively, the condition for maximum profit may be written as

$$P_i/P = \frac{W}{\alpha P} (N_i/K_i)^{1-\alpha} \exp(-\epsilon_p) \quad (i = 1 \ldots F). \qquad (6)$$

---

[1] We have already defined unemployed individuals as those who are seeking work. In this context we must suppose that they are looking for work at wages higher than those currently on offer. If wages are uniform across the economy and are known to be so, this is obviously a fruitless activity. So either we must suppose that the 'unemployed' in this framework are not looking for work and so are not truly unemployed by our definition, or we must suppose that lying behind this simple aggregate model is a labour market with some inter-sectoral stochastic variation leading to cross-section wage variability and search, none of which is made explicit (see Lucas and Prescott, 1974, for example). Either way round, unemployment is essentially 'voluntary'.

[2] These results follow from a household (index j) utility function of the form

$$U_j = \left\{ F^{1/(1-\theta)} \left[\sum_{i=1}^{F} C_{ij}^{(\theta-1)/\theta} \right]^{\theta/(\theta-1)} \right\}^{\gamma} (M_j'/P)^{1-\gamma},$$

where
$$P = \left[\frac{1}{F} \sum_{i=1}^{F} P_i^{(1-\theta)} \right]^{1/(1-\theta)}$$

$$Y_i = \sum_j C_{ij}, \quad Y = \left(\sum_i \sum_j P_i C_{ij} \right)/P.$$

Equation (4) also incorporates money market equilibrium, that is $\sum_j M_j' = M$. See Blanchard and Kiyotaki (1987) for more details.

On the basis of this, we are now in a position to write down the aggregate model.

An Aggregate Competitive Model

Demand side. From (4) and the aggregate version of (5) we have, in logs

$$y = a_0 + (m - p), \tag{7}$$

$$y - k = \alpha(n - k) + \epsilon_p, \tag{8}$$

where $a_0 = \log(\gamma) - \log(1 - \gamma)$. In order to concentrate on unemployment, we redefine demand in terms of deviations from full capacity output, $\bar{y}$. The latter is defined as

$$\bar{y} - k = \alpha(l - k), \tag{9}$$

where the productivity shock is set equal to zero. Demand relative to full capacity, σ, is now defined as

$$\sigma = y - \bar{y} \tag{10}$$

and (7), (8) can be rewritten as

$$\sigma = a_0 + (m - p) - \bar{y}, \tag{11}$$

$$\sigma = -\alpha u + \epsilon_p. \tag{12}$$

Since the economy is symmetric in all goods, $P_i = P$, all i and hence the maximum profit condition, (6), can be written in logs as

$$p - w = \alpha_0 + (1 - \alpha)(n - k) - \epsilon_p \quad (\alpha_0 = -\log\alpha), \tag{13}$$

which is simply the aggregate labour demand function. This can be rewritten in terms of unemployment as

$$p - w = \alpha_0 - (1 - \alpha)u - (1 - \alpha)(k - l) - \epsilon_p. \tag{14}$$

This has price as the dependent variable because it enables us to extend the model conveniently to an imperfectly competitive product market. Indeed we shall generally refer to this as the pricing rule, while recognising its inappropriateness for the present competitive context.

Under the competitive labour market assumption, $u^s = u$ and consequently the labour supply equation (2) can be written as a wage equation of the form

$$w - p = (w - p)^* + 1/\beta_1(\beta_0 + z - u). \tag{15}$$

The basic macro-model now consists of equations (11), (12), (14), (15), which determine u, σ, w and p at given levels of k, z, ϵ_p, $m - \bar{y}$. In order to separate the long run equilibrium from short run fluctuations, we suppose that both m and z are subject to shocks of the form

$$m = m^* + \epsilon_m, \quad z = z^* + \epsilon_z.$$

We define long run equilibrium u^*, σ^*, w^*, p^* by setting $\epsilon_p = \epsilon_m = \epsilon_z = 0$. Solving yields

$$u^* = \beta_0 + z^* \tag{16}$$

$$(w-p)^* = -\alpha_0 + (1-\alpha) u^* + (1-\alpha)(k-l) \tag{17}$$

$$\sigma^* = -\alpha u^* \tag{18}$$

$$\sigma^* = a_0 + (m^* - p^*) - \bar{y}. \tag{19}$$

A number of features of this long run equilibrium are worth noting. Unemployment depends only on the labour supply variables, z^*. Capital accumulation influences real wages but not unemployment and the money stock only affects the price level. The fact that unemployment is unaffected by capital accumulation is a consequence of the long run zero elasticity of labour supply. Suppose, for example, that labour supply is backward bending in the long run, so that (1) may be rewritten as

$$n^s = \beta_{01} + \beta_1(w-p) - \beta_2(w-p)^* - z, \quad \beta_2 > \beta_1. \tag{1a}$$

Then equilibrium unemployment becomes

$$u^* = \frac{\beta_0 + z^* + (\beta_2 - \beta_1)(k-l-\alpha_0)}{1 - (\beta_2 - \beta_1)(1-\alpha)}. \tag{16a}$$

So, as capital accumulation proceeds, long run unemployment rises, essentially because of the income effect on labour supply. Such an effect is probably an undesirable property of any model of unemployment, since it is inconsistent with the absence of any trend in unemployment over the last century.[3]

Turning to the short run of the model, we obtain

$$u - u^* = \frac{\epsilon_z - \beta_1 \epsilon_p}{1 + \beta_1(1-\alpha)}. \tag{20}$$

So unemployment fluctuations in this kind of competitive model derive from productivity and labour supply shocks. Nominal shocks have no effect because unemployment is determined solely by the price setting equation (14) and the wage equation (15), that is, by labour demand and labour supply. Nominal shocks have no impact on either of these schedules and cannot, therefore, influence unemployment. This is the foundation of the real business cycle model which is thus our first substantive topic.

The Real Business Cycle Model

As the name indicates, this model is essentially concerned with fluctuations. Furthermore, as in the seminal paper of Kydland and Prescott (1982), the

---

[3] This effect does, of course, depend on the labour force not adjusting with labour supply. If we follow Lucas and Rapping (1969) and define the labour force as

$$l = \beta'_{01} + (\beta_1 - \beta_2)(w-p)^*,$$

then the effect disappears.

fundamental source of these fluctuations is the productivity shock, ϵ_p. Since that time, there has been a veritable explosion of work along these lines, the basic idea being to see how much can be explained within a strictly competitive paradigm. The focus is very much on the United States economy which, as we have already seen, has been dominated by cyclical fluctuations in the post-war period.

In our discussion of this model, we concentrate on a number of specific areas where potential problems may arise. These include the sources of persistence, the size of the labour supply elasticity, β_1, the sources of the productivity shocks and the impact of government expenditure.

The Sources of Persistence

As we can see from the time series in Fig. 1, unemployment fluctuations exhibit a great deal of serial correlation. What can explain this? The most obvious possibility is that productivity shocks themselves are serially correlated (see Kydland and Prescott, 1982, for example, or King et al., 1988, for a more comprehensive analysis). At first sight this seems quite plausible, at least to anyone who has experienced the residual serial correlation which appears when measures of output are regressed on sets of input measures, at any level of aggregation. However, until autonomous productivity shocks are explicitly identified, it is rather difficult to go any further. We shall have more to say on this in a later section.

A second possibility derives from costs of adjustment in factor demands. In the original Kydland and Prescott paper, this took the form of delays in the implementation of investment plans. It is clear, however, that standard employment adjustment costs will do the trick. In such a model, the aggregate labour demand equation (13) will take the form

$$p - w = \alpha_0 (1 - \alpha) \left[(1 + \lambda) n - \lambda n_{-1} - k \right] - \epsilon_p, \qquad (13a)$$

where λ is increasing in costs of adjustment. Unemployment fluctuations then follow the pattern

$$(u - u^*) = \frac{(1 - \alpha) \lambda \beta_1}{1 + \beta_1 (1 + \lambda)(1 - \alpha)} (u - u^*)_{-1} + \frac{\epsilon_z - \beta_1 \epsilon_p}{1 + \beta_1 (1 + \lambda)(1 - \alpha)}. \qquad (20a)$$

Comparison with (20) then immediately reveals that persistence is increasing in λ and hence in the level of adjustment costs.

Inventory dynamics are a third possibility. In response to a positive productivity shock, inventories will rise, leading to lower output and employment in the future as the excess inventories are consumed. For our present purpose, this is not very helpful since this tends to generate negative serial correlation. Positive serial correlation can however be generated via capital accumulation (see Long and Plosser, 1983, for example). A positive productivity shock leads to increased output, saving and hence increases in future capital and therefore future output. As Fischer (1988) indicates, this effect is unlikely to be large.

Habit formation in household utility functions provides yet a further possibility, for then current labour supply will depend on last period's employment. Kydland and Prescott (1982) allow for this kind of effect. Finally once we explicitly allow for the processes by which workers find jobs and firms fill vacancies, this will automatically generate dynamics. Such general equilibrium search models will be considered in more detail in due course.

The Size of the Short-run Labour Supply Elasticity

It is clear from (20) that in order to translate productivity shocks into unemployment fluctuations, we must have a sufficiently large short run labour supply elasticity, β_1. Given real wage fluctuations, it must be large enough to generate the appropriate fluctuations in the supply of labour. To see the sort of thing that is required, note the average cyclical (detrended) movements in log hours per year and log real wages for male heads of household during the 1970s, reported in Table 2. The numbers indicate that if these are to be consistent with movements along a short run labour supply curve, a short run

Table 2

Average Changes in Detrended Log Hours, Log Real Wages *

| | All observations (1,531) | | |
Date	(1) Change in log hours	(2) Change in log wage	(3) Ratio (1)/(2)
1970–3	0·016	0·017	0·94
1974–5	−0·028	−0·030	0·93
1976–7	0·014	0·010	1·40
1978–9	−0·016	−0·021	0·76
Weighted average	—	—	0·99

* Panel Survey of Income Dynamics (male heads of households, 21–64); the numbers are derived from Abowd and Card (1983), table 2.

real wage elasticity of around unity is required for this group. (For similar evidence referring to aggregate employment, see Kennan, 1988.) Luckily, *for this same group of individuals*, we have a lot of relevant evidence. MaCurdy (1981), Altonji (1986) and Ham (1986) all present estimates and their numbers indicate that the true elasticity is very likely to be between zero and 0·5. It would therefore appear that the estimated short-run elasticity is simply not big enough (see also Hall, 1980; Ashenfelter, 1984; Nickell, 1987). Ham (1986) pursues this issue further and finds that if individuals experience unemployment in any particular year, hours of work in that year do not lie on their labour supply curve. The status of these microestimates of short run labour supply elasticities is, however, open to dispute. We know the measurement error problem is very serious and since hourly earnings are typically computed as annual earnings divided by measured hours, investigators must rely heavily on their instruments to remove the spurious negative correlation between hours and hourly earnings. Nevertheless, the most sophisticated micro investigation to date (Abowd and Card, 1989) finds little support for a labour supply interpretation of earnings and hours movements.

On the question of the macro and micro discrepancy, Heckman (1984) points out that if the macro-elasticities and the micro-elasticities do not refer to the same groups, this kind of evidence is not valid. Although this objection applies to the evidence in Ashenfelter (1984), for example, it does not apply to the numbers discussed above which refer to the same individuals. More subtle composition effects, such as those described in Heckman and MaCurdy (1988), may however, enable even this discrepancy to be explained.

Another way of explaining the macro-micro discrepancy is advanced in Hansen (1985) and Rogerson (1988). They develop models involving non-convexities in labour supply (for example, fixed costs of going to work, see also Hall, 1987a). This, when combined with labour contracts, generates a high aggregate labour supply response even though individuals have an apparently low willingness to substitute working hours intertemporally. However, the evidence of Abowd and Card (1987) is not favourable to this form of contract model although the results of Beaudry and DiNardo (1989) are somewhat more positive.

Another aspect of the life-cycle model which is relevant here is the fact that if we have additive intertemporal separability in household utilities, then consumption and leisure must move together so long as the real wage remains unchanged (and they are both normal, see Barro and King, 1984). It is this outcome which causes the rejection of the intertemporal substitution model in Mankiw *et al.* (1985), although it could also be interpreted as a rejection of additive separability. Altonji (1982), Eichenbaum *et al.* (1988) also produce negative evidence although Alogoskoufis (1987) is rather more enthusiastic.

What are Productivity Shocks?

Presumably productivity shocks refer to factors such as the introduction of new products or technological innovations. Detailed evidence on the sources of these shocks is, however, in short supply. Prescott (1986) simply suggests that they might be synonymous with fluctuations in total factor productivity as measured by the Solow 'residual'. There is some doubt as to whether such fluctuations can be thought of as reflecting exogenous technology shocks. The Solow residual tends to be strongly procyclical. This is typically interpreted as arising from labour hoarding with workers simply supplying more effort in booms, when there is more work to be done. In other words, these fluctuations simply represent the response to shocks from other quarters rather than autonomous movements. (See Mankiw, 1989 and Hall, 1987b for further discussion, and Hamilton, 1983 for an analysis of the relevance of oil price shocks.)

Another approach started in 1982 when Lilien noted the positive correlation between unemployment fluctuations and inter-industry 'turbulence', as measured by the standard deviation of employment changes across sectors. Further examination of this correlation and related issues appears in Evans (1987), Davis (1987), Topel (1986), Rogerson (1987) and Holzer (1989a). The general idea is that autonomous intersectoral demand shifts lead to expansion in some industries and contraction in others. If the supply of labour to the expanding industries is inelastic in the short run, then employment will fall by more in the contracting industries than it rises in the expanding industries. Unemployment will then rise. During this process, it is clear that vacancies will also increase, as there is essentially a short run increase in mismatch. In fact as Abraham and Katz (1986) point out, vacancies fall as unemployment rises. Furthermore, Murphy and Topel (1987a) note that as unemployment rises, intersectoral movements of labour tend to decline although, as the work of Loungani and Rogerson (1989) indicates, this is by no means undisputed. Nevertheless the balance of the evidence tends to suggest that both unemployment and turbulence tend to rise and fall simultaneously as the consequence of other shocks, rather than the latter causing the former. Finally, it is worth noting that once oil shocks are controlled for, the turbulence–unemployment correlation tends to disappear in any event (see Loungani, 1986).

Temporary Shifts in Government Purchases

Although real business-cycle models tend to focus on productivity shocks, there is general agreement that a temporary expansion of government purchases will lead to a reduction in unemployment (see Barro, 1981, for example). The question then arises as to the mechanism which brings this about in the competitive context. The answer has to be via the real interest rate effect on labour supply. In response to the increase in government purchases and the consequent increase in demand for goods and money, real interest rates rise. As we have already noted, in a life-cycle context working today then becomes more attractive than working tomorrow, labour supply expands and unemployment falls. Evidence on this effect is not clear-cut. Neither Altonji (1982) nor Lucas and Rapping (1969) obtain any positive results and none of the microeconometric studies (e.g. Altonji, 1986; MaCurdy, 1981, or Ham, 1986) even bother to investigate this issue. Hall (1980) produces some positive results but only by forcing the real wage and real interest rate effects to be the same. Only Alogoskoufis (1987) appears to produce any significant favourable evidence. This interpretation of the mechanism therefore remains open to doubt.

Alternative Competitive Models Generating Real Fluctuations

General equilibrium search models. These represent a comprehensive attempt to get behind the notions of supply and demand in the labour market. The idea is actually to model the process by which unemployed workers find jobs, and employers with unfilled jobs find workers. Although we include this discussion under the competitive models head, this is not quite correct since wage setting, following job matches between workers and firms, is almost bound to involve some element of bilateral monopoly (see Mortensen, 1982, for example).

The general structure of such models (see Diamond, 1981, 1982; Pissarides, 1985; Howitt, 1988, for example) is to start by specifying job-matching and job separation processes and then to allow atomistic firms and workers to maximise subject to these matching and separation technologies. Unemployment exists in equilibrium because of the break-up of job matches which provides a flow into unemployment. These separations result from firm specific shocks, hence the affinity to the real business cycle framework.

Unlike the standard real business cycle model, however, the equilibrium level of unemployment is typically not optimal. Sub-optimality arises because of various kinds of externalities. For example, increased hiring by one firm reduces unemployment and thus raises the costs of hiring for other firms. Alternatively more search effort by firms makes it cheaper for workers to find jobs and vice-versa.

With regard to dynamics, models of this type exhibit persistence in response to serially uncorrelated shocks. If there is a favourable shock hiring increases and unemployment falls. As productivity returns to normal, the lower unemployment rate reduces hiring until unemployment returns to normal (see Pissarides, 1985, for a complete dynamic analysis which includes an explicit treatment of vacancies as well as unemployment). Overall, these models add a welcome touch of realism to the analysis of unemployment in an equilibrium context.[4]

Nonlinear deterministic models of fluctuations. The real business-cycle model can be thought of as essentially a linear difference equation model driven by stochastic shocks. An alternative, discussed in Grandmont (1985), is to have endogenous fluctuations driven by periodically varying, self-fulfilling expectations. The following simple model is taken from Grandmont (1989). Consider an overlapping generations model where individuals, who live two periods, work and save in the first period and consume their savings in the second. Suppose N_t is first-period labour supply which produces output $Y_t = N_t$. Consumption in the second period is C_{t+1} which must, in equilibrium, equal the output produced by the next generation, since goods cannot be stored. Then the individual's choice problem is to solve

$$\text{Max } V_1(N^* - N_t) + V_2(C_{t+1})$$

$$\text{s.t. } P_t N_t = P_{t+1} C_{t+1},$$

P being the present value price of goods. The first order condition reduces to

$$N_t V_1'(N^* - N_t) = C_{t+1} V_2'(C_{t+1}) \tag{21}$$

and since, in equilibrium, $N_t = Y_t, C_{t+1} = Y_{t+1}$ and V_1 is monotone, (21) can be rewritten as a difference equation

$$Y_t = \chi(Y_{t+1}). \tag{22}$$

The existence of cycles depends crucially on the shape of the function χ. If intertemporal substitution dominates, χ is increasing and cycles of period greater than 1 cannot exist. However, if there is extreme conflict between

---

[4] A complete analysis is in Pissarides (1989). Good surveys are to be found in Mortensen (1986) or Sargent (1987).

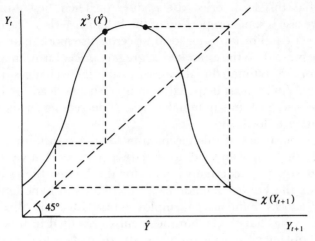

Fig. 3. A χ function with conflicting income and substitution effects.

substitution and income effects, χ could have the shape given in Fig. 3. It is clear from this figure that $\chi(\chi[\chi(\hat{Y})]) = \chi^3(\hat{Y}) < \hat{Y}$. However, it is easy to check that for Y close to zero, $\chi^3(Y) > Y$. So the function χ^3 has a fixed point Y^*, i.e. $\chi^3(Y^*) = Y^*$. This demonstrates the existence of a cycle of order 3, that is, one in which output returns to the same level every third period. This cycle would be based on a certain pattern of expectations concerning future prices which is self-fulfilling. Incidentally, Grandmont also notes that by a theorem of Sarkovskii, the existence of a cycle of order 3 implies infinitely many cycles, with at least one of every order greater than 3.

Research is now proceeding into the possibility of such cycles without rather extreme assumptions concerning income effects, by considering productive investment (see Woodford, 1986; Reichlin, 1986; Farmer, 1986; and Benhabib and Laroque, 1988, for example). The results are of some interest, but until we have some empirical evidence on such models they are unlikely to enter mainstream thinking on unemployment.

The Role of Nominal Shocks

The competitive model set out at the beginning of this section allows no role for nominal shocks in generating unemployment fluctuations (see equation (20)). The classic method for generating such a role in the competitive context is to allow for the absence of full information, as in the seminal paper of Lucas (1972). Thus there are local labour markets and on the supply side of the market, workers are concerned with the aggregate price level, which they do not know prior to making their labour supply decisions. Firms, on the other hand, are only concerned with the price in their own market. There are also local shocks and aggregate shocks. Suppose there is an unexpected increase in the money supply. Then prices and wages rise in the local labour market and workers have to estimate the change in the aggregate price. Since local prices may rise either because of general inflation or because of a local shock, workers are unsure what this local price rise is due to. Their best estimate of the aggregate price rise is some proportion of the local price rise. The consequence in labour market equilibrium is for local prices to rise more than wages which themselves rise more than the estimated aggregate price. Firms' real wages thus fall whereas workers' estimated real wages rise and these changes support a rise in employment. Only unanticipated nominal shocks lead to employment changes whose size, per unit nominal shock, is decreasing in the variance of aggregate relative to local shocks.

These two implications of this mechanism for the transmission of nominal shocks have both been subjected to extensive empirical investigation. For example Barro (1977), Liederman (1980) for the United States and Attfield *et al.* (1981) for the United Kingdom, all consider the hypothesis that only unanticipated shocks influence unemployment. However, there are good reasons for believing that the favourable results presented in these papers are very fragile. Problems of specification (Small, 1979; Gordon, 1982; Mishkin, 1982; Alogoskoufis and Pissarides, 1983; Pesaran, 1983) and identification (Pudney, 1982) bedevil this kind of empirical testing. However, the weight of the evidence is against the basic hypothesis (that only unanticipated shocks matter).

The second implication, that the real effects of nominal shocks are larger, per unit of shock, the smaller is the variance of the shocks, has been subject to a number of cross country investigations (Lucas, 1973; Froyen and Waud, 1980; Alberro, 1981) which have not provided any strong evidence against. However, as Ball *et al.* (1988) indicate, alternative interpretations can be placed on the data correlation.

This kind of asymmetric information framework is not the only way to introduce non-neutralities into a competitive model. An alternative is to introduce restrictions on the technology of monetary transactions such as the so-called cash-in-advance constraint. Essentially money received from sales only accrues after agents have made their consumption decisions. Hence the consumption decision is constrained by the existing stock of money. In such models, changes in money growth, even if anticipated, typically have real effects although they tend to go 'the wrong way', that is faster money growth is associated with lower output (see Eichenbaum and Singleton, 1986 or Lucas, 1987, for a general discussion).

It is clear that generating real effects from nominal shocks in the competitive context is quite tricky. In a world where all agents are price takers, generating what, in effect, reduces to price stickiness, is always going to require considerable ingenuity. However, once we allow agents to set prices, then the whole process moves into the domain of behaviour and price stickiness can be analysed in a relatively standard fashion. So it is natural to move on to models of imperfect competition, which we do in the next section.

II. IMPERFECT COMPETITION IN THE PRODUCT MARKET

In this section, we allow for price setting behaviour on the part of firms but retain a competitive labour market. As a consequence, unemployment will be of the same type as in the previous section. That is, the unemployed are simply those who are looking for work at wages higher than those currently on offer (see footnote 1) and unemployment is voluntary. Since we are essentially concerned with fluctuations, this is not a serious problem. Generally speaking, the same pattern of fluctuations would be observed even if we had a non-competitive labour market and unemployment was, to some extent, involuntary. This is not to say, however, that non-competitive elements may not magnify the fluctuations under certain circumstances (see Ball and Romer, 1987, for example).

In terms of our basic model, the switch from price taking to price setting behaviour merely implies that the price equation (14) now has the form

$$p - w = \alpha_0' - (1 - \alpha) u - (1 - \alpha) (k - l) - \epsilon_p, \qquad (14a)$$

where $\alpha_0' = -\log \alpha + \log [\theta/(\theta - 1)] > \alpha_0$. Thus, the price mark-up on marginal cost rises by the standard imperfect competition term, $\theta/(\theta - 1)$, θ being the demand elasticity. This will only influence unemployment if the long run labour supply schedule is not vertical as in Blanchard and Kiyotaki (1987), for example. In this paper, the long run labour supply schedule is upward sloping and hence employment falls (unemployment rises) as θ falls. This corresponds to the case in equation (16a) where $\beta_1 > \beta_2$ which implies u^* is increasing in α_0.

If unemployment shifts with the demand elasticity, this may allow government purchases to influence unemployment by influencing the elasticity of demand facing firms. Thus, if the government sets the level of nominal purchases at the firm level, this effectively introduces a unit elastic element into demand. Then any increase in government purchases (relative to the money stock) will tend to reduce the 'average' elasticity facing firms, raise the mark-up and hence raise unemployment (see Wren-Lewis, 1985, for example).

However, the key implication of introducing non-competitive firms is to open up the possibility of nominal inertia in price setting. This refers to prices responding sluggishly to other nominal changes, particularly shifts in wage costs. Thus suppose, for example, that prices in our basic model are set before wages are revealed, so that the price equation (14a) becomes

$$p - w^e = \alpha_0' - (1 - \alpha) u - (1 - \alpha) (k - l) - \epsilon_p. \qquad (14b)$$

Prices are set on the basis of expected rather than actual wages. Then even if there are no productivity or labour supply shocks ($\epsilon_p = \epsilon_z = 0$) and even if we assume rational expectations, unemployment will still fluctuate because of money supply shocks, with equation (20) taking the form

$$u - u^* = -\beta_1 \alpha \epsilon_m, \qquad (20a)$$

ϵ_m being the money supply shock. Furthermore, serial correlation in unemployment can be generated via the mechanisms already discussed in the previous section (employment adjustment costs, for example).

Nominal Inertia in Price Setting

Costs of changing prices. In order to analyse nominal inertia in price setting, we first focus on the costs of changing prices. These costs are not well documented although the fact that some costs must be incurred goes without saying. Prices must be relabelled, catalogues and menus reprinted. Such costs are often termed 'menu' costs. An additional cost, emphasised by Okun (1981), for example, is that associated with customer dissatisfaction if prices change too frequently or erratically. The importance of all this is hard to gauge. As Carlton (1986) notes, there are many changes in price which are very small (less than $\frac{1}{2}\%$) which would tend to indicate that menu costs are small. However, as Carlton (1985) emphasises, the extent to which firms allow fluctuations in demand to be absorbed by changes in delivery delays rather than price changes is considerable, so some significant costs of price change must be perceived. Furthermore, as Mankiw (1985), and Akerlof and Yellen (1985) note, since the optimal price is a stationary point, deviations of price away from the optimum only have second order costs for the firm. However, such deviations may have first order effects because of the negative externality involved. The stickiness in one firm's price contributes to aggregate price rigidity which exacerbates fluctuations in output thereby harming all the other firms (see Ball *et al.*, 1988 or Ball and Romer, 1989*b*). However, Ball and Romer also demonstrate that although the fluctuations generated may be first order, the average welfare losses caused are only second order; that is, of the same order as the private costs to the firms generated by the price rigidity causing the fluctuation.

Quadratic adjustment costs. Costs of changing prices have a fixed element, the menu cost, and a smooth element arising, perhaps, from customer dissatisfaction. The latter element is emphasised in the quadratic adjustment cost model developed in Rotemberg (1982) and combined with employment adjustment costs by Dolado (1986). This combination has several consequences. First, if the price adjustment costs have the simple form $b_p(p_{it}-p_{it-1})^2$, then lagged prices will appear in the price setting equation. However, it might be argued that customer dissatisfaction only arises if the firm deviates from expected aggregate inflation. Then adjustment costs would have the form, $b_p[p_{it}-p_{it-1}-(p_t^e-p_{t-1})]^2$ and only price surprises would appear in the price setting equation. This latter would seem more realistic for, as Sims (1988) notes,

'But if there were such a thing as an economy with a rock-solid inflation rate of 40%, plus or minus 2%, per year, institutions would surely adapt, so that prices would be announced in catalogs and wage contracts with smooth growth paths paralleling the smooth aggregate price path. Nominal rigidity would set in about this price path in much the same form as we see around the zero inflation rate in low-inflation economies' (p. 77).

The second consequence of the interaction between price and employment adjustment costs is that prices will depend positively on both the level *and the change* of economic activity. Thus, as demand expands, employment adjustment costs ensure that marginal costs rise by more in the short-run than in the long-run and this effect is transmitted directly to prices. Third, the more important are employment adjustment costs, the faster prices must adjust. This arises because employment adjustment costs make output shifts more sluggish and prices must change in order to compensate.

Fixed costs of changing prices. These will automatically lead to prices changing only at discrete intervals. Even if these intervals are short at the micro level, this may lead to considerable stickiness at the aggregate level as the delays are added over a large number of stages of production (see Blanchard, 1987, for both theory *and* evidence). This effect is exacerbated if there is staggering, that is, firms changing prices at different times. The question of when staggering can be an equilibrium phenomenon is a tricky one, however, in the light of the fact that, typically, the higher the proportion of a firm's competitors who change their prices, the bigger the incentive for the firm to change its own price. This 'bunching' tendency may be counteracted by firm specific shocks (see Ball and Romer, 1989*a*). Alternative possibilities are discussed in Ball and Cecchetti (1988), and Parkin (1986).

A second approach to this issue is based on the Barro (1972) and Sheshinski and Weiss (1977) analysis of the optimal price setting behaviour of a firm facing fixed costs of changing prices. If the firm operates in an environment where aggregate inflation proceeds at a constant rate, the optimal policy is an (S, s) rule. Thus if the firm's optimal price without adjustment costs is p_i^*, which rises at the constant aggregate inflation rate, the strategy is to raise its price p_i to a level $S + p_i^*$ each time p_i^* reaches $p_i - s$, S, s being constants depending on the cost of adjustment and aggregate inflation. The optimality of such (S, s) rules depends crucially on the specific assumptions of the model and is only robust to very special extensions (see Sheshinski and Weiss, 1983 or Benabou, 1989). Furthermore, if nominal demand in the economy rises smoothly, Caplin and Spulber (1987) demonstrate that the aggregate price level rises in proportion even if individual firms are only raising prices at discrete intervals according to an (S, s) rule. There is, then, no aggregate price inertia and neutrality prevails. This result breaks down, however, if nominal demand falls as well as rises or if it jumps. Possible consequences are discussed in Tsiddon (1987) and in Blanchard and Fischer (1989, chapter 8), the overall conclusion being that aggregate prices again exhibit some inertia.

In general, therefore, fixed costs of adjustment will lead to nominal inertia in aggregate price setting but the precise analytical form of this inertia is hard to discern, except under certain special cases. One point, however, does seem to emerge. The faster and more smoothly nominal demand is rising, the closer one gets to the Caplin–Spulber neutrality result. So it seems possible that the higher is the general level of inflation, the less important is the role of price inertia (see also Ball *et al.*, 1988). This is essentially because prices are rising more frequently and so remain fixed over shorter intervals.

Overall, therefore, imperfect competition in the product market allows the introduction of a sound behavioural foundation for price stickiness which, in its turn, enables nominal shocks to generate real fluctuations. The extent to which nominal as opposed to real shocks are the predominant cause of economic fluctuations remains an open question (see Shapiro, 1987, and Blanchard and Quah, 1987, for some preliminary work on sorting this out).

III. IMPERFECT COMPETITION IN THE LABOUR MARKET

If wages were determined in a more or less competitive fashion and this was a transparently obvious feature of labour markets, it is unlikely that unemployment and unemployment statistics would excite a great deal of interest. Indeed, proponents of the real business cycle approach do not devote much space to questions of unemployment because if everyone is on their labour supply function, unemployment is not a very important indicator.[5] However, the fact that unemployment in many countries has been two or three times higher throughout the 1980s than it was throughout the 1960s is hard for most people to square with the notion of a competitive labour market, particularly when such a high proportion of the unemployed have very long durations[6] and live in relative poverty. Indeed, for many, it is transparently obvious, and has been so since the 1930s, that unemployment reflects a waste of resources and severely penalises those who are subjected to it, mainly unskilled and semi-skilled workers.[7] Not surprisingly this has given rise to a variety of theories of non-competitive wage determination, which we consider in this section.

Nominal Inertia in Wage Setting

As with nominal price stickiness, nominal inertia in wage setting is important because it provides a transmission mechanism for demand shocks. It is essentially non-competitive because to generate a convincing theory of such nominal inertia, the agents who set wages must be identified. As with price setting, if there are fixed costs associated with changing or renegotiating wages, then we will observe wage changes only at discrete intervals. Since this is what we do observe, this notion has some appeal.

Most of the work in this area has been concerned with setting out the consequences of nominal wage stickiness rather than its causes, although presumably models based on fixed costs of adjustment could easily be constructed. Fischer (1977), Taylor (1979, 1980) are the basic papers. As with price setting, there has been a lot of interest in the stability or otherwise of staggering (see Fethke and Policiano, 1984, 1986) which has added force in the light of the fact that, in some countries, notably Japan, wage contracts are synchronised. Issues relating to persistence are discussed in Taylor (1983) and Jackman (1984) where the latter demonstrates that staggered wage bargains

---

[5] This is perhaps not quite correct. For example, unemployment could be very high in a competitive labour market because unemployment benefits were extremely generous. This fact would be of great importance in the sense that most people would consider this to be a significant waste of resources.

[6] In the United Kingdom, for example, the proportion of the unemployed with durations exceeding one year is more than 40%. The corresponding figure in Belgium is over 60%!

[7] In 1984, the unemployment rate in Britain was 18·4% for unskilled and semi-skilled workers compared with an average of 12·1%. The corresponding figures for the United States are 10·4% and 6·6% (in 1987).

will generate persistent effects of nominal shocks even if unions are fully informed and have rational expectations. The most comprehensive empirical analysis is in Benabou and Bismut (1988). So while we have a good understanding of the consequences of staggering and nominal wage stickiness, we do not, as yet, have a very comprehensive theory underlying it. As we shall see, most non-competitive theories of wage determination generate equilibrium real wages which differ from competitive levels, rather than nominal inertia. In some respects this is no bad thing. While they may not be much good at explaining why demand shocks have real effects, they are capable of generating 'true' unemployment in long run equilibrium.

Implicit Contracts

The original implicit contract models due to Baily (1974), Gordon (1974), and Azariadis (1975) examine the consequence of optimal labour contracts between risk averse workers and risk neutral firms. These contracts exhibit a constant (state independent) real wage with the firm essentially absorbing the income fluctuations. Unfortunately it also turns out that, in bad states, there is what might be described as 'overemployment inefficiency', that is, the marginal product of labour is smaller than the reservation wage[8] (see Pissarides, 1979 and Akerlof and Miyazaki, 1980). Furthermore, once we allow firms to pay workers when they are not employed, this inefficiency disappears (see Grossman and Hart, 1981, for example). So a fully efficient contract becomes a possibility, with the pattern of compensation across states being determined to optimise risk sharing.

Further progress was made with the introduction of asymmetric information (Calvo and Phelps, 1977; Grossman and Hart, 1981), where only the firm is assumed to be fully informed about the state of the world, ex post (see Hart, 1983; Rosen, 1985, and Hart and Holmstrom, 1987 for surveys). In order that the firm has no incentive to lie about the state, ex post efficiency cannot be sustained. However, the precise form of the inefficiency is highly susceptible to the assumptions concerning worker's utility functions and the relative degree of risk aversion of firms and workers, with overemployment inefficiencies being a frequent outcome. Furthermore, the predicted form of the labour contracts is much more complicated than those actually observed (see Oswald, 1986). This has led to some scepticism about the value of these models as a foundation for a theory of unemployment, perhaps most trenchantly expressed in Stiglitz (1986).

Efficiency Wages

The fundamental idea underlying efficiency wage models is that firms set wages and gain some benefit from paying higher wages which offset the direct cost. The benefits arising from paying higher wages may arise in a number of ways.

[8] This is sometimes described as overemployment. This is somewhat misleading since it has been taken to mean that employment is higher than in a competitive world. If labour supply is inelastic, in a simple equivalent competitive model everyone is employed, so the latter could hardly be correct. The misunderstanding arises because in standard contract theory, the reservation wage is treated as exogenous. In general equilibrium with unemployment, this is not the case.

(i) If individual effort is not costlessly observable, higher wages raise the cost of job loss which encourages effort and enables the firm to economise on monitoring (see Calvo, 1979, or Shapiro and Stiglitz, 1984, for example). (ii) Higher wages reduce turnover and this benefits the firm if higher quitting imposes real costs (see Stiglitz, 1974, 1985; Salop, 1979). (iii) Higher wages enable firms to attract a higher quality pool of job applicants which is beneficial in situations where there is imperfect observability of worker quality (see Weiss, 1980). (iv) Higher wages simply improve morale and increase productivity (see Akerlof 1982, 1984).

In order to see how such models may lead to long run unemployment, consider the following simple 'shirking' model (type (i) above). The firm's revenue has the form $AR[e(W/\overline{W}, u)\, N]$ where e refers to effort, N to employment and A to a multiplicative demand or productivity factor. Effort is an increasing function of both wages relative to those elsewhere, $W/\overline{W}$, and unemployment, u, since the cost of job loss is increasing in both these factors. The firm then chooses wages and employment to solve

$$\max_{W,\,N} AR[e(W/\overline{W}, u)\, N] - WN.$$

The first order conditions are

$$AR'e_1\, N/\overline{W} = N, \tag{23}$$

$$AR'e = W, \tag{24}$$

which leads to a wage equation of the form[9]

$$e_1(W/\overline{W}, u)\, W/\overline{W} = e(W/\overline{W}, u). \tag{25}$$

If the economy consists of a large number of identical firms of this type, then in general equilibrium, $W = \overline{W}$ and equilibrium unemployment is given by

$$e_1(1, u) = e(1, u). \tag{26}$$

In general, u will differ from the competitive level.[10] Another point worth noting, for future reference, is that wages at the firm level depend only on the aggregate wage and unemployment (from eqn. (25)). Changes in the general level of productivity at the firm level which influence revenue multiplicatively, as measured by A, have no impact on firm level wage setting, although they will, of course, influence wages in general equilibrium.

Even if efficiency wages are confined to a part of the economy rather than occurring across the board, it is still possible to have unemployment so long as it is easier to obtain a job in the efficiency wage sector from unemployment rather than from a job in the competitive sector. This type of unemployment may be thought of as 'wait' or 'queue' unemployment. The unemployed are queuing up for a job in the higher wage sector rather than working in the competitive sector. The level of unemployment is such as to make the

---

[9] This equation is sometimes known as the Solow condition (see Solow, 1979).
[10] Further models along similar lines may be found in Yellen (1984), Johnson and Layard (1986).

unemployed indifferent between waiting for an efficiency wage sector job and working in the lower wage competitive sector. This is similar to the Harris–Todaro (1970) model of urban unemployment in developing countries (see Hall, 1975 and Johnson and Layard, 1986). Quite why it is easier to obtain an efficiency wage job while unemployed rather than while working is not entirely clear, however.[11] On-the-job search is quite a widespread activity with some 6% of employed workers in the United Kingdom engaging in it in 1984 and around 4% in the United States in 1976 (Rosenfeld, 1977, and Burgess, 1989, have further details).

A major objection to the notion that workers receive higher wages to make them perform better is the so-called 'bonding critique'. An alternative to efficiency wages is that workers post a performance bond when they take up a job which they forfeit if they perform badly. Efficiency wages are then not required and the resulting unemployment disappears (see Carmichael, 1985). Indeed, it has been argued that the existence of rising wage profiles in jobs reflects this kind of bond payment (see Carmichael, 1983) although they may not act as a complete replacement for it (Akerlof and Katz, 1986). Objections to the bonding critique may be based on capital market imperfections (Akerlof and Katz, 1989) or on the incentives the firm has to declare that performance is inadequate and collect the bond. Thus Carmichael (1985) implicitly assumes that firms never cheat. However, the most powerful objections to bonding are to be found in MacLeod and Malcomson (1989). They demonstrate that in an equilibrium which is defined as the perfect equilibrium of a repeated game, it is possible for workers to receive a rent from employment even if full bonding is allowed.[12]

Evidence for efficiency wages comes in a variety of forms. Since efficiency wages are associated with wage premia which do not correspond to worker quality or compensating differentials, the search for such premia is an obvious strategy. Documenting the benefits which accrue to a firm from higher wages is also clearly important.

The basic notion of equalising differentials is that all workers with the same characteristics, working in jobs with the same characteristics, should obtain the same wage. Furthermore wages should adjust so that pay in jobs with different characteristics should be such that identical workers should be indifferent to different jobs.[13] This view has long been questioned. Thus Cannan (1914) argued that if there were equality of net advantages, 'we should find well-to-do parents in doubt whether to make their sons civil engineers or naval stokers, doctors or roadsweepers' (p. 207). Many studies find large pay disparities across apparently similar individuals and establishments (for example Slichter, 1950; Lester, 1952; MacKay et al., 1971).

Pursuing this issue somewhat further, Krueger and Summers (1988) estimate standard wage equations and find that controlling for a host of individual

[11] It could be argued that working in the low wage competitive sector sends out a bad signal to employers. On the other hand, it could equally be argued that being unemployed sends out a bad signal.

[12] They also show that if markets are analysed under the assumption that all rents accrue to the short side of the market, then the only equilibrium would be one with zero employment in the efficiency wage sector.

[13] For an excellent survey, see Rosen (1986).

characteristics including union membership, there are extremely large residual differences across industries. In order that these should reflect genuine premia of the efficiency wage type, the following possibilities must be ruled out. First, unobserved differences in labour quality. Krueger and Summers, utilising panel data, find that the change in wages when an individual switches industry is of the same order of magnitude as the industry wage differential. There are, however, two important problems here. The measurement error problem and the endogeneity problem. The former refers to the severe impact on the results of misclassifying industry changes, the latter to the fact that industry changing is a matter of individual choice. Murphy and Topel (1987b), for example, attempt to deal with the first problem and find that a relatively high proportion of the industry differential reflects unmeasured quality effects. However, because of the temporal aggregation implicit in their annual data, their estimate of the impact of unmeasured quality is upward biased. Gibbons and Katz (1987) probably get closer to the truth by concentrating on workers who change industry as a result of plant closures, where the job change is more likely to be both accurately classified and exogenous. Their results are generally consistent with those of Krueger and Summers (as, incidentally, are those of Blackburn and Neumark, 1988).

The second possibility to be ruled out is that the industry differentials simply reflect compensating differences. When Krueger and Summers include measures of job attributes in their regressions, the impact on the industry effects is negligible. Furthermore, as had already been noted by Freeman (1981), fringe benefit differentials tend to expand wage differences. However, this evidence is not wholly convincing since more capable workers will tend to take jobs with better working conditions. Since the pure cross-sections do not control adequately for ability, the findings on job attributes may be spurious and Krueger and Summers do not quote any panel data evidence on this issue. However, Dickens and Katz (1987) find that inter-industry wage relativities are very similar across different occupations. This is difficult to square with compensating differentials since it is hard to see why job attributes should differ in the same way across two industries for both production line workers and clerks, for example. Finally, there is the fact that quit rates are higher where wages are lower (Pencavel, 1972). Under compensating differentials, this would not be the case.

The last possibility to be ruled out is that these industry wage differentials are simply temporary consequences of intersectoral demand shifts. In fact, the differentials are extremely stable over time. For example Krueger and Summers find that the correlation between the industry premia in 1974 and 1984 is 0·97.

So we have stable industry wage premia which appear on top of those arising from differences in worker quality and compensating differentials. This is clearly a necessary condition for efficiency wages. To go further in this direction, we must demonstrate both that firms benefit from higher wages and that the level of such benefits differs significantly across industries. Here, the evidence so far is rather thin. As noted above, higher wages reduce quitting

(Pencavel, 1972; Freeman, 1980). In addition, higher relative wages improve productivity (Wadhwani and Wall, 1988), higher wages generate higher rates of job application (Holzer *et al.*, 1988) and higher wages lead to lower hiring/training costs (Holzer, 1989*a*). Furthermore, Kaufman (1984) provides some relevant facts following a series of interviews with British employers in 1982, a period of severe recession. A majority of employers, including half the non-union firms, believed they could find qualified workers at lower wages than they currently paid. Their main argument for not paying lower wages was that work effort would be reduced. Furthermore, several felt that paying lower wages would be unfair to their employees. Both these arguments are, of course, consistent with efficiency wage notions.

Overall, therefore, we have some evidence in favour of the efficiency wage story but it is not, as yet, overwhelming (see Katz, 1986 for a useful survey).

Union Bargaining

The basic model of union wage bargaining involves a union with some preferences on real wages and employment. Assume the union's preferences can be expressed as a utility function of the form $V(W, N)$, $V_1, V_2 > 0$ and the firm is concerned with profits, $\Pi(W, N)$ where W is the wage, N is employment. (In this section we ignore the distinction between real and nominal wages, because prices are assumed constant and uniform throughout.) Then if the firm and the union bargain over both wages and employment, and the bargaining process leads to an efficient outcome, then wages and employment will lie on the contract curve,

$$V_W/V_N = \Pi_W/\Pi_N. \tag{27}$$

If, on the other hand, the firm sets employment unilaterally, then employment must lie on the labour demand curve,

$$\Pi_N = 0. \tag{28}$$

These two possibilities can only be consistent if the union is indifferent to employment ($V_N = 0$). This could happen if, for example, layoffs were undertaken on a last in, first out (LIFO) basis (or indeed on any other predetermined and publicly known basis). The majority of union members would then be indifferent to employment if they were only concerned with their own immediate job prospects (see Oswald, 1986, for example). However, the LIFO principle is not uniquely decisive, as a survey reported in Oswald and Turnbull (1985) makes clear. So we certainly cannot rule out the possibility of there being some conflict between equations (27) and (28). These alternatives have been extensively discussed in McDonald and Solow (1981), Nickell (1982), Oswald (1985). This issue is of some importance since if the firm sets employment, wages will generally turn out higher and employment lower, in partial equilibrium, than if bargaining is efficient. This result does not, however, carry over to general equilibrium as we shall see.

A number of studies have attempted to discriminate between these two possibilities, notably Brown and Ashenfelter (1986), MaCurdy and Pencavel (1986), Bean and Turnbull (1987), Carruth *et al.* (1986), Card (1988) and

Alogoskoufis and Manning (1989). The evidence provided in these papers is not very clear cut, in part because the empirical results are not very convincing and in part because there are any number of reasons why the wage-employment data may not lie on a *standard* labour demand curve. Efficiency wages, for example, would lead directly to the presence of outside wages in labour demand. The last named of the above papers is perhaps the most satisfactory in the sense that it embeds both the above models in the overarching framework set out in Manning (1987) which we discuss below. More persuasive evidence is, in fact, provided in Oswald (1987) and Oswald and Turnbull (1985) based on the results of surveys of both British and United States unions. The question posed was, 'Does your union normally negotiate over the number of jobs as well as over wages and conditions?' The replies were:

	No	Yes	No answer/unclear	Total replies
United States	16	2	1	19
Britain	10	3	5	18

Two further facts are relevant. First, United States contracts typically include a 'management rights' clause asserting, for example, that the company 'will determine the extent of any required labor force adjustment'. Second, employment is continuously adjusted via natural wastage and the firm's hiring policy, whereas wages are typically negotiated formally at discrete intervals of the year or more in length. So negotiations about employment would have to be a continuous, and thus very costly, process. It is, of course, always possible to argue that, despite the fact that explicit contracts state that firms determine employment, firms and workers make implicit deals to move towards an efficient outcome. There is, however, no strong evidence that this is the case.

While bargaining over employment is unusual, bargaining over working conditions including effort, in general, and manning ratios, in particular, is quite prevalent.[14] This is not, however, the same as bargaining over employment since, for given manning ratios, employment can be changed, in the long run, by varying the number of machines, and in the short run, by varying the number of machines in use and the number of shifts per machine.

Implications for Unemployment

Assuming that unions bargain over wages but firms set employment, what are the implications for wage determination and unemployment? First we must specify the bargaining outcome. The standard model which is used is that due to Nash (1953), who provides an axiomatic justification. Strategic justifications are given by Bishop (1964) and Binmore *et al.* (1986). The Nash bargaining outcome solves

$$\max \left[V(W, N) - \bar{V} \right]^{\beta} \left[\Pi(W, N) - \bar{\Pi} \right]^{1-\beta},$$

where the *status quo* points, $\bar{V}, \bar{\Pi}$, refer to the union utility levels and profits

---

[14] In Britain in 1980 (1984), 92 (78)% of union establishments bargained over physical working conditions and 76 (55)% bargained over manning ratios.

which would arise if there were a conflict, i.e. a strike or lock-out (see Binmore *et al.*, 1986). The parameter β reflects the relative strength of the union in the bargain. So in this context, the efficient bargain solves

$$\max_{W, N} (V - \bar{V})^{\beta}(\Pi - \bar{\Pi})^{(1-\beta)}, \tag{29}$$

whereas the labour demand or 'right to manage' model solves

$$\max_{W, N} (V - \bar{V})^{\beta}(\Pi - \bar{\Pi})^{(1-\beta)} \tag{30}$$

$$\text{s.t. } \Pi_N = 0.$$

A formulation, due to Manning (1987), which incorporates both of these is a sequential bargain where in stage 1, wages solve

$$\max_{W} \{V[W, N(W)] - \bar{V}\}^{\beta_1}\{\Pi[W, N(W)] - \bar{\Pi}\}^{1-\beta_1}, \tag{31}$$

where $N(W)$ is the level of employment arising from the second stage bargaining with given wages, namely

$$\max_{N} [V(W, N) - \bar{V}]^{\beta_2}[\Pi(W, N) - \bar{\Pi}]^{1-\beta_2}. \tag{32}$$

The parameters β_1, β_2 reflect the bargaining power of the union in the wage and employment bargains respectively. The efficient bargain has $\beta_1 = \beta_2$ whereas the 'right to manage' bargain has $\beta_2 = 0$. A special case of this latter is the so-called monopoly union model, where the union sets the wage and the firm sets employment ($\beta_1 = 1, \beta_2 = 0$). *A priori*, this seems a somewhat unlikely case. There is no evidence in its favour and it may safely be ignored. The Manning (1987) framework is the obvious one to use as the basis for an econometric analysis of the type of bargaining (see Alogoskoufis and Manning, 1989; Nickell and Wadhwani, 1989*b* and Andrews and Harrison, 1988). Its main drawback is its static nature. Dynamic bargaining models are rare although a start has been made by Lockwood and Manning (1988) and Espinosa and Rhee (1989).[15]

A variety of functional forms for the union objective, V, have been utilised including Stone–Geary (Dertouzos and Pencavel, 1981) and the augmented addilog (Pencavel, 1984).[16] However, the most popular is the utilitarian union objective, namely

$$V(W, N) = \begin{cases} NU(W) + (M - N)\,\tilde{U} & (M \geqslant N) \\ MU(W) & (M < N), \end{cases} \tag{33}$$

where M is the exogenous membership prior to the bargain, U is the utility function of the representative member and $\tilde{U}$ is the expected utility of a member if he or she does not obtain a job in the firm. This objective is, in fact,

---

[15] Dynamising the monopoly union model is, however, straightforward – see Minford (1983), for example.
[16] Farber (1986) has further details.

quite hard to work with because of the 'kink' as employment hits membership. Much of the work that uses this objective simply ignores the second possibility, implicitly assuming that $M \geqslant N$. Such models then lead to very simple general equilibrium models of unemployment. For example, suppose that outside expected utility has the form

$$\tilde{U} = U(\overline{W})\left[1 - \omega(u)\right] + U(B)\,\omega(u) \quad (\omega' > 0). \tag{34}$$

$\overline{W}$ is the outside wage, B is the benefit level and $\omega(u)$ is the proportion of the period which the individual spends unemployed.

If we now take the firm's profit function to have the form

$$\Pi(W, N) = AR(N) - WN,$$

where AR is revenue, and assume that $\tilde{U}$ is available to workers on strike because they can work elsewhere, whereas firms get nothing, then the Nash objective has the form

$$\{N[U(W) - \tilde{U})]\}^{\beta}[AR(N) - WN]^{1-\beta}.$$

The consequence of bargaining for each firm is to generate a wage and employment level as a function of β and the variables contained in $\tilde{U}$, namely $\overline{W}, B, u$. For example, suppose U has the constant elasticity form

$$U = W^{\alpha}/\alpha \quad (\alpha \leqslant 1)$$

and we define η as the labour demand elasticity ($\eta = R'/NR''$) and S_R as the share of labour ($S_R = NR'/R$). Then the wage equation in the right to manage model in a log linear form is

$$w = \overline{w} + \frac{1}{\alpha}\log\left[\frac{|\eta|(1 - S_R) + \gamma S_R}{(|\eta| - \alpha)(1 - S_R) + \gamma S_R}\right] + \frac{1}{\alpha}\log\left[1 - \omega(u)(1 - b^{\alpha})\right], \tag{35}$$

where $\gamma = (1 - \beta)/\beta$ and $b = B/\overline{W}$, the benefit replacement ratio. Thus we find that the wage is a mark-up on outside wages, where the mark-up is decreasing in the elasticity of labour demand, $|\eta|$, and the unemployment rate, u, and increasing in union bargaining power, β, and the benefit replacement ratio, b. Furthermore, as in the efficiency wage equation (25), the wage is independent of the firm specific productivity term, A. Suppose we have a fully unionised economy consisting of a large number of identical firm–union pairs. Then, in general equilibrium, we must have $w = \overline{w}$ and hence, from (35), u must satisfy[17]

$$\omega(u) = \frac{\alpha(1 - S_R)}{(1 - b^{\alpha})[|\eta|(1 - S_R) + \gamma S_R]}. \tag{36}$$

So equilibrium unemployment is increasing in the replacement ratio, b, union bargaining power, β, and decreasing in worker risk aversion, α, and the

---

[17] Note that, in general, equation (36) is only an implicit equation for u because both S_R and η are functions of N. Thus if L is the labour force and F is the number of firm–union pairs, S_R and η are functions of $(1 - u)L/F = N$. If R is constant elasticity, however, then both η and S_R are constants.

elasticity of demand for labour, $|\eta|$. A further interesting result arises if we consider the equivalent formula for the efficient bargain model. In this case equilibrium unemployment, u', is given by

$$\omega(u') = \frac{\alpha(1 - S_R)}{(1 - b^\alpha)(1 + \gamma S_R)}. \tag{37}$$

Then it is easy to show that if firms face constant elasticity demand curves and have a Cobb–Douglas technology, then $|\eta|(1 - S_R) = 1$ and hence $u = u'$. In this case, equilibrium unemployment is the same under both 'right to manage' and efficient bargaining despite the fact that in partial equilibrium, the latter generates lower wages and higher employment. However, once the endogeneity of the outside opportunity, $\tilde{U}$, is brought into play, this employment difference disappears although wages end up higher in the efficient bargain, because bargaining over employment as well as wages increases the effectiveness of the union (see Pissarides, 1986, appendix 7A; Layard and Nickell, 1988; Manning, 1988; Johnson and Layard, 1986 for further models).

More complex equilibrium unemployment models in the union context arise once we allow for two sectors. We can, of course, have queue models which we have already discussed in the efficiency wage context. However, the most complete analysis of such models is to be found in Jackman, Layard, Nickell and Wadhwani (1989, chapter 2). They find, for example, that while unemployment unambiguously rises with a *ceteris paribus* increase in union power, an increase in the coverage of the union sector has an ambiguous impact. The key parameter here is the elasticity of supply to the competitive sector. If this is high, then extending union coverage may be harmful to employment because of its depressing effect on non-union wages (see Minford, 1983, for example). If it is low, then the impact can go the other way. This may help to explain why, across countries and time periods, there is no clear relationship between aggregate unemployment and union coverage. Freeman (1987) reports the same across United States states, controlling for other relevant variables.

Levels of Bargaining

One aspect of unionised economies which is particularly important for unemployment determination is the level at which wage bargaining takes place. This varies from completely decentralised, as in the United States, to completely centralised, as in Austria (see Flanagan *et al.*, 1983, for details). There are two forces at work here. The higher the level of centralisation, the more inelastic the demand for labour which exerts upward pressure on wages. The idea here is simply that as we move from firm level bargains to industry level bargains, for example, product demand elasticities, and hence labour demand elasticities, will fall. However, if there is complete centralisation, the alternative to employment is unemployment since there are no 'alternative' jobs. This reduces outside opportunities in a conflict and weakens bargaining strength. Furthermore, the unemployment consequences of higher wages are brought starkly into focus which concentrates the mind of union bargainers. This reduces upward pressure on wages. The upshot is that highly centralised or highly decentralised bargaining tend to produce lower wage pressure than intermediate level bargaining. (Calmfors and Horn, 1986; Calmfors and Driffill, 1988; Jackman, Layard, Nickell and Wadhwani, 1989, chapter 2, provide full analyses).

Insiders and Wages

As we have seen, in both the simple efficiency wage equation (25) and the simple union wage equation (35), the firm level wage equations allow no role for firm specific productivity effects to influence wages. This is not a general result. In the union context it arises, at least in part, because we have not taken proper account of the full union objective, equation (33), since we have ignored the membership constraint (i.e. we have assumed $M \geqslant N$). As we have already noted, however, dealing with this kink is rather tricky analytically and it is simpler to smooth it out by incorporating some level of uncertainty in the model.

Suppose that firms face uncertain levels of demand, say, and that wages are bargained before this uncertainty is revealed. Then, when the uncertainty is revealed, firms set prices, output and employment given the wage. Assuming that layoffs are determined by random draw, the union is now simply concerned with the expected utility of a representative member.

Consider the following model where, for simplicity, we assume a competitive product market. Then, *ex-post*, the firm chooses employment to solve

$$\max_{N} AP^{e} f(N) \, \tilde{\epsilon} - WN,$$

where $\tilde{\epsilon}$ is the revealed random variable (mean unity), A is the productivity term and W is the bargained wage. Employment and profits are thus given by

$$N = N(W/AP^{e}\tilde{\epsilon}), \quad \Pi = W\tilde{\Pi}(W/AP^{e}\tilde{\epsilon}). \tag{38}$$

The members have first call on available jobs and so an individual's probability of layoff is zero if $M \leqslant N$, and is $1 - \mathrm{E}(N \mid N < M)/M)$ if $M > N$. The overall layoff probability L is given by

$$L = \mathrm{Prob}\,(N < M)\{1 - [\mathrm{E}(N \mid N < M)/M]\}$$

$$= L(M, W/AP^{e}) \quad (L_{1}, L_{2} > 0). \tag{39}$$

Expected utility for a union member is thus given by

$$(1 - L)\,W + L\overline{W}[1 - \omega(u)\,(1 - b)]$$

assuming risk neutrality on the part of workers. (Note that under risk neutrality $\tilde{U} = \overline{W}[1 - \omega(u)] + B\omega(u) = \overline{W}[1 - \omega(u)\,(1 - b)]$.) So if we assume status quo points as before, the wage will solve the Nash bargain problem

$$\max_{W} ([1 - L(M, W/AP^{e})]\{W - \overline{W}[1 - \omega(u)\,(1 - b)]\})^{\beta}[W\Pi(W/AP^{e})]^{1-\beta},$$

where the firm is concerned with expected profit. Note that this problem is equivalent to

$$\max_{W} \{[1 - L(M, W/AP^e)][W/\overline{W} - 1 + \omega(u)(1-b)]\}^\beta [(W/\overline{W})\,\Pi(W/AP^e)]^{1-\beta}.$$

In general, the solution has the form

$$W = F(\overline{W}, AP^e, M, u, b, \beta), \quad F_1, F_2, F_5, F_6 > 0, \quad F_3, F_4 < 0, \qquad (40)$$

with F homogeneous of degree 1 in $\overline{W}$ and AP^e. Unlike the previous wage models, wages are now influenced both by aggregate factors related to the general labour market, $\overline{W}, u, b$ and by firms/union specific factors, AP^e, M, β. In particular wages are inversely related to initial membership, which is the foundation of the insider-outsider model. Indeed this model is very similar to that discussed in Lindbeck and Snower (1987) and is a more general form of the basic model in Blanchard and Summers (1986). A more general version still may be found in Nickell and Wadhwani (1989a).

If we log-linearise (40), we can write it in the form

$$w = \mu_{01} + \mu_{02}\beta + \mu_1(p^e + a - \delta_1 m) + (1 - \mu_1)(\overline{w} - \delta_2 u + \delta_3 b), \qquad (41)$$

where μ_1 is the 'weight' attached to firm specific or insider factors in wage determination. In this framework, we might specify membership as initial employment, n_{-1}, where these are termed the insiders. Obviously more general formulations are possible (see Lindbeck and Snower, 1987) but the important point is that such models generate a negative relationship between wages and lagged employment. The theoretical foundations for such insider effects on wage determination need not be restricted to union models. A number of alternatives are discussed in Lindbeck and Snower (1986; 1988), Solow (1985), Nickell and Wadhwani (1989a) although see Fehr (1988) for critical remarks on some of these models. There is also extensive evidence on both the importance of firm specific factors in wage determination and, to a lesser extent, on the negative relationship between lagged employment and wages. Positive evidence on the former is to be found in surveys of wage bargainers (Gregory et al., 1987; Blanchflower and Oswald, 1987) and in econometric analyses at the industry, firm and establishment level (Nickell and Wadhwani, 1989a; Blanchflower et al., 1990; Brunello and Wadhwani, 1989; Holmlund and Zetterberg, 1989). It is clear from the first and the last two of these papers that estimates of the insider weight, μ_1, vary substantially between countries, being close to zero in Scandinavia, around 0·15 in Britain and West Germany, and about 0·3 in Japan and the United States. The fact that firm specific factors are not important in the centralised wage setting regimes operational in Scandinavia is not surprising. The high estimates for Japan and the United States are, however, of some interest given that the insider weight, μ_1, reflects non-competitive forces. Looking at it another way, however, it can also be viewed as a measure of 'flexibility' in the sense that it captures the extent to which wages adjust to stabilise employment within firms. This nevertheless remains a profoundly non-competitive tendency. Further results include the fact that insider effects are more important in more highly unionised firms/industries (Nickell and Kong, 1988; Holmlund and Zetterberg, 1989) and outside effects, particularly from aggregate unemployment, are more important in small firms (Brunello and Wadhwani, 1989; Blanchflower, 1989).

Positive evidence on the role of lagged employment is far harder to find. Some very weak favourable evidence is reported using United Kingdom firm level data in Nickell and Wadhwani (1989a) but no evidence is found at the industry level in five countries[18] by Holmlund and Zetterberg (1989) or in Canadian contract data by Christophides and Oswald (1988).

The importance of the lagged membership/employment effect arises from its macroeconomic implications. If we set $m = n_{-1}$ in equation (41) and aggregate over the whole economy, we simply set $w = \bar{w}$ and solve out. This yields an aggregate equation of the form

$$w = \mu_{01}/\mu_1 + (\mu_{02}/\mu_1)\,\beta + p^e + a - \frac{(1-\mu_1)}{\mu_1}\,\delta_2\,u - \delta_1\,n_{-1} + \frac{(1-\mu_1)}{\mu_1}\,\delta_3\,b \quad (42)$$

or, given a constant labour force, l, and putting real wages on the left,

$$w - p = (\mu_{01}/\mu_1 - \delta_1\,l) - (p - p^e) + (\mu_{02}/\mu_1)\,\beta$$
$$+ a - \frac{(1-\mu_1)}{\mu_1}\,\delta_2\,u + \delta_1\,u_{-1} + \frac{(1-\mu_1)}{\mu_1}\,\delta_3\,b. \quad (43)$$

So the membership/insider effect generates a positive lagged unemployment term in the wage equation. This implies that a rise in unemployment has a bigger downward impact on wages in the short run than in the long run. This is often termed a hysteresis effect, the idea being that the position of the economy today depends not only on what is happening today, but on where it was yesterday. Just as with employment adjustment costs, such effects generate persistence in the aggregate economy.

It is important to recognise, however, that such membership or insider hysteresis is not the only source of persistence which can arise from wage setting behaviour. Unemployment exerts downward pressure on wages because high unemployment raises the cost of job loss, by making it harder to find alternative employment. But the level of unemployment only acts as a good proxy for the cost of job loss if its composition is independent of its level. For example, suppose that the long-term unemployed either search less hard for work or are considered to be less desirable workers by prospective employers. Then the higher the proportion of long-term unemployed in the unemployment pool, the weaker will be the effective competition for jobs per unemployed worker, and the easier it will be for an unemployed entrant to find work. So, for a given level of unemployment, the higher the proportion of long-term unemployed, the less effective is unemployment in holding down wages. This has two implications. First, if unemployment rises, the proportion of long-term unemployed tends to fall in the short run as the number of new entrants increases. However, if

[18] Sweden, Norway, Finland, Germany, United States.

unemployment stays at its new higher level, this effect disappears and the proportion of long term unemployed tends to increase. So the short run effect of a change in unemployment is greater than its long-run effect – precisely a hysteresis phenomenon. Second, in the long run, higher unemployment is associated with a higher proportion of long-term unemployed and hence the downward pressure on wages increases less than proportionally to unemployment – this introduces a long run concavity effect. More formally, suppose the downward pressure on wages has the form

$$(\delta_{21} - \delta_{22}\rho_u)\, u,$$

where ρ_u is the proportion of long-term unemployed. Next suppose that ρ_u is related to u as described above; that is

$$\rho_u = \gamma_0 - \gamma_1 \frac{\Delta u}{u} + \gamma_2 u.$$

So the combined effect has the form

$$(\delta_{21} - \gamma_0\, \delta_{22})\, u + \delta_{22}\, \gamma_1\, \Delta u - \delta_{22}\, \gamma_2\, u^2,$$

which exhibits both hysteresis and concavity.

The potential importance of long-term unemployment was first emphasised in Layard and Nickell (1986) although the possibility of hysteresis arising from the impact of unemployment on labour supply had already been noted in Phelps (1972). Blanchard and Diamond (1989 b) provides a formal theoretical foundation. There is some evidence in favour of the importance of long-term unemployment notably in Nickell (1987) and Franz (1987), using aggregate data, and in Nickell and Wadhwani (1989) using firm-based data. Blackaby and Manning (1988) find the long-term proportion reduces the impact of unemployment in an individual cross section but Blanchflower and Oswald (1989) find this effect to be insignificant once enough non-linearity in the unemployment effect is included. At a more aggregate level, Jackman, Layard, Nickell and Wadhwani (1989, chapter 9), find that the coefficient on the hysteresis term (Δu) in a set of country specific wage equation is significantly related to the long-term unemployed proportion in a cross section of OECD countries. Finally, surveys regularly show that employers discriminate systematically against long-term unemployed applicants (Meager and Metcalf, 1988; Robinson, 1988; Ebmer, 1989).

Other Topics in Wage Determination

As should be clear from previous sections, we can write a model of aggregate wage determination as a real wage equation, where real wages are influenced by nominal inertia (that is, they fall (rise) if nominal variables run ahead of (behind) expectations), productivity terms, the level and rate of change of unemployment and a series of other factors which, so far, include union bargaining power and the generosity of the benefit system. Such a model would include the labour supply formulation, given in (15), as a special case.

Our purpose in this section is to examine other possible factors which may influence wage determination. These will include any factors which influence the effectiveness of the unemployed as job seekers and any variables which may directly increase pressure on wages if workers have a tendency to resist falls in their real incomes.

The Effectiveness of the Unemployed as Job Seekers

It is clear that in almost any model of wage determination, a reduction in effective labour supply at given levels of unemployment will tend to raise wages, since it tends to reduce the cost of job loss. There are two obvious factors which reduce effective labour supply (aside from the long-term unemployed proportion which we have already discussed). These are the generosity of the benefit system and the extent to which the skills of the unemployed do not match those required in the available job vacancies.

The fact that the generosity and availability of unemployment benefits influences unemployment duration is well documented in microeconometric studies (a selection from the many papers on this issue might include, Ehrenberg and Oaxaca, 1976; Classen, 1977; Lancaster, 1979; Nickell, 1979; Kiefer and Neumann, 1979; Atkinson et al., 1984; Narendranathan et al., 1985; Solon, 1985; Katz and Meyer, 1988. Other references may be found in Mortensen, 1986.) The key to the importance of benefits, however, lies in the extent to which these labour supply effects influence wages. Here the evidence is much thinner and most estimated wage equations contain no such effect. However some positive results may be found in Minford (1983), Beenstock et al. (1985), and Layard and Nickell (1986).

Turning to the mismatch question, the evidence on the impact of changes in mismatch on wages is again rather thin. Some may be found in Layard and Nickell (1986), Modigliani et al. (1986), and Dolado et al. (1986), but there is nothing very systematic (see also Jackman and Roper, 1987, for a general discussion).

On the broader issue of the effectiveness of the unemployed as job seekers, it is clear that if they become less effective, then the number of vacancies should rise relative to unemployment. Over a standard cycle, vacancies and unemployment will move in opposite directions, generating the so-called UV or Beveridge Curve. So a fall in the effectiveness of the unemployed will generate an outward movement of this curve (see Holt, 1970; Hall, 1975; Pissarides, 1986a; Jackman, Layard, Nickell and Wadhwani, 1989; Jackman, Layard and Pissarides, 1989; Budd et al., 1988; Blanchard and Diamond, 1989a, for theoretical foundations and evidence). This suggests that one might take the actual shift of the UV curve as a measure of changes in the effectiveness of the unemployed and relate this directly to wages. This has been tried with a modicum of success by Bean et al. (1986a).

Real Wage Resistance and the Wedge

Until now we have ignored the important distinction between the real wage as perceived by employers and the consumption wage relevant to workers. In a closed economy with no taxes, this distinction is more or less absent but once we allow for taxation and imports then it becomes a crucial factor. If we suppose that w reflects (log) labour costs and p is the (log) value-added price index (GDP deflator), then $w-p$ is the real wage relevant for labour demand (real product wage). The net wage received by workers may be written as $w-t_1-t_2$ where t_1 is the tax rate on labour falling on firms (e.g. social security taxes) and t_2 is the income tax rate. The price index relevant to employees is the consumer price index p_c and the wedge between the real product wage and the real consumption wage is given by $t_1+t_2+p_c-p$. The main elements influencing p_c-p are the rate of excise tax and the price of imports relative to GDP. So the wedge is increasing in both tax rates on labour and goods, and the real price of imports.

Suppose this wedge rises. Then if real product wages are to remain unchanged, real consumption wages must fall. Any resistance to this fall will lead to upward pressure on real (product) wages. This is, in essence, a tax incidence question and there is quite a lot of evidence that increases in the tax wedge do indeed raise wage pressure, at least in the short run (see Bean *et al.*, 1986*b*; Newell and Symons, 1985; Knoester, 1983; Knoester *et al.*, 1987; Modigliani *et al.*, 1986; Padoa Schioppa, 1989, for example).

IV. THE MACROECONOMICS OF UNEMPLOYMENT

A Simple General Model

We can summarise much of our previous discussion within a very simple framework which has much in common with that set out in Rowthorn (1977), Carlin and Soskice (1985), Blanchard (1986), and Layard and Nickell (1987).

We begin with a slight generalisation of the demand side set out in the first section. Demand relative to full utilisation output, σ, we write as

$$\sigma = \sigma_1 x + \sigma_2(m-p) - \bar{y}, \tag{44}$$

where x reflects a measure of fiscal policy (see equation (11)). Then the simple Cobb–Douglas technology implies

$$\sigma = -\alpha u + \epsilon_p, \tag{45}$$

which is simply a repeat of equation (12).

Our discussion of pricing/employment behaviour leads us to a general pricing equation of the form

$$p-w = \beta_0 - \beta_{11}(p-p^e) - \beta_{12}(w-w^e) - \beta_2 u - \beta_{21}\Delta u - \beta_3(k-l) - \beta_4\epsilon_p, \tag{46}$$

where the price and wage surprises reflect nominal inertia (see section II), the hysteresis term (Δu) arises from labour adjustment costs, for example (see equation (13*a*), section I) and otherwise it simply follows the standard competitive model (equation (14), section I). Furthermore, it is easy to show in all these models that

$$\beta_4 > 0, \tag{47}$$

because the marginal product of labour must rise (marginal cost must fall) at given employment when there is a favourable technology shock.

Our extensive analysis of wage models leads to a general wage equation of the form

$$w-p = \gamma_0 - \gamma_{11}(p-p^e) - \gamma_{12}(w-w^e) - \gamma_2 u - \gamma_{21}\Delta u + \gamma_3(k-l) + z_w. \quad (48)$$

Again the price and wage surprises reflect nominal inertia (see section III), the Δu term captures either insider effects or long-term unemployment effects, $k-l$ is the productivity term and z_w includes all the other factors generating wage pressure such as benefits, unions, mismatch, and real wage resistance arising from changes in the wedge.

As in section I, we investigate the dynamics of this model by subjecting it to shocks. Thus we suppose that m, x, z_w are random variables which have the form

$$m = m^* + \epsilon_m, \quad x = x^* + \epsilon_x, \quad z_w = z_w^* + \epsilon_w. \quad (49)$$

Equilibrium in this model is defined by zero shocks ($\epsilon_p = \epsilon_m = \epsilon_x = \epsilon_w = 0$) and no surprises ($p-p^e = w-w^e = 0$). The equilibrium level of unemployment is given by

$$u^* = \frac{\gamma_0 + \beta_0 + z_w^* + (\gamma_3 - \beta_3)(k-l)}{\gamma_2 + \beta_2}. \quad (50)$$

Note first that equilibrium unemployment will move secularly in this economy as productivity rises (i.e. $k-l$ goes up) unless $\gamma_3 = \beta_3$. Since such secular movements do not occur in practice, there must be reasons why this parameter restriction holds in the long run. In fact in bargaining and other models of wage determination where productivity effects enter directly, this will typically be the case[19] (see Jackman, Layard, Nickell and Wadhwani, 1989, chapter 8, for example). So, from now on, we shall suppose that $\gamma_3 = \beta_3$.

The second point worth remarking is that despite the fact that this framework subsumes a variety of forms of non-competitive behaviour in both product and labour markets, the equilibrium level of unemployment is unaffected by fiscal and monetary policy, depending only on autonomous wage pressure, z_w, and the mark-up in the price equation, β_0. There are a variety of ways in which this result may break down. As we have already pointed out, if fiscal policy changes the demand elasticity facing firms, it will influence u^* by changing the price mark-up, β_0 (see Wren-Lewis, 1985). More generally, as Grandmont (1989) notes, demand multipliers can be induced via supply side substitution effects (ruled out here by the one-good nature of the model). These can be intersectoral, as in Hart (1982), Dixon (1988) or intertemporal as in Kahn and Mookherjee (1988), Jullien and Picard (1989). These models often have so-called 'Keynesian features' but are, in fact, much the same as real business cycle models which incorporate a real impact of government expenditures via the real interest rate effect on labour supply.

A third point to note concerns the status of this equilibrium in the open economy context. One of the elements of z_w^* is the wedge between the product wage and the consumption wage. In an open economy this wedge is influenced

---

[19] This is essentially because own productivity effects enter the wage equation via the firm's 'ability to pay'. This itself is clearly directly related to the price-productivity relationship in price setting.

by the real price of imports. If this rises and there is real wage resistance, then wage pressure will increase and equilibrium unemployment will go up. This suggests, therefore, that if the government can lower the real price of imports, by appreciating its currency, it can reduce equilibrium unemployment. Of course, in order to achieve the higher level of activity, it must simultaneously ensure a rise in demand, but a suitable mix of monetary and fiscal policy can produce the desired result. Therefore, in an open economy, we can have multiplicity of no surprise equilibria with different unemployment rates (see Modigliani et al., 1986, for example). However, corresponding to each will be a different trade deficit, with higher deficits being associated with lower unemployment. There remains, therefore, a unique equilibrium associated with trade balance, for example (or indeed with whatever level of deficit or surplus is deemed to be a sustainable equilibrium level). (See Carlin and Soskice, 1985; Layard and Nickell, 1986, or Alogoskoufis, 1989 for further details.)

Before we investigate the dynamic behaviour of the model it is worth mentioning three sets of parameters which will prove to be significant. The first set are the nominal inertia parameters $(\beta_{11}, \beta_{12}, \gamma_{11}, \gamma_{12})$ which will generally lie between zero and one. The second group reflect the impact of the level of economic activity on price and wage setting, namely $(\beta_2, \beta_{21}, \gamma_2, \gamma_{21})$, while the third group are the hysteresis terms $(\beta_{21}, \gamma_{21})$.

Under model consistent expectations, the response of unemployment to shocks is given by

$$(u - u^*) = \frac{(\beta_{21} + \gamma_{21})}{(\beta_2 + \gamma_2 + \beta_{21} + \gamma_{21})} (u - u^*)_{-1}$$

$$- \frac{1}{\Delta} [(1 + \beta_{11})(1 + \gamma_{12}) - (1 - \beta_{12})(1 - \gamma_{11})] (\sigma_1 \epsilon_x + \sigma_2 \epsilon_m)$$

$$+ \frac{1}{\Delta} [(1 + \beta_{11})(1 + \gamma_{12}) - (1 - \beta_{12})(1 - \gamma_{11}) - (1 + \gamma_{12}) \sigma_2 \beta_4] \epsilon_p$$

$$+ \frac{1}{\Delta} [\sigma_2 (1 - \beta_{12})] \epsilon_w, \tag{51}$$

where

$$\Delta = \alpha[(1 + \beta_{11})(1 + \gamma_{12}) - (1 - \beta_{12})(1 - \gamma_{11})]$$
$$+ \sigma_2 [(\beta_2 + \beta_{21})(1 + \gamma_{12}) + (1 - \beta_{12})(\gamma_2 + \gamma_{21})] > 0.$$

Taking each term in turn, it is clear that persistence is generated by hysteresis (Δu effects) in both wage *and* price setting. If the change effects of economic activity on price and wage setting $(\beta_{21}, \gamma_{21})$ are large relative to the level effects (β_2, γ_2), then shocks may drive the economy out of equilibrium for long periods of time. If there are no level effects, then we have a pure hysteresis model with no equilibrium, and unemployment following a random walk. (Blanchard and Summers, 1986, for example.)

Turning to the impact effect of the shocks, we can first consider those from the demand side. Their impact on unemployment is increasing in nominal inertia, both in price and wage setting $(\beta_{11}, \beta_{12}, \gamma_{11}, \gamma_{12})$, and decreasing in the size of the activity effects on price and wages $(\beta_2, \beta_{21}, \gamma_2, \gamma_{21})$. The fact that wage and price stickiness are important for the transmission of demand shocks is, of course, a standard result but it is worth emphasising the role of activity effects in stabilising the economy.

The parameter which captures the impact of real balances on demand, σ_2, also has an important part to play. If this parameter is small, fiscal policy shocks tend to have a larger impact relative to those arising from monetary policy. This, of course, corresponds to the situation where the demand for goods is interest inelastic and the demand for money is interest elastic.

Favourable technology shocks have two kinds of impact on unemployment. Nominal inertia tends to induce a rise in unemployment but this is offset in part or in whole by the negative effect on prices at fixed nominal demand which remains even if price/wage stickiness is wholly absent.

Finally we have (transitory) wage shocks. Their negative impact on both unemployment and output is attenuated by nominal inertia and is eliminated entirely if β_{12} is unity. This occurs because if prices are set before the wage shock is revealed, then the wage shock has no impact on prices and hence no impact on demand, output or employment. As with demand shocks, bigger activity effects on wage and price setting reduce the real impact of wage shocks and tend to stabilise the economy.

Turning now the *impact effect of these shocks on real wages*, it is straightforward to show that positive technology shocks tend to raise real wages and the same is true of positive wage shocks. The former occurs essentially because the demand for labour is raised. The latter is obvious. More interesting is the impact of demand shocks on the real wage. Using (51) and (48), it is easy to show that real wages will fall in response to a positive demand shock if and only if

$$(\beta_{11} + \beta_{12})(\gamma_2 + \gamma_{21}) < (\gamma_{11} + \gamma_{12})(\beta_2 + \beta_{21}). \tag{52}$$

So a demand increase and the corresponding rise in employment will be associated with a falling real wage if wages are stickier than prices $(\gamma_{11} + \gamma_{12} > \beta_{11} + \beta_{12})$ and activity has a bigger impact on price setting than on wage setting $(\beta_2 + \beta_{21} > \gamma_2 + \gamma_{21})$. On the other hand, if prices are unaffected by the level of activity $(\beta_2 = \beta_{21} = 0)$, as with mark-up pricing, then real wages will tend to rise as a result of a demand expansion.

Finally, with regard to price surprises, it is easy to show that demand and wage shocks lead to positive surprises whereas favourable technology shocks generate negative surprises. To summarise, therefore, positive demand shocks rely on price/wage stickiness for their favourable real effects and can be associated with real wage movements in either direction. Positive technology shocks tend to raise real wages and also employment unless nominal inertia is very strong. Positive wage shocks tend to raise real wages and lower employment but their real effects are attenuated by price/wage stickiness.

Finally the persistence of all these shocks depend critically on the extent of hysteresis in both price and wage-setting.

Before looking at the relationship between this model and the so-called NAIRU model, it is worth commenting on a particular feature of the demand side. Implicit in this model is that, given the chosen price, firms supply whatever is demanded. This yields, via the production function, the relationship (45) between demand and unemployment. It is possible to have models where firms do not supply whatever is demanded either for reasons of cost, that is the marginal cost of doing so is too high, or for reasons of physical capacity, that is they simply do not have enough capital. In the longer run, of course, we might expect capacity to adjust but, in the short run, there can obviously be rationing of this kind. This will lead to further dynamics in the model (in fact it is essentially another type of hysteresis) although it will not change its longer run properties. Empirical models of this type include Sneesens and Dreze (1986) and Lambert (1988), for example. Bean (1989) provides a comprehensive investigation of the capital shortage question.

The NAIRU and the Unemployment–Inflation Tradeoff

In the period since Phillips' original paper in 1958, the notion of the unemployment–inflation tradeoff has been a central facet of macroeconomics. Yet, in the model of the previous section, inflation was not, apparently, mentioned. Nevertheless there is an unemployment–inflation tradeoff implicit in this model so long as price-wage expectations take a particular form. Suppose, for example, that expectations are not model consistent, but take the simple form

$$p^e = p_{-1}, \quad w^e = w_{-1}. \tag{53}$$

Then if we add (46) and (48), we have what is effectively the supply side of the model, which can be written as

$$u = \frac{(\beta_{21}+\gamma_{21})\,u_{-1}-(\gamma_{11}+\beta_{11})\,\Delta p-(\gamma_{12}+\beta_{12})\,\Delta w-\beta_4\,\epsilon_p+\gamma_0+\beta_0+\epsilon_w}{(\beta_2+\gamma_2+\beta_{21}+\gamma_{21})}. \tag{54}$$

This represents an unemployment–inflation tradeoff of the simplest kind, where unemployment can be permanently reduced at the expense of a higher inflation rate. However, as Friedman (1968) and Phelps (1968) pointed out, the notion that the expectations formation mechanism given in (53) would remain stable in the face of a high rate of inflation seems unlikely.

The next step is to move up a derivative and suppose that expectations take the form[20]

$$(p^e - p_{-1}) = (p_{-1} - p_2), \quad (w^e - w_{-1}) = (w_{-1} - w_{-2}).$$

[20] In fact all that is really required is for the inflation expectations process to have a unit root.

In this case, the expectations mechanisms is correct for stable inflation rates, however high, and the equivalent equation to (54) is

$$u = \frac{(\beta_{21} + \gamma_{21}) u_{-1} - (\gamma_{11} + \beta_{11}) \Delta^2 p - (\gamma_{12} + \beta_{12}) \Delta^2 w - \beta_4 \epsilon_p + \gamma_0 + \beta_0 + z_w}{(\beta_2 + \gamma_2 + \beta_{21} + \gamma_{21})}.$$

(55)

This is the unemployment–inflation tradeoff in a NAIRU model; that is unemployment can only be kept below its equilibrium in the long run by having rising inflation. Equilibrium unemployment is consistent with stable inflation at any level.[21]

Despite the fact that the assumed expectations formation mechanism would surely change if the government systematically tried to use this tradeoff by having consistently rising inflation, this equation is not bad as a description of the state of affairs in most OECD economies over the last 20 years. For example, if we take a pooled time series–cross section regression for 19 OECD countries from 1956–85 we find that

$$\Delta^2 p_{it} = a_i + b_i t - 0{\cdot}32 u_{it} - 0{\cdot}48 \Delta u_{it}$$
$$(4{\cdot}5) \qquad (3{\cdot}0)$$

where i is the country subscript, t the time subscript. Thus there is both a well defined tradeoff and considerable evidence of hysteresis.

Explaining Unemployment in the Long Run

It is clear from the previous sections that any real explanation of long run shifts in unemployment must come from the supply side. While it is obviously true that when unemployment is high, demand must be low (unless there are short-run capacity constraints), it is to a supply side equation of the type exemplified by (55) that one must look to obtain any real understanding of the processes involved. And over the long term, the surprise terms $\Delta^2 p$, $\Delta^2 w$ must average out to zero and so the focus must be on the wage pressure terms, z_w. However, the long run could easily represent a very considerable time if the level of persistence in the economy is very high. Thus if the parameters β_{21}, γ_{21} are large relative to β_2, γ_2, then the impact of past demand shocks and hence inflationary surprises could go on for many years. This fact, when combined with the difficulty of actually identifying the wage pressure variables, has meant that convincing empirical work in this area remains somewhat thin on the ground despite considerable expenditure of effort. Thus it is not too difficult to explain the rise in unemployment in most countries between the 1960s and the late 1970s by some combination of rises in the wedge (including the real import price shocks of 1974 and 1979), increases in industrial militancy, increases in the generosity and coverage of the benefit system and increases in mismatch (see the papers in Bean *et al.*, 1986*b* or Newell and Symons, 1985). However,

---

[21] Somewhat misleadingly, NAIRU stands for non-accelerating inflation rate of unemployment. This description has slipped a derivative since it is the price level which is not accelerating, while the rate of inflation is merely unchanging.

it is far harder to explain why unemployment has remained very high into the late 1980s in many European countries when the adverse demand and import price shocks of the early 1980s have generally been reversed. Either the degree of persistence is extremely high, as mooted in Blanchard and Summers (1986), or there are supply side factors which remain imperfectly understood and have yet to see the light of day.

Explaining Cross-country Differences

One of the most intriguing features of the pattern of unemployment in the post-war period is the tremendous variance in the experiences of different countries (see table 1). This is particularly interesting in view of the fact that the commodity price shocks of 1974 and 1979 hit all of them, although by no means equally. There are a number of facts which stand out in Table 1. First, in every country unemployment is higher in the 1980s than in the 1960s. Second, in the first group of countries (the EC group), unemployment is vastly higher in the 1980s than in the 1960s whereas in the non EC countries of Europe and in Japan, the rise in unemployment is generally very modest. North America and Oceania are somewhere in between.

In order to explain these differences, there are two approaches. The first is what might be termed a reduced form approach. That is, to isolate features of the labour or product markets across countries and to relate these directly to some measure of economic performance. This approach may be found in the seminal work of Bruno and Sachs (1984) and McCallum (1983) as well as in Gordon (1987), Freeman (1988), Barro (1988). The alternative approach is somewhat more structural and involves first estimating the parameters of a simple model which explains unemployment in a number of countries and then relating these parameters to features of the labour and product markets in those countries. This has been attempted by Grubb *et al.* (1982), Bean *et al.* (1986a), Newell and Symons (1985; 1987), Jackman, Layard, Nickell and Wadhwani (1989, chapter 9), Alogoskoufis and Manning (1988), Calmfors and Driffill (1988).

What facts emerge from these studies? First, one useful fact concerning the ability of simple models to explain cross-country differences in unemployment patterns. Consider the long-run solution to equation (55) omitting $\Delta^2 w$ terms. This gives

$$u = \frac{\gamma_0 + \beta_0}{\beta_2 + \gamma_2} - \frac{\gamma_{11} + \beta_{11}}{\beta_2 + \gamma_2} \Delta^2 p + \frac{z_w - \beta_4 \epsilon_p}{\beta_2 + \gamma_2}, \qquad (56)$$

where the coefficient of $\Delta^2 p$ is often termed nominal wage rigidity (NWR) whereas that on the shock terms $(\beta_2 + \gamma_2)^{-1}$ is termed real wage rigidity (RWR). NWR is, in fact, the unemployment cost of reducing inflation by one point whereas RWR is the unemployment effect of a unit increase in wage pressure. In Jackman, Layard, Nickell and Wadhwani (1989, chapter 9), the relevant parameters are estimated for 19 countries and a measure of the wage pressure shocks between the period 1969–73 and 1980–5 is obtained. Then if Δu

is the change in unemployment between the two periods, the following cross-section regression was obtained

$$\frac{\Delta u}{\text{total shock}} = 0.002 - \underset{(7.2)}{1.02} \frac{NWR\Delta(\Delta^2 p)}{\text{total shock}} + \underset{(10.5)}{1.84} RWR$$

$$(R^2 = 0.93, N = 19).$$

Thus some 93% of the cross-country variation in unemployment change per unit shock can be explained within this simple framework.[22]

Turning now to the importance of labour market institutions, probably the most important feature that has been studied is the structure of wage bargaining which ranges from completely centralised in Austria, say, to completely decentralised in the United States. Following Crouch (1985), Bruno and Sachs (1984) constructed an index of the degree of centralisation of wage bargaining or 'corporatism' which produces a ranking of all the countries. They then discovered that more corporatist countries (essentially the small non-EC countries of Europe) performed better in response to the first oil shock. This generated some controversy, essentially because, as we have already noted in section III, a high level of *decentralisation* should also work well. Both Freeman (1988) and Calmfors and Driffill (1988) pursue this critique with some success, although the former is antipathetic to the whole business of corporatism indices on the not unreasonable grounds that their construction is a very subjective activity. He prefers to use an index of wage dispersion, arguing that high dispersion reflects decentralised, flexible wage determination, and low dispersion reflects centralisation. He duly finds that both high and low wage dispersion are associated with superior performance relative to middle ranking levels of dispersion. McCallum (1983) follows the same line independently and concludes that a superior labour market indicator is the degree of social consensus, as proxied by strike levels in the 1950s and 1960s. This is a key correlate of superior performance during the 1970s, at least on the inflation front.

Those pursuing the more structural approach also make use of the corporatism concept and typically relate it to the parameter which measures the impact of unemployment on wage setting, γ_2, which is, in fact, the key determinant of RWR. Bean *et al.* (1986) discover the γ_2 parameter to be positively related to corporatism whereas Alogoskoufis and Manning (1988) find it to be positively related to the Calmfors and Driffill adjusted index, which allocates high positions to the most and the least centralised systems. Jackman, Layard, Nickell and Wadhwani (1989, chapter 9), on the other hand, find their estimate of γ_2 to be only weakly related to corporatism using any measure. But this is not the only factor that influences γ_2. Jackman *et al.* also discover that it is very strongly related to the period of availability of unemployment benefit. That is, the longer the duration of benefit, the smaller the impact of

[22] This regression also includes a dummy for Spain to take account of the huge wage shock she sustained at the end of the Franco era.

unemployment on wages and hence the higher RWR. This is, of course, perfectly consistent with our discussion of wage setting where unemployment has its effect via fear of job loss. Finally, they also find some evidence that γ_2 is positively related to the proportion of small firms in the economy, which again accords with the evidence noted in section III, where wages in small firms were found to be more responsive to labour market forces than those in large firms.

Having dealt with impact of activity levels on wage setting, what information is there on the correlates of persistence? On the price side, we noted that persistence or hysteresis arises from employment adjustment costs. The main result, reported in Jackman, Layard, Nickell and Wadhwani (1989, chapter 9) is that there is some evidence of an inverse relationship between the price hysteresis parameter (β_{21}) and the proportion of workers with a current job tenure of less than 2 years (which incidentally varies widely from a high of 39% in the United States to a low of just 13% in Italy!). It seems reasonable to suppose that this latter figure is negatively correlated with employment adjustment costs.

On the wage front, the basic result already mentioned is that the wage hysteresis parameter (γ_{21}) is positively related to the long-term unemployed proportion which, in its turn, is positively related to benefit duration. There is also evidence of a negative relationship between γ_{21} and the proportion of employees in small firms, which hints at the importance of insiders who are perhaps less likely to be found in the small firms sector.

Finally we come to nominal inertia. The other major result of Bruno and Sachs (1984) was that aside from corporatism, the key determinant of a good performance following the first oil shock was the presence of a high degree of nominal inertia in wage setting and this was, in turn, related to the frequency and degree of indexation of wage bargaining. That nominal inertia should reduce the impact of a supply side shock should come as no surprise, given the results in the previous section.

CONCLUDING REMARKS

It should be obvious from what has gone before that a great deal has been achieved in the last two decades. In particular we have a much better understanding of the role of both expectations and imperfectly competitive forces in generating fluctuations, we have begun to lay the micro-foundations of labour market behaviour, and we have a deeper grasp of the role of shocks from different sides of the labour and product markets. However, there remains a great deal of unfinished business. With regard to the questions thrown up by unemployment fluctuations, the first outstanding one is how far can the real business cycle model be pushed? Can it be applied successfully in those countries where unemployment movements are more dramatic than in the United States or is it simply a parochial affair? Can the mysterious productivity shocks be successfully and convincingly identified?

Turning to the neo-Keynesian alternative, just how important is nominal inertia? For example, Newell and Symons (1988) are quite prepared to deny its existence in wage setting, in more or less all OECD countries. A great deal more needs to be done before we understand the microeconomics of both price and wage setting, particularly at the level of the firm. We have very little systematic information on contracts and agreements, particularly on the price side, and even if we did have a lot of information, it is not at all clear how it should be handled. The gap here between micro and macro appears particularly wide.

Concerning overall levels of unemployment, pinning down the supply side factors which determine levels in the long run has proved to be very tricky. The whole business is made more confusing because of the apparent presence of very long lasting dynamics. Hysteresis effects are clearly of great importance, with the data giving the appearance of economies being 'stuck' for long periods at very high unemployment levels following shocks which apparently have irreversible effects. These irreversibilities are, however, sometimes more apparent than real. Thus, for example, in the late 1930s in Britain it was thought that there was a substantial irreducible minimum number of unemployed who were deemed unemployable. By 1941, they were all working (not in the armed forces).

The differences between countries are very suggestive but we have only scratched the surface when it comes to really understanding the forces at work. It does appear to be the case that some countries work better than others, but the extent to which the appropriate institutions can be transferred from one country to another is not even close to being understood. Overall, a lot has been achieved, but we remain a long way from a generally accepted view of the fundamental causes of unemployment.

REFERENCES

Abowd, J. M. and Card, D. M. (1983). 'Intertemporal substitution in the presence of long term contracts.' Industrial Relations Section Working Paper No. 166, Princeton University.
—— and —— (1987). 'Intertemporal labor supply and long-term employment contracts.' *American Economic Review*, vol. 77, pp. 50–68.
—— and —— (1989). 'On the covariance structure of earnings and hours changes.' *Econometrica*, vol. 57, pp. 411–46.
Abraham, K. and Katz, L. (1986). 'Cyclical unemployment: sectoral shifts or aggregate disturbances?' *Journal of Political Economy*, vol. 94, pp. 507–22.
Akerlof, G. (1982). 'Labor contracts as partial gift exchange.' *Quarterly Journal of Economics*, vol. 87, pp. 543–69.
—— (1984). 'Gift exchange and efficiency-wage theory: four views.' *American Economic Review*, vol. 74, pp. 79–83.
—— and Katz, L. F. (1986). 'Do deferred wages dominate involuntary unemployment as a worker discipline device?' University of California, Berkeley, mimeo.
—— and —— (1989). 'Workers' trust funds and the logic of wage profiles.' *Quarterly Journal of Economics*, vol. 104, pp. 525–36.
—— and Miyazaki, H. (1980). 'The implicit contract theory of unemployment meets the wage bill argument.' *Review of Economic Studies*, vol. 47, pp. 321–38.
—— and Yellen, J. L. (1985). 'A near-rational model of the business cycle, with wage and price inertia.' *Quarterly Journal of Economics*, vol. 100 (Suppl.), pp. 823–38.
Alberro, J. (1981). 'The Lucas hypothesis on the Phillips curve: further international evidence.' *Journal of Monetary Economics*, vol. 7, pp. 239–50.
Alogoskoufis, C. S. (1987). 'On intertemporal substitution and aggregate labour supply.' *Journal of Political Economy*, vol. 95, pp. 938–60.

—— (1989). 'On fiscal policies, external imbalances and fundamental equilibrium exchange rates.' Centre for Economic Policy Research, Discussion Paper No. 322.

—— and Manning, A. (1988). 'On the persistence of unemployment.' *Economic Policy*, vol. 5, pp. 2–43.

—— —— (1989). 'Tests of alternative wage employment bargaining models with an application to the UK aggregate labour market.' Birkbeck College, Discussion Paper in Economics, 89/5.

—— and Pissarides, C. (1983). 'A test of price sluggishness in the simple rational expectations model: UK 1950–80.' ECONOMIC JOURNAL, vol. 93, pp. 616–28.

Altonji, J. (1982). 'The intertemporal substitution model of labour market fluctuations: an empirical analysis.' *Review of Economic Studies*, vol. 49, pp. 783–824.

—— (1986). 'Intertemporal substitution in labor supply.' *Journal of Political Economy*, vol. 94, pp. S176–215.

Andrews, M. J. and Harrison, A. (1988). 'Testing for efficient contracts in unionised labour markets.' University of Manchester, Department of Econometrics, D.P. No. ES201.

Ashenfelter, O. (1984). 'Macroeconomic analyses and microeconomic analyses of labor supply.' *Carnegie–Rochester Conference Series on Public Policy*, No. 21, pp. 117–55.

Atkinson, A. B., Gomulka, J., Micklewright, J. and Rau, N. (1984). 'Unemployment benefit, duration and incentives in Britain.' *Journal of Public Economics*, vol. 23, pp. 3–26.

Attfield, C. L. F., Demery, D. and Duck, N. W. (1981). 'Unanticipated monetary growth; output and the price level: U.K., 1946–77.' *European Economic Review*, vol. 16, pp. 367–85.

Azariadis, C. (1975). 'Implicit contracts and underemployment equilibria.' *Journal of Political Economy*, vol. 83, pp. 1183–202.

Baily, M. N. (1974). 'Wages and employment under uncertain demand.' *Review of Economic Studies*, vol. 41, pp. 37–50.

Ball, L. and Cecchetti, S. G. (1988). 'Imperfect information and staggered price setting.' *American Economic Review*, vol. 78, pp. 999–1018.

—— Mankiw, N. G. and Romer, D. (1988). 'The new Keynesian economics and the output–inflation trade-off.' *Brookings Papers on Economic Activity*, vol. 1, pp. 1–65.

—— and Romer, D. (1987). 'Real rigidities and the non-neutrality of money.' NBER, Working Paper No. 2476, Cambridge, Mass.

—— and —— (1989a). 'The equilibrium and optimal timing of price changes.' *Review of Economic Studies*, vol. 56, pp. 179–98.

—— and —— (1989b). 'Are prices too sticky?' *Quarterly Journal of Economics*, vol. 194, pp. 507–24.

Barro, R. (1972). 'A theory of monopolistic price adjustments.' *Review of Economic Studies*, vol. 34, pp. 17–26.

—— (1977). 'Unanticipated money growth and unemployment in the United States.' *American Economic Review*, vol. 67, pp. 101–15.

—— (1981). 'Output effects of government purchases.' *Journal of Political Economy*, vol. 89, pp. 1086–121.

—— (1988). 'The persistence of unemployment.' *American Economic Review (Papers and Proceedings)*, vol. 78, pp. 32–7.

—— and King, R. (1984). 'Time separable preferences and intertemporal substitution models of the business cycle.' *Quarterly Journal of Economics*, vol. 99, pp. 817–40.

Bean, C. (1989). 'Is there a capital shortage?' *Economic Policy*, vol. 8, pp. 11–54.

—— Layard, R. and Nickell, S. (1986a) (editors). *Unemployment. Economica* (Supplement), vol. 53.

—— —— and —— (1986b). 'The rise in unemployment: a multi-country study.' *Economica* (Supplement on Unemployment), vol. 53, pp. S1–22.

—— and Turnbull, P. (1987). 'Employment in the British coal industry: a test of the labour demand model.' ECONOMIC JOURNAL, vol. 97, pp. 1092–104.

Beaudry, P. and DiNardo, J. (1989). 'Long-term contracts and equilibrium models of the labor market: some favourable evidence.' Industrial Relations Section Working Paper 252, Princeton University.

Beenstock, M. and others (1985). 'A medium term macroeconomic model of the U.K. economy, 1950–82.' City University Business School, London, mimeo.

Benabou, R. (1989). 'Optimal price dynamics and speculation with a storable good.' *Econometrica*, vol. 57, pp. 41–80.

—— and Bismut, C. (1988). 'Wage bargaining and staggered contracts: theory and estimation.' CEPREMAP Discussion Paper No. 8810, Paris.

Benhabib, J. and Laroque, G. (1988). 'On competitive cycles in productive economies.' *Journal of Economic Theory*, vol. 45, pp. 145–70.

Binmore, K., Rubinstein, A. and Wolinsky, A. (1986). 'The Nash bargaining solution in economic modelling.' *Rand Journal of Economics*, vol. 17, pp. 176–88.

Bishop, R. (1964). 'A Zeuthen–Hicks theory of bargaining.' *Econometrica*, vol. 32, pp. 410–7.

Blackaby, D. H. and Manning, D. M. (1988). 'The North–South divide: questions of existence and stability.' University College of Swansea, mimeo (forthcoming, ECONOMIC JOURNAL).

Blackburn, M. and Neumark, D. (1988). 'Efficiency wages, inter-industry wage differentials and the return to ability.' University of South Carolina, mimeo.

Blanchard, O. (1986). 'The wage price spiral.' *Quarterly Journal of Economics*, vol. 101, pp. 543–65.

—— (1987). 'Individual and aggregate price adjustment.' *Brookings Papers on Economic Activity*, vol. 1, pp. 57–122.

—— and Diamond, P. (1989a). 'The Beveridge curve.' *Brookings Papers on Economic Activity*, vol. 1, pp. 1–76.

—— and —— (1989b). 'Long term unemployment and wage determination.' MIT Economics Department, mimeo.

—— and Fischer, S. (1989). *Lectures in Macroeconomics*. Cambridge, Mass.: MIT Press.

—— and Kiyotaki, N. (1987). 'Monopolistic competition and the effects of aggregate demand.' *American Economic Review*, vol. 77, pp. 647–66.

—— and Quah, D. (1987). 'The dynamic effects of aggregate demand and supply disturbances.' *American Economic Review*, vol. 79, pp. 655–73.

—— and Summers, L. (1986). 'Hysteresis and the European unemployment problem.' *NBER Macroeconomics Annual*, vol. 1, pp. 15–78.

Blanchflower, D. (1989). 'Fear, unemployment and pay flexibility.' University of Surrey, mimeo.

—— and Oswald, A. (1987). 'Internal and external influences upon pay settlements: new survey evidence.' *British Journal of Industrial Relations*, vol. 26, pp. 363–70.

—— and —— (1989). 'The wage curve.' Centre for Labour Economics, D.P. No. 340, London School of Economics (forthcoming, *Scandinavian Journal of Economics*).

—— Garrett, M. and Oswald, A. (1990). 'Insider power in wage determination' (forthcoming, *Economica*, vol. 57).

Brown, J. N. and Ashenfelter, O. (1986). 'Testing the efficiency of employment contracts.' *Journal of Political Economy*, vol. 94, pp. 540–87.

Brunello, G. and Wadhwani, S. (1989). 'The determinants of wage flexibility in Japan: some lessons from a comparison with the UK using micro-data.' Centre for Labour Economics, W.P. No. 1116, London School of Economics.

Bruno, M. and Sachs, J. (1984). *The Economics of Worldwide Stagflation*. Oxford: Basil Blackwell.

Budd, A., Levine, P. and Smith, P. (1988). 'Unemployment, vacancies and the long-term unemployed.' ECONOMIC JOURNAL, vol. 98, pp. 1071–91.

Burgess, S. (1989). 'Unemployment flows and turnover in Britain: some facts.' Bristol University Economics Department D.P. No. 88/229.

Calmfors, L. and Driffill, J. (1988). 'Centralization of wage bargaining and macroeconomic performance.' *Economic Policy*, vol. 6, pp. 13–61.

—— and Horn, H. (1986). 'Employment policies and centralised wage-setting.' *Economica*, vol. 53, pp. 281–302.

Calvo, G. (1979). 'Quasi-Walrasian theories of unemployment.' *American Economic Review (Papers and Proceedings)*, vol. 69, pp. 102–7.

—— and Phelps, E. (1977). 'Appendix: employment contingent wage contracts.' *Carnegie-Rochester Conference Series on Public Policy*, vol. 5, pp. 160–8.

Cannan, E. (1914). *Wealth*, 3rd edition. London: Staples Press.

Caplin, A. and Spulber, D. (1987). 'Menu costs and the neutrality of money.' *Quarterly Journal of Economics*, vol. 102, pp. 703–26.

Card, D. (1988). 'Unexpected inflation, real wages and employment determination in union contracts.' Industrial Relations Section W.P. No. 232, Princeton University.

Carlin, W. and Soskice, D. (1985). 'Real wages, unemployment, international competitiveness and inflation: a framework for analysing closed and open economies.' University College, Oxford, mimeo.

Carlton, D. (1985). 'Delivery lags as a determinant of demand.' University of Chicago, Graduate School of Business, mimeo.

—— (1986). 'The rigidity of prices.' *American Economic Review*, vol. 76, pp. 637–58.

Carmichael, L. H. (1983). 'Firm-specific human capital and promotion ladders.' *Bell Journal of Economics*, vol. 14, pp. 251–8.

—— (1985). 'Can unemployment be involuntary? Comment.' *American Economic Review*, vol. 75, pp. 1213–4.

Carruth, A. A., Oswald, A. J. and Findlay, L. (1986). 'A test of a model of trade union behaviour: the coal and steel industries in Britain.' *Oxford Bulletin of Economics and Statistics*, vol. 49, pp. 59–78.

Christofides, L. N. and Oswald, A. J. (1988). 'Real wage determination in collective bargaining agreements.' Centre for Labour Economics, Working Paper No. 1062, London School of Economics.

Classen, K. (1977). 'The effect of unemployment insurance on the duration of unemployment and subsequent earnings.' *Industrial and Labor Relations Review*, vol. 30, pp. 438–44.

Crouch, C. (1985). 'Conditions for trade union wage restraint.' In *The Politics of Economic Stagflation* (ed. L. Lindberg and C. S. Mail). Washington: Brookings Institution.

Davis, S. (1987). 'Allocative disturbances and specific capital in real business cycle theories.' *American Economic Review*, vol. 77, pp. 326–31.

Dertouzos, J. N. and Pencavel, J. H. (1981). 'Wage and employment determination under trade unionism: the international typographical union.' *Journal of Political Economy*, vol. 89, pp. 1162–81.

Diamond, P. A. (1981). 'Mobility costs, frictional employment and efficiency.' *Journal of Political Economy*, vol. 89, pp. 798–812.

—— (1982). 'Wage determination and efficiency in search equilibrium.' *Review of Economic Studies*, vol. 49, pp. 217–27.

Dickens, W. and Katz, L. (1987). 'Inter-industry wage differences and industry characteristics.' In *Unemployment and the Structure of Labor Markets* (ed. K. Lang and J. Leonard). New York: Basil Blackwell.

Dixon, H. (1988). 'Unions, oligopoly and the natural range of unemployment.' ECONOMIC JOURNAL, vol. 98, pp. 1127–47.

Dolado, J. (1986). 'Intertemporal employment and pricing decision rules in UK manufacturing.' Oxford Institute of Economics and Statistics, Applied Economics D.P. No. 18, University of Oxford.

—— Malo de Molina, J. L. and Zabalza, A. (1986). 'Spanish industrial unemployment: some explanatory factors.' *Economica* (Supplement on Unemployment), vol. 53, pp. S313–53.

Ebmer, R. (1989). 'Some micro evidence on unemployment persistence.' Johannes Kepler University, Linz, Austria, mimeo.

Ehrenberg, R. G. and Oaxaca, R. L. (1976). 'Unemployment insurance, duration of unemployment and subsequent wage growth.' *American Economic Review*, vol. 66, pp. 754–66.

Eichenbaum, M. and Singleton, K. T. (1986). 'Do equilibrium real business cycle theories explain postwar U.S. business cycles?' *NBER Macroeconomics Annual*, vol. 1, pp. 91–134.

Eichenbaum, M., Hansen, L. and Singleton, K. (1988). 'A time series analysis of representative agent models of consumption and leisure.' *Quarterly Journal of Economics*, vol. 103, pp. 51–78.

Espinosa, M. P. and Rhee, C. (1989). 'Efficient wage bargaining as a repeated game.' *Quarterly Journal of Economics*, vol. 104, pp. 565–88.

Evans, G. W. (1987). 'Sectoral imbalance and unemployment in the United Kingdom.' London School of Economics, mimeo.

Farber, H. S. (1986). 'The analysis of union behaviour.' In *The Handbook of Labor Economics* (ed. O. Ashenfelter and R. Layard). Amsterdam: North-Holland.

Farmer, R. E. A. (1986). 'Deficits and cycles.' *Journal of Economic Theory*, vol. 40, pp. 77–88.

Fehr, E. (1988). 'Do cooperation and harassment explain involuntary unemployment?' Discussion Paper 1988–7. Vienna: University of Technology.

Fethke, G. and Policiano, A. (1984). 'Wage contingencies, the pattern of negotiations and aggregate implications of alternative contract structures.' *Journal of Monetary Economics*, vol. 14, pp. 150–70.

—— and —— (1986). 'Will wage setters ever stagger decisions?' *Quarterly Journal of Economics*, vol. 101, pp. 867–77.

Fischer, S. (1977). 'Long term contracts, rational expectations and the optimal money supply rule.' *Journal of Political Economy*, vol. 85, pp. 191–205.

—— (1988). 'Recent developments in macroeconomics.' ECONOMIC JOURNAL, vol. 98, pp. 294–339.

Flanagan, R. J., Soskice, D. W. and Ulman, L. (1983). *Unionism, Economic Stabilization, and Incomes Policies: European Experience*. Washington: Brookings Institution.

Franz, W. (1987). 'Hysteresis, persistence and the NAIRU: an empirical analysis for the Federal Republic of Germany.' In *The Fight Against Unemployment, Macroeconomic Papers from the Center for European Policy Studies* (ed. R. Layard and L. Calmfors). Cambridge, Mass.: MIT Press.

Freeman, R. B. (1980). 'The exit–voice tradeoff in the labor market, unionism, job tenure, quits, and separations.' *Quarterly Journal of Economics*, vol. 94, pp. 643–73.

—— (1981). 'The effect of trade unionism on fringe benefits.' *Industrial and Labor Relations Review*, vol. 34, pp. 489–509.

—— (1987). 'Union density and economic performance: an analysis of U.S. states.' Centre for Labour Economics, Working Paper No. 1001, London School of Economics.

—— (1988). 'The impact of labor market institutions and constraints on economic performance.' *Economic Policy*, vol. 6, pp. 64–78.

Friedman, M. (1968). 'The role of monetary policy.' *American Economic Review*, vol. 58, pp. 1–17.

Froyen, R. T. and Waud, R. N. (1980). 'International evidence on output-inflation trade-offs.' *American Economic Review*, vol. 70, pp. 409–21.

Gibbons, R. and Katz, L. (1987). 'Unmeasured ability and inter-industry wage differences.' MIT, mimeo.

Gordon, D. (1974). 'A neo-classical theory of Keynesian unemployment.' *Economic Inquiry*, vol. 12, pp. 431–59.

Gordon, R. J. (1982). 'Price inertia and policy ineffectiveness in the United States, 1890–1980.' *Journal of Political Economy*, vol. 90, pp. 1087–117.

—— (1987). 'Productivity, wages, and prices inside and outside manufacturing in the U.S., Japan and Europe.' *European Economic Review*, vol. 31, pp. 685–732.

Grandmont, J. M. (1985). 'On endogenous competitive business cycles.' *Econometrica*, vol. 53, pp. 995–1045.

—— (1989). 'Keynesian issues and economic theory.' CEPREMAP Discussion Paper No. 8907, Paris.

Gregory, M., Lobban, P. and Thomson, A. (1987). 'Pay settlements in manufacturing industry, 1979–84:

a micro-data study of the impact of product and labour market pressures.' *Oxford Bulletin of Economics and Statistics*, vol. 49, pp. 129–50.

Grossman, S. and Hart, O. (1981). 'Implicit contracts, moral hazard, and unemployment.' *American Economic Review*, vol. 71, pp. 301–7.

Grubb, D., Jackman, R. and Layard, R. (1982). 'Wage rigidity and unemployment in OECD countries.' *European Economic Review*, vol. 21, pp. 11–40.

Hall, R. E. (1975). 'The rigidity of wages and the persistence of unemployment.' *Brookings Papers on Economic Activity*, vol. 2, pp. 301–50.

—— (1980). 'Labor supply and aggregate fluctuations.' *Carnegie–Rochester Conference Series on Public Policy*, no. 12, pp. 7–33.

—— (1987*b*). 'Market structure and macroeconomic fluctuations.' *Brookings Papers on Economic Activity*, vol. 1, pp. 285–322.

Hamm, J. (1986). 'Testing whether unemployment represents life-cycle labour supply behaviour.' *Review of Economic Studies*, vol. 50, pp. 559–78.

Hamilton, J. D. (1983). 'Oil and the macroeconomy since World War II.' *Journal of Political Economy*, vol. 91, pp. 228–48.

Hansen, G. (1985). 'Indivisible labor and the business cycle.' *Journal of Monetary Economics*, vol. 16, pp. 309–28.

Harris, J. and Todaro, M. (1970). 'Migration, unemployment and development. A 2-sector analysis.' *American Economic Review*, vol. 55, pp. 126–42.

Hart, O. (1982). 'A model of imperfect competition with Keynesian features.' *Quarterly Journal of Economics*, vol. 97, pp. 109–38.

—— (1983). 'Optimal labour contracts under asymmetric information: an introduction.' *Review of Economic Studies*, vol. 50, pp. 3–35.

—— and Holmstrom, B. (1987). 'The theory of contracts.' In *Advances in Economic Theory, Fifth World Congress* (ed. T. Bewley). Cambridge University Press.

Heckman, J. (1984). 'Comments on the Ashenfelter and Kydland papers.' *Carnegie–Rochester Conference Series on Public Policy*, no. 21, pp. 209–24.

—— and McCurdy, T. E. (1988). 'Empirical tests for labor–market equilibrium: an evaluation.' *Carnegie–Rochester Conference Series on Public Policy*, vol. 28, pp. 231–59.

Holmlund, B. and Zetterberg, J. (1989). 'Insider effects in wage determination: evidence from five countries.' Uppsala University, Sweden, mimeo.

Holt, C. (1970). 'How can the Phillips curve be moved to reduce both inflation and unemployment?' In *Microeconomic Foundations of Employment and Inflation Theory* (ed. E. Phelps). New York: Norton.

Holzer, H. J. (1989*a*). 'Employment, unemployment and demand shifts in local labor markets.' NBER Working Paper 2858, February, Cambridge, Mass.

—— (1989*b*). 'Wages, employer costs, and employee performance in the firm.' NBER Working Paper 2830, Cambridge, Mass.

—— Katz, L. and Krueger, A. (1988). 'Job queues and wages: new evidence on the minimum wage and inter-industry wage structure.' NBER Working Paper 2561, Cambridge, Mass.

Howitt, P. (1988). 'Business cycles with costly search and recruiting.' *Quarterly Journal of Economics*, vol. 103, pp. 147–64.

Jackman, R. (1984). 'Money wage rigidity in an economy with rational trade unions.' In *Recent Advances in Labour Economics* (ed. G. Hutchinson and J. Treble). London: Croom Helm.

—— and Roper, S. (1987). 'Structural unemployment.' *Oxford Bulletin of Economics and Statistics*, vol. 49, pp. 9–36.

—— Layard, R., Nickell, S. and Wadhwani, S. (1989). Draft of *Unemployment*. Oxford University Press, Oxford (forthcoming).

—— —— and Pissarides, C. (1989). 'On vacancies.' *Oxford Bulletin of Economics and Statistics*, vol. 51, pp. 377–95.

Johnson, G. and Layard, R. (1986). 'The natural rate of unemployment: explanation and policy.' In *The Handbook of Labor Economics* (ed. O. Ashenfelter and R. Layard). Amsterdam: North-Holland.

Jullien, B. and Picard, P. (1989). 'Efficiency wage and macroeconomic policy: a dynamic model with rational expectations.' CEPREMAP, Paris, mimeo.

Kahn, C. and Mookherjee, D. (1988). 'A competitive efficiency wage model with Keynesian features.' *Quarterly Journal of Economics*, vol. 103, pp. 609–45.

Katz, L. F. (1986). 'Efficiency wage theories, a partial evaluation.' NBER Macroeconomics Annual, vol. 1, pp. 235–72.

—— and Meyer, B. D. (1988). 'The impact of the potential duration of unemployment benefits on the duration of unemployment.' Industrial Relations Section W.P. No. 241, University of Princeton.

Kaufman, R. T. (1984). 'On wage stickiness in Britain's competitive sector.' *British Journal of Industrial Relations*, vol. 22, pp. 101–12.

Kennan, J. (1988). 'Equilibrium interpretations of employment and real wage fluctuations.' Domestic Studies Program, Working Papers in Economics, E-88-23, Hoover Institution, Stanford University.

Kiefer, N. and Neumann, G. (1979). 'An empirical job-search model with a test of the constant reservation wage hypothesis.' *Journal of Political Economy*, vol. 87, pp. 89–108.

King, R. and Plosser, C. (1984). 'Money, credit, and prices in a real business cycle economy.' *American Economic Review*, vol. 74, pp. 363–80.

—— —— and Rebelo, S. (1988). 'Production, growth and business cycles II. New directions.' *Journal of Monetary Economics*, vol. 21, pp. 309–41.

Knoester, A. (1983). 'Stagnation and the inverted Haavelmo effect: some international evidence.' *De Economist*, vol. 131, pp. 548–84.

—— and van der Windt, N. (1987). 'Real wages and taxation in ten OECD countries.' *Oxford Bulletin of Economics and Statistics*, vol. 49, pp. 151–69.

Krueger, A. and Summers, L. (1988). 'Efficiency wages and the inter-industry wage structure.' *Econometrica*, vol. 56, pp. 259–94.

Kydland, F. E. and Prescott, E. F. (1982). 'Time to build and aggregate fluctuations.' *Econometrica*, vol. 50, pp. 1345–70.

Lambert, J.-P. (1988). *Disequilibrium Macro-models Based on Business Survey Data*. Cambridge: Cambridge University Press.

Lancaster, T. (1979). 'Econometric methods for the duration of unemployment.' *Econometrica*, vol. 47, pp. 939–56.

Layard, R. and Nickell, S. (1986). 'Unemployment in Britain.' *Economica* (Supplement on Unemployment), vol. 87, pp. S121–70.

—— and —— (1987). 'The labour market.' In *The Performance of the British Economy* (ed. R. Dornbusch and R. Layard). Oxford: Clarendon Press.

—— and —— (1988). 'Is unemployment lower if unions bargain over employment?' Centre for Labour Economics, Working Paper 955R, London School of Economics (forthcoming, *Quarterly Journal of Economics*).

Lester, R. (1952). 'A range theory of wage differentials.' *Industrial and Labor Relations Review*, vol. 5, pp. 483–500.

Liederman, L. (1980). 'Macroeconometric testing of the rational expectations and structural neutrality hypotheses for the United States.' *Journal of Monetary Economics*, vol. 6, pp. 69–82.

Lilien, D. M. (1982). Sectoral shifts and cyclical unemployment.' *Journal of Political Economy*, vol. 90, pp. 777–93.

Lindbeck, A. and Snower, D. J. (1986). 'Wage setting, unemployment, and insider-outsider relations.' *American Economic Review*, vol. 76, pp. 235–9.

—— and —— (1987). 'Union activity, unemployment persistence and wage-employment ratchets.' *European Economic Review*, vol. 31, pp. 157–67.

—— and —— (1988). 'Cooperation, harassment, and involuntary unemployment: an insider-outsider approach.' *American Economic Review*, vol. 78, pp. 167–88.

Lockwood, B. and Manning, A. (1988). 'Dynamic wage and employment determination with endogenous union membership.' London: Birkbeck College, mimeo.

Long, J. and Plosser, C. (1983). 'Real business cycles.' *Journal of Political Economy*, vol. 91, pp. 39–69.

Loungani, P. (1986). 'Oil price shocks and the dispersion hypothesis, 1900–1980.' Rochester Center for Economic Research, Working Paper No. 33. University of Rochester.

—— and Rogerson, R. (1989). 'Cyclical fluctuations and sectoral reallocation: evidence from the PSID.' *Journal of Monetary Economics*, vol. 23, pp. 259–74.

Lucas, R. E. (1972). 'Expectations and the neutrality of money.' *Journal of Economic Theory*, vol. 4, pp. 103–24.

—— (1973). 'Some international evidence on output-inflation trade-offs.' *American Economic Review*, vol. 63, pp. 326–34.

—— (1987). *Models of Business Cycles*. Oxford: Basil Blackwell.

—— and Prescott, E. (1974). 'Equilibrium search and unemployment.' *Journal of Economic Theory*, vol. 7, pp. 188–209.

—— and Rapping, L. (1969). 'Real wages, employment and inflation.' *Journal of Political Economy*, vol. 77, pp. 721–54.

MacLeod, W. B. and Malcomson, J. (1989). 'Wage premiums and profit maximisation in efficiency wage models.' Centre for Labour Economics, D.P. No. 337, London School of Economics.

MaCurdy, T. E. (1981). 'An empirical model of labor supply in a life-cycle setting.' *Journal of Political Economy*, vol. 89, pp. 1059–85.

—— and Pencavel, J. (1986). 'Testing between competing models of wage and employment determination in unionized labor markets.' *Journal of Political Economy*, vol. 94, pp. 53–139.

MacKay, D., Boddy, D., Brock, J., Diack, J. and Jones, N. (1971). *Labour Markets Under Different Employment Conditions*. London: George Allen and Unwin.

Mankiw, N. G. (1985). 'Small menu costs and large business cycles: a macro-economic model of monopoly.' *Quarterly Journal of Economics*, vol. 100, pp. 225–52.

——— (1989). 'Real business cycles: a new Keynesian perspective.' *Journal of Economic Perspectives*, vol. 3, pp. 79–90.

——— Rotemberg, J. J. and Summers, L. H. (1985). 'Intertemporal substitution in macroeconomics.' *Quarterly Journal of Economics*, vol. 100, pp. 225–51.

Manning, A. (1987). 'An integration of trade union models in a sequential bargaining framework.' ECONOMIC JOURNAL, vol. 97, pp. 121–39.

——— (1988). 'Unemployment is probably lower if unions bargain over employment.' London: Birkbeck College, mimeo.

McCallum, J. (1983). 'Inflation and social consensus in the seventies.' ECONOMIC JOURNAL, vol. 93, pp. 784–805.

McDonald, I. M. and Solow, R. M. (1981). 'Wage bargaining and employment.' *American Economic Review*, vol. 71, pp. 896–908.

Meager, N. and Metcalf, H. (1988). 'Recruitment of the long-term unemployed.' Institute of Manpower Studies Report No. 138, University of Sussex.

Minford, P. (1983). 'Labour market equilibrium in an open economy.' *Oxford Economic Papers* (November Supplement), vol. 35, pp. 207–44.

Mishkin, F. S. (1982). 'Does anticipated monetary policy matter? An econometric investigation.' *Journal of Political Economy*, vol. 90, pp. 22–51.

Modigliani, F., Padoa Schioppa, F. and Rossi, N. (1986). 'Aggregate unemployment in Italy: 1960–83.' *Economica* (Supplement on Unemployment), vol. 53, pp. S245–74.

Mortensen, D. (1982). 'The matching process as a noncooperative bargaining game.' In *The Economics of Information and Uncertainty* (ed. J. J. McCall). Chicago: University of Chicago Press.

——— (1986). 'Job search and labor market analysis.' In *The Handbook of Labor Economics* (ed. O. Ashenfelter and R. Layard). Amsterdam: North-Holland.

Murphy, K. M. and Topel, R. (1987a). 'The evolution of unemployment in the United States: 1968–1985.' *NBER Macroeconomics Annual*, vol. 2, pp. 11–57.

——— and ——— (1987b). 'Unemployment, risk and earnings: testing for equalizing wage differences in the labor market.' In *Unemployment and the Structure of Labor Markets* (ed. K. Lang and J. Leonard). New York: Basil Blackwell.

Narendranathan, W., Nickell, S. and Stern, J. (1985). 'Unemployment benefits revisited.' ECONOMIC JOURNAL, vol. 95, pp. 307–29.

Nash, J. F. (1953). 'Two-person cooperative games. *Econometrica*, vol. 21, pp. 128–40.

Newell, A. and Symons, J. (1985). 'Wages and unemployment in OECD countries.' Centre for Labour Economics, D.P. No. 219, London School of Economics.

——— and ——— (1987). 'Corporatism, laissez-faire, and the rise in unemployment.' *European Economic Review*, vol. 31, pp. 567–601.

——— and ——— (1988). 'The Phillips curve is a real wage equation.' Centre for Labour Economics, Working Paper No. 1038, London School of Economics.

Nickell, S. (1979). 'Estimating the probability of leaving unemployment.' *Econometrica*, vol. 47, pp. 1249–66.

——— (1982). 'A bargaining model of the Phillips curve.' Centre for Labour Economics, D.P. No. 130, London School of Economics.

——— (1987a). 'Why is wage inflation in Britain so high?' *Oxford Bulletin of Economics and Statistics*, vol. 49, pp. 103–28.

——— (1987b). 'The short-run behaviour of labour supply.' In *Advances in Econometrics, Fifth World Congress* (ed. T. F. Bewley), pp. 177–96. Cambridge: Cambridge University Press.

Nickell, S. J. and Kong, P. (1988). 'An investigation into the power of insiders in wage determination.' Institute of Economics and Statistics, Applied Economics D.P. No. 42, University of Oxford.

——— and Wadhwani, S. (1989a). 'Insider forces and wage determination.' Centre for Labour Economics, D.P. No. 334, London School of Economics (forthcoming, ECONOMIC JOURNAL).

——— and ——— (1989b). 'Employment determination in British industry: investigations using macro-data.' Centre for Economic Policy Research, D.P. No. 320, London.

Okun, A. (1981). *Prices and Quantities: A Macroeconomic Analysis*. Washington: The Brookings Institution.

Oswald, A. J. (1985). 'The economic theory of trade unions; an introductory survey.' *Scandinavian Journal of Economics*, vol. 87, pp. 160–93.

——— (1986). 'Unemployment insurance and labour contracts under asymmetric information: theory and facts.' *American Economic Review*, vol. 76, pp. 365–78.

——— (1987). 'Efficient contracts are on the labour demand curve: theory and facts.' Centre for Labour Economics, Discussion Paper No. 284, London School of Economics.

——— and Turnbull, P. (1985). 'Pay and employment determination in Britain: what are labour contracts really like?' *Oxford Review of Economic Policy*, vol. 1, pp. 80–97.

Padoa Schioppa, F. (1989). 'Union wage setting and taxation.' Universita di Roma 'La Sapienza', Rome, mimeo (forthcoming, *Oxford Bulletin of Economics and Statistics*).

Parkin, M. (1986). 'The output–inflation tradeoff when prices are costly to change.' *Journal of Political Economy*, vol. 94, pp. 200–24.

Pencavel, J. H. (1972). 'Wages, specific training, and labor turnover in U.S. manufacturing industries.' *International Economic Review*, vol. 13, pp. 53–64.

—— (1984). 'The trade off between wages and employment in trade union objectives.' *Quarterly Journal of Economics*, vol. 99, pp. 215–31.

Pesaran, H. (1982). 'A critique of the proposed tests of the natural rate-rational expectations hypothesis.' ECONOMIC JOURNAL, vol. 92, pp. 529–54.

Phelps, E. (1968). 'Money wage dynamics and labor market equilibrium.' *Journal of Political Economy*, vol. 76, pp. 687–711.

—— (1972). *Inflation Policy and Unemployment Theory*. New York: Norton.

Phillips, A. W. (1958). 'The relation between unemployment and the rate of change of money wage rates in the United Kingdom 1861–1957.' *Economica*, vol. 25, pp. 283–99.

Pissarides, C. (1979). 'Contract theory, temporary layoffs and unemployment: a critical assessment.' In *Microeconomic Analysis* (AUTE Meetings, 1979) (ed. D. Currie, D. Peel and W. Peters), pp. 51–71. London: Croom Helm.

—— (1985). 'Short-run equilibrium dynamics of unemployment, vacancies, and real wages.' *American Economic Review*, vol. 75, pp. 676–90.

—— (1986a). 'Unemployment and vacancies in Britain.' *Economic Policy*, vol. 3, pp. 499–559.

—— (1986b). 'Equilibrium effects of tax-based incomes policies.' In *Incentive-Based Incomes Policies* (ed. D. Colander). Cambridge, Mass.: Ballinger.

—— (1989). *Equilibrium Unemployment Theory*. Oxford: Basil Blackwell.

Prescott, E. C. (1986). 'Theory ahead of business cycle measurement.' *Federal Reserve Bank of Minneapolis, Quarterly Review*, Fall, pp. 9–22.

Pudney, S. (1982). 'The identification of rational expectations models under structural neutrality.' *Journal of Economic Dynamics and Control*, vol. 4, pp. 117–22.

Reichlin, P. (1986). 'Equilibrium cycles in an overlapping generations economy with production.' *Journal of Economic Theory*, vol. 40, pp. 89–102.

Robinson, P. (1988). 'Why are the long-term unemployed locked out of the labour market and what can be done about it?' Campaign for Work Research Paper, vol. 1, no. 2, London.

Rogerson, R. (1987). 'An equilibrium model of sectoral reallocation.' *Journal of Political Economy*, vol. 95, pp. 824–34.

—— (1988). 'Indivisible labour lotteries and equilibrium.' *Journal of Monetary Economics*, vol. 21, pp. 3–16.

Rosen, S. (1985). 'Implicit contracts, a survey.' *Journal of Economic Literature*, vol. 23, pp. 1144–75.

—— (1986). 'The theory of equalizing differences.' In *The Handbook of Labor Economics* (ed. O. Ashenfelter and R. Layard). Amsterdam: North-Holland.

Rosenfeld, C. (1977). 'The extent of job search by employed workers.' *Monthly Labor Review*, vol. 100, pp. 58–62.

Rotemberg, J. J. (1982). 'Sticky prices in the United States.' *Journal of Political Economy*, vol. 90, pp. 1187–211.

Rowthorn, R. (1977). 'Conflict, inflation and money.' *Cambridge Journal of Economics*, vol. 1, pp. 215–39.

Salop, S. (1979). 'A model of the natural rate of unemployment.' *American Economic Review*, vol. 69, pp. 117–25.

Sargent, T. J. (1979). *Macroeconomic Theory*. New York: Academic Press.

—— (1987). *Dynamic Macroeconomic Theory*. Cambridge, Mass.: Harvard University Press.

Shapiro, C. and Stiglitz, J. E. (1984). 'Equilibrium unemployment as a worker discipline device.' *American Economic Review*, vol. 74, pp. 433–44.

Shapiro, M. D. (1987). 'Are cyclical fluctuations in productivity due to demand shocks or supply shocks?' NBER Working Paper 2147, February, Cambridge, Mass.

Sheshinski, E. and Weiss, Y. (1977). 'Inflation and costs of price adjustment.' *Review of Economic Studies*, vol. 44, pp. 287–304.

—— and —— (1983). 'Optimum pricing policy under stochastic inflation.' *Review of Economic Studies*, vol. 50, pp. 513–29.

Sims, C. A. (1988). 'Comments and discussion.' *Brookings Papers on Economic Activity*, vol. 1, pp. 75–9.

Slichter, S. (1950). 'Notes on the structure of wages.' *Review of Economics and Statistics*, vol. 32, pp. 80–91.

Small, D. H. (1979). 'Unanticipated monetary growth and unemployment in the United States: comment.' *American Economic Review*, vol. 69, pp. 996–1003.

Sneessens, H. R. and Dreze, J. H. (1986). 'A discussion of Belgian unemployment combining traditional concepts and disequilibrium economics.' *Economica* (Supplement on Unemployment), vol. 53, pp. S89–120.

Solon, G. (1985). 'Work incentive effects of taxing unemployment benefits.' *Econometrica*, vol. 53, pp. 295–306.

Solow, R. (1979). 'Another possible source of wage stickiness.' *Journal of Macroeconomics*, vol. 1, pp. 79–82.

—— (1985). 'Insiders and outsiders in wage determination.' *Scandinavian Journal of Economics*, vol. 87, pp. 411–28.

Stiglitz, J. E. (1974). 'Wage determination and unemployment in L.D.C.'s: the labor turnover model.' *Quarterly Journal of Economics*, vol. 88, pp. 194–227.

—— (1985). 'Equilibrium wage distributions.' ECONOMIC JOURNAL, vol. 95, pp. 595–618.

—— (1986). 'Theories of wage rigidity.' In *Keynes' Economic Legacy: Contemporary Economic Theories* (ed. Butkiewicz *et al.*). New York: Praeger.

Taylor, J. B. (1979). 'Staggered wage setting in a macro model.' *American Economic Review (Papers and Proceedings)*, vol. 68, pp. 108–13.

—— (1980). 'Aggregate dynamics and staggered contracts.' *Journal of Political Economy*, vol. 88, pp. 1–23.

—— (1983). 'Union wage settlements during a disinflation.' *American Economic Review*, vol. 73, pp. 981–93.

Topel, R. (1986). 'Local labor markets.' *Journal of Political Economy*, vol. 94, pp. 111–43.

Tsiddon, D. (1987). 'On the stubbornness of sticky prices.' Columbia University, mimeo.

Wadhwani, S. and Wall, M. (1988). 'A direct test of the efficiency wage model using micro-data.' Centre for Labour Economics D.P. No. 313, London School of Economics.

Weiss, A. (1980). 'Job queues and layoffs in labor markets with flexible wages.' *American Economic Review*, vol. 56, pp. 96–117.

Woodford, M. (1986). 'Stationary sunspot equilibria in a finance constrained economy.' *Journal of Economic Theory*, vol. 40, pp. 128–37.

Wren-Lewis, S. (1985). 'Imperfect competition and effective demand in the long run.' National Institute of Economic and Social Research, D.P. No. 98.

Yellen, J. L. (1984). 'Efficiency wage models of unemployment.' *American Economic Review*, vol. 74, pp. 200–5.

5

TAX POLICY: A SURVEY*

J. A. Kay

I. THE BASIS OF TAX POLICY

I.1 *The Changing Background*

Public finance is one of the oldest branches of economics. For centuries economic policy consisted of little else. But in the twentieth century the range of issues with which tax policy is concerned has widened greatly. In Victorian – or frontier – days the primary function of government was the provision of public goods – defence, police, a system of contract law and a mechanism for its enforcement. The task of tax policy was to obtain funds for these purposes with the minimum of fuss and expenditure. But in modern states public goods are a minor part of overall state activity (Table 1). Much of government expenditure is devoted to the provision to users, at prices well below cost, of private goods such as health and education. Income maintenance is another principal function. Together these categories total more than half of public spending for all the countries of Table 1. The essential nature of fiscal activity now is either to raise taxes on some commodities to permit subsidies on others, or to impose taxes on some individuals to make grants to others. The link between tax and spending is now close and symmetric. But this symmetry is rarely reflected in the theory, or the practice, of tax policy.

For most of this century, taxation has assumed an increasing share of national income. But by the end of the 1970s, the continuing rise provoked the beginnings of a so-called tax revolt, whose most famous manifestation was California's Proposition 13, which set a constitutional limit on state taxation. Dissatisfaction with both rates and structures of taxation has become increasingly widespread. The 1980s have seen an unprecedented pace of tax reform. In 1986 the Congress of the United States passed an Act providing for a major restructuring of its direct tax system. The New Zealand government has implemented one of the most radical reassessments of its system of taxation ever undertaken by a Western country. Britain has seen two important sets of tax reform measures, in 1984 and 1988. Japan and West Germany, despite strong political opposition, have begun the process of restructuring their fiscal systems. Tax reform is on the political agenda almost everywhere.

There are obvious common elements to these developments, which are related to a much wider reliance on market forces rather than state intervention in economic policy generally. Lower direct tax rates on a broader base have been a theme almost everywhere. These have been introduced in both the personal and the corporate sector. Cuts in the highest rates of tax have been

* This chapter was first published in the ECONOMIC JOURNAL, vol. 100, March 1990. I am grateful for comments on an earlier draft of this paper to (particularly) Sijbren Cnossen, Paul Geroski, Michael Keen and the referees and editor. Opinions are entirely mine.

Table 1

Government Expenditure by Economic Function (1981)

	As % of total expenditure				
	France	Germany	Japan	UK	US
Public goods	15·2	13·8	12·1	17·8	25·6
Merit goods	32·5	29·0	36·2	31·5	31·1
Income maintenance	35·0	33·9	20·0	21·1	23·7
Economic services	7·9	9·9	17·4	8·3	9·8
Debt interest	4·4	4·4	10·4	10·6	8·2
Other	2·4	4·4	1·3	4·6	0·5

Source: Saunders and Klau (1985), Table 9: categories follow their definitions. Note: UK 1979, US 1978: figures do not add to 100% because of differences in classification.

particularly marked, and almost all countries have reduced sharply the number of different tax rates in their schedule. The primary concern of this paper is to relate the changing climate of policy analysis to the changing climate of policy itself.

I.2 *The Policy Issues*

The article is written around six central questions which the framers of tax policy might ask, as follows.

What should the tax base be?

Taxes may be levied on income, wealth or expenditure, on rents or on profits, on the consumption of tobacco, or the ownership of a motor vehicle. Most governments employ a mixture of all of these, but they draw revenue from them in different proportions and the tax mix changes over time. The issues involved in choosing a tax base are the subject of Section II.

What should the rate structure be?

Commodities may be charged at different rates, or uniformly: incomes may be taxed proportionately or progressively. Benefits interact with taxes to determine the distributional effects of the tax structure and their consequences for work incentives. These issues are considered in Section III.

To what extent can the tax system be used constructively to pursue objectives other than the pursuit of revenue?

Taxes do not only raise revenue: they also influence the ways in which markets operate. Section IV considers how tax policy should, and should not, be used to pursue these objectives. But the design of policy also has non-economic aspects. The process of raising tax may be as much a matter of public concern as the consequences. And taxes are imposed by politicians and bureaucrats who may have objectives other than the pursuit of social welfare. These broader issues are the subject of Section VIII.

What are the economic effects of taxation?
Taxation affects the distribution of income, the allocation of resources, and the welfare of individual households. One of the principal tasks of the economist concerned with fiscal policy is to measure these influences. Section V examines how the incidence of taxation is determined.

How should fiscal relationships between different governments and levels of government be handled?
As the world economy becomes more international, the interactions between different tax regimes are of increasing significance. At the same time, relations between the various levels of government within countries are increasingly fraught. These questions are the subject of Section VI.

How should the tax system be administered and enforced?
Significant resources are employed in the collection of taxes, and the 'black economy' is the subject of extensive and extravagant discussion. Section VII considers what economic analysis has to say on these subjects.

In the concluding Section IX I sketch answers to these six questions.

I.3 *Tax Analysis and Tax Policy*

The strategy of this paper is to examine, in each area it considers, both the evolution of ideas and the evolution of policy. The connections between analysis and actions are not always apparent, and it is wise to be clear about the nature of the influence which one can, and cannot, expect. Finance Ministers will never rise and say that 'satisfied that the distribution of skills in the population is semi-continuous, and cognisant of Pontryagian's maximum principle, I am pleased to announce that the tax schedule for 1989-90 contains a finite number of discontinuities'. Those scholars who criticise Ministers for their ignorance of the calculus of variations, and those practical men who criticise those who do understand the calculus of variations for being too academic, are equally victims of a misunderstanding about the relationship between ideas and policy.

Everyone is in the grip of some theory – even those who affect to despise theory. I was present on one occasion when, bemused by the debate between Hicksian and Schanz–Haig–Simons concepts of income, a senior policy administrator asked why we could not simply stick with 'the common-sense definition'. The point was not that there were no principles underlying what he thought should and should not be included in income: patently there were, or he could never have discharged his job in a consistent and efficient manner. It was rather than he had never before been invited, or required, to articulate what they were. An important merit of such articulation is that it is then possible to see how these principles might require modification in the light of changing conditions, and to work out the best means of implementation. Everyone who discusses economic policy uses economic theory. They use it better if they know which theory it is they use, but they use it all the same.

The influence of intellectual debate on policy, though indirect, is ultimately

profound. It could hardly be otherwise. Politicians and senior administrators
rarely have wholly novel ideas of their own. While Henderson (1986) has
written of DIY economics – and there is plenty of evidence of that in the
superficial utterances which characterise much political debate in this area –
tax policy is too complicated for truly DIY constructions to survive for long.
Policy ideas are drawn from a climate determined by popular opinion,
journalism and informed practitioners, and, in the long run, it is scholarship
effectively communicated which is the primary influence on that climate.

The lags which that process generates are variable, but often long. It is,
clearly, paradoxical that the comprehensive income tax concept should have
had its greatest impact on policy in the 1980s. An idea most clearly articulated
in 1938 (Simons, 1938), it won the general support of the academic community
in the 1950s and 1960s but, as I describe in Section II, consensus has largely
collapsed in the last decade. But we should not be surprised. As Keynes
explained in his conclusions to the General Theory, few people readily
assimilate new ideas after the age of 25 or so, and hence the ideas which
influence policy are rarely the newest. Keynes' discussion remains the most
perceptive analysis of the influence of ideas on policy and it is appropriate that
it should come from the economist whose influence on policy has been the
greatest.

It is often tempting for scholars to believe that the best route to policy
influence is to whisper in the Minister's ear but, in reality, that whisper will be
lost in the clamour of vested interests and day-to-day political pressures.
It is in the broader climate of opinion that good ideas will tend, over time, to
outlive the bad, and rational argument to defeat the protestations of the self-
interested. Amid the demands for 'relevant' research, it is easy to forget that
the principal route by which scholars exert influence is – as it always has been
– through their students.

II. THE TAX BASE

II.1 *Changes in the Tax Structure*

Where do governments derive their tax revenue? In Fig. 1, I show how the
British government finances its expenditure, and how this has changed over the
last 25 years. Some key trends are very clear. We see the rising importance of
social security taxes, and of VAT. National insurance contributions have
grown steadily. VAT, introduced in Britain in 1973, has increased greatly in
significance and raises far more revenue than did purchase tax, the wholesale
sales tax which it replaced. Personal income tax makes much the same
contribution to revenue as in the 1960s. Most other taxes – excises on particular
commodities, the corporate income tax, other taxes on capital – are in relative
decline.

These trends seem to be universal. Stiglitz (1988) provides a similar
discussion of the changing composition of US taxation. Over the same period,
in that country, the federal government has drawn relatively more from social
security taxes, much the same from personal income tax, and less from
corporation tax and from excises. State taxes on property and on retail sales

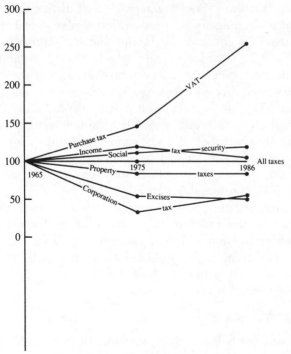

Fig. 1. Relative growth of different taxes.

have diminished in importance – the United States has no VAT. Table 2 attempts, as far as possible, to extend these comparisons across the OECD, and the UK and US pattern seems to be repeated. VAT and social security grow rapidly; specific commodity taxes and capital and property taxation are less important.

Table 2

Composition of Tax Revenues, OECD, 1965 and 1986

	1965	1986
Personal income tax	26·3	31·5
Corporate income tax	9·2	7·9
Social security taxes	18·2	24·2
Property taxes	8·0	4·9
General consumption taxes	1·7	15·5
Specific consumption taxes	23·2	12·8

Source: *OECD Revenue Statistics*, 1988. Note: Totals do not add to 100%.

It is apparent that there are common forces driving the development of the tax system across the Western world. It is less apparent what these factors are. To assess this, we need to look behind the bald description of these particular taxes and see how the tax base is constructed. In the evolutionary process which governs the changing tax mix, there are obvious winners and losers among the taxes themselves. What are the characteristics that distinguish one group from the other? What is the range of tax bases which modern fiscal systems employ?

We impose taxes on income: on labour income (through social security taxes) and on a rather broader concept which includes some capital income (personal income tax) which we also attempt to tax in other ways (through capital gains tax and corporation tax). We charge tax on the purchase of particular goods – as with the excises on petrol, alcohol and tobacco. And we tax general consumption – mostly by VAT, although some countries still have wholesale or retail sales taxes. We tax economic rents – specifically through resource rent taxation, and more widely by means of the corporate income tax. And we tax wealth. Most countries have some charge on residential property and many have a tax on tangible personal assets.

In the modern state, then, we tax income, consumption, rents and wealth and that is broadly the order of their importance. Increasingly, we raise revenue from labour income and from consumption. In the following parts of this section, I discuss some of the problems associated with the construction of the tax base. In the light of that analysis, I return to Section II.5 to consider why the tax base overall is evolving as it is.

II.2 *The Income Tax Base*

The comprehensive (or Schanz–Haig–Simons) income tax has long been seen as the ideal against which income taxes should be judged (as in Goode, 1976 or Pechman, 1977). Such a tax is based on an accretion concept of income, and measures it by reference to the increase in value of an individual's assets during the period of assessment. Thus, all capital gains on tangible wealth (although not on human capital) would be subject to tax, as would the accumulation of income on behalf of a household or individual (as, for example, within a corporation, a life insurance or pension fund, or a trust). By the early 1970s, support for the comprehensive income ideal was so great that the concept of the 'tax expenditure' was introduced to describe deviations from the comprehensive income base (Surrey, 1973). For Surrey and those who shared his view, such deviations should be costed, and appraised, on much the same basis as any positive item of public expenditure.

Yet the application of the Schanz–Haig–Simons tax base raises a variety of practical problems. It is not generally feasible to levy tax on accrued capital gains. But to impose a charge only on realisations reintroduces a bias in favour of capital gains and raises a possible need for income averaging if gains are realised in erratic and lumpy amounts. The latter problem is eased if the income tax schedule has a simple rate structure, and when the number of rate bands was reduced to two in both the United States and United Kingdom, the opportunity was taken to equalise the rates of tax on income and on capital gains.

The comprehensive income base also requires adjustment for the effects of inflation on personal wealth. It is important here to note the distinction (Meade, 1978) between bracket indexation – the regular reappraisal of the money amounts which trigger liability to a higher rate of tax – and capital/income indexation – the measurement of income in a period of inflation. Bracket indexation is required for many taxes but the issue of capital/income indexation arises only for taxes based on individual and corporate income. The first version of the US tax reform package (US Treasury, 1984) put forward the set of computations required for capital/income indexation but the associated complexity found little favour with policy makers and this aspect of the plan was dropped from subsequent proposals.

Inflation not only affects the incidence of income tax but acts as a tax in its own right. And to the extent that inflation is a monetary phenomenon, it is associated with the economic consequences of budget deficits. In the last fifteen years, it has been common in many countries for the government deficit to be of a magnitude which would make it one of the largest two or three taxes. Revenues obtained by the state sector, however derived, influence the level of private consumption both now and in the future and so the deficit has incidence and economic effects analogous to those of any explicit tax. Careful analysis of these issues has, however, so far revealed as much complication as enlightenment. Although governments have been running deficits, the real value of public-sector net worth may have been increasing, since inflation has simultaneously been reducing the cost of servicing nominal liabilities. The public-sector balance-sheet may present a very different picture from that suggested by a simple comparison of net receipts and outflows in any particular year (Hills, 1984). However, the concept of a public-sector balance-sheet itself raises difficulties. All government liabilities should be matched by rational expectations of future tax rates, and these expectations may, in turn, have consequences for individual wealth and individual consumption.

II.3 *Taxing Income versus Taxing Consumption*

It is conventional to distinguish direct from indirect taxation. The *Oxford English Dictionary* defines an indirect tax as 'one which is not levied directly on the person on whom it ultimately falls'. In a world in which the formal responsibility for payment of almost all taxation rests on corporations – few taxes are collected directly from individuals – and in which the incidence of taxation is an issue of complexity, such a definition is difficult to sustain. In common usage, the distinction between direct and indirect taxes reflects three different aspects of tax structures which, though related, are themselves distinct. These are the choice between taxes on income and taxes on consumption: the choice between taxes on commodities and taxes on individuals: and the choice between a source or origin and a destination basis for taxation. I address the first of these issues here: the other two questions are considered at III.1 and VI.1 respectively.

In popular discussion, the distinction between income and expenditure taxation is commonly seen as a choice between the personal income tax and a general commodity tax such as VAT. Actually, this equivalence greatly underestimates the range of possibilities. Since Fisher and Fisher (1942) and Kaldor (1955) it has been well known that a consumption tax could be levied as a direct tax on individuals rather than as an indirect tax on the commodities they consume. This is achieved not by requiring individuals to record every item of personal expenditure, but as a residual calculation of the net receipts of the household during the period of assessment. A variety of studies in the 1970s explored in considerable detail how such a proposal would work in practice (Andrews, 1974; US Treasury, 1977; Meade, 1978; Lodin, 1978; Graetz, 1980). It is very much open to question whether the 'income tax' as it operates in most countries is closer to the comprehensive income tax ideal or to this net receipts based tax. For this reason it is now common to talk of a hybrid income-consumption tax (Aaron *et al.*, 1988), or at least it would be common if the phrase were less cumbersome.

Under a comprehensive income tax deferred consumption is taxed more heavily than current consumption, while an expenditure tax taxes both equally. While this is sometimes seen as, in itself, an argument in favour of consumption taxation (John Stuart Mill was only the first to deplore the double taxation of savings and more recently the very low personal savings rates of the United Kingdom and United States have caused concern), the elimination of one distortion in an inevitably imperfect tax system is not in itself a sufficient argument. Tax reform packages should not be assessed by counting the number of distortions and arguments based on 'double taxation' ignore the fact that it is the relative level of taxation, not the number of occasions on which tax is charged, which is relevant to economic decisions. And if savings are positive, an equal yield consumption tax requires a higher rate than the corresponding income tax: we may have to choose between *more* distortions and *greater* distortions.

It is far from clear that the rate of tax on the return on life-cycle savings should be zero, but one simple set of assumptions which does generate this result is a utility function which is separable as between consumption and labour and also homothetic with respect to consumption at different periods of the life cycle (Atkinson and Stiglitz, 1976). In such a framework, all commodities should be taxed uniformly and in the present context, it would follow that present and future consumption should be taxed at the same rate. Since these assumptions are not completely implausible, this result seems encouraging for the supporters of expenditure taxation, but it has become apparent that further realistic developments of the model structure – such as the inclusion of overlapping generations – destroy the simplicity of the initial result (Atkinson and Sandmo, 1980). It is evidently unlikely that this type of argument will lead to any clearcut demonstration of the superiority of either income or expenditure taxation on efficiency grounds and much of the recent debate has concentrated on other issues.

Early arguments for expenditure taxation relied heavily on equity arguments. Kaldor (1980 a, p. 58) contrasted the Indian prince running down his stock of gold with the beggar outside the palace gates, each of whom would pay no tax because they had no income. But it has since become clearer that this comparison is misleading. If the assets of the Indian prince were the proceeds of a lifetime's savings from taxed income, then the fact that he pays no *additional* tax when he spends would simply be a consequence of the neutrality between present and future consumption which the expenditure tax seeks to achieve. The force of the example arises because the reader is inclined to believe – no doubt correctly – that the prince's assets are the product of inheritance rather than thrift. Kaldor's arguments are therefore more correctly addressed to the taxation of gifts and bequests than to the choice between income and expenditure taxation.

This life-cycle perspective does, however, put the equity issues in a different light. Should the *timing* of consumption influence an individual's tax payment? Under a consumption tax, everyone with the same present value of lifetime consumption (which, in the absence of gifts and bequests, must equal the present value of lifetime labour income) will pay the same tax. Over an individual's lifetime consumption and labour income tax bases are essentially equivalent. The central difference between a comprehensive income tax and a consumption tax is that (by a variety of devices) the former taxes the yield on life-cycle savings: the latter (by a variety of devices) does not. Under a comprehensive income tax, those who consume early pay more than those who consume late.

It is difficult to construct convincing reasons why this should be so and at this point the expenditure tax seems to have the better of the equity arguments. In response, however, Goode (1980) and other adherents of the comprehensive income tax have sought to query the validity of the life-cycle perspective. In their eyes, the distribution of the tax burden between an individual aged 25 and the same individual aged 75 is a public policy issue of essentially the same kind as that raised by the distribution of the tax burden between two individuals at the same stage in their life cycle. The income tax assesses the consumption possibilities available to all at any moment in time and imposes an equal charge on those with equal possibilities. Thus the choice in equity between income and expenditure taxation may hinge on whether capital markers are sufficiently efficient and accessible, and individuals sufficiently far-sighted, to make the life-cycle perspective a realistic one.

A surprising aspect of this recent debate has been the change in the direction of administrative arguments. When Kaldor first described a modern expenditure tax, his conception was viewed as interesting, esoteric but impractical. Yet in a classic exposition of the practical case for an expenditure tax, however, the American lawyer, W. D. Andrews, wrote:

'On balance, therefore, a consumption-type or cash flow personal income tax would represent an incomparably simpler tax to administer than either the present hybrid or a true accretion-type tax.
What must now be considered is whether a consumption-type personal income tax, even if easier to administer, would be as fair and as desirable from the standpoint of economic incentives as would an accretion-type tax. Interestingly, there is a considerable body of economic literature arguing that a consumption-type tax would be more desirable, but assuming it to be less capable of practical implementation.'

(Andrews, 1974, p. 1165).

This shift of opinion results partly from the clearer understanding of the administration of the expenditure tax which emerged from the work of Andrews and, particularly, the Meade Committee, and partly from changes in the relative administrative burdens of activities involving judgement compared with those demanding mechanical record-keeping. I return to the implications of that theme for tax policy below.

II.4 *Corporation Taxes*

A comprehensive income tax of the Schanz–Haig–Simons type has immediate implications for the structure of corporation tax. The income of companies is, ultimately, that of the shareholders and ideally that income should be attributed to them and taxed accordingly. This proposal was considered most extensively in Canada (Carter, 1966) but has not, in the end, been adopted anywhere. The recent trend to simplification of income tax rate schedules has, however, made this option look considerably more realistic and recent reforms in Australia (which came close to full integration in 1986) and in New Zealand have achieved a high degree of integration between personal and corporate income taxes by providing not only for full imputation but equivalence in rates.

The United States continues to base company taxation on a classical corporation tax structure. This divorces entirely the liability of the corporation from that of the shareholders, so that dividends are taxed twice, first as the income of the company and subsequently as the income of the shareholders. But the most common system is now one of partial imputation, in which the corporate tax gives the shareholder a credit against some part of his own personal tax liability. This system is deployed (in slightly different guises) in France, Germany and the United Kingdom, and in the 1970s formed the basis of a proposed directive for the approximation of company tax structures across the European Community.

But this directive was rejected by the European Parliament on the sensible ground that harmonisation of aspects of the rate structure would mean little if there was no harmonisation of the tax base. Different countries compute taxable profits in different ways. Economists differ in their interpretation of the significance of these choices and differences. These issues pose a more fundamental question. What is it that corporation tax taxes?

The traditional answer is that corporation tax is a levy on capital employed within the corporate sector. That view governs most of the literature on the incidence of the tax, discussed in Section V below, and it is probably still true that most policy-makers who determine rates and structures of company tax do so in the belief that they are setting a tax on corporate capital and that its incidence falls principally on the shareholders of the firm concerned. A line of thought inaugurated by Stiglitz (1976) challenges this conventional wisdom. It notes that companies can substitute debt for equity capital, and do. The availability of generous investment allowances often means that the overall effect of corporation tax is to subsidise investment rather than to penalise it. And in a global capital market, the prospect that any single small country will derive much revenue from taxing corporate capital is limited: if it seeks to do so, it will simply drive that capital elsewhere.

So how is it that corporation tax can raise revenue? If the tax were indeed a tax on corporate capital, then it would not generate any yield, because capital would flow to different forms of financing, or to activities and jurisdictions which would escape the tax or minimise its burden. Investment is channelled into activities which are subject to corporation tax because – and only because – such investment is necessary to exploit immobile production opportunities. This tax on companies is then essentially a tax on immobile rents earned within the corporate sector. It is a tax on entrepreneurship (in the broadest sense of the term) not on capital employed. The rents of entrepreneurship may be derived from the opportunity to use scare factors in production (allowing companies to exploit your mineral deposits) or to deploy scare factors for local consumption (allowing companies to sell Coca-Cola to your nationals). In less developed countries, corporation tax revenue mainly arises from one or other of these sources and from the monopoly rents earned by local cartels (especially in the finance and distribution sectors). The reality of the tax in Western economies is probably little different. The full implications of these insights for the structure of company taxation and, particularly, for its international aspects have yet to be fully explored.

As with personal income, corporate income requires adjustment for inflation. This issue has received more attention in the corporate than in the personal sector, partly because of the accountancy profession's interest in the apparently related task of adjusting company financial statements for the effects of inflation. Although several systems of inflation accounting have won transitory professional favour, governments everywhere have been reluctant to follow these systems for tax purposes, partly because of their perception of the subjectivity of many of the adjustments involved. In practice, they have preferred to make *ad hoc* adjustments which have similar effect. These have included allowing LIFO methods of accounting for stocks and considerably accelerating the rate at which depreciation allowances may be claimed on fixed assets.

It is not apparent, however, that the inflation accounting debate is very relevant to the structure of corporation tax. The belief that one is central to the other is predicated on the twin assumptions that corporation tax is indeed a tax on company income, and that if a true measure of that income could be found, it would be both possible and desirable to impose corporation tax on it. But the new view of corporation tax, described above, casts doubt on this whole set of arguments. The proliferation of *ad hoc* adjustments can then be viewed not as an inexcusable failure by revenue authorities to support progressive account-ants, but as a pragmatic recognition of the realities of the nature of the tax base. It is likely, in fact, that the common association of the distinct issues of reforming corporation tax and improving financial reporting, of levying tax on companies and assessing corporate income in periods of inflation, has led to all these tasks being performed less effectively than might otherwise have been the case.

Many of the changes made to the corporation tax base which provided relief for stock appreciation and improved depreciation provisions took the company tax system towards the cash flow basis elaborated in the Meade Report (Meade, 1978). Such a system would imply that all business expenditures – whether capital or current – were fully deductible for corporation tax purposes, and analogously all receipts would be taxable. The R base for a cash flow tax imposes a charge on the net operating cash flow of the business. The S base levies tax only on net distributions to shareholders. Thus the two bases differ by the amount of any net financial flows (borrowing, debt repayment and cash accumulation) to or from the company concerned. Such a tax is a logical counterpart of the new view of corporation tax incidence. It allows for full deductibility of all capital costs and yields revenue only by virtue of the rents which are earned by the corporations subject to the tax.

II.5 *Monitoring the Tax Base*

It is now time to return to the issues with which this section began. Why has the tax base evolved as it has? To tax something it is necessary to be able to measure it and monitor it. But what we can measure, or monitor, rarely corresponds to what economic or social considerations would lead us to tax. The stately homes of England still bear the marks of the window tax. The window tax was not imposed because daylight was thought to be unhealthy. Its proponents wished to impose a tax related to the size and luxuriousness of property and they thought that the number of windows was a proxy variable for these characteristics which they could easily observe. That proxy was imperfect and it became a worse proxy as the gentlemen of England blocked up their least necessary windows. The problem of defining the tax base is that of resolving the tension between what can easily and accurately be defined and controlled and what is economically relevant. And proxy variables tend to change their meaning when reliance is placed upon them – a fiscal version of Goodhart's law.

In a modern economy, we mostly monitor and measure transactions. A sells a commodity, or his labour, to B, and we record the amount that is paid. We transform this into a tax base by a variety of processes. We may choose to net and aggregate transactions – we define the tax base to be the sum of all sales of tobacco products, or as total receipts less certain expenditures, or as the aggregate of all property purchases by an individual. And we may introduce hypothetical transactions – the amount for which an asset could have been sold, the value of stocks and work in progress, or the price at which a good which is transferred between different parts of a multinational corporation would have been exchanged between arm's length traders.

The more complex is any of these processes of transformation, the less satisfactory the tax base is likely to be. It is worth noting, however, that the problems of recording large amounts of information are less than those of analysing large numbers of hypothetical transactions, and that advancing technology has greatly helped us with recording while the increasing sophistication of modern financial systems raises the costs of analysis. Modern taxes which work badly are, in the main, those which are largely divorced from real transactions. Sometimes this divorce reaches levels of complete absurdity. Domestic rates – the British property tax – were based on what the property concerned could have been rented for in 1973. Since there was virtually no market in rented residential property in 1973, the base of the tax was in practice determined by reference to what the valuation officer had already decided other property might have been rented for in 1973. Almost the only merit of such a tax base is that it belongs to a world of such unreality that it is difficult for the taxpayer to challenge any assessment, and that is a merit only to those who have to administer the tax. And this unreality may undermine confidence in the system in the long run, as has indeed proved to be the case.

More commonly, however, the tax base relates partly to real and partly to hypothetical transactions. Income tax on earned income or on interest and dividends received falls into the first of these categories: fringe benefits, and many of the calculations need to compute trading income, or accrued income from capital, fall into the second. The calculation of corporation tax liability is still further removed from any information contained in primary records. The direction of the trends shown in Fig. 1 and Table 2 is systematically towards those taxes which have a transactions base and away from those which do not. VAT and social security taxes fall clearly into the first of these categories. Taxes on wealth, corporation tax and tax on capital income, fall decisively into the second. Personal income tax – an amalgam of a tax on labour income (everywhere dominant in terms of its contribution to revenue) and a tax on income from capital (everywhere dominant in terms of its contribution to administrative complexity) lies somewhere in between, and so do taxes on gifts and bequests.

III. TAX STRUCTURES

III.1 *The Structure of Indirect Taxation*

In the 1920s, Pigou posed a question for the young mathematician Frank Ramsey and the answer (Ramsey, 1927) remains a classic of mathematical economics. What structure of commodity taxation would raise a given sum in revenue at minimum loss of welfare? A problem of this kind is now most conveniently handled using duality methods, so that we maximise an indirect utility function $V(\mathbf{q})$ subject to a constraint $(\mathbf{q}-\mathbf{p})\,\mathbf{x}(\mathbf{q}) = R$ where $\mathbf{q}$ is the consumer price vector, $\mathbf{p}$ represents consumer prices (so that taxes are $\mathbf{t} = (\mathbf{q}-\mathbf{p})$), $\mathbf{x}$ is the resulting vector of consumption, and R is desired tax revenue. Attaching a Lagrange multiplier λ to the constraint gives:

$$-\alpha x_i + \lambda \sum_j t_j \frac{dx_j}{dq_i} + x_i = 0 \quad \forall_i,$$

where α is the marginal utility of income (dV/dm). Substituting the Slutsky equation in this expression and defining (following Diamond, 1975) the social marginal utility of income (which includes the value of associated tax receipts) as

$$\mu = \alpha + \lambda \sum_j t_j \frac{dx_j}{dm}$$

gives

$$\sum_j \frac{dx_i}{dq_j} t_j = \frac{\lambda - \mu}{\lambda} \ \forall_i.$$

Thus the change in the income compensated demand for each commodity should be such that if the derivatives of these compensated demand functions were constant (which could only locally be true) the proportionate reduction in demand would be the same for all commodities. Loosely, but conveniently, this has often been formulated as an inverse elasticity rule: impose higher taxes on goods for which the elasticity of demand is relatively low.

As the capacity to estimate complete demand systems from disaggregated expenditure data has been developed, a number of attempts have been made to compute a set of optimal commodity tax rates in a Ramsey type model – see, for example, Atkinson and Stiglitz (1972), Deaton (1977), Harris and MacKinnon (1979), Heady and Mitra (1982). The functional forms assumed in the estimation of complete demand systems do, however, themselves impose restrictions on the cross-elasticities of demand between commodities and – particularly – with labour. Since these are central to the theoretical calculation of efficient tax rates, this is a serious difficulty.

Before considering applications of this analysis, however, it is worth examining the formulation of the Ramsey problem more carefully. The framework supposes either a single consumer, or a distribution of endowments between consumers capable of equalising the marginal utility of income α across all consumers, or a social welfare function V that treats this as having been equalised. But if there were no distributional concerns, would not a poll tax be superior to any system of commodity taxes? If we must look for goods which are inelastically demanded, then the commodity that best meets that criterion is life itself, so why not tax it?

This response to the inverse elasticity rule is, in the end, a devastating one, but it is worth teasing out two paradoxes which emerge. Why is it that an erroneous principle – tax goods that people will go on consuming anyway – can be so influential not only in the literature of public finance but also in popular discussion of tax policy? It is not because of the impact of Ramsey's analysis on decision makers – governments taxed salt and other necessities centuries before articles on tax policy appeared in the ECONOMIC JOURNAL. But the reason they did so was that there were, at that time, many restrictions on the other ways in which revenue could be raised – the market economy was limited and so were the resources of the state. Thus the practical solution to an optimal tax problem is contingent on the constraints imposed on the instruments available – lump sum taxation is best, but you should tax salt if you can tax nothing else. This sensitivity of structure to available weapons is as recurrent a theme of the modern literature as it is of the experience of tax practitioners. The irrelevance of Ramsey's formulation is directly attributable to his over-specification of the relevant constraints.

There is a second paradox here in the relationship between policy and analysis. Political discussion continues, in broad terms, to assign distributional objectives to direct taxes and the raising of revenue to indirect taxation. But our analysis of Ramsey's problem illustrates that if there were no distributional issues, it would be appropriate to raise taxes principally by direct methods, and it is largely because there are such distributional questions that the need for commodity taxation arises.

A comprehensive framework which has formed the basis of subsequent analysis of these issues is that of Diamond and Mirrlees (1971). This allows varying producer prices, alternative constraints on the range of tax instruments available to the government, and many individuals who vary in abilities, tastes and social marginal valuation of their income. An important conclusion of their analysis is that productive efficiency remains desirable even under general assumptions which allow substantial allocative inefficiency, or which render allocative inefficiency inevitable. It follows from this that the case against indirect taxes on intermediate goods (other than those implied by externality or other market failure considerations) is strong, and that commodity taxes should, as far as possible, fall only on final consumption.

Thus we come – as Ramsey should perhaps have come – to the basic question of why we should tax commodities at all when it is possible to tax individuals. The output of particular commodities may itself be an objective of public policy. Externalities arise where the effects of production or consumption relate to people other than those who choose the level of production or consumption (river pollution and attractive gardens), while merit goods (Musgrave, 1959) are commodities where the level of an individual's consumption is thought to be of direct social interest in itself (and not just through its effects on others). But commodity taxes may also be justified on distributional grounds if there are constraints on the ways in which individuals can be taxed. While ideally we might hope to levy lump sum taxes on individuals, or households, the need to impose tax on observable variables may lead us to choose consumption of individual commodities as an instrument instead.

Although the term 'merit goods' sometimes refers either to goods which yield positive externalities, or to those consumed by low income households, Musgrave's definition confines it to commodities which (presumably un-informed) households would consume in inappropriately small quantities (education, housing) or inappropriately large amounts (alcohol, cigarettes) if left to their own devices. These justifications typically ease into one or other of the alternatives, however, reflecting the reduced appeal today of purely paternalistic arguments. Such distributional arguments depend, as noted above, on the existence of constraints on the ways in which individuals may be taxed. The rationale for imposing taxes on goods consumed by high-income households is weak if, as is generally the case, we can observe directly whether households have high incomes or not.

Consumption of commodities may convey additional information, however, in one or other of two ways (Deaton, 1977, 1981). Leisure is inherently untaxable. Thus there may be advantage in the differential taxation of goods and services whose consumption is complementary with leisure (squash rackets and long novels). And there may be commodities whose consumption is correlated with earning capacity (rather than earnings themselves). This is an important distinction. If everyone would buy a villa in the South of France if they were rich, we could tax either the rich or villas in the South of France, with identical results. If some people would buy villas in the South of France, and others luxury yachts, then we could either tax the rich or we could tax both the owners of villas and the owners of yachts, but it is probably easier to tax the incomes of the rich. If some rich people would buy villas and others would eat a lot, it is definitely better to tax high incomes than to tax housing and food. If, however, affluent people go to opera not only because they can afford it, but because a liking for opera is associated with taste, cultivation and other factors that promote worldly success, then opera-going conveys information about unobservable characteristics additional to income or wealth itself and might appropriately be taxed. Related arguments may favour the use of non-linear tariff schedules for particular commodities (a means of getting at rich people who eat a lot). The opportunities to do this are mainly confined to services where subsequent arbitrage between individuals who face different marginal prices is impossible or costly, such as telephone or electricity usage.

Thus differential commodity taxation may be justified by the relationship between consumption of the commodity concerned and either the ability to earn or the utility of leisure. If, however, utility functions are homothetic with respect to consumption of individual commodities and separable as between consumption and effort, homotheticity rules out the first of these rationales and separability the second. Then it is easy to show that all commodities should be taxed at the same rate. (An equivalent argument was used above to suggest the potential superiority of the expenditure tax.) And, of course, in this framework there is no difference between a general commodity tax and an income tax since no inter-temporal issues arise.

Indirect taxes – whether imposed on particular commodities or on consumption in general – may be implemented in various ways. Broad commodity categories may be taxed at either wholesale or retail level. But as traditional patterns of distribution have broken down, and services have come to take a larger share of consumer expenditure, wholesale sales taxes have encountered increasing problems of administration. Retail sales taxes have always proved more difficult to operate than those collected at earlier stages of the production process. In the last twenty years, most countries have introduced a value added tax and this tax is now in force in 20 of 24 OECD members and in about 60 states worldwide (Gillis et al. 1989). An invoice based VAT – the common model – is charged on gross output. Tax levied on inputs which are purchased from other registered traders may be deducted on computing liability. VAT thus provides a systematic mechanism for taxing final consumption while relieving transactions in intermediate goods. VAT also lends itself reasonably readily to differentiation across commodity types.

Goods selected for especially high rates of commodity taxation are sometimes placed in higher rate bands under VAT but are also frequently the subject of particular excise duties. While VAT is necessarily proportional to the value of output, an excise tax may be based either on the retail or wholesale price (an *ad valorem* tax) or on the physical quantity of the commodity (a specific tax). Within the European Community, for example, tobacco products are subject to both – there is a specific tax per cigarette and an *ad valorem* tax based on the retail price of the cigarettes concerned. *Ad valorem* taxation leads to lower quality production and (in the oligopolistic markets in which excised commodities are generally produced) to lower profits and to lower prices (Kay and Keen, 1983, 1987).

III.2 *Direct Tax Schedule*

How redistributive should income tax be? The issue was keenly debated by the nineteenth-century theorists collected in Musgrave and Peacock (1957), and Musgrave (1959) surveys the conflict between the varying principles of minimum aggregate sacrifice, equal absolute sacrifice, and equal proportional sacrifice. A related, but more recent, approach is one which has been attributed to Rawls (1971), whose maximin principle (taken as the maximisation of the welfare of the least fortunate) has provided an alternative, if hardly more plausible, quantifiable maximand.

It has always been apparent that the shape of the tax schedule reflected a tradeoff between equity considerations demanding high degrees of progressivity and efficiency factors militating against them, but it was not until Mirrlees (1971) that a framework for careful analysis of these issues was developed. The theory is both complex and subtle, and rather few general results emerge. One rather striking implication is that marginal tax rates should approach zero at both the top and bottom ends of the income distribution (Sadka, 1976; Seade, 1977) – a marked contrast to actual tax schedules – but simulations have suggested that these end point results are not robust and may be misleading guides to appropriate rates in ranges which are not literally the end points of the distribution, so that practical conclusions for policy should not readily be drawn from these arguments.

Nonetheless, there is a striking contrast between this low–high–low pattern of marginal tax rates and the high–low–high patterns often observed in practice (Kay and King, 1989). The latter pattern is the result of the interaction of tax and benefits at the lower end of the income distribution, and the operation of higher rates of income tax at the upper end. The dichotomy between what we do and what we perhaps should do has been used as an argument for the compromise of a linear income tax (Meade, 1978) – based on an intercept or tax threshold and a single marginal rate of tax. This rationale is not terribly convincing, but calculation of the appropriate shape of linear income tax is a good deal easier than the analysis required when wholly general functions are admitted (Sheshinski, 1972), while calculations have suggested that the difference between an optimal linear income tax and an optimal general income tax may not be too great in practice (Mirrlees, 1971; Stern, 1976). Since a linear income tax has significant administrative advantages (in particular, it allows withholding at a single rate), it has been the subject of increasing attention.

A more informal approach to the analysis of income tax schedules derives

from the extensive discussion surrounding the 'Laffer curve'. The Laffer curve
– first drawn, it is alleged, on a napkin in a Washington restaurant – begins
from the observation that tax rates of zero and 100% both raise zero tax
revenue. Thus there must be a tax rate somewhere within that range at which
maximum revenue is derived. Although not strictly correct as a matter of
mathematics (it is possible, and not at all implausible, that tax revenues are
steadily increasing in tax rates throughout the range from zero to 100%),
(Malcolmson, 1986) the Laffer curve does correctly draw attention to the
possibility that reductions in the rates of certain taxes might induce more tax
revenue rather than less.

That observation, however, does not demonstrate that this Laffer range is
likely to be observed in real life (Fullerton, 1982). While assertions like Laffer's
do appear to have been influential in persuading the Reagan administration
that reductions in tax rates could be implemented without substantial losses in
revenue (Stockman, 1986) the result in practice appears to have been the
emergence of a large budget deficit. Nevertheless, it has been suggested that
even if the overall tax burden has not reached a point at which a lower average
tax rate would yield additional revenue, this might be true of particular
elements within the overall structure. Thus Lindsey (1987) and Minford (1983)
have drawn attention to the ways in which income tax revenues from the
higher rates of tax have increased even though those rates themselves have been
reduced. But this reflects a widening of pre-tax income differentials generally
(Dilnot and Kell, 1988) for reasons which may be only loosely related to the
change in shape of the tax schedule. Particular taxes may sometimes respond
to lower rates with higher yield. Capital gains tax may be a good example,

Table 3

Tax Schedules Internationally

	Number of rate brackets		Initial rate		Maximum rate	
	1975	1988/9	1975	1988/9	1975	1988/9
Australia	7	5	20	24	65	49
Canada	13	3	9	17	47	29
France	13	13	5	5	60	57
Germany	*	*	22	19 (1990)	56	53 (1990)
Ireland	6	3	26	32	72	56
Italy	32	7	10	10	72	50
Japan	19	5	10	10	75	50
Netherlands	10	3 (1990)	27	35†	71	60 (1990)
New Zealand	22	2	19	24	57	33
Sweden	11	3	7	5	56	42
UK	10	2	35	25	83	40
US	25	3	14	15	70	33

Source: Cnossen and Messere (1989).
* Not applicable: the German tax schedule is based on a polynomial formula.
† Not comparable: includes social security contributions.

where a lower rate reduces the penalty on portfolio rearrangement and may thus promote an (albeit temporary) spurt in revenue.

The two directions of change suggested by this discussion – a move towards linear tax schedules and reductions in the highest rates of tax – have been striking features of the evolution of tax structures during the last decade (Table 3). Both Britain and the United States have reduced the number of rate brackets to two, and the maximum rates have fallen from 98% and 70% respectively to 40% and 28%. (The US picture is complicated by the superposition of state and local income taxes and the existence of a withdrawn exemption which raises the effective rate to 33% over a wide range of incomes.) Similar trends are evident in almost all countries.

III.3 *Tax Progressivity*

These movements appear to reduce the progressivity of the tax system substantially, and there is no doubt that this was often both the intention and the outcome. This effect is easily exaggerated, however, for two related reasons. One is that the top rates of tax frequently served little more than symbolic purposes – few people were subject to them, their effect was readily avoided in practice, and their contribution to total revenue slight. A second is that there is much confusion about what is meant by progressivity.

Popular discussion often interprets progressivity to mean that the marginal rate of tax is increasing in income and some more serious literature (e.g. Blum and Kalven, 1953) uses the term progressivity in this way. But this interpretation sometimes reflects a failure to distinguish clearly between average and marginal tax rates – a linear tax schedule with an allowance equal to average incomes and a 100% marginal rate is the most progressive tax schedule of all. A more subtle confusion, however, is that the term progressivity is used to refer both to the inequality reducing effect of taxation and to the structure of the tax schedule itself.

It is clear that there is a distinction between these two concepts. Income tax is, for example, usually the most effective of taxes in reducing inequality. But taxes on capital gains or inheritance have the – distinct – property of falling mainly on rich people. The distribution of the burden of these latter taxes is more concentrated in the higher-income groups but, simply because income tax raises so much more revenue, it does more to reduce inequality. Since the concept of inequality exists, and is reasonably well understood, it seems better to reserve the term progressivity for the narrower concept of concentration of the tax burden. Inequality reduction will then be a function not only of the progressivity of a tax but also of its yield (Kakwani, 1977).

It is impossible to arrive at a complete ordering of inequality except by reference to some explicit criterion function, but a partial ordering is often possible – as when one distribution is generated from another by a sequence of transfers (Rothschild and Stiglitz, 1970, 1971; Atkinson, 1970). Similarly, comparisons between the progressivity of alternative tax schedules are generally ambiguous. However, it is possible to identify changes as either unambiguously increasing or reducing the progressivity of tax schedules since structural changes may be definitely progressivity enhancing or diminishing (Hemming and Keen, 1983), and this allows a partial ordering on progressivity to be derived.

III.4 *Taxation, Benefits and Social Security*

The introduction to this paper noted the essential inter-relationship of tax and benefit systems when social-security expenditure is the largest single element in the government's budget – as it is in most Western countries. In most economies, however, tax and benefit systems have historically developed in different ways. As a result there is little integration between the mechanisms by which taxes are levied and benefits delivered, and also little integration between the criteria and schedules that are applied to each. As the coverage of benefits has become more extensive, the problems posed by these inter-relationships or their absence has become more acute. The *poverty trap* is the phenomenon by which high withdrawal rates of means tested benefits paid to low income households interact with initial tax rates on earnings to generate very high overall marginal tax rates, sometimes in excess of 100%. The *unemployment trap* results when replacement rates – the proportion of post-tax earnings which are replaced through the benefit system when a worker loses his job – rise to high levels (Dilnot *et al.* 1984).

At the same time, the growth of social security contributions as a source of state revenue means that this second tax on earnings is now comparable to – and in some countries more important than – income tax itself. It is a common experience that the overall effect of these two schedules taken together has properties which are not characteristic of either and which it is unlikely would be the product of any explicit policy.

A negative income tax – which would bring together all tax and benefits in a single structure – is often advocated as a means of resolving these problems. Low-income households would not only be exempt from tax: they would receive payments. It would be possible to have a schedule of rates at which low incomes were supplemented independent of, or integrated with, the overall income tax schedule itself. Such schemes were widely advocated in the United States in the 1960s – see, for example, Tobin *et al.* (1967); Diamond (1968); and more recently Levitan (1980). Similar proposals have been put forward in the United Kingdom by Prest (1970) and Polanyi and Polanyi (1973). And the tax credit scheme put forward by Britain's Conservative government in the 1970s, although not in the end adopted, had close affinities to a negative income tax.

Different in approach, but formally identical in structure, is a social dividend (Rhys Williams, 1943) or basic income guarantee scheme (Parker, 1982). Such a system promises all citizens an assured annual income, which is paid directly to those not in employment (or conceivably to everyone whether in work or not). The aggregate cost is then recovered through general income taxation.

The principle behind these schemes contrasts sharply with the social insurance concept which has formed the basis of the benefit systems of most

European countries (Kohler and Zacher 1982). Social insurance rests on two basic principles – the contingency principle and the contributory principle. Under the contingency principle payment results from the occurrence of a contingency associated with the need for income support, like sickness or unemployment, rather than from low income itself. The contributory principle implies that entitlement to benefit is derived from personal contributions, analogous to premiums paid to a private insurance scheme, rather than from general revenues. Both of these principles have been heavily eroded in practice. The contingency principle has been emasculated by the growth of income-related payments to supplement contingent benefits which are perceived as inadequate. The contributory principle has been undermined by the steady transformation of social-security contributions into a tax on earned income. But the rhetoric of social insurance continues to influence the discussion of social-security policies even though the reality has long faded.

It is apparent from the contrast between these two principles that a benefit system is likely to make use of two kinds of information – contingent data on household circumstances, and assessments of household income and wealth. Benefit systems have traditionally been based on the first, and tax systems on the second. The two directions proposed for radical reform of tax and benefits – negative income tax on the one hand and a reassertion of the social insurance principle on the other – involve polarisation of the reformed system around one or other of these alternatives.

Yet the key to a balance between effectiveness, equity and economy in tax and benefit administration is the use of both contingent and income related information. By 'tagging' benefits (Akerlof, 1978) the use of lump sum information improves the tradeoff between efficiency and equity. If benefits are wholly or partly based on factors which are correlated with income (but are not income itself) the same redistribution can be achieved with lower marginal tax rates. The evolution of both tax and benefit systems in practice has reflected this. The calculation of tax liability has been sensitive to household circumstances, while the assessment of benefit has been increasingly related to household income. An integrated system is one which makes use of information on both.

The future of income support, and its relationship with the tax system, is now an issue in many countries as the expanding social security budgets of the 1960s and 1970s come under increasing pressure. Yet while political concern is clear, public discussion is often less than coherent. If the UK experience is any guide, the obstacles to progress lie less in the need for further analysis of structure and concepts than in the difficulties of reconciling administrative traditions with a long and independent history.

III.5 *The Theory of Tax Reform*

The models described in the preceding sections of this paper seek to define conditions which would characterise an optimal tax system. The tax systems we observe patently fall far short of that. The theory of the second best queries the relevance of applying principles derived from the analysis of a full optimum in these circumstances. It is then necessary to ask whether the theory of optimal taxation yields prescriptions which can be applied to imperfect tax systems. The developing theory of tax reform (Feldstein, 1976; Guesnerie, 1977) is a response to that challenge.

A move towards lump sum taxation, away from distortionary taxes, is always potentially welfare improving provided the new set of distortionary taxes is optimally chosen (Atkinson and Stern, 1974). This implies that a suitably chosen path towards a more efficient system will lead to a steady increase in welfare. The issue is much less clear, however, if the choice of commodity tax reforms is constrained, or if we are seeking to look at changes in the structure of commodity taxation itself.

Ahmad and Stern (1983) use standard techniques from cost benefit analysis to assess the marginal social cost of revenue from alternative taxes. The optimum is, evidently, the point at which that cost is the same for all taxes. Any piecemeal reform can then be appraised by comparison of the shadow prices of the instruments involved. Hatta (1986) argues that under the conditions which make uniform commodity taxation optimal, moves towards greater uniformity in rates are generally welfare improving, but Deaton (1987) shows that the conditions under which this is likely to be true are generally rather somewhat restrictive. The theory of income tax reform has yet to be far developed.

But it should be understood that the primary purpose of optimal tax theory is not to allow the computation of numerical estimates of what tax rates should be. In this field of economics, as of others, the primary role of models is to illuminate what Hahn has called 'the grammar of arguments': to discriminate between valid and invalid assertions and to distinguish the circumstances in which they do or do not command such validity.

The grammar developed in this section of the paper shows how many popular, and influential, tax policy arguments contain syntactical errors. It is, for example, important to look at distributional issues in relation to the whole range of tax instruments available, and not to the distributional effect of each tax individually. It follows that the arguments commonly used to justify the zero-rating of food under VAT, for example, are probably rather weak. So are those arguments for taxing tobacco heavily which are based on assertions about its elasticity of demand. Many of the reasons for imposing very high rates of tax in the highest ranges of the income distribution appear to rest on misconceptions. All these observations stress the importance of looking at each issue in tax policy in the context of the system as a whole.

IV. TAXATION AND MARKET FAILURE

IV.1 *Commodity Taxation to Relieve Market Failure*

In Sections II and III of this paper I have considered the conventional objectives of taxation – to raise revenue for governments with due regard to issues of efficiency and equity. There may also be a role for corrective taxation – taxation whose purpose is to achieve welfare gains rather than to minimise welfare losses.

A conventional taxonomy of sources of market failure identifies monopoly, non-convexities, externalities and information problems. Taxation is rarely the best, or the second best, response to the problems created by the existence of monopoly, although the rates (Green, 1961), or structure (Kay and Keen, 1983) of commodity taxation may be influenced by the existence of monopoly which cannot be attacked in other ways – or has not been. Nor does tax policy often offer a solution to the deficiencies of markets in information or to the problems of markets in which information is imperfect. The market failures to which tax policy is commonly and properly addressed are those associated with externalities, public goods, and the exploitation of natural resources.

It has long been argued that taxation is a more appropriate mechanism than regulation for dealing with the consequences of external effects (Pigou, 1947; Sandmo, 1975). If the regulatory authority were perfectly informed about the costs and preferences of those causing, or influenced by, the externality, there would be no reason to prefer one instrument to the other. The regulator could either prescribe the optimal level of smoke emissions, or impose a tax on smoke emissions which led the polluter to choose the optimal level. The volume of smoke released would be identical. The two instruments might have different distributional consequences, but Pareto-efficient outcomes would be achieved in each case.

The choice is a real one because the regulator is imperfectly informed. The resolution of that choice therefore hinges on the nature of that lack of information and the costs of error. If we can assess the damage done by noisy aircraft but are ignorant of the costs to airlines of reducing noise, taxation may be an appropriate remedy. If, on the other hand, we wish to control the effects of highly toxic pollutants and do not know the structure of the polluters' costs, we may do better to prescribe quantities instead (Weitzman, 1974).

Whatever the conclusions of economic analysis, policy-makers have tended to prefer regulation to the use of fiscal policy. But there are clear indications of a change in trend. It is now common to levy charges for industrial pollution, especially of water. The use of tax policy to encourage the introduction of unleaded petrol in several European countries is a striking example of the extension of the principle that the polluter pays from producers to consumers. Denmark and Sweden have introduced a range of environmental taxes on consumer goods, penalising commodities such as pesticides, disposable tableware and non-returnable containers.

In most countries, however, it remains difficult to detect any coherent rationale for those goods which are singled out for especially high rates of commodity taxation. Almost all countries impose special taxes on alcoholic drinks, tobacco, motoring and betting. But the reasons why Anglo-Saxon countries have penalised mechanical lighters and playing cards, and continental European ones tea, coffee and sugar, are mostly hidden in the mists of time. Externalities do provide some basis for these taxes, especially those on petrol and (to a lesser degree) on alcohol and tobacco (Cnossen, 1983).

Is there some other market failure which these taxes serve to remedy? Another rationale for these excises derives from the kind of paternalism contained in Musgrave's concept of merit goods. But these high taxes reflect mainly a mixture of long tradition and the apparent willingness of voters to accept punitive rates of taxation on consumption about which the taxpayer himself (or herself) already feels more than a little guilty. As was noted in Section I, duties on specific commodities are rapidly diminishing in overall significance.

IV.2 *Taxation and Public Goods*

If the function of nineteenth-century government was to provide public goods, much of nineteenth-century public finance theory was concerned with systems to secure the efficient provision of such goods (Musgrave and Peacock, 1957). Wicksell demonstrated that the simultaneous determination of tax shares and expenditures in an assembly requiring unanimity would lead to optimal provision, since only Pareto-efficient outcomes could be approved. The time and costs of implementing this solution make something less than unanimity necessary. But to permit anything less than unanimity invites strategic behaviour in which coalitions are formed to promote redistribution from minorities to majorities.

The Lindahl solution (Johansen, 1973) would charge each taxpayer an amount equal to his marginal valuation of the public good times the amount provided. If the Samuelson conditions for optimal provision were met, and the public good produced under constant cost conditions, this would exactly finance the level of efficient output. But the issue of how the information necessary to compute such taxes might be derived has always been unresolved. Some progress here has at last been made.

An incentive compatible mechanism is one in which the self-interest of each agent lies in revealing correct information. The Vickrey auction (the normal practice in the English saleroom) achieves this by effectively requiring the successful bidder to pay only the amount that the next highest bidder offers, eliminating incentives to strategic behaviour. Moreover, the equilibrium reached is (if only the participants knew it) an equilibrium dominant in strategies – it doesn't matter why your opponent bids as he does. The Clark–Groves mechanism (Clark, 1971; Groves and Loeb, 1975) extends this principle to public goods by making the marginal cost of social provision to each individual equal to the difference between the cost and the aggregate of reported willingness to pay by all others. However, we need to solve two problems simultaneously – that of obtaining the information needed to ensure optimal provision of the public good and of raising exactly the finance needed to pay for it. Groves and Ledyard (1977) showed that a Nash equilibrium (rather than an equilibrium in dominant strategies) might be consistent with the achievement of both objectives.

These important theoretical contributions have generated a developing literature, but one that still leaves us some considerable distance from seeing what an incentive compatible mechanism for revealing preferences for public goods might mean in practice. Since, as we saw in Section I, public goods are now a minor part of total public expenditure, it is inevitable that a preliminary to this will involve tax hypothecation: we would need to reveal simultaneously our preference for defence expenditure and defence taxation. Revelation processes are still some way from telling us how to solve the problems of collective provision and strategic behaviour involved in the management of a household or a cricket club, far less those involved in the running of a great society.

IV.3 *Taxation and Resources*

As concern about the environment has grown, so has interest in taxation problems related to the extraction and use of natural resources. There are two central, related issues. For some countries (including many LDCs and even recently the United Kingdom) rents derived from natural resources are an important part of the tax base. At the same time, there is concern that markets may not produce efficient patterns of resource utilisation. Taxation is one of the instruments of public policy which may be used to influence this. The reason the two issues are linked is that one major source of this inefficiency may be the absence of well-defined property rights in the resource. When the state intervenes to correct this, it is natural for it also to appropriate the rents which it establishes and protects.

For many resources – particularly oil – direct production costs are small relative to revenues. Such rents are attractive bases for taxation. The rates of tax which result are generally far higher than any to be found elsewhere in the tax structure – the marginal rate of tax on North Sea oil revenues has typically been around 90% – but this poses a number of problems. Distortions are almost inescapable when tax rates of this magnitude are imposed and the complexity of regimes where multiple taxes interact almost guarantees this result. The marginal cost of expenditures to the companies concerned is low and may even be negative. Where it is low, there are incentives to engage in activities whose benefits are intangible or accrue indirectly – corporate advertising which extols the excellence of the company and the public-spirited concerns of its executives, or the production of wonderful but uneconomic television programmes like Brideshead Revisited. When the effective marginal tax rate exceeds 100%, the company may engage in wasteful expenditures through 'gold plating' of its assets.

Most countries tax rents through a multiplicity of tax instruments. Royalties are levied on gross revenues. Corporation tax is imposed on profits. But to identify the profits attributable to a resource discovery it is generally necessary first to ring fence the discovery itself and then to impose some arbitrary capital structure; unless distinct activities of integrated companies are identified in this way it is generally possible to transfer the rents from natural resources to an alternative jurisdiction which will tax them at the lower rates applied to profits by a suitable choice of financing. Governments have rarely been satisfied with the revenues they earn from resource rents and have often levied ad hoc taxes. Britain has had, at various times, Advance Petroleum Revenue Tax and Supplementary Petroleum Duty. The cash-flow basis which makes liability independent of financing arrangements is particularly well suited to the taxation of resource rents. Taxes loosely based on this concept (such as Britain's Petroleum Revenue Tax) have been widely employed and more explicit cash-flow concepts advocated (Garnaut and Clunies Ross, 1975, 1979; Part, 1982).

Bidding for licences appears to offer a simpler means of taxing rent. In a competitive auction, the government might succeed in extracting the whole of the rent and in ensuring that resource companies, rather than governments, bear the risks associated with price and production uncertainties. However, there is an important difference between an auction for an Old Master (where all agree what the object is but disagree in their perception of what the painting is worth) and an auction for a block of land acreage (where, if all agreed on what the object was, there would also be a common view of its value). These latter auctions are characterised by the 'winner's curse' – the blocks you are awarded are those in which your geologists have overestimated the value of the acreage concerned. As a result, it does not pay to bid up to your full valuation and only rarely will the outcome be efficient. For these reasons, or others, governments have sometimes made use of auctioning procedures but have usually done so only in conjunction with more conventional taxes on resource rents.

The path of resource extraction over time is only efficient under specific conditions and taxation may be a means of influencing that path (Dasgupta and Heal, 1979, chapter 12). This is particularly important for common property resources, such as fisheries (Gordon, 1954). However, the effects of resource taxation depend not only on current taxes but also on anticipated future levels. Since experience shows that resource taxation rarely diminishes, this creates incentives to accelerate depletion. Governments wishing to control extraction paths will mostly do better to exercise such influence directly, and mostly have.

V. THE EFFECTS OF TAXATION

V.1 *The Concept of Incidence*

The effects of taxation are generally analysed by reference to its incidence. I shall approach the issue by dividing it into three parts. The first question – the subject of incidence itself – is concerned with identifying who pays any particular tax, and with the aggregate distribution of liabilities. In considering this subject we are especially concerned with the distribution among households, but often also with the way in which tax is allocated between different factors of production or categories of taxpayer. At the same time, however, the tax structure itself changes the equilibrium configuration of prices and outputs in the economy. Consumers buy fewer heavily taxed goods, production levels differ, and the relative costs of outputs and inputs are changed. The second question involves the measurement of these effects – the impact of taxation on labour supply, savings, risk-taking or commodity demand. As a result of these changes in the quantities of goods and services which are produced or purchased, the tax system has welfare consequences distinct from the pattern of gains and losses which result from tax payments themselves. Deadweight losses are suffered by consumers who choose to consume less of the taxed commodities, and may indeed fall on some who do not pay any tax at all. On the other hand, if the imposition of a tax on a particular factor of production leads to a rise in its price, the loss to the supplier of that factor may be less than the amount he has to pay in tax. The third question raised is therefore how to measure and analyse the amount and distribution of welfare losses which result from the tax system.

The reader should be warned that, although this framework is, in my view, both the most appropriate way of assessing the effects of taxation and the most useful means of interpreting the extensive literature on the subject, the usage is not a conventional one. The treatment adopted here sees tax incidence as essentially a static characteristic of a particular equilibrium. In contrast, an assessment of the effects which taxation has on behaviour must be based on a comparison between that equilibrium and a hypothetical alternative equilibrium (which will need to be specified for the purposes of the analysis). Thus I side with Lady Hicks, who argued that 'there is a distinct and important meaning in the social accounting sense of incidence, and further, this is a calculation which can be made with a fair degree of statistical accuracy and completeness' (Hicks, 1946, p. 49) rather than with Kotlikoff and Summers (1987) who assert (p. 1043) that 'the measurement of tax incidence is not an accounting exercise; rather it is an analytical characterisation of economic equilibria under alternative assumptions about taxation'.

In this latter sense, the term 'incidence' is commonly employed to describe both the distribution of tax payments and the effects of taxation, so that, for example, Harberger's seminal demonstration of the consequences of corporation tax for the way in which capital is deployed in a two-sector model of the economy is entitled 'The incidence of the corporation income tax' (Harberger, 1962). The phrase 'differential incidence' reflects the need for a specified counterfactual equilibrium when incidence is interpreted in this way, although the specification of this counterfactual is rarely taken very seriously even by those who claim to employ the concept of differential incidence: thus Okner and Pechman's classic empirical study of the incidence of the US tax system claims to be based on a comparison between the effects of the actual tax structure and a proportional income tax (Pechman and Okner, 1974, p. 12), but the diligent reader will find no subsequent mention of the proportional income tax anywhere in that volume. For the purposes of this paper, I distinguish sharply between the three aspects defined above – tax incidence, the effects of taxation, and the welfare consequences.

V.2 Tax Incidence

The confusion described in the preceding paragraph is partly generated by the common difference between the legal liability for payment of a tax and its incidence. My employer is required to deduct income tax from my wages and pay it to the Inland Revenue, but the signature on the cheque is not a fact of much economic significance: the employer is acting as agent in this transaction and it is no more helpful to say that he pays the tax than it is appropriate to say that the bank which actually transfers the funds to the account of the

Inland Revenue is paying the tax. In an essentially analogous way, tobacco tax is paid by tobacco manufacturers or wholesalers when the commodity concerned is removed from a bonded warehouse, but the wholesaler too is acting in an agency function and the tax is incident on those who smoke the cigarettes or grow tobacco.

In both these examples, the tax system drives a wedge between producer prices of factors and commodities and the prices paid to, or received by, households. In such cases, it is easy to measure the tax payment as the difference between the value of factor supplies, or consumption, at consumer and producer prices (Dilnot *et al.* 1990). Where taxes do not fall at the production boundary – as, for example, with taxes imposed on intermediate goods – the analysis of incidence is more complex and requires a framework of accounting prices analogous to that used in cost-benefit analysis (see, for example, Little and Mirrlees, 1974; Stern, 1987).

The incidence of taxation, measured in this way, reveals the relative burden of taxation on different factors of production, or commodities, or in different countries or regions. OECD has prepared international comparisons of average rates of tax on earnings and on commodities (OECD, 1988) while Kay and Sen (1983) show how the relative tax rates on labour and capital vary across countries. These comparisons of tax rates are conceptually relatively straightforward, but assessment of the relative incidence of corporation tax in different countries is much more complex. The effective rate of tax on corporate activities is not only a function of the legal rate of corporation tax itself but is also dependent on the structure of the tax and its relationship to the personal income tax.

The most extensive attempt to answer these questions is that of King and Fullerton (1984), who compute effective marginal tax rates on specific investment activities on a comparable basis for the United States, United Kingdom, Germany and Sweden. The procedure ascribes a tax rate to each major type of investment (fixed assets, stocks, etc.) and to each form of finance (debt, equity, etc.). King and Fullerton consider two alternative assumptions about the nature of the taxed equilibrium – one in which post-tax rates of return are equalised and another in which pre-tax rates are identical.

These economic analyses are concerned with the incidence of particular taxes on factors and activities. Political judgments are much exercised with the way in which taxes are distributed among households. Empirical studies of aggregate tax incidence have been undertaken for several countries: Australia (Warren, 1979, 1986), Canada (Gillespie, 1976), Denmark (OECD, 1988), France (Cazenove and Morrisson, 1974), Ireland (National Economic and Social Council, 1975), but the most extensive analyses, both in scope and in range of years covered, are those of the Brookings Institution for the United States and the Central Statistical Office for the United Kingdom.

The approach adopted in both these groups of studies seeks to assess the relationship between aggregate tax paid (and, in some cases, benefits received) and original income (what households earn before payment of tax and receipt of benefits). The common conclusion is that taxes are, in aggregate, a good deal less progressive than is generally thought, and that, with possible exceptions in the lowest and highest levels of original income, the tax system may be regarded as approximately proportional. Most of the progressivity of the fiscal system taken as a whole results from benefits rather than taxation. A progressive income tax is broadly offset by the regressive impact of other tax instruments.

The conclusion has, however, been challenged by critics of the methodology employed, which is broadly similar across these studies. There are two main issues. One problem (Browning and Johnson, 1979; Browning, 1986) is that the incidence of any particular tax is not independent of the assumptions made about the incidence of any other tax (including negative taxes, such as benefits). Thus, for example, the tax system will appear more progressive if benefit levels are assumed to be fixed in real terms than if they are fixed in nominal terms (and hence reduced in value by the necessity of paying commodity taxes on the resulting expenditure). The overall incidence of the fiscal system taken as a whole is not affected by this observation, but the division of its progressivity between tax and benefits is.

A second issue concerns the attribution of taxes, particularly those on intermediate goods. The common treatment of these as general commodity taxes makes their distributional impact regressive, but Dilnot et al. (1990) suggest that these taxes may be better treated as origin- rather than destination-based (see Section VI.1) and should be treated as (progressive) general factor taxes. This substantially influences the assessment of incidence and Dilnot et al. (1984) argue that the overall impact of the UK tax system is not only progressive but has become substantially more so over time.

V.3 The Effects of Taxation

Tax analysis is particularly concerned with the incentive to work, with effects on savings and investment, and with consequences for risk-taking behaviour. The effects of taxation on labour supply are among the most politically controversial issues in tax policy. The sign of the effect is, of course, ambiguous, since if leisure is a normal good a positive income effect increasing work effort may outweigh a negative substitution effect, but it may be that political concern is related to the welfare consequences of taxation rather than with the quantity of labour or effort as such.

Empirical study of the effects of taxation on labour supply was stimulated by the experimental negative income tax studies undertaken in the United States in the 1960s, when participants were invited to substitute alternative earnings schedules for their own. Analysis of the results has remained controversial, and the modelling of non-linear budget constraints, which are faced by most households, remains a difficult matter of econometric technique. A current consensus, however, suggests that substitution effects are generally large for secondary earners (particularly married women) but that the earnings/leisure substitution elasticity is generally small for male principal earners. (Brown (1983), Hausman (1985) provide good surveys of the evidence.) There may also be substantial effects of taxation on retirement and participation decisions.

Different factors govern the effects of taxation at the upper end of the distribution, where it is implausible (or unimportant) to look for effects on the quantity of labour supplied: quality matters more. The classic interview study remains that of Break (1957) reproduced by Fields and Stanbury (1971), while similar approaches have been adopted by Barlow *et al.* (1966) and Holland (1977). Most of this work is consistent with a small positive outcome, although Fiegehen and Reddaway (1981), who focus explicitly on the impact on international mobility, find no significant effect.

Since the reduction of top tax rates has been one of the most important developments in tax policy in the 1980s, this paucity of evidence – both in number of studies and in the indication of magnitudes of effect – is at first sight disturbing. There is a sense, however, in which this technical focus may miss the point. The top rates of tax in the United Kingdom have always been unimportant in terms of their contribution to revenue. These tax structures serve more as a statement of social values than a nicely balanced reconciliation of the trade-off between labour supply and incentives implicit in Mirrlees-type models, and their effect may be less on the quantity of effort than on managerial attitudes and individual career choices. Thus, the broad historical analyses of social attitudes to managers, business and high incomes of Barnett (1986) or Weiner (1982) may have more relevance to an understanding of the ways in which taxation influences the decisions of high earners than the more formal structure of economic analysis.

The wedge between rates of return to savers and the return on capital is the result of the combined effect of the personal income tax, acting as a tax on lifetime accumulation, and the corporation tax as a tax on capital employed within the corporate sector. As concern has grown (Boskin, 1987; Bovenberg, 1988) about the low savings rate of the United States (and more recently the United Kingdom) relative to Pacific competitors, this macroeconomic concern has increasingly influenced the direction of microeconomic analysis.

Just as the effect of income tax on labour supply is ambiguous, so is the influence of a tax on capital income on savings. The tax raises the price of future consumption relative to that of present consumption, favouring immediate gratification. At the same time it also reduces potential consumption in both periods, and the first period effect reflects the overall balance of the two factors (Feldstein, 1978). Although some studies (Boskin, 1978) have produced empirical evidence to suggest that the elasticity of substitution between present and future consumption is large, this conclusion remains controversial. More recent work has concentrated more on the issue of how the amount and pattern of savings is influenced by the differential treatment of different kinds of savings (Meade, 1978; Carroll and Summers, 1987). The provision of state pensions may have substantial negative influences on savings behaviour (Feldstein, 1974; Hemming, 1977), and the tax-advantaged status of private pensions (whether funded or not) may also affect both the amounts which are saved and the ways in which savings are translated into investment (Feldstein, 1976c).

To the extent that corporation tax is a tax on capital employed in the corporate sector – and we saw at Section II.4 above that this proposition was less clear-cut than is commonly assumed – it acts as a disincentive to investment, and it certainly discriminates between different types of investment and different mechanisms for financing that investment. Attempts to address the former problem of negative effects on overall investment, particularly by accelerated depreciation provisions, have tended to increase the latter problem of discriminatory treatment of different kinds of investment, and thus have led to a long policy cycle in which investment credits became increasingly generous throughout the 1960s and 1970s only to be extensively withdrawn in the 1980s.

Domar and Musgrave (1944) first observed that a positive income tax was likely to encourage risk-taking: essentially, the government becomes a partner in any speculative transaction and so reduces the cost of risk-bearing to the originator. Subsequent analysis (Stiglitz, 1969) has emphasised the dependence of this result on two propositions of doubtful empirical validity – the symmetrical treatment of both income and capital gains (a recent development in both the United Kingdom and United States) and the existence of full offset for losses. The equalisation of tax rates on income and capital gains is a major step towards such symmetry. At the same time, the tax codes of Britain, the United States and other countries have facilitated the taxpayer's ability to match trading losses against other income, but limited the opportunity to allow such deductions for passive income derived from ventures in which the taxpayer is not an active participant. This reflects an anxiety to improve loss offset provisions for genuinely risky activities while reducing opportunities to use them as a means of tax avoidance.

V.4. *The Welfare Effects of Taxation*

The deadweight loss from taxation is the cost which the taxpayer (or the individual who avoids taxation by reorganising his behaviour) incurs in addition to the amount of the tax he pays. It is the loss which is eliminated by lump-sum taxation and minimised by an optimal tax system. The rigorous analysis of deadweight loss has been simplified considerably by the use of duality methods (Diamond and McFadden, 1974; Kay, 1980). Deadweight loss becomes simply the additional amount the taxpayer would be willing to give up if he were subject to lump-sum taxation instead and can be described by simple comparison of expenditure functions. When producer prices are constant, these suggest a natural price vector at which these expenditure functions can be compared.

When producer prices are variable, two complications emerge. The relevant reference price vector is no longer obvious, although the attractive properties of Debreu's coefficient of resource utilisation (Debreu, 1951; Kay and Keen, 1988) suggest that the producer prices of the efficient counterfactual equilibrium provide a suitable basis. Moreover, there are welfare consequences which follow from the change in the producer price vector itself. There are gains or losses from taxing goods subject to economies or diseconomies of scale – an idea familiar since Pigou (1947). For a small open economy, there may also be benefits from changing the terms on which trade takes place with the rest of the world – the tax policy analogue of the optimal tariff of trade theory.

The empirical analysis of the welfare effects of taxation has, appropriately, paralleled the development of general equilibrium models, and it is no accident that the contributions of Harberger (1964) are seminal to both. Despite this, Harberger's approach to welfare analysis was based on the summation of a series of partial equilibrium estimates ('adding welfare triangles'), and it is now apparent that this procedure does not, even approximately, measure the aggregate costs of taxation in a general equilibrium model. The structures devised by Shoven, Whalley and associates were partly designed to enable the effects of discontinuous changes in tax systems to be modelled (Shoven and Whalley, 1973). More commonly, however, estimates have been made of the welfare gains from the implementation of incremental tax reform (see, for example, Atkinson *et al.*, 1980; Ahmad and Stern, 1983), or of changes in particular policy areas (King, 1983).

Such analysis can look at the effect of changes in tax rates or, more ambitiously, at the effect of changes in tax structures. Auerbach and Kotlikoff (1987) develop a life-cycle model which illuminates the choice between income and expenditure as tax bases. They find significant gains from a switch to consumption taxation but demonstrate that these gains are sensitive to the specification of transitional arrangements.

The policy reaction is apparent. The distortions in savings and investment which result from the deficiencies of the personal and corporate income tax bases have become central to the political debate on the effects of taxation. The shift in emphasis from specific, discriminatory duties on particular commodities to general consumption taxation is possibly the most marked of the trends in the evolution of the tax base shown in Section I. Policy-makers have come increasingly to recognise the size of these economic costs of taxation relative to the direct operating costs which naturally exercise tax administrators.

V.5 *General Equilibrium Models of Taxation*

One of the first models of the tax structure to be developed in a general equilibrium framework was Harberger's (1962) analysis of the incidence of the corporate income tax. The Harberger framework allows both for substitution of capital and labour within the corporate sector and for the mobility of capital between corporate and non-corporate activities. The corporate tax therefore induces changes in the capital intensity of both the taxed and the untaxed sector and so influences factor incomes from all sources.

Harberger's approach allowed identification of the variables on which the incidence of the taxes he analysed depended, but it was when the techniques of Scarf (1969, 1973) became available that it became possible to compute general equilibrium models of taxation. The model of Shoven and Whalley (1973), for example, closely follows the Harberger framework and allows estimation of the distributional impact of tax reforms as well as of the changes in the use of factors. The parameters employed are calibrated to reproduce particular features of the observed equilibrium (they are prescribed rather than estimated). Piggott and Whalley (1985) present a more recent development of this framework for the UK economy.

Although it is clear that a full analysis of the effects of taxation requires a general equilibrium approach, this type of model has perhaps proved a less fruitful line of development than initial excitement suggested. The problem, essentially, is that there is a trade-off to be made between the detail with which the tax system itself is modelled and the comprehensiveness of the analysis of its effects. Such a trade-off is, indeed, apparent in the Harberger model itself. Harberger treats the corporate income tax as a proportional tax on the return on capital employed within the corporate sector but, as we have seen, this is not an accurate representation of any of the many varieties of corporation tax which are imposed in real economies. More careful description of the corporate tax to be considered would, however, not only be highly time and country specific, but would also require a detailed specification of the characteristics of the company sector itself. In the last decade, for example, as many as half the firms liable to corporation tax in the United Kingdom have been tax-exhausted – they have no current tax liability and can offset accumulated losses against future gains. This means that the marginal rate of tax is individual to the firm and that the behaviour of tax liability, or investment and financing behaviour, may be very different from that which would arise if the corporate sector were to be treated as a single unit. Non-linearities in the personal tax system make aggregation problems equally serious there.

A major advantage of a general equilibrium approach is that it clarifies, in a straightforward way, the issues defined in Section V.1. Any specific equilibrium is characterised by a distribution of tax payments – across individuals, by sectors. Thus we can read off the incidence of a particular tax, or the tax system. The welfare consequences of any structure can be assessed, either in absolute terms, or by reference to a particular counterfactual equilibrium. And if such a counterfactual is specified, then the impact of a tax change on the quantity of any particular commodity produced or consumed, or on the income or welfare of an individual or household, can be assessed and measured.

V.6 *Tax Incidence and Tax Policy*

Although an appreciation of the incidence of taxation is perhaps the key contribution which economic analysis can make to tax policy, it is difficult to suppress a feeling of disappointment in surveying the state of knowledge. One subject – the labour supply of labour income groups – has been studied intensively, and although some disagreement persists, there are now widely accepted conclusions. Our understanding of the effects of taxation on savings and investment is advancing also. But we still know relatively little about how taxes affect the choice of methods of savings and investment, or about how taxes influence entrepreneurship and risk-taking, although these questions are central to political debate.

New modelling techniques and data availability have enhanced our capacity to understand the distributional impact of taxation, but our ability to make comparisons internationally, or even for a single country over time, is still limited. The theory of welfare loss from taxation is now well understood but empirical applications are only just beginning.

As my discussion of general equilibrium approaches was designed to illustrate, empirical analysis of the effects of taxation requires the development of models which achieve an appropriate balance between essential detail and inessential complication, and the skill of the model-builder or model-user lies in the capacity to make that distinction. Moreover, the difference between the essential and the inessential will be contingent on the specific question which is addressed, and thus the search for all purpose, comprehensive models of the tax system is never likely to be successful. One approach (Atkinson and Sutherland, 1987) involves the development of simple, user-friendly frameworks within which the modeller, or armchair Chancellor, can prescribe whatever detail and parameters seem to him appropriate. Another is to add simple behavioural assumptions to the very disaggregated models based on samples of firms and households of the kind which have traditionally been used by revenue authorities to predict the fiscal consequences of planned changes. These models can also be linked to the public-sector components of econometric macro models. Whatever lines of development prove ultimately most fruitful, it is already clear that the opportunities made available by the increased speed and efficiency of computing are revolutionising the opportunities available for detailed understanding of the economic consequences of taxation. There is much work still to be done.

VI. INTERNATIONAL AND LOCAL TAXATION

VI.1 Multiple Jurisdictions

The castles of the Rhine were built by barons to enable them to levy tax on the traffic which passed by on the river below. Even in medieval days, however, the exercise was not without problems. Excessive tolls led to the diversion of cargo to routes that were less convenient but also less expensive. The amount which any one baron could collect was contingent on the levies of all other barons. Some sites were busier or more commanding than others and some tollkeepers had more powerful cannon. These problems were handled, if not resolved, by a mixture of conventions and rules, negotiation and outright warfare, until ultimately agreements were made, or enforced, on the limits of competing jurisdiction. In due course a *zollverein* was formed and ultimately a German state with agreed procedures for sharing revenues between the various authorities within the federation was established.

Today, the mechanisms for settling conflicting claims are more civilised but the underlying problems of levying tax in an interdependent world with independent fiscal jurisdictions have changed little. There is the issue of distortion – the inefficient diversion of economic activity to alternative regimes: the issue of jurisdiction – the reconciliation of competing claims to the same tax base: and the issue of enforcement – which arises from the unwillingness, or inability, of countries to impose each other's tax codes, and the varying capacity which they have to implement their own. These questions arise both for the organisation of international taxation and in the relationships between local and central governments in a unitary state, although the scholarly literatures on these two subjects are worlds apart.

The reasons these issues matter is that there is mobility between different jurisdictions. We shall principally be concerned with three kinds of mobility. There is mobility of goods and services, which allows trade to take place across borders, and taxation may inhibit this (or indeed encourage it). Factors of production may be mobile – here we are mainly concerned with the movement of capital across borders. And individuals themselves can change jurisdictions. This matters for tax policy principally because people who move generally take with them their labour, the opportunity to tax their capital, and the place where they normally consume.

In analysing the effects of taxation in open economies, there is an important distinction between source- or origin-based taxes and those which have a destination base. As the structure of a value added tax demonstrates, consumption is equal to the total of incomes generated at each stage of production and, over some suitable time frame, the reverse is also true. A broad-based tax may be charged by reference to the place of consumption (the destination principle) or the location of production (the origin principle). Although it is typically the case that income taxes are levied on the origin principle and consumption taxes on a destination basis, there is nothing inherent in the structure of these taxes that requires this result. This may be seen by considering the effects of a proposal which has been considered in a number of countries – and to a limited degree adopted in Japan – which is that VAT should be levied on an accounts rather than an invoice basis. The practical equivalence of indirect taxes, consumption taxes and destination-based taxes is, however, reinforced by GATT rules which seek to restrict the degree to which direct taxes may be refunded on exports. The opportunity to shift the tax system from an origin to a destination basis, thus stimulating exports and discouraging imports, has been put forward as an argument for the adoption of VAT in many of the countries which have introduced this tax, although in a world of floating exchange rates the force of this observation seems very limited (Tait, 1989). A perceived merit of VAT is that the zero-rating of exports fulfils the requirements of the destination principle, in a simple and systematic way, while other indirect taxes tend to fall at least in part on exported commodities. The distinction between origin and destination taxes is important in assessing the incidence of particular taxes.

VI.2 *Efficiency Aspects of International Taxation*

Countries may increase their welfare by imposing optimal tariffs, and it may similarly be possible to increase natural income in beggar-my-neighbour fashion by discriminatory domestic taxation (the European Court required Britain to bring its duty on imported wine into line with the rates it charges on domestically produced beer). But if the maximisation of global welfare were our objective, we could apply many of the efficiency results that apply to the analysis of a single country's tax system to the problems of international taxation. Perhaps the most important of these results is the Diamond–Mirrlees conclusion that aggregate production should be efficient. It would follow that just as no taxes should be imposed on transactions between firms, no taxes should be imposed on transactions between countries, and international trade would then take place at producer prices.

VAT levied on a destination basis achieves precisely this happy result. A uniform VAT, levied on imports and rebated on exports, is equivalent to a proportional tax on factor incomes in the country concerned (Grossman, 1980). So although countries differ greatly in the balance between direct and indirect taxation, they do not gain trade advantages from each other by doing so. If VAT were to be imposed on an origin basis, however, trade distortions would occur if countries charged it at different rates. It follows that countries which impose VAT must either harmonise their rates or make border tax adjustments if trade is to be efficient.

Where taxes are imposed on *intermediate* goods, trade distortions and production inefficiencies will occur. Taxes on business property and motor fuel may have this effect and so may exemptions within the VAT structure (as a result of the inability of business purchasers to reclaim VAT charged on the production of exempt goods). And it is difficult to apply the destination principle to services. An American who takes a cashmere sweater home from Harrods will have the VAT he pays refunded, but if he has his hair cut at the same time he gets no relief, and if the purpose of his visit was to take legal advice, he may or may not pay VAT, depending on whether or not the transaction is classified as an international service.

Tax may be levied on income by reference either to the source of the income, or the residence of its recipient – you can charge tax by reference to where the income came from, or where it went, or both. Or at least you can try: as the speed of international capital movement increases, the opportunities for definitive identification of either where it came from or where it went diminish. The outcome may seek to achieve capital import neutrality (capital is taxed at the same rate regardless of where it originates), or capital export neutrality (capital is taxed at the same rate regardless of where it is used). If the residence principle is used, capital will tend to migrate to where it is most efficiently deployed. If the source of income is what matters, capital will move to wherever it is taxed most lightly. Thus a residence basis does not require uniformity of the tax base and rates to secure efficiency in the use of capital, but the source principle does require such harmonisation. Individual income is mainly taxed on a residence basis. In addition, however, we purport to tax capital income by means of corporation tax. Applying the residence principle rigorously to corporate income would mean that we charged tax by reference to where the ultimate shareholder lives. We do not do this; instead, we look at the location of the corporation. The considerable problems which both the source and residence bases of capital income taxation pose are further discussed below under the heading of jurisdiction.

There may be inefficiencies arising from the movement of people. Internationally, these are not of great significance. Deadweight losses arise when people choose to live somewhere lacking amenities, like Jersey, because the lower tax rate compensates for the disadvantages of the locale, and more direct costs can arise if excessive taxation of expatriates discourages mobility. LDC's may find that redistributive taxes result in a loss of skilled personnel, and exit taxes have been proposed to deal with this (Bhagwati, 1976). But taxation is a minor influence on where most people choose to live, relative to the claims of family, friends, culture and language. A study designed to document the flood of executive talent from the United Kingdom in response to punitive taxes on earnings in the 1970s could locate only the merest trickle (Fiegehen and Reddaway, 1982).

VI.3 *Efficiency Aspects of Local Taxation*

In the context of local taxation, however, this mobility of individuals between jurisdictions has been seen as a positive boon. The Tiebout model (Tiebout, 1956) sees movement between local authority areas as a mechanism which permits the formation of local authority 'clubs' in which households with similar incomes and preferences gather together and secure the optimal level of provision of public goods which those incomes and preferences would imply. The Tiebout model is, of course, an unrealistic polar case. The opposite pole is one in which there is little possibility of movement between heterogeneous communities and in which local public expenditures are too small for differences in services and taxes between communities to be an important influence on where households choose to live. In such a world these differences will be capitalised into house prices (Oates, 1969) and local expenditures will be determined by political mediation between the conflicting requirements of different groups of residents (Bruechener, 1979). Note that this capitalisation through property values does *not* depend on a property tax being the mechanism of local government finance. A local income tax or poll tax would be capitalised into house prices in a similar way.

If mobility of individuals is less important than trade in goods or the flight of capital in the context of international taxation, the ordering is reversed when local taxation is at issue. Local governments in most countries do not impose sales taxes on goods and services, nor do they tax capital: where they do – as in the United States – the range of rates which they charge is limited and so is the potential for consequential production inefficiencies. Efficiency issues in local taxation therefore relate to household mobility and local choice of tax and service levels.

So which is the more persuasive model of local government? Harmonious communities of identical residents, whose happy coincidence of needs ensures that each election involves only unanimous acclamation of the continuation of agreed policies? Or beleaguered heterogeneous authorities subject to swings of political control as divergent groups seek to protect their taxes, services and property values? In reality, both caricatures are recognisable – the American polarisation of cities into decaying centres and complacent suburbia represents the Tiebout model in action, while Britain has seen politicised authorities at war with minorities of their own residents and with central government. Few countries which give significant functions to multiple levels of government have escaped problems in the relationships between these levels of government.

Much of this conflict results from the effects of local government activity on the distribution of income. There are several aspects to this (Tresch, 1981). Central government may redistribute between local authorities. This is, in a sense, a counter-Tiebout measure – in a Tiebout equilibrium there would generally be no reason to redistribute between authorities (as distinct from between individuals). Such a grant programme restricts the mobility which would bring a Tiebout equilibrium about (Inman, 1975) and may reduce the marginal cost of £1 of local public expenditure to local residents (Cripps and Godley, 1976). At the same time, however, local government may assume a redistributive role in conflict with or in addition to that attempted by central government. Even if this is restrained, subsidiary authorities may set the level of spending with an eye to the distributional consequences of their expenditure levels rather than the preferences of local residents for public services (Inman and Rubinfield, 1979).

It is concern for these issues that has provoked policies which seek to structure the grant system in such a way that extra spending by a local authority falls wholly on local residents, and towards a benefit, rather than ability to pay, view of the proper structure of local taxation. Hence the British proposal to replace the domestic property tax by a poll tax on local residents. Such a substitution has, of course, significant implications for the progressivity of the tax structure taken as a whole, and, to the extent that tax capitalisation operates, for the level of local property prices (Hughes, 1988).

VI.4 *Problems of Jurisdiction*

Although the consequences of problems of distortion and of jurisdiction generally interact, they are in principle clearly distinct. Distortion is an issue because the same activity or transaction might take place under alternative tax systems so long as there are multiple tax regimes even if the revenues from all of them accrue to the same government. Jurisdiction is an issue because revenues may accrue to different exchequers, and would arise even if all countries had identical tax systems so long as there are different authorities. There is an issue of jurisdiction when there are two barons with castles on the same river. There is a problem of distortion when two parallel rivers, perhaps with different ease of navigation, each have their own baron. The reason the problems are often interrelated is that when you take your cargo to another river, the baron you leave behind is often unwilling to let the matter rest there. Mobility of goods or factors commonly leads both to distortion and to arguments over jurisdiction.

Property taxes are a popular means of financing local government throughout the world because issues of jurisdiction are so easily resolved. A building has a well-defined location, it is easy to determine what that location is, and it can only ever be in one place at a time. Other local taxes – whether on income, consumption or on residence itself – are not so simple to implement.

But the most serious problems of jurisdiction are those which apply to corporate taxes. Suppose that a Swiss pharmaceutical company discovers a new drug in its laboratories in the United States. The product is manufactured in Belgium and sold in West Germany at a price which reflects a very large mark-up on the cost of materials used. Where does the profit on the transaction, or series of transactions, arise? It is likely that all four countries involved will wish to demand a share of the income generated and there are no obvious mechanisms for resolving their competing claims. Indeed as technology advances, activities develop which may have no physical location at all – satellite broadcasting, or computer instigated screen-based share trading.

None of the devices which tax administrators have created to resolve these problems works well in practice. Jurisdiction is generally based on corporate residence, by inappropriate analogy between individuals and corporations, and the British courts have struggled for a century with the intrinsically meaningless question of where a company is resident. Double tax treaties give ad hoc relief, in certain circumstances, to multiple claims to tax on the same income. An 'arm's length' principle is invoked to impute prices for transactions which, although internal to the company, nevertheless cross international barriers. But where, as is increasingly the case, the transaction is in specific factors under conditions of bilateral monopoly, this arm's length principle can provide no guide, since there are no markets in the factors concerned. It is worth noting that the question of where the Swiss drug company's profits arose is one to which there is no answer even in principle. Even with complete information and boundless goodwill – which is very far from being the case in practice – one method of apportionment is as arbitrary as any other. In an integrated economy, such as the United States, an agreed apportionment formula and the adoption of a tax base which is more or less common to all states is the only way in which multiple local corporation tax jurisdictions can be made to operate. Attempts to extend this principle internationally have encountered vigorous resistance and arguments over unitary taxation have been a major diplomatic issue between Europe and the United States in the 1980s.

In general, jurisdictional issues are much less important for local taxation within a single state than they are internationally. The fundamental difference between the relations between sovereign states in the international economy, and between local authorities in the domestic economy, is that in the second case there is a single overriding national government which can determine conflicting jurisdictional claims. This distinction is less important in the United States, where the constitution reserves substantial powers to the states, than it is in Britain.

Governments have responded to the problems of the absence of such an over-reaching supra-national authority by throwing up fiscal barriers around their frontiers. For as long as commodity taxes have been imposed, excise officers have battled with smugglers to ensure that tax due is properly collected. In the twentieth century, the smuggling of capital has become more important than the smuggling of goods. The fiscal frontiers which result may be necessary to enable taxes to be collected, but at the same time they impede innocent trade. As the world economy becomes more integrated, the ability of governments to maintain such barriers is eroded – exchange controls on capital movements have largely collapsed in the face of the growth of an international capital market. At the same time, those fiscal barriers which remain become more irksome and more costly, and institutions such as the European Community which are concerned to promote economic integration between states have sought to remove or reduce them.

The European Commission's plans to complete the internal market in 1992 involve reducing artificial incentives to cross-border shopping by requiring approximation of VAT systems and harmonisation of other commodity taxes among the twelve states of the Community. The proposals are based on an average of the (widely dispersed) rates currently in force in different countries, rather than on a determination of the best commodity tax system for the Community as a whole: thus they are described as 'convergence by reference to point of departure, not point of arrival'. The scheme represents a much more powerful sledgehammer than is needed to crack the nut of family shopping trips to South Antrim or Luxembourg, and so far no substantive progress has been made towards implementation. It is likely that in due course some more modest proposals targeted directly on the problems at issue will be brought forward (Cnossen and Shoup, 1987; Lee et al. 1988).

International capital movements make it necessary to consider how income which arises in one country for the benefit of someone living elsewhere should be taxed in both the jurisdictions involved. As described above, the basic principles are those of source and residence. Traditional capital exporters (Britain and the United States) have sought to apply a residence principle, while traditional capital importers (most other countries) have looked to the source of income. All countries have seen a reduction in source taxation as a means of attracting capital, or as a necessary response to similar action by others. The residence principle is difficult to enforce because it is difficult to monitor the investment income which your residents earn in other countries unless they remit it. The practical consequence is that effective tax rates are lower on capital if it is exported than if it is employed domestically, and that LDCs in particular not only collect little revenue from the taxation of capital income but discover that the process of collecting little revenue itself encourages capital flight overseas (Williamson and Lessard, 1987).

This problem can, in principle, be tackled through international collaboration. The European Community has proposed a common withholding tax on investment income paid to its residents although the scheme was withdrawn following opposition from those countries which do in fact attract deposits from customers in other member states. The weakness of such collaboration is that it needs to involve all countries, or most, and as the number who participate increases so does the gain to any country which chooses to remain outside the scope of such collaboration (Bird and McLure, 1989). The trail that turns to Liechtenstein or Panama generally runs cold and cold it is likely to remain. The alternative solution is to develop, or accept, taxes which are more robust to such problems: a realistic assessment is that the ability of developed countries to enforce tax on income from capital is likely to diminish in line with the current experience of LDCs.

VII. ENFORCEMENT, ADMINISTRATION AND COMPLIANCE

VII.1 *Tax Avoidance*

If a tax is imposed, consumption or use of the taxed commodity will generally fall. (Some of the well-known qualifications to this proposition have already been discussed.) Tax is thus avoided. But tax avoidance means something narrower than this. Tax avoidance arises where the potential taxpayer is able to reduce his liability while substituting an essentially equivalent transaction. If whisky is taxed, and I drink less of it, I avoid tax: but if I escape tax on whisky while still drinking a golden liquid whose flavour is redolent of the peat of the Scottish highlands, I engage in tax avoidance.

Legal avoidance is commonly distinguished from illegal evasion. Avoidance occurs when full disclosure of the relevant facts to the tax authority would still imply no tax liability. Evasion depends on concealment of material facts. The French language translates avoidance as 'evasion' and evasion as 'fraud'. Evidently there is a cultural as well as a linguistic difference here. The distinction between avoidance and evasion is useful, but like that between white and blue collar crime, ultimately proves hard to maintain. The manner in which facts are disclosed is often critical to how the taxman will interpret them. And legislation in several countries – such as Australia – and judicial decision in others – such as the United Kingdom – have sought to turn avoidance into evasion by declaring void transactions whose purpose is to minimise tax rather than to serve a commercial purpose. But it is not often possible to create sensible results by knocking out one of a series of transactions, and these measures have enjoyed little success, although they have eliminated some ludicrously artificial avoidance schemes.

It might seem that economists (as opposed to lawyers or moral philosophers) would have little to say about tax avoidance, and indeed they have said little. Friends of Nicholas Kaldor would not have expected him to share this unaccustomed reticence, but the insight contained in his comment (Kaldor, 1980b, p. 18) that 'the existence of widespread tax avoidance is evidence that the system, not the taxpayer, stands in need of radical reform', has not received proper attention, either from tax administrators (who perceive tax avoidance as engrained as original sin, and as intractable), or from economists who have seen the study of tax avoidance as less intellectually, if more financially, rewarding than relaxing the assumptions of optimal tax theorems.

Kaldor's point, of course, is that economic concepts differ in their robustness in practical application. In specific cases, this is recognised. Thus the adherents of the comprehensive income tax have displaced the Hicksian concept of income (income is what a man can consume during a period and still expect to be as well off at the end of the period as at the beginning) by the Schanz–Haig–Simons measure (income is what a man could have consumed during a period of account without reducing his wealth). They reason correctly, that tax inspectors would find the task of assessing expectations harder than the task of measuring outcomes.

In Section II.5 I contrasted the robustness of alternative tax bases, emphasising the importance of the directness of the relationship between the tax base and observable transactions. Income tax avoidance falls over-whelmingly into one or other of two categories, representing the main cases where income accrues but there is no transaction. One is the accumulation of unrealised accretion. The other is the incidence of payment in kind. The most common of these fringe benefits are cars, food and accommodation, insurance and education expenses (OECD, 1988). If fringe benefits are perfectly substitutable for personal expenditure, then tax is forgone but no deadweight loss is incurred; if the substitution is imperfect, then remuneration through this mechanism is costly. If the company provides me with a more (or indeed less) luxurious car than I would have chosen for myself, then part of the resulting tax saving will be dissipated in efficiency losses (Ashworth and Dilnot, 1986). The paradoxical conclusion is that the more successful the tax system is in outlawing attractive fringe benefits – which are highly substitutable for earnings – the greater are the distortions which may result.

Such an attack may be made by charging employees with tax on the value of the benefit, or by refusing the cost of deduction to the employer (as with partial or complete disallowance of expenditure on business entertainment). Australia and New Zealand have developed this latter approach by imposing a general fringe benefit tax on employers. This seems to reflect a political reluctance to attack employee privileges directly rather than any principled solution to the problem, which is not to say that the solution is without merit.

VII.2 *Tax Evasion*

The economics of tax evasion is part of the economics of the criminal activity generally (Ehrlich, 1973) and it has been shown that the amount of such evasion will diminish with the probability of detection and the penalties which result (Isachsen and Strom, 1980). The analysis might have been more interesting if it had reached the opposite conclusion, or it had found a means of modelling Gilbert's widely shared anxiety to make the punishment fit the crime, which is presumably why in practice we fine tax evaders sums related to the tax unpaid rather than subject them to solitary confinement for life. Sandmo (1981) makes the important point that tax evasion cannot be assumed to be welfare reducing. The moonlighting plumber might prefer to stay at home rather than participate in the formal economy, and if he takes his ill-gotten gains to the pub where he is required to pay VAT and excise duty it is even conceivable that the black economy produces no net revenue loss (Peacock and Shaw, 1982).

The measurement of the 'black economy' has been a subject of considerable controversy and – necessarily – ill-informed speculation. Tanzi (1982) has collected a range of estimates – while Pedone's (1981) estimate that 40% of Italian VAT is evaded may be credible, comparable figures for North

European or North American economies are not. High conjectures have been put forward by Fiege (1979) and Guttman (1977) who base their analysis on the presumption that illegitimate transactions are mainly financed with cash and seek to reconcile, with difficulty, their assertions of large increases in the size of the black economy with reductions in the velocity of circulation of narrow money. The Inland Revenue has claimed that the black economy might be around 7·5% of national income. While this figure has been widely repeated no account of its basis has been provided and Peacock (1988) has cynically suggested that it derives mainly from a political balance between the desire to seek additional powers and resources and the implications of incompetence inherent in a higher figure. The best assessments are those derived from the Taxpayer Compliance Measurement Programme of the United States and the most careful overall appraisal of the arguments is that of Smith (1986) who concludes that for the United Kingdom a figure in excess of 5% requires the support of faith rather than evidence.

VII.3 *Tax Compliance and Administration*

When economists talk about the costs of imperfect tax systems, they are pointing to the deadweight losses from taxation discussed in Section V.4. When tax administrators talk about the costs of taxation they have in mind more tangible matters. These concern the salaries of revenue officials, the costs of the red tape in which they surround their papers and their customers. There are also the fees paid to accountants, and the air fares to exotic locations such as Leichtenstein and the Netherlands Antilles where a surprisingly large proportion of world financial transactions appear to take place, given the modest gross domestic products of these jurisdictions. The first two categories of expenditure – official salaries and red tape – are *central administrative* costs, the second two categories – advisory fees and junkets to foreign parts – are *compliance* costs, the expenditures incurred by taxpayers themselves in meeting the requirements of the tax authorities, or minimising their liabilities to them.

Administrative costs and compliance costs are both substitutable and complementary. There is a spectrum of mechanisms of administration ranging from that in which the entirely passive taxpayer has the required sum extracted from his pocket by the revenue authorities (income tax on earnings deducted at source is close to that) to that in which the taxpayer himself computes the tax due and voluntarily remits it to the exchequer. Neither of these extremes of revenue enforcement and self-assessment work. Even PAYE requires that employers submit information about their workforce, and wholly voluntary levies unsupported by elements of official coercion rarely yield much revenue. Different governments have chosen different points along that spectrum for their various taxes. In Britain, income tax is generally heavily dependent on revenue enforcement while VAT is self-assessed with random official audit. Complementarity between taxpayer costs and the burden of tax collection arises because avoidance activity by taxpayers necessitates compensating responses by the revenue authorities and (perhaps) vice versa. A sort of mutual arms race occurs, in which the diffuse nature of the army of taxpayers ensures that no truce is possible. The outcome – increasingly complex legislation and litigation – is apparent at all the weak points of the tax structure, particularly in areas of the personal and corporate income taxes.

Public choice theory would suggest that officials have incentives to increase the resources devoted to tax collection, the private sector to minimise them (Forte and Peacock, 1981; Peacock, 1981). It would follow total costs are likely, other things equal, to be reduced the further along the spectrum to self-assessment specific administrative procedures are located (Barr *et al.* 1977). In line with a trend to privatisation of public services much more widely (Kay, 1987) tax administration has moved towards self-assessment both in the way in which existing taxes are handled and in the style and structure of new taxes, such as VAT.

Administrative costs can generally be measured by reading the government accounts, but the measurement of compliance costs requires a research programme. A series of studies by Sandford has formed part of such a programme. Sandford (1973) and Sandford *et al.* (1989) review the administrative and compliance costs of the British tax system as a whole and set them at about 4% of revenue derived.

Although there is a clear distinction between administrative and compliance costs, on the one hand, and deadweight losses, on the other, there is also an important connection. It is clearly not worth spending £2 or even £1 to collect £1 of tax, but how much is it worth spending? The answer is given by the shadow price of tax revenue, which would be derived from the dual of the optimal tax calculation (if we had an optimal tax system) or from the analysis of the welfare impact of tax reforms (since we do not). If we set the shadow price at £1.25 for example (£1 of tax collected imposes welfare losses of this amount) it would follow that we should expand enforcement activity to, but not beyond, the point at which an additional 25p of collection costs brings in an extra £1.25 of receipts.

VII.4 *Improving Enforcement*

Administration and enforcement of taxation is generally discussed in a rather narrow framework. Statutes exist: the obligation of revenue officials is to enforce them. While this is of course true, it means that there is little or no serious discussion of what makes some structures easier to enforce than others. Indeed discussion of the administrative issues associated with tax reform proves, in most cases, a depressing experience: what is possible is equated with what is familiar; what exists is assumed to 'work' and so what does not currently exist is, of necessity, 'difficult'.

Nevertheless, some progress is made. One of the reasons governments have so strikingly increased their reliance on VAT is that VAT is a good tax to administer. This is partly because the tax base is relatively clear, transactions oriented, and comprehensive: and partly because, since it is a modern tax, systems for implementing it have been instituted free of the historical baggage which lumbers the administration of – particularly – personal and corporate income taxes. The most important factor facilitating, or inhibiting, tax enforcement is the choice of the tax base. Many of the issues here have already been considered in Section II.

It is apparent that there are large differences between countries in the effectiveness of their tax administration, although I know of no attempt to quantify the issue. Nevertheless, the impression that the countries of northern Europe collect a much higher proportion of tax due than those of the south seems general among tax practitioners. It is probable that my inclination to avoid, or evade, depends on my perception of the extent to which others do so, which allows multiple equilibria and probable instability of equilibria. If this is so, the gains from maintaining public confidence in the efficiency and equity of tax administration may be very large, and the persistent circulation of exaggerated claims about the significance of the black economy deeply damaging: the belief that 'everyone is doing it' is dangerous if everyone *is* doing it, and more dangerous if everyone is not.

VIII. POSITIVE ISSUES IN TAX POLICY

VIII.1 Tax Policy and Public Choice

Most of this paper has been written for concerned citizens anxious to identify what is good in tax policy. This is appropriate if the objective is to ask what tax structures ought to be, but is not necessarily relevant in asking what tax structures are. Tax systems are the product of a democratic process in which politicians bid for the votes of what may not always be an altruistic electorate. And tax systems – and, perhaps, the politicians themselves – are managed by bureaucrats whose self-interest may differ from those of their political masters or the public they are employed to serve. The principal-agent literature (Grossman and Hart, 1983) is concerned with the design of structures which induce agents, who possess superior information and have effective control of day-to-day decision-making, to pursue the objectives of their principal. It is in this area that the normative and positive theories of public finance interact.

Voters express their preferences for both public goods and redistribution through the ballot box. The problems of securing stable equilibria from voting mechanisms are well known (Arrow, 1951; Riker, 1982) unless preferences are single peaked or restricted in some analogous way (Plott, 1967). Log-rolling or vote trading mechanisms may increase the likelihood of such a stable equilibrium by the creation of omnibus packages (Buchanan and Tullock, 1962; Becker, 1983). However, log-rolling creates its own disadvantages. Legislators may trade mutual support for packages favouring their own constituents and hence support inefficiently large programmes (Stigler, 1971; Weingast *et al.* 1981). Rent-seeking behaviour may itself absorb much of the potential efficiency gains from programmes.

Redistribution policies are intrinsically multi-dimensional and hence preference restrictions are less likely to hold. Roberts (1977) analyses majority voting for the parameters of a linear tax schedule, and shows that an equilibrium outcome is achievable provided 'hierarchical adherence' is maintained – the rich remain (relatively) rich whatever tax schedule is in force.

Aumann and Kurz (1977) describe redistribution games in which majorities vote taxes to redistribute a fixed total income among themselves. They show that marginal tax rates are likely to exceed 0·5. Aumann and Kurz, and subsequent commentators, have suggested that this rate is implausibly high: while estimates of the overall average of marginal tax rates do not exist for most countries, calculations for the United Kingdom, which is around average for *average* tax rates, show an average of *marginal* tax rates significantly above 0·5 (Dilnot *et al.* 1984).

Bureaucrats are assumed to have an interest in expanding bureaucracy: thus Brennan and Buchanan (1980) begin with a leviathan who enjoys a perpetual franchise to extract resources from voter/consumers. They propose constitutional curbs designed to limit the power to tax. They also favour narrower tax bases and taxes on goods in elastic supply. The contrast to Ramsey-type rules could hardly be more marked, and is intentional. For Brennan and Buchanan, and those who share their stance, the inefficiency of the tax system is seen as a positive benefit, limiting the amount likely to be raised; their criteria of optimality are virtually the reverse of those of the welfarist approach. Their projected constitution also includes a balanced budget provision intended to limit government's capacity to divert resources from future generations.

These desires for statutory limitations are reflected in the tax revolt of the late 1970s, and demands for general constitutional limitations on taxation and budget deficits (although political sentiments contrast sharply with experience). The very effectiveness of VAT as a revenue-raising instrument has been seen by some groups as a reason for opposing its introduction into the United States. The positive theory of tax policy explains why it may be rational to impose restrictions on the size and shape of tax policies which democratic governments may choose.

VIII.2 *The Mechanisms of Taxation*

These demands reflect the rejection of a welfarist view of tax policy. In its extreme form (Nozick, 1974) this implies evaluation of tax policy by reference to process, rather than end states. Almost all constitutions protect their citizens against oppressive taxation, so that the introduction of a federal income tax in the United States required a constitutional amendment. In Britain, such constitutional protection is thought to be secured, inexplicably, by prohibiting anyone but government ministers from putting expenditure proposals to Parliament and excluding financial matters from the consideration of the House of Lords.

If tax policy may restrict rights, tax policies may also be used to secure them (Dasgupta, 1986; Helm, 1989). The 'right' to housing, food or other necessities is often used as a reason why these items should be subject to low rates of tax, if taxed at all. Yet it is difficult to see how a right is secured by a low price. In Sen's famous paradox, which demonstrates the potential incompatibility of liberalism and Paretanism (Sen, 1970), individuals are guaranteed the right to choose what books they read, or whether they sleep on their back or their belly: but given the illiberal preferences which prevail in society, they find it profitable to allow others to come and sort out their libraries or turn them over in bed. But the essence of liberalism is not captured by the ability to require others to pay for being illiberal. A right is a right, not a trading counter.

It is apparent that we are using the word 'right' in two senses here. One relates to the initial distribution of endowments in a welfarist framework. The right to be free of pollution is not an absolute guarantee of crystal clear water and the purest of air, but a statement of the principle that the polluter pays. But the right to shelter – if there is such a right – is absolute. It is not something I can trade off for gewgaws, and the right to dispose of one's own labour is not consistent with slavery even if slavery is a voluntary contract entered freely by both parties. Rights are then met by public provision or prohibition, not subsidies or taxes. The right to shelter is met by low-cost public housing, not mortgage interest tax relief: the evil of slavery killed by its prohibition, not by a stamp duty on slave contracts. Taxation may interfere with life, liberty and the pursuit of happiness: it can even encourage it, but it cannot enforce it.

There is a different reason for supposing that the process of government activity matters as well as the end result. The process may itself be seen as an objective in itself. The notion of taxpaying as a badge of citizenship lies as deep in fiscal history as the tea in Boston harbour, and may reflect a contractarian view of the state (Gough, 1957). More recent versions of the same argument can be found in the view that everyone, regardless of means, should pay at least 20 % of the local community charge, or poll tax: and, from a different political perspective, there are those who support universalist benefit systems because they expose the whole community to the same tax and transfer mechanism.

In daily life, the process of taxation mainly concerns the uncongenial activity of communication with revenue authorities. Their power to gather information varies considerably across countries (and this would be a major problem if international co-operation in tax enforcement were to advance). Britain's administration is unusually circumscribed, probably reflecting the system's nineteenth-century origins. In Britain and the United States, disclosure of information about individual taxpayers is not just misconduct by tax officers but a criminal offence (this has now been the subject of specific legislation in Britain), while in Sweden tax returns are, like other government documents, public information.

VIII.3 *Horizontal Equity*

Few comprehensive discussions of tax policy, or tracts on public finance, fail to contain a discussion of horizontal equity – the principle that similar individuals should be treated similarly. For some, this is simply a welfarist requirement – 'the equal taxation of equals is implied directly by utilitarianism and does not require a separate principle of horizontal equity' (Feldstein, 1976a). Unfortunately, this is not generally true: Stiglitz (1982) illustrates cases where random taxation may prove to be optimal, either *ex ante* or *ex post*.

I suspect most people would share the view that such a structure was wrong, even if it was efficient, with objections to randomness in government action which extend far beyond tax policy. There are rarely explicit stochastic elements in tax structures, but effective randomness arises, often in a serious way, when legislation is poorly enforced or so badly conceived that it cannot be enforced. Tax then falls arbitrarily on some, for whom avoidance or evasion is difficult, or who consider it immoral, while others escape.

The principle of horizontal equity is sometimes used to rule out discrimination on grounds of race or sex (Atkinson and Stiglitz, 1980). But it is evidently not the horizontal equity principle that is doing the work here. Differences in race and sex not only exist but are, unfortunately, economically relevant, which is mostly why we are concerned about racial or sexual discrimination in the first place. Moreover, the choice of what are and are not acceptable bases for discrimination within the tax system is one which changes over time. Nineteenth-century legislators not only saw nothing inappropriate in discriminating between men and women in the tax structures they designed: it would have been impossible, given the social values and systems of property ownership which then prevailed, for them to have done anything else.

Horizontal equity appears most relevant to the choice of the tax unit: how individuals and families should be taxed. Here, there is a fundamental conflict between two underlying objectives – the desire to respect the right of individuals to be treated as individuals, which points to the individual as the appropriate unit, and the purpose of relating tax liability fairly to the whole of an individual's circumstances, which suggests a unit or household basis (Kay and King, 1989). There are as many resolutions to this problem as there are countries in the world (Morris and Warren, 1981; Kay and Sandler, 1982), but there is some evidence that the trend is towards an individual basis (Spencer, 1986).

It is difficult to think of any practical problem in fiscal policy which has been illuminated by the application of the principle of horizontal equity. It has, perhaps, provided a focus around which a number of substantive issues can be considered. When, if ever, is randomness in taxation acceptable? What variables are admissible in assessing tax liability and what are not? Is there a conflict in the design of the tax unit between efficiency and individual rights? But the ethical questions involved in each of these subjects are imported from elsewhere, not derived from the principle of horizontal equity. The assertion that people in similar circumstances should be treated similarly invariably degenerates to a discussion of what is meant by similar.

IX. THE EVOLUTION OF TAX POLICY

IX.1 *Directions of Reform*

The tax systems of most Western countries have changed markedly in the last two decades. In this same period there has been extensive academic debate on tax policy: conferences have been held, new journals have been founded, new ideas have surfaced, and a lively debate has developed. What is the association between these scholarly activities and the evolution of policy?

Although different countries have implemented tax reform in different ways, there are clear common themes around the world. Each of these principal themes has clear precursors in the literature surveyed in this paper. The overall growth of public spending has been slowed, and governments have imposed – often artificial – restraints on the aggregate levels of taxation and spending (Section VIII.1). Within that structure, there has been a shift in the relative importance among broad-based taxes away from the taxation of income from capital in the personal or corporate sector towards consumption taxes and social security taxes on earned income (Section II.3).

VAT has been generally adopted as the standard model of commodity taxation, with greater uniformity of rates and little taxation of intermediate goods. Exceptions to the rule of uniformity have reflected less the distributional characteristics of the commodity (Section III.1) and increasingly the social impact of such consumption (Section IV.1). The income tax structure has seen major reductions in the top rates of tax – indeed this is true of all tax schedules – and considerable simplification of rate schedules (Section III.2). Stiglitz (1987) finds these movements in contradiction to the thrust of the optimal tax literature: my own judgement is that they reflect a better appreciation that the complexities which have characterised income tax schedules in the past rarely served the purposes which were intended. Corporation tax has been increasingly integrated with personal income tax (Section II.4).

There are some important areas where policy is incoherent. Corporation tax systems have moved from relative parsimony towards investment to great generosity, and back, with the consistency of direction of a drunken driver. The income tax base has been transformed in ways which reflect the requirements of the comprehensive income tax – as in the equalisation of income and capital gains tax rates – but has also moved towards a consumption base – with the exemption of the yield from an increasingly wide range of life-cycle savings from income tax. In both cases, the indecisive direction of policy is a mirror of a vigorous and unresolved academic debate. And if policy-makers have failed to address the issue of the tax unit effectively, that failure is mirrored in a dearth of substantive analysis.

In Section I, I explained how analysis influences policy, and the indirect nature of that influence. It follows that our concern should not be to present complex optimal tax formulae into which policy-makers can insert parameters which reflect their own preferences: this technocratic view of the political process bears no relationship to the reality of a democratic society. It is true that ideally there is a distinct optimal tax rate for every individual and every transaction: but the effect of applying that in practice is to hand the determination of tax policy over to vested interests and smart lawyers. The task of analysis is to define and elucidate simple principles which can be widely communicated and widely understood.

IX.2 The Evolution of Tax Policy

So what are these principles? In Section I, I put forward six key questions which policy-makers might ask economists to answer. There are no definitive answers nor a universal consensus: here I describe a personal view.

What should the tax base be? The tax base should, as far as possible, be based on real transactions, not hypothetical ones. This favours taxes such as VAT and a tax on labour income, but taxes on capital and capital income rarely met these criteria. Taxes on capital are no longer of much significance anywhere; socialist governments around the world promise to introduce wealth taxes but rarely implement them with much success. However, the taxation of capital income dies extremely hard. Once it is recognised that corporation tax is primarily a tax on rent, rather than on capital, it becomes apparent that taxes on capital income have never raised much revenue.

But the rhetoric of tax policy suggests that we did not mean it to be like that. The 1980s have seen a reversion to some of the principles of the comprehensive income tax. An issue for the next decade is whether that is the wave of the future, or whether the lesson of these reforms is that the best we can do within that framework is still rather poor. Charles McClure, one of the architects of the US tax reform packages, has framed the question clearly. Was 1986 tax reform's finest hour, or did it represent the death throes of the comprehensive income tax?

My judgement is that the second of these positions is closer to the truth. The comprehensive income tax fails on a mixture of political and administrative difficulties and, particularly, much of the complexity of the existing tax code is attributable to those areas where the logic of the income tax demands a base far removed from day-to-day transactions. The weaknesses of the tax in these areas not only creates an administrative burden for taxpayers and revenue authorities but leads to avoidance and distortion which undermine the broader economic functions of the tax.

The challenge for the next decade and the next century is to broaden the range of instruments consistent with the transactions base. In particular, the capacity of VAT and existing means of taxing labour income to secure distributional objectives is very limited. The transformation of the income tax into a progressive personal expenditure tax, and of the corporation tax into a tax based on corporate cash flows, provide the solutions to these problems. It should be appreciated that the object of taxing expenditure, rather than relying on the existing and evolving income tax, is not to exempt owners of capital from tax: it is to ensure that some tax is in fact paid on accumulations of wealth. At last, there are signs that policy-makers are coming to appreciate that the *effective* progressivity of the tax system, especially in the higher ranges of the income distribution, is much more influenced by the choice of the tax base than by the level of the rates.

But what should the rate structure be? I believe there is a strong case, based firmly in economic analysis, for rate structures which are simple, broad-based and non-discriminatory. This is not because tax theory can show – say – that uniform commodity taxation is optimal. Theory can never prove a proposition like that, not only because uniform commodity taxation is shown to be ideal only in certain very special circumstances, but because theory can never, in itself, make the case for any specific policy prescription. What it can do – and has done – is to show that most of the objectives of the kind of discrimination we observe are not achieved, or would be better achieved in other ways, and that there are no very clear rules for identifying empirically those commodities which should be taxed at different rates or what these different rates should be. If that is so, then it is better to have uniformity than to open an argument in which rationality will play only a minor role. Trade theorists are familiar with the argument that although free trade is not necessarily ideal it is better than any other likely outcome. So we should have a single rate, comprehensive VAT. Although there are arguments for differentiation, the patterns of discrimination which currently exist are the product of distributional objectives – mostly better pursued by other instruments – and other reasons which are generally weaker still.

As far as the structure of taxation on labour income, or expenditure, is concerned, this approach suggests a single system which incorporates income tax, social security contributions and principal means tested benefits. Within that structure, minimising the number of marginal rates has some administrative advantage, and reduces the distortions which result from the dispersion of rates across taxpayers. The elaborately differentiated rate structures which prevailed in most countries last decade were not the product of careful analysis of the distributional implications and incentive effects of tax systems. Indeed in many cases they were not the product of any analysis at all: decorative castles with crenellated turrets and no foundations. Two or three rates of tax are still enough to offer considerable flexibility, and one might well be enough. A growing international consensus seems to put the maximum rate which can realistically be operated at between 50 and 60%. You can vote for higher rates but you cannot make them effective: 98% of nothing is nothing.

What should be the corrective role of taxation? Here taxes should be concentrated on those specific market failures – particularly externalities – for which fiscal instruments are appropriate. In the face of environmental concerns, taxation is a good means of persuading both individuals and firms to undertake their own cost-benefit analysis of activities and their consequences. But most other social and economic policy objectives are better achieved by other means. Fiscal intervention in the housing market – much of it unintended – has been almost wholly malign, and the favouring and disfavouring of different forms of investment and finance has done little for the efficiency of the corporate sector. In these areas we do better to seek fiscal neutrality. It is encouraging that we are indeed moving in these directions.

What effects do taxes have? The consequences of tax policies are many, wide ranging and often not what their authors envisaged. Partly this is because the general equilibrium consequences of a change are rarely readily apparent. Perhaps more important is that the effect of deviations between theoretical and actual taxes are often as important as those between actual taxes themselves, and distortions between different types of activity – as, particularly, in the savings and investment markets – may be much more significant than any tax-induced encouragement or discouragement of the activity as a whole.

Certainly less is known about the economic consequences of taxation than we might feel entitled to expect. The distributional effects of taxation have been much studied, but in spite of that there is no clear verdict on how that has changed over time, nor are there well founded comparisons between countries. Empirical analysis of labour supply is now extensive, and that of savings behaviour increasingly so, but most other incentive effects are still the subject of conjecture rather than empirical evidence. Questions such as the effects of taxation on entrepreneurship, which exercise politicians – and rightly so – have been very little studied. As in some other areas of empirical economics, there is a tendency to produce new answers to old questions rather than to address new questions.

The fiscal relationship between different governments and levels of government and the question of *how the tax system should be administered and enforced* is often left to tax practitioners, not always with success. International aspects of taxation are generally the subject of pragmatic negotiation between administrators, with *ad hoc* solutions based largely on ill-defined concepts of equity and perceptions of national interest which lack any analytical or empirical base. There is probably no area of tax policy where further research effort is so clearly required. Better international co-ordination will ameliorate some problems, but may actually increase others: the progress of economic integration similarly helps to resolve some issues while making others more acute.

The key to future policy is to strike a balance between Utopian solutions which require impossible degrees of international co-operation and excessive pragmatism which resolves administrative confusion but aggravates economic distortion. (The Cockfield proposals for harmonising Europe's indirect taxes exemplify the first and the existing international network of double tax treaties the second.) The solution is to devise structures which fit easily together in an international context. The existing structure of corporation tax clearly does not meet these requirements: nor does a residence basis for the taxation of capital income. It is, for example, unlikely that countries will ever be very successful in taxing activities which take place wholly within other jurisdictions. This might sound the most obvious of points, but its implications for the structure of international taxation, which could no longer retain any element of residence basis, are revolutionary. Another of the attractions of cash flow based taxes is their long-term potential for offering solutions to these problems.

Domestic administration and enforcement is subject to similar requirements. Solutions do not lie in appeals to the moral sense of taxpayers, or in the continued accretion of powers by the revenue authorities. Tax avoidance and evasion are problems of the tax system, not of the social system: if laws are difficult to implement, the first resort should be to frame a better law not to appeal to the moral sense of taxpayers. The best approach is to concentrate resources on taxes which are robust to problems of administration and enforcement. It is apparent that tax avoidance, particularly, is heavily concentrated in certain very limited areas of the tax structure – principally again those associated with income from capital – which also contribute very little to revenue. A primary merit of the expenditure tax is that it is an enforceable means of achieving the objects of these taxes.

IX.3 *The Tax System as a Whole*

I have stressed the importance of looking at the tax system as a whole, and it is worth spelling out what such a structure, taken as a whole, might be like. Revenue would come from three principal sources: a broad-based VAT, a payroll tax and a tax which might still be called an income tax but would be one of the several versions of cash flow or expenditure taxation. The rate schedule would probably involve only a single rate with a generous exemption, and benefits to low-income households would be paid through the same mechanism. Corporate taxation would fall more explicitly on rents, probably through the adoption of a cash-flow base. Differential commodity taxation, and the discriminatory taxation of producer goods, would be confined to corrective taxes on externalities. The principal mechanism of enforcement would be self-assessment with audit.

We are already – mostly – moving in these directions. We would do so more effectively if the analytic basis of tax policy were more widely understood.

REFERENCES

Aaron, H. J., Galper, H. and Pechman, J. A. (eds.) (1988). *Uneasy Compromise: Problems of a Hybrid Income-Consumption Tax*. Washington: Brookings Institution.

Ahmad, E. and Stern, N. H. (1983). 'Theory of reform and Indian indirect taxes.' *Journal of Public Economics*, vol. 25, pp. 259–95.

Akerlof, G. A. (1978). 'The economics of "tagging".' *American Economic Review*, vol. 68, pp. 8–19.

Andrews, W. D. (1974). 'A consumption type or cash flow personal income tax.' *Harvard Law Review*, vol. 87, pp. 1113–88.

Arnott, R. and Stiglitz, J. (1986). 'Moral hazard and optimal commodity taxation.' *Journal of Public Economics*, vol. 29, pp. 1–24.

Arrow, K. J. (1951). *Social Choice and Individual Values*, 2nd ed. (1963). New York: John Wiley.

Ashworth, M. and Dilnot, A. W. (1987). 'Company cars taxation.' *Fiscal Studies*, vol. 8, no. 4, pp. 24–38.

Atkinson, A. B. (1970). 'On the measurement of inequality.' *Journal of Economic Theory*, vol. 2, pp. 244–63.

—— and Sandmo, A. (1980). 'The welfare implications of capital income taxation.' ECONOMIC JOURNAL, vol. 90, pp. 529–49.

—— and Stern, N. H. (1974). 'Pigou, taxation and public goods.' *Review of Economic Studies*, vol. 41, pp. 119–28.

—— —— and Gomulka, J. (1980). 'On the switch from direct to indirect taxation.' *Journal of Public Economics*, vol. 14, pp. 195–224.

—— and Stiglitz, J. E. (1972). 'The structure of indirect taxation and economic efficiency.' *Journal of Public Economics*, vol. 1, pp. 97–119.

—— and —— (1976). 'The design of tax structures: direct versus indirect taxation.' *Journal of Public Economics*, vol. 6, pp. 55–75.

—— and —— (1980). *Lectures on Public Economics*. Maidenhead: McGraw-Hill.

—— and Sutherland, H. (1987). *TAXMOD*. London: London School of Economics.

Auerbach, A. J. and Feldstein, M. S. (1985). *Handbook of Public Economics*, vol. 1. Amsterdam: North Holland.

—— and —— (1987). *Handbook of Public Economics*, vol. 2. Amsterdam: North Holland.

—— and Kotlikoff, L. J. (1987). *Dynamic Fiscal Policy*. Cambridge: Harvard University Press.

—— and Kurz, M. (1977). 'Power and taxes.' *Econometrica*, vol. 45, pp. 1137–61.

Barlow, R., Brazer, H. and Morgan, J. (1966). *Economic Behaviour of the Affluent*. Washington, D.C.: Brookings Institution.

Barnett, C. (1986). *The Audit of War*. London: Macmillan.

Barr, N. R., James, S. R. and Prest, A. R. (1977). *Self-Assessment for Income Tax*. London: Heinemann.

Becker, G. S. (1983). 'A theory of competition among pressure groups for influence.' *Quarterly Journal of Economics*, vol. 98, pp. 371–410.

Bhagwati, J. N. (1976). 'The international brain drain and taxation: A survey of issues.' In *The Brain Drain and Taxation* (ed. J. N. Bhagwati). Amsterdam: North Holland.

Bird, R. M. and McLure, C. E. (1989). 'The personal income tax in an interdependent world' (forthcoming in (ed. S. Cnossen) *The Future of the Personal Income Tax*, North Holland, 1990).

Blum, W. J. and Kalven, H. (1953). *The Uneasy Case for Progressive Taxation*. London: University of Chicago Press and Phoenix Books.

Boskin, M. J. (1978). 'Taxation, saving and the rate of interest.' *Journal of Political Economy*, vol. 86, pp. S3–27.

—— (1987). 'Increasing the National Savings Rate.' Paper given at Americans for Generational Equity Conference, Washington, D.C.

Bovenberg, A. L. (1988). *Private Savings in the US: Measurement and Analysis of Trends*. Washington: IMF.

Bradford, D. F. (1986). *Untangling the Income Tax*. Cambridge: Harvard University Press.

Break, G. F. (1957). 'Income taxes and incentives to work: an empirical study.' *American Economic Review*, vol. 47, pp. 529–49.

Brennan, G. and Buchanan, J. M. (1980). *The Power to Tax: Analytical Foundations of a Fiscal Constitution*. Cambridge: Cambridge University Press.

Brown, C. V. (1981) (ed.). *Taxation and Labour Supply*. London: Allen & Unwin.

—— (1983). *Taxation and the Incentive to Work*, 2nd ed. Oxford: Oxford University Press.

Browning, E. K. (1986). 'Tax incidence, indirect taxes and transfers.' *National Tax Journal*, vol. 38, pp. 525–34.

—— and Johnson, W. R. (1979). *The Distribution of the Tax Burden*. Washington, D.C.: American Enterprise Institute.

Bruechener, J. K. (1979). 'Property values, local public expenditure and economic efficiency.' *Journal of Public Economics*, vol. 11, pp. 223–45.

Buchanan, J. M. and Tullock, G. (1962). *The Calculus of Consent*. Ann Arbor: University of Michigan Press.

Carroll, C. L. and Summers, L. H. (1987). 'Why have private savings rates in the US and Canada diverged?' *Journal of Monetary Economics*, vol. 20, pp. 249–79.

Carter Commission (1966). *Report of the Royal Commission on Taxation*. Ottawa: Government Printer.

Cazenove, P. and Morrisson, G. (1974). 'Income redistribution: France, Great Britain and the United States.' *Revue Economique*, vol. 25, pp. 635–71.

Clark, E. (1971). 'Multipart pricing of public goods.' *Public Choice*, vol. 8, pp. 19–33.

Cnossen, S. (1983). 'Harmonisation of indirect taxes in the EEC.' *British Tax Review*, pp. 232–53.

—— and Messere, K. (1989). 'Survey and evaluation of research income tax systems in OECD member countries.' In *The Personal Income Tax: Phoenix from the Ashes?* (eds S. Cnossen and R. M. Bird). Amsterdam: North Holland.

—— and Shoup, C. S. (1987). 'Coordination of value-added taxes.' In *Tax Coordination in the European Community* (ed. S. Cnossen). Deverten: Kluwer.

Cripps, F. and Godley, W. A. (1976). 'Local government finance and its reform: a critique of the Layfield Committee's Report.' Cambridge: Department of Applied Economics.

Dasgupta, P. (1986). 'Positive freedom, markets and the welfare state.' *Oxford Review of Economic Policy*, vol. 2, no. 2, pp. 25–36.

Dasgupta, P. and Heal, G. (1979). *Economic Theory and Exhaustible Resources*. Cambridge: Cambridge University Press.

Deaton, A. S. (1977). 'Equity, efficiency and the structure of indirect taxation.' *Journal of Public Economics*, vol. 8, pp. 299–312.

—— (1981). 'Optimal taxation and the structure of preferences.' *Econometrica*, vol. 49, pp. 1245–60.

—— (1987). 'Econometric issues for tax design in developing countries.' In *The Theory of Taxation of Developing Countries* (ed. D. Newbery and N. Stern). Oxford: Oxford University Press for the World Bank.

Debreu, G. (1951). 'The coefficient of resource utilisation.' *Econometrica*, vol. 19, pp. 273–92.

Diamond, P. A. (1965). 'National debt in a neoclassical growth model.' *American Economic Review*, vol. 55, pp. 1125–50.

—— (1975). 'A many person Ramsey rule.' *Journal of Public Economics*, vol. 4, pp. 335–47.

—— (1968). 'Negative taxes and the poverty problem.' *National Tax Journal*, vol. 31, pp. 288–303.

—— and McFadden, D. I. (1974). 'Some uses of the expenditure function in public finance.' *Journal of Public Economics*, vol. 3, pp. 3–21.

—— and Mirrlees, J. A. (1971). 'Optimal taxation and public production I: production efficiency and II: tax rules.' *American Economic Review*, vol. 61, pp. 8–27 and pp. 261–78.

Dilnot, A. W., Kay, J. A. and Keen, M. J. (1990). 'Allocating taxes to households – a methodology.' *Oxford Economic Papers*, forthcoming.

—— —— and Morris, C. N. (1984). *The Reform of Social Security*. Oxford: Oxford University Press.

—— and Kell, M. (1988). 'Top rate tax cuts and incentives: some empirical evidence.' *Fiscal Studies*, vol. 8, pp. 86–107.

Domar, E. D. and Musgrave, R. A. (1944). 'Proportional income taxation and risk-taking.' *Quarterly Journal of Economics*, vol. 58, pp. 388–422.

Dreze, J. and Stern, N. (1987). 'The theory of cost benefit analysis.' In *Handbook of Public Economics*, vol. 2 (ed. A. J. Auerbach and M. S. Feldstein). Amsterdam: North Holland.

Ehrlich, I. (1973). 'Participation in illegitimate activities: a theoretical and empirical investigation.' *Journal of Political Economy*, vol. 81, pp. 521–65.

Feldstein, M. H. (1974). 'Social security, induced retirement and aggregate capital accumulation.' *Journal of Political Economy*, vol. 82, pp. 905–26.

—— (1976a). 'On the theory of tax reform.' *Journal of Public Economics*, vol. 6, pp. 77–104.

—— (1976b). 'Personal taxation and portfolio composition: an econometric analysis.' *Econometrica*, vol. 44, pp. 631–50.

—— (1976c). 'Perceived wealth in bonds and social security: a comment.' *Journal of Political Economy*, vol. 84, pp. 331–6.

—— (1978). 'The rate of return, taxation and personal savings.' ECONOMIC JOURNAL, vol. 88, pp. 482–7.

—— (1987) (ed.). *The Effects of Taxation on Capital Accumulation*. Chicago: University of Chicago Press.

Fiege, E. L. (1979). 'How big is the irregular economy?' *Challenge*, vol. 22, pp. 5–13.

Fieghen, G. C. and Reddaway, W. B. (1981). *Companies, Incentives and Senior Managers*. Oxford: Oxford University Press.

Fields, D. B. and Stanbury, W. J. (1971). 'Income taxes and incentives to work: some additional empirical evidence.' *American Economic Review*, vol. 61, pp. 435–43.

Fisher, I. and Fisher, H. W. (1942). *Constructive Income Taxation: a Proposal for Reform*. New York: Harper.

Forte, F. and Peacock, A. T. (1981). 'Tax planning, tax analysis and tax policy.' In *The Political Economy of Taxation* (ed. A. T. Peacock and F. Forte). Oxford: Blackwell.

—— and Roskamp, W. (1981). *Reform of Tax Systems*. Wayne University Press.

Fullerton, D. (1982). 'On the possibility of an inverse relationship between tax rates and government revenues.' *Journal of Public Economics*, vol. 19, pp. 3–23.

Garnaut, R. and Clunies Ross, A. (1975). 'Uncertainty, risk aversion and the taxing of natural resource projects.' ECONOMIC JOURNAL, vol. 85, pp. 271–87.

—— and —— (1979). 'The neutrality of the resource rent tax.' *Economic Record*, vol. 55, pp. 193–201.

Gillespie, W. I. (1976). 'On the redistribution of income in Canada.' *Canadian Tax Journal*, vol. 24, pp. 419–50.

Gillis, M., Shoup, C. S. and Sicat, G. (eds) (1989). *Value Added Taxation in Developing Countries*. Washington, D.C.: World Bank.

Goode, R. (1976). *The Individual Income Tax*. Washington, D.C.: Brookings Institution.

—— (1980). 'The superiority of the income tax.' In *What should be taxed – income or expenditure?* (ed. J. Pechman). Washington, D.C.: Brookings Institution.

Gordon, H. S. (1954). 'The economic theory of a common property resource.' *Journal of Political Economy*, vol. 62, pp. 124–42.

Gough, J. W. (1957). *The Social Contract*. Oxford: Clarendon Press.

Graetz, M. J. (1980). 'Expenditure tax design.' In *What should be taxed: income or expenditure?* (ed. J. A. Pechman). Washington, D.C.: Brookings Institution.

Green, H. A. J. (1961). 'The social optimum in the presence of monopoly and taxation.' *Review of Economic Studies*, vol. 29, pp. 66–78.

Grossman, G. M. (1980). 'Border tax adjustments: do they distort trade?' *Journal of International Economics*, vol. 10, pp. 117–28.

Grossman, S. J. and Hart, O. D. (1983). 'An analysis of the principal–agent problem.' *Econometrica*, vol. 51, pp. 7–45.

Groves, T. and Ledyard, J. (1977). 'Optimal allocation of a public good: a solution to the free rider problem.' *Econometrica*, vol. 45, pp. 783–810.

—— and Loeb, M. (1975). 'Incentives and public inputs.' *Journal of Public Economics*, vol. 4, pp. 311–26.

Guesnerie, R. (1977). 'On the direction of tax reform.' *Journal of Public Economics*, vol. 7, pp. 179–202.

Guttman, P. M. (1977). 'The subterranean economy.' *Financial Analysts Journal*, November/December, pp. 22–7 and 34.

Harberger, A. C. (1962). 'The incidence of the corporation income tax.' *Journal of Political Economy*, vol. 70, pp. 215–40.

—— (1964). 'Taxation, resource allocation and welfare.' In *The Role of Direct and Indirect Taxes in the Federal Revenue System*. (ed. J. Due) Princeton, New Jersey: Princeton University Press.

Harris, R. G. and MacKinnon, J. G. (1979). 'Computing optimal tax equilibria.' *Journal of Public Economics*, vol. 11, pp. 197–212.

Hatta, T. (1977). 'A theory of piecemeal policy recommendations.' *Review of Economic Studies*, vol. 44, pp. 1–21.

—— (1986). 'Welfare effects of changing commodity tax rates towards uniformity.' *Journal of Public Economics*, vol. 29, pp. 99–112.

Hausman, J. A. (1985). 'Labour supply.' In *Handbook of Public Economics*, vol. 1 (ed. A. J. Auerbach and M. S. Feldstein). Amsterdam: North Holland.

Heady, C. J. and Mitra, P. K. (1982). 'Restricted redistributive taxation, shadow prices and trade policy.' *Journal of Public Economics*, vol. 17, pp. 1–22.

Helm, D. R. (1989) (ed.). *The Economic Borders of the State*. Oxford: Oxford University Press.

Hemming, R. C. L. (1977). 'The effect of state and private pensions on retirement behaviour and personal capital accumulation.' *Review of Economic Studies*, vol. 44, pp. 169–72.

—— and Keen, M. (1983). *Journal of Public Economics*, vol. 20, pp. 373–80.

Hendershott, P. A. (1987). 'Tax changes and capital allocation in the 1980s.' In *The Effects of Taxation on Capital Accumulation* (ed. M. Feldstein). Chicago: Chicago University Press.

Henderson, P. D. (1986). *Innocence and Design*. Oxford: Blackwell.

Hicks, U. K. (1946). 'The terminology of tax analysis.' ECONOMIC JOURNAL, vol. 56, pp. 38–05.

Hills, J. (1984). *Savings and Fiscal Privilege*. London: Institute for Fiscal Studies.

Holland, D. M. (1977). 'Effect of taxation on incentives of higher income groups.' In *Fiscal Policy and Labour Supply*. London: Institute for Fiscal Studies.

Hughes, G. (1988). 'Rates reform and the housing market.' In *The Reform of Local Government Finance in Britain* (ed. S. A. Bailey and R. Paddison). London: Routledge.

Inman, R. P. (1975). 'Grants in a metropolitan economy.' In *Financing the New Federalism* (ed. W. Oates). Baltimore: Johns Hopkins.

—— and Rubinfield, D. L. (1979). 'The judicial pursuit of local fiscal equity.' *Harvard Law Review*, vol. 92, pp. 1662–750.

Isachsen, A. J. and Strom, S. (1980). 'The hidden economy: the labour market and tax evasion.' *Scandinavian Journal of Economics*, vol. 82, pp. 304–11.

Johansen, L. (1963). 'Some notes on the Lindahl theory of determination of public expenditures.' *International Economic Review*, vol. 4, pp. 346–58.

Kakwani, N. C. (1977). 'Measurement of tax progressivity.' ECONOMIC JOURNAL, vol. 87, pp. 71–80.

Kaldor, N. (1955). *An Expenditure Tax*. London: Allen & Unwin.

—— (1980a). 'Indian tax reform.' In *Reports on Taxation II*. London: Duckworth.

—— (1980b). 'Memorandum of dissent.' In *Reports on Taxation I*. London: Duckworth.

Kay, J. A. (1980). 'The deadweight loss from a tax system.' *Journal of Public Economics*, vol. 13, pp. 111–20.

—— (1987). *The State and the Market: the UK Experience of Privatisation*. Occasional Paper 25. New York and London: Group of 30.

—— and Keen, M. J. (1983). 'How should commodities be taxed?' *European Economic Review*, vol. 23, pp. 339–58.

—— —— (1987). 'Alcohol and tobacco taxes: criteria for harmonisation.' In *Tax Coordination in the European Community* (ed. S. Cnossen). Deverten: Kluwer.

—— —— (1988). 'Measuring the inefficiencies of tax systems.' *Journal of Public Economics*, vol. 35, pp. 265–87.

—— and King, M. A. (1989). *The British Tax System*, 5th ed. Oxford: Oxford University Press.

—— and Sandler, C. (1982). 'The taxation of husband and wife.' *Fiscal Studies*, vol. 3, no. 2, pp. 173–87.

—— and Sen, J. (1983). 'The comparative burden of business taxation.' *Fiscal Studies*, vol. 4, no. 3, pp. 23–8.

Keith Committee (1983). *Report of the Committee on Enforcement Powers of the Revenue Departments* (Chmn Lord Keith). London: HMSO.

King, M. A. (1983). 'Welfare analysis of tax reforms using household data.' *Journal of Public Economics*, vol. 21, p. 2.

—— and Fullerton, D. (eds) (1984). *Taxation of Income from Capital*. Chicago: University of Chicago Press.

Kohler, P. H. and Zacher, H. F. (eds) (1982). *The Evolution of Social Insurance*. London: Frances Pinter.

Kotlikoff, L. and Summers, L. (1987). 'Tax incidence.' In *Handbook of Public Economics*, vol. 1 (ed. A. J. Auerbach and M. S. Feldstein). Amsterdam: North Holland.

Lee, C., Pearson, M. and Smith, S. (1988). 'Fiscal harmonisation: an analysis of the European Commission's proposals.' *IFS Report* no. 28, London.

Levitan, S. A. (1980). *Programs in Aid of the Poor for the 1980s*. Baltimore: Johns Hopkins.

Lindsay, L. (1987). 'Individual taxpayer response to tax cuts 1982–4.' *Journal of Public Economics*, vol. 33, pp. 173–206.

Little, I. M. D. and Mirrlees, J. A. (1974). *Project Appraisal and Planning for Developing Countries*. London: Heinemann.

Lodin, S.-O. (1978). 'Progressive expenditure tax – an alternative.' Stockholm: LuberForlag.

Malcolmson, J. (1986). 'Some analytics of the Laffer curve.' *Journal of Public Economics*, vol. 29, pp. 263–79.

Meade, J. E. (chmn) (1978). *The Structure and Reform of Direct Taxation*, Report of a Committee chaired by Prof. J. E. Meade. London: Allen & Unwin for Institute of Fiscal Studies.

Minford, A. P. *et al.* (1983). *Unemployment: Cause and Cure*. Oxford: Martin Robertson.

Mirrlees, J. A. (1971). 'An exploration in the theory of optimum income taxation.' *Review of Economic Studies*, vol. 38, pp. 175–208.

—— (1986). 'The theory of optimal taxation.' In *Handbook of Mathematical Economics*, vol. 3 (ed. K. J. Arrow and M. Intriligator). Amsterdam: North Holland.

Morris, C. N. and Warren, N. A. (1981). 'Taxation of the family.' *Fiscal Studies*, vol. 2, pp. 26–46.

Musgrave, R. A. (1953). 'General equilibrium aspects of incidence theory.' *American Economic Review*, vol. 43, pp. 504–17.

—— (1959). *The Theory of Public Finance*. Maidenhead: McGraw-Hill.

—— and Peacock, A. T. (eds) (1957). *Classics in the Theory of Public Finance*. London: Macmillan.

National Economic and Social Council (Ireland) (1975). *Income Distribution – a Preliminary Report*. Dublin: The Stationery Office.

Nozick, R. (1974). *Anarchy, State and Utopia*. New York: Basic Books.

OECD (1985). *Issues in International Taxation*. Paris.

—— (1987). *Issues in International Taxation 2*. Paris.

—— (1988). *The Taxation of Fringe Benefits*. Paris.

Oates, W. (1969). 'The effects of property taxes and local spending on property values.' *Journal of Political Economy*, vol. 77, pp. 957–71.

Parker, H. (1982). *The Moral Hazard of Social Benefits*. London: IEA.

Part, A. (chairman). (1982). *Report of a Committee on North Sea Oil Taxation*. London: Institute for Fiscal Studies.

Peacock, A. T. (1981). 'Fiscal theory and the "market" for tax reform.' In *Reform of Tax Systems* (ed. F. Forte and W. Roskamp). Wayne University Press.

—— (1988). 'The philosophy of tax reform: a public choice perspective.' Paper prepared for Institute of Economics Affairs Conference, unpublished.

—— and Forte, F. (eds) (1981). *The Political Economy of Taxation*. Oxford: Blackwell.

—— and Shaw, G. K. (1982). 'Tax evasion and tax revenue loss.' *Public Finance*, vol. 37, no. 2.

Pechman, J. A. (ed.) (1977). *Comprehensive Income Taxation*. Washington, D.C.: Brookings Institution.

—— and Okner, B. A. (1974). *Who Bears the Tax Burden?* Washington, D.C.: Brookings Institution.

Pedone, A. (1981). 'Italy.' In *The Value-Added Tax: Lessons from Europe* (ed. H. J. Aaron). Washington, D.C.: Brookings Institution.

Pigou, A. C. (1947). *A Study in Public Finance*, 3rd ed. London: Macmillan.

Piggott, J. (1988). 'General equilibrium computations applied to public sector issues.' In *Surveys in Public Sector Economics* (ed. P. G. Hare). Oxford: Blackwell.

—— and Whalley, J. (1985). *UK Tax Policy and Applied Equilibrium Analysis*. Cambridge: Cambridge University Press.

Plott, C. R. (1967). 'A notion of equilibrium and its possibility under majority rule.' *American Economic Review*, vol. 57, pp. 787–806.

Polanyi, G. and Wood, J. B. (1974). *How Much Inequality?* London: IEA.

—— and Polanyi, P. (1973). 'Tax credits: a reverse income tax.' *National Westminster Bank Review*, February, pp. 20–34.

Prest, A. R. (1970). 'The negative income tax: concepts and problems.' *British Tax Review*, November–December, pp. 352–65.

Pyke, D. J. (1987). *The Political Economy of Tax Evasion*. Hume Paper 6. Edinburgh: David Hume Institute.

Ramsey, F. P. (1927). 'A contribution to the theory of taxation.' ECONOMIC JOURNAL, vol. 37, pp. 47–61.

Rawls, J. (1971). *A Theory of Justice*. Cambridge, Mass.: Harvard University Press.

Rhys Williams, Lady J. (1943). *Something to Look Forward To*. London: Macdonald.

Riker, W. (1982). 'Implications from the disequilibrium of majority rule for the study of institutions.' *American Policy Science Review*, vol. 74, pp. 432–46.

Roberts, K. W. S. (1977). 'Voting over income tax schedules.' *Journal of Public Economics*, vol. 8, pp. 329–40.

Rothschild, M. E. and Stiglitz, J. E. (1970). 'Increasing risk I: a definition.' *Journal of Economic Theory*, vol. 2, pp. 225–43.

—— and —— (1971). 'Increasing risk II: its economic consequences.' *Journal of Economic Theory*, vol. 3, pp. 66–84.

Sadka, E. (1976). 'On income distribution, incentive effects and optimal income taxation.' *Review of Economic Studies*, vol. 43, pp. 261–8.

Samuelson, P. A. (1954). 'The pure theory of public expenditure.' *Review of Economics and Statistics*, vol. 37, pp. 350–6.

Sandford, C. (1973). *The Hidden Costs of Taxation*. London: Institute for Fiscal Studies.

—— Godwin, M. and Hardwick, P. (1989). *Administrative and Compliance Costs of Taxation*. Bath: Fiscal Publications.

Sandmo, A. (1975). 'Optimal taxation in the presence of externalities.' *Swedish Journal of Economics*, vol. 77, pp. 86–98.

—— (1981). 'Income tax evasion, labour supply and the equity efficiency trade-off,' *Journal of Public Economics* vol. 16, pp. 265–288.

Saunders, P. and Klau, F. (1985). 'The role of the public sector.' *OECD Economic Studies*, Paris.

Scarf, H. E. (1969). 'An example of an algorithm for calculating general equilibrium prices.' *American Economic Review*, vol. 59, pp. 669–77.

—— with collaboration of Hansen, T. (1973). *The Computation of Economic Equilibria*. New Haven, Connecticut: Yale University Press.

Seade, J. K. (1977). 'On the shape of optimal tax schedules.' *Journal of Public Economics*, vol. 7, pp. 203–36.

Sen, A. K. (1970). 'On the impossibility of a Paretian liberal.' *Journal of Political Economy*, vol. 78, pp. 152–7.

Sheshinski, E. (1972). 'The optimal linear income tax.' *Review of Economic Studies*, vol. 39, pp. 297–302.

Shoven, J. and Whalley, J. (1973). 'General equilibrium with taxes: a computational procedure and an existence proof.' *Review of Economic Studies*, vol. 40, pp. 475–89.

Simons, H. C. (1938). *Personal Income Taxation: the Definition of Income as a Problem of Fiscal Policy*. Chicago: University of Chicago Press.

Smith, S. (1986). *Britain's Shadow Economy*. Oxford: Clarendon Press.

Spencer, N. (1986). 'Taxation of husband and wife: lessons from Europe.' *Fiscal Studies*, vol. 7, no. 3, pp. 83–90.

Stern, N. H. (1976). 'On the specification of models of optimum income taxation.' *Journal of Public Economics*, vol. 6, pp. 123–62.

Stigler, G. J. (1971). 'The theory of economic regulation.' *Bell Journal of Economics*, vol. 2, pp. 3–21.

Stiglitz, J. (1969). 'The effects of income, wealth and capital gains taxation on risk-taking.' *Quarterly Journal of Economics*, vol. 83, pp. 262–83.

—— (1976). 'The corporation tax.' *Journal of Public Economics*, vol. 5, pp. 303–11.

—— (1987). 'Pareto efficient and optimal taxation and the new welfare economics.' In *Handbook of Public Economics*, vol. II (ed. A. Auerbach and M. Feldstein). Amsterdam: North Holland.

—— (1988). *Economics of the Public Sector*. New York: Norton.

Stockman, D. A. (1986). *The Triumph of Politics*. New York: Harper & Row.

Surrey, S. S. (1973). *Pathways to Tax Reform*. Cambridge, Mass.: Harvard University Press.

Tait, A. A. (1989). 'The value added tax: revenue, inflation and the foreign trade balance.' In *Value Added Taxation in Developing Countries* (ed. M. Gillis, C. S. Shoup and G. Sicat). Washington, D.C.: World Bank.

Tanzi, V. (ed.) (1982). *The Underground Economy in the US and Abroad*. Lexington, Mass.: Lexington Books.

Tiebout, C. M. (1956). 'A pure theory of local expenditures.' *Journal of Political Economy*, vol. 64, pp. 416–24.

Titmuss, R. M. (1962). *Income Distribution and Social Change*. London: Allen & Unwin.

Tobin, J., Pechman, J. A. and Mieskowski, P. M. (1967). *Is a Negative Income Tax Practicable?* Washington, D.C.: Brookings Institution.

Tresch, R. (1981). *Public Finance: a Normative Theory*. Plano, Texas: Business Publications.

United States Treasury (1977). *Blueprints for Basic Tax Reform*. Washington, D.C.: Government Printing Office.

—— (1984). *Tax Reform for Fairness, Simplicity and Economic Growth*. Washington, D.C.: Department of the Treasury.

Warren, N. A. (1979). 'Australia tax incidence in 1975–6: some preliminary results.' *Australian Economic Review*, vol. 3, pp. 19–30.

—— (1986). 'The distributional impact of changing the tax mix in Australia.' In *Changing the Tax Mix* (ed. J. G. Head). Sydney: Australian Tax Research Foundation.

Weiner, M. J. (1981). *English Culture and the Decline of the Industrial Spirit*. Cambridge: Cambridge University Press.

Weingast, B., Shepsle, K. and Johnsen, C. (1981). 'The political economy of benefits and costs: a neoclassical approach to distributive policy.' *Journal of Political Economy*, vol. 89, pp. 642–64.

Weiss, L. (1976). 'The desirability of cheating incentives and randomness in the optimal income tax.' *Journal of Political Economy*, vol. 84, pp. 1343–52.

Weitzman, M. L. (1974). 'Prices vs quantities.' *Review of Economic Studies*, vol. 41, pp. 477–91.

Whalley, J. (1975). 'A general equilibrium assessment of the 1973 United Kingdom tax reform.' *Economica*, vol. 42, pp. 139–61.

Williamson, J. and Lessard, D. R. (1987). *Capital Flight: The Problem and Policy Responses*. Washington, D.C.: Institute for International Economics.

INDEX

Abraham, K. G., 22, 145
ad valorem taxation, 201
adaptive expectations hypothesis, 61
Adelman, F. and I., 13
adjustment costs model of labour, 21, 152
aggregate demand and supply, 22–3
Ahmad, E., 206
Akerlof, G. A., 2, 30, 32, 150
Alogoskoufis, C. S., 145, 158, 174
Altonji, J. G., 18, 143
Andrews, W. D., 193
ARIMA models, 67
Arrow, K. J., 23
Artis, M. J., 104
Ashenfelter, O., 18
asset pricing model, 6
Auerbach, A. J., 216
Aumann, R. J., 230
Australia, 83, 89, 117, 194
autoregressive models, 67
Azariadis, C., 25, 153

Baily, M. N., 25, 153
Ball, L., 31, 150
Bank of England, 89, 91, 96, 112, 116–17
banks and banking system, 34
    competition in, 108, 110, 111, 121
    and financial innovations, 87, 98, 108–9
    and government bills, 116–17
    and monetary base control, 112–15
    and money supply, 82–5, 92, 95–6,
      103
bargaining model of trade unions, 157–8
    implications for unemployment of, 26–7,
      158–65
Barker, T. S., 59
Barnett, W. A., 2
Barro, R. J., 1, 2, 10, 19, 24, 35, 37, 62,
    85, 151
base drift, 89

Bean, C., 166, 174
Benassy, J. -P., 6
Bernanke, B., 34
Bernheim, B. D., 35
Bils, M. J., 17
Black, F., 34
'black economy', 226–7, 229
Blackaby, D. H., 165
Blanchard, O. J., 2, 31, 32, 35, 48, 165,
    173
Blanchflower, D., 165
Blinder, A. S., 16, 34
bonds
    government, 35–6, 88, 95–6, 116–17,
      121–2
    for performance, 27, 155
Boschen, J., 10
Box, G. E. P., 67
Brazil, 36
Brennan, G., 230
Britain *see* United Kingdom
Brown, B. W., 66
Brunner, K., 1, 120
Bruno, M., 174, 175
bubbles, speculative, 34–5
Buchanan, J. M., 230
buffer stock money, 101–2
Buiter, W. H., 61
Burns, T., 48, 50, 68, 77
business cycles, 11–14
    money and theory of, 8–11
    propagation mechanisms of, 13, 14–22
    and unemployment, 12, 20–1, 141–5

Cairncross, A., 48, 49, 50, 51–2, 77
Callaghan, James, 89
Calvo, G. A., 85
Campbell, J. Y., 12
Canada, 83, 89, 96
Cannan, E., 155